Employee Benefits and Labor Markets in Canada and the United States

William T. Alpert
and
Stephen A. Woodbury
Editors

2000

W.E. Upjohn Institute for Employment Research
Kalamazoo, Michigan

Library of Congress Cataloging-in-Publication Data

Employee benefits and labor markets in Canada and the United States / William T. Alpert and Stephen A. Woodbury, editors.
    p. cm.
  Includes bibliographical references and index.
  ISBN 0–88099–206–9 (alk. paper) — ISBN 0–88099–205–0 (paper : alk. paper)
   1. Employee fringe benefits—Canada—Costs—Congresses. 2. Employee fringe benefits—United States—Costs—Congresses. 3. Labor costs—Canada—Congresses. 4. Labor costs—United States—Congresses. 5. Labor market—Canada—Congresses. 6. Labor market—United States—Congresses. I. Alpert, William T. II. Woodbury, Stephen A.

HD4928.N6 E463 2000
331.12'0971—dc21

00–031999

The facts presented in this study and the observations and viewpoints expressed are the sole responsibility of the authors. They do not necessarily represent positions of the W.E. Upjohn Institute for Employment Research.

Cover design by J.R. Underhill.
Index prepared by Leoni Z. McVey.
Printed in the United States of America.

Judy Gentry, editor at the Upjohn Institute from 1977 until her retirement in 1996, passed away while this volume was in production. Over the years, she edited the writing of scores of labor economists with intelligence and sensitivity. We miss her and dedicate this book to her memory.

CONTENTS

Introduction

William T. Alpert
University of Connecticut
and
The William H. Donner Foundation

Stephen A. Woodbury
Michigan State University and *W.E. Upjohn Institute*

Some of the most important personal consumption items that individuals receive are closely tied to work and are provided or financed by employers, either voluntarily or by government mandate. In the United States and Canada, as in most industrialized countries, these benefits include retirement income, health care, income during times of unemployment (in the form of unemployment insurance), income and medical care in the event of workplace injury (workers' compensation), and life insurance. Employers' expenditures on these employee benefits have grown dramatically in the last 50 years and now are on the order of one-third of total labor costs in most industrialized countries (Hart et al. 1988).

This volume brings together 14 original research chapters on various aspects of the employee benefits systems of Canada and the United States. Preliminary versions of some of the papers in the volume were presented at a conference held in the mid 1990s sponsored and supported by the William H. Donner Foundation and the W.E. Upjohn Institute for Employment Research. In planning the volume, our intention has been to use a Canadian–U.S. comparison to highlight the basic economic features of employee benefits and the policy issues that are connected with them.

There are substantial differences between the employee benefit systems of Canada and the United States; the most striking are in the two countries' health care systems. In Canada, health care is provided through a system of provincial and territorial plans funded by the federal government out of general revenues, whereas in the United States

1

health care is provided through a mixed private/public system financed largely by employer contributions and payroll taxes. Because the Canadian provincial and territorial plans are funded out of general revenues, they are not perceived as an employer cost, as they are in the United States.

The differences between Canada and the United States in other social insurance programs are less stark, although the differences are nonetheless substantial. For example, government involvement in the provision of retirement income takes the form of three major programs in Canada, as opposed to just one in the United States. Public pensions are more generous and private pension plans are correspondingly less important in Canada than in the United States (see the chapters by Gunderson, Hyatt, and Pesando (p. 381) and by Dorsey (p. 413) in this volume).

The existence and magnitude of employee benefits pose numerous economic questions that are important to public policy. In organizing the volume, we have grouped these questions under four headings: labor supply and worker availability, labor demand, labor-market adjustment and equity, and pensions. We place issues such as whether the availability of benefits (or lack thereof) create incentives or disincentives to work under the heading of labor supply, treated in Part I. (To some extent, these issues are also treated in chapters on labor-market adjustment. For example, the chapters by Olson (p. 295) and by Hunt-McCool, McCool, and Dor (p. 325) address the labor-supply implications of the U.S. health care system, which essentially requires an individual to work in order to be covered by health insurance.) Issues stemming from the status of employee benefits as a cost of labor (do employee benefits create incentives that alter the level or mix of employment?) are labor-demand issues, treated in Part II. The potential for employee benefits to affect worker turnover, tenure, and wages are adjustment issues, treated in Part III. Finally, Part IV centers on issues related to retirement income programs, both public and private.

Differences between Canada and the United States in employee benefits and labor costs offer a natural laboratory in which to examine the impacts of differing policies on labor market outcomes in the two countries. In both the United States and Canada, however, there is a dearth of research that is both rigorous and policy-relevant on the linkages between labor markets and the provision of these benefits by employers or the government. We hope that the research presented in this volume helps fill the gap.

CHAPTER SUMMARIES

In his overview chapter ("Does the Composition of Pay Matter?"), Sherwin Rosen addresses an essential question and places the issues posed by employee benefits in their proper economic context. Rosen views employment-related benefits as consumption decisions that have been centralized so as to become collective or group decisions, delegated partly to firms and partly to governments. He offers three economic reasons for the centralization of certain consumption decisions. First, there may be economies of scale in the provision of some goods; that is, joint provision of a common good may reduce transaction and other costs that would be incurred if decisions were made individually. Rosen notes that such economies take on special importance as a motive for employer-provided benefits when certain benefits escape taxation. Second, some goods may be viewed as inputs that enhance productivity—hence, firms paternalistically provide some goods to improve their workers' welfare and productivity. Similarly, enduring employment relationships and employment security may be viewed and analyzed in light of their effects on workers' productivity. Third, an insurance rationale—or an intertemporal consistency problem, as Rosen calls it—motivates many employee benefit programs. Rosen emphasizes the moral hazard that social provision of health, retirement, and other benefits may produce and discusses the principle that public provision of such benefits may merely offset or substitute for their private provision. Rosen applies these three analytical insights in discussions of military compensation and of compensation in the former Soviet Union. Overall, Rosen's sweeping and comprehensive essay offers a framework for future economic research on employee benefits.

Part I of the volume comprises three chapters that treat the relationship between employee benefits and the supply of labor.

In Chapter 1 ("Child Care and the Supply of Labor in Canada and the United States"), Charles Michalopoulos and Philip Robins address differences between Canada and the United States in child-care arrangements and the working patterns of women. The growth of the labor-force participation rate of married women has been accompanied by the growing use of day-care centers and caregivers who are not family relatives and the declining use of parental care and family relatives. Significant controversy has surrounded the extent to which the child-care choices and labor-force decisions of women are affected by government policies that subsidize child care. Michalopoulos and Robins analyze pooled Canadian and U.S. data with the goal of obtaining improved estimates of the effect of subsidies on child-care choices and labor supply of mothers. They describe the broad similarities and specific differences between the two countries' child-care policies (both countries provide general and targeted child-care subsidies through their personal income tax systems) and present data describing the methods of child care in each country. They then estimate the impact of child-care prices and subsidies on both the primary form of child care used by families and the labor-force behavior of mothers. The authors' empirical results suggest that the form of child care chosen and employment of the mother are influenced mainly by the husband's earnings, ethnicity, and location. There is little evidence that child-care prices and subsidies influence the form of child care in the two countries. Neither do child-care prices and subsidies appear to be major determinants of whether mothers work full time, part time, or not at all.

In Chapter 2 ("An Economic Model of Employee Benefits and Labor Supply: An Application of the Almost Ideal Demand System"), Paul Fronstin turns to an essential question that has rarely been addressed in empirical research: Does the mix of compensation influence labor supply and, if so, how? He addresses this question by estimating a system of demand equations for leisure and employee benefits using data from the 1993 Current Population Survey. His estimation proceeds in two stages. In the first stage, he estimates a bivariate probit model of labor supply (the probability of working) and employee benefits (the probability of participating in a salary-reduction pension plan). In the second stage, he estimates selectivity-corrected share equations for leisure and pension contributions. The central (and novel) result in Fronstin's chapter is his estimate of the cross-price elasticity between leisure and pension contributions, which he finds is essentially zero; that is, pensions, unlike wages, have minimal effect on the supply of labor. Fronstin's other results of estimation are in keeping with existing empirical findings; for example, he finds that pensions and wages are highly substitutable. Although limited by the unavailability of data on other aspects of compensation, Fronstin's innovative study points the way to further exploration of the relationship between labor supply and employee benefits when improved data do become available.

As the labor-force participation of women has grown, so has the importance of family and medical leave benefits. In Chapter 3 ("The Economics of Family and Medical Leave in Canada and the United States"), Eileen Trzcinski and William T. Alpert provide a description of the family and medical leave policies of both Canada and the United States, noting that family and medical leave provisions have (potentially) two components—the provision of wage replacement benefits during the leave and the guarantee of the same or similar job upon return from the leave. In Canada, each province mandates family and medical leave that includes both wage replacement and a job guarantee, whereas in the United States, the Family and Medical Leave Act (FMLA) of 1993 provides only a job guarantee, and this only in firms with 50 or more workers. Trzcinski and Alpert use data on more than 2,700 firms from the 1988 Small Business Administration's Employee Leave Survey to describe the incidence of family leave policies in the United States before enactment of the FMLA. They use the same data to model the determinants of each of the main components of family and medical leave—paid leave and a job guarantee. Their modeling efforts are more successful in tracing the factors that are correlated with paid leave provision than the factors that are correlated with a job guarantee upon return from a leave. They interpret their results to suggest that different theoretical approaches are needed to understand the incidence of paid leave and a job guarantee and to predict the impacts of further legislative mandates.

Part II of the volume turns to an examination of the relationship between employee benefits and the demand for labor. Payroll taxes are used to finance all three of the major social insurance programs in the United States: Social Security, workers' compensation, and unemployment insurance. The most persistent criticism facing social insurance programs financed by employer contributions has been that they raise labor costs and thereby reduce both employment and the competitiveness of U.S. business. In Chapter 4 ("Payroll Taxation, Employer Mandates, and the Labor Market: Theory, Evidence, and Unanswered Questions"), Jonathan Gruber appraises this and other criticisms of mandated employer contributions in the United States. Gruber reviews programs that are financed by payroll taxes and discusses the theory and evidence on the labor-market effects of payroll taxes and employer mandates (including various complications such as minimum wages and group-specific mandates). He also presents some new evidence on the influence of employer mandates on wages at both the individual and firm levels. He then considers the implications for efficiency and equity of changing the method of financing social insurance programs from the payroll tax to the income tax. This highly useful chapter highlights what is known about the labor-market effects of payroll taxation and employer mandates, develops and presents new evidence, and points the way to fruitful avenues for further research.

In Chapter 5, Masanori Hashimoto continues this line of inquiry with a theoretical treatment of the relationship between employee benefits and labor demand ("Fringe Benefits and Employment"). Hashimoto's model differs from previous models of employee benefits by considering the entire market for benefits rather than focusing solely on the decisions of firms. In this setting, changes in employee benefits can occur because workers' tastes for benefits change, because the cost of providing benefits changes, or because of changes in government mandates. Whether increases in employee benefits reduce employment, then, depends on the cause of the increase in benefits. Increases in benefits that follow from reduced benefit costs or from increased demand for benefits by workers (resulting from favorable tax treatment, for example) will increase employment. Increases in benefits that follow from increased government mandates, on the other hand, are likely to lead to employment losses. Hashimoto also reports the results of some sensitivity tests of his model's results.

Part III of the volume includes four chapters that consider the implications of employee benefits for worker turnover, wages, and equity. The first three chapters in Part III focus mainly on a peculiar feature of health insurance provision in the United States—that most individuals who are covered by private health insurance are covered through an employer-provided plan and that employer-provided health insurance often covers all members of a worker's family. It stands to reason that this link between the job and the availability of health insurance could affect the behavior of workers in a variety of ways.

In Chapter 6 ("Family Health Benefits and Worker Turnover"), Dan Black examines a previously unexplored aspect of the link between health benefits and turnover. Although much attention has focused on so-called preexisting conditions clauses as a source of "job lock," Black notes that the family coverage provisions of many employer-provided health insurance plans are an even more likely avenue by which employer-provided health insurance could affect worker turnover. Black's theoretical treatment shows that the existence of employer-provided family health coverage can alter the value that a worker places on alternative job offers, increasing or decreasing the likelihood of turnover depending on specific circumstances. Black then uses April 1993 Current Population Survey (CPS) data to document the extent of double coverage by employer-provided health insurance. As a test of his theory, he uses the same data to estimate models (for men and women) of job change in which the probability of recent job change depends on coverage by a spouse's health insurance plan (among other variables). Black finds that workers (both men and women) who are covered by the employer-provided health insurance of their spouses are about 50 percent more likely than others to have changed jobs in the last year, suggesting in turn that the existence of employer-provided spousal benefits substantially distorts incentives to change jobs and reduces the efficiency of labor markets.

In Chapter 7 ("Part-Time Work, Health Insurance Coverage, and the Wages of Married Women"), Craig Olson examines whether employer-provided health insurance influences the labor-supply decisions and wages of married women. Using CPS data from 1983 and 1993, he first shows that women who are married to men without health-insurance coverage are more likely to have jobs that provide health insurance than are women married to men who do have health insurance coverage. In other words, wives whose husbands do not provide health insurance have a higher demand for health insurance than wives whose husbands do provide health insurance. In turn, married women who are not covered by their husbands' health insurance may increase their work hours in order to obtain health insurance coverage at work (part-time jobs are less likely than full-time jobs to offer health insurance). Olson's empirical results using 1993 data support this notion; in contrast, his results for 1983 show no impact of husbands' health insurance coverage on wives' work hours. Olson argues that this change was caused by the decline in health insurance coverage among men during the 1980s; that is, as health insurance coverage among men fell, more women increased their work hours to gain eligibility for employer-provided health benefits.

In Chapter 8 ("Employer-Provided versus Publicly Provided Health Insurance: Effects on Hours Worked and Compensation"), Janet Hunt-McCool, Thomas McCool, and Avi Dor further examine the impact of employment-based health insurance on labor-market behavior and outcomes. In particular, they examine differences in the behavior of married women who are and are not covered by the employer-provided health insurance of their husbands. They view women who are covered by their husbands' health insurance as "virtual Canadians," in that their decisions about labor-force participation and labor supply are independent of employers' health insurance offers (as is the case under a system of public health care like Canada's). On the other hand, women who are not covered by their husbands' health insurance are likely to consider employers' health insurance offers in making labor-supply decisions. Using data from the 1987 National Medical Expenditure Survey, they estimate two-stage models of wages, earnings, compensation, and health insurance premiums (the first stage of their models creates controls for possible selection in the matching of women to men who do or do not have jobs that provide family health benefits). Their results are consistent with two hypotheses: 1) women who are not covered by their husbands' health insurance select jobs that provide health insurance and 2) these women are willing to sacrifice wage income for health insurance. Hunt-McCool, McCool, and Dor, like Black, suggest that efficiency and social welfare are reduced by the U.S. system of providing health care provision.

As employee benefits have grown as a share of total compensation, their potential to have important implications for the distribution of income has also grown. Few studies of income distribution, however, have considered employee benefits. In Chapter 9 ("Employee Benefits and the Distribution of Income and Wealth"), Daniel Slottje, Stephen Woodbury, and Rod Anderson examine household data that include information on health insurance expenditures (the National Medical Care Expenditure Survey and the National Medical Expenditure Survey) or pension wealth (the 1983 and 1989 Surveys of Consumer Finances) in an effort to better understand how employee benefits influence income distribution. They find that employer contributions to health insurance, although more unequally distributed than personal income, are distributed in such a way that they slightly reduce the overall distribution of income. They find that the distribution of private pension wealth is about as unequal as the distribution of private nonretirement wealth overall, although private pensions smooth the high end of the wealth distribution. These findings suggest that neither health insurance nor private pensions can be seen as a major force behind increasing inequality in the distribution of income or wealth.

Part IV of the volume comprises four chapters that focus on pensions and public policy toward retirement income in Canada and the United States. In Chapter 10 ("Public Pension Plans in the United States and Canada"), Morley Gunderson, Douglas Hyatt, and James Pesando offer a highly useful analytical description and comparison of the government programs that provide retirement income in Canada and the United States. They compare the contributions to and benefits from both public and private pensions, discuss the extent to which public pensions replace earnings, and examine how public pensions transfer income both within and between generations. The authors also treat the potential effects of the Canadian and U.S. public pension plans on work incentives, retirement, and the demand for labor. The authors' emphasis on comparing the Canadian and U.S. systems brings into relief the essential features of any public retirement system and highlights the problems facing any government program that provides retirement income.

Whereas Gunderson, Hyatt, and Pesando focus on public pensions, Stuart Dorsey describes and reviews the literature on private pensions in Canada and the United States in Chapter 11 ("Current Policy Issues Toward Private Pensions in Canada and the United States"). He begins with a brief review of the history of private pensions in Canada and the United States, then describes and compares the main features of government intervention into private pensions—tax policy and regulation—which are remarkably similar in the two countries. The bulk of Dorsey's chapter is devoted to discussing four specific policy issues that confront both Canada and the United States in considering the future of private pensions: the extent of private pension coverage, the portability of private pensions, tax policy toward private pensions, and the problem of indexing pension benefits for inflation. In all of these discussions, Dorsey highlights the results of research and the relevance of research to policy toward private pensions.

In Chapter 12 ("Labor-Market Effects of Canadian and U.S. Pension Tax Policy"), James Pesando and John Turner examine a special feature of pension policy in both Canada and the United States: the tax-favored treatment of employer contributions to pension plans. Neither in Canada nor in the United States are employer contributions to private pensions subject to the personal income tax, creating an incentive for workers to receive compensation in the form of contributions to a private pension plan. Pesando and Turner's main goal is to trace the influence of this favorable tax treatment on the extent of pension coverage. In addition, they examine how the tax treatment of pensions affects three other outcomes: the generosity of pension plans, whether private pension plans are funded through employer or worker contributions, and whether pensions take the form of defined-benefit or defined-contribution plans. The authors pay special attention to two important differences between Canada and the United States. First, worker contributions to private pension plans in Canada are tax deductible regardless of whether the worker participates in a defined-benefit or a defined-contribution plan, whereas a worker in the United States must participate in a 401k (or similar) plan for his or her contributions to be tax deductible. Second, in Canada, workers face a lower limit on the amount they can save through the pension system.

The volume closes with an empirical analysis of a worrisome trend—the decline in private pension coverage that occurred among young men during the 1980s. In Chapter 13 ("Did the Decline in Marginal Tax Rates during the 1980s Reduce Pension Coverage?"), Patricia Reagan and John Turner use Current Population Survey data from 1979, 1988, and 1993 to examine the reasons for this decline. Their analysis stems from the reasoning that, because employer contributions to private pensions are not subject to the personal income tax, the incentive for workers to be covered by pensions (and to receive compensation in the form of contributions to a private pension plan) rises as the marginal personal income tax rate rises. Reagan and Turner's careful modeling efforts suggest that a 1-percentage-point increase in the marginal income tax rate leads to a 0.4-percentage-point increase in pension coverage rates. It follows that the drop in marginal tax rates that occurred during the 1980s was an important factor in the reduced pension coverage of young men.

ACKNOWLEDGMENTS

The William H. Donner Foundation and the W.E. Upjohn Institute generously supported this project, and we are grateful for that support. We thank the authors for their cooperation in bringing their chapters to completion and for their patience during what has been a far longer gestation period than either of us expected or desired. We are especially grateful to the following reviewers who provided detailed comments and helpful criticism on drafts of the chapters:

Laurie J. Bassi, American Society for Training and Development
Charles Beach, Queen's University
William Custer, Employee Benefit Research Institute
Randall W. Eberts, W.E. Upjohn Institute
Ronald G. Ehrenberg, Cornell University
William Even, Miami University (Ohio)
Paul Fronstin, Employee Benefit Research Institute
John H. Goddeeris, Michigan State University
Daniel S. Hamermesh, University of Texas
Andrew J. Hogan, Michigan State University
Susan N. Houseman, W.E. Upjohn Institute
Douglas Hyatt, University of Toronto
Louis S. Jacobson, Westat, Inc.
Jean Kimmel, W.E. Upjohn Institute
Paul L. Menchik, Michigan State University
Sigurd Nilsen, United States General Accounting Office
Leslie Papke, Michigan State University
Patricia Reagan, Ohio State University
Bruce C. Vavricek, Congressional Budget Office
William Wascher, Board of Governors of the Federal Reserve
    System
Ging Wong, Human Resources Development Canada

Reference

Hart, Robert A., David N. F. Bell, Rudolf Frees, Seiichi Kawasaki, and Stephen A. Woodbury. 1988. *Trends in Non-Wage Labour Costs and Their Effects on Employment.* Brussels and Luxembourg: Office for Official Publications of the European Communities.

Does the Composition of Pay Matter?

Sherwin Rosen
University of Chicago

THE ISSUES

Why are people paid in so many different ways? Most pay is in cash, but some is in kind. These days, a part usually is deferred until retirement, occasionally another part is paid "up front," and some goes to purchase certain things, such as social security and unemployment insurance, that are legally tied to job holding and payroll taxes. How different allocations of pay among these and many other components affect the allocation of resources and economic performance is the main problem for the economic analysis of employee benefits.

Consumption per person is the ultimate measure of economic performance. After all, the economic role of productive capacity and other inputs in the economy derives from their contributions to sustaining consumption and improving the living standards of citizens over the long term. In primitive times, when transportation costs were so large that gains from exchange and the development of markets were extremely limited, specific acts of production and work hardly could be separated from specific acts of consumption. Robinson Crusoe had to carefully coordinate the consumption of particular goods with their production because exchange with others was not possible. Work and consumption essentially were joint decisions. Virtually all compensation was in kind.

The modern economy, with its extensive market structures and extraordinary division of labor, achieves much of its high standard of living by exploiting specialization and gains from trade. As always, personal command over consumption still is determined by the productivity of one's labor and other resources, but consumption decisions are not nearly so tied to specific, personal acts of production. If all pay were in cash, virtually all personal consumption decisions would be independent of personal income sources. None whatsoever would be tied to particular acts of work, and each person would purchase precisely the most desired consumption bundle, independent of what others chose. Needless to say, this is not the way things are always done.

We have moved a long way from Robinson Crusoe, but many personal consumption items and other forms of spending are closely tied to work. Compensation is a complicated package of payments, promises, and obligations in most modern labor markets. Important aspects of compensation are provided in kind, often in the form of bundles of goods that are purchased in common by all workers in an organization. Fringe benefits, such as health and retirement plans, typically have many uniform features among all workers in a firm. The effort and attention paid to these items suggest that much is at stake in the precise form in which compensation is paid today.

THE EFFICIENCY OF MONETARY PAY: GENERALIZED PURCHASING POWER

Economies of information make decentralization through some form of market system the standard "default" paradigm for economics. In theory, it is the utility-maximizing allocation of work, output, consumption, and investment that determines potential economic welfare, given tastes and technology. How is this allocation achieved? If preferences were fully known and transactions were costless, people could equally well hire agents to purchase goods on their behalf to choose among particular items themselves. The same utility-maximizing outcome would be achieved in either case.

However, if tastes are private information and not easily known or conveyed to others, vast resources are saved by decentralization. Decisions are made more efficiently. Individual consumers are in the best position to make the most informed choices on their own behalf. Delegating or contracting it to others is bound to lead to misallocations in most cases. There are considerable savings from not having to communicate all possible preferences to others, not only to avoid misunderstandings, but also for hired agents to make the right choices should unusual circumstances and unexpected opportunities arise. In addition, individual choice avoids potential conflicts of interest and control problems of delegating decisions to people who have independent interests and agendas of their own. Who will spend a person's money in that person's best interests? The person or someone else? This, of course, is the fundamental argument for the desirability—indeed, the necessity—of decentralized individual decision making to efficiently allocate resources. Why then, should compensation be paid in any other form?

The most important reason arises from Alfred Marshall's observation that workers must deliver their own work themselves. Insofar as there is utility or disutility in specific acts of work, work locations, work associates, etc., these must be appropriately accounted in final consumption and considered as payments in kind.[1] Even in the absence of these technological tie-ins and consumption (or possibly investment) aspects of work, however, there are other economic reasons for consumption decisions to be "centralized" in collective or group decisions, sometimes tied to work decisions and at least partially delegated through firms, and other times delegated to government or other agencies.

One reason is potential economies of scale in the provision of some types of goods. Another is a form of externality, where the consumption of one person affects the welfare of others in ways that cannot be fully priced nor fully internalized socially by purely private choices. A third is intertemporal externality or consistency problems, where adverse individual outcomes are shared by the community at large.

Economies of Scale

Economies of scale is the most familiar, indeed, the stock argument for the provision of public goods through collective or public choice. Joint provision of a common good to many consumers saves transaction costs that otherwise would be incurred if individuals make the decisions for themselves, completely independent of each other. Saving transactions costs in these cases typically requires that the administrative agency purchase a standardized good or a very limited range of goods; otherwise, the economy of scale tends to be lost. Collective choices, therefore, necessarily involve some loss of freedom relative to making independent individual choices. Individuals in the group do not always get exactly what they desire most under these restrictions, and this represents the private and social costs of buying goods collectively through group consensus rather than individually.

Such costs are not voluntarily incurred unless there are corresponding benefits. It is rational to subvert one's specific preferences to common, group-chosen consumption standards if the good can be obtained cheaply enough. Goods provided in this way tend to cater to median preferences in the group, but if the system is stable, the goods must be close enough to the preferences of any member to make continued participation worthwhile. Otherwise, members would defect, and the group would either change its character or disappear altogether.

In advanced market economies, perhaps the most important cause for components of pay to take this form is tax avoidance. To a first approximation (but see below), the firm cares about the total cost of an employee, not how the cost is allocated among various components of compensation. Furthermore, all costs are equally counted as expenses in calculating income, corporate or otherwise, for assessing tax liabilities of the firm. To the extent that the tax system finds it difficult to tax in-kind income of workers, there are obvious incentives for firms and workers to agree to convert income into tax-free, in-kind forms. Some ways of doing so are easier than others (Woodbury and Huang 1991).

Tax authorities everywhere are loathe to impute income to "intangibles" for tax purposes because of the difficulties of doing so without costly disputes and substantial differences of opinion. An obvious example is the failure to impute rent on owner-occupied housing in calculating the personal income tax. A less obvious example is imputing taxable income for jobs with desirable amenities, such as good working conditions, location, office quality, air-conditioning, and other. Income taxes encourage on-the-job consumption of such items because it is too costly to calculate their monetary equivalents in each individual case. Obviously, these forms of pay are of greater value the greater the marginal tax rate. Progressive income taxation implies that these forms of pay are of greater value to higher-wage workers than they are to lower-wage workers.

The monetary value of many other things, such as company-provided meals, housing, club memberships, and work clothing are easier to assess, and they are often included in income for individual income-tax purposes. Other important benefits, such as the employer's share of contributions to retirement or to health insurance, however, have easily imputed value but still are exempted from taxable income by law. It is interesting to note that many in-kind pay provisions in the United States and Canada originated in periods such as wartime, when nominal wage controls were used to suppress inflation. There is a natural tendency toward "wage drift" in those circumstances: using wage and price controls to suppress inflation gives strong incentives for workers and employers to look for ways to increase worker incomes exempt from regulation. Provision of company-owned housing to employees often was used for this purpose in Europe in the post World War II era. World War II money wage controls are said to be the origins of firm-provided health insurance to workers in the United States.

Externalities and Productivity

Next, consider goods that have "productive consumption" attributes, that is, goods having important linkages between personal consumption and personal productivity. The consumption of many goods affects productivity directly, some for the good, others for the bad. In a fully decentralized and complete market economy, private consumption decisions would take these productivity by-products fully into account because individuals would confront the full costs and benefits of their decisions. For instance, if an act of consumption, such as drinking, causes one's productivity to fall, the person rationally anticipates an extra charge in the form of reduced wages while under the influence and properly takes that into account in deciding where, when, and how much to drink.

In practice, many markets are incomplete and too costly to operate. In such cases, these by-product effects on others are not fully priced and not always fully internalized by private decisions. A worker who gets drunk and has to skip work might get docked a day's pay, but typically doesn't have to compensate co-workers for the bother and extra effort they must exert to make up for the absence. Usually these imperfections arise because transactions costs make it too expensive for firms and workers to contract directly on worker output.

Rather, transactions costs are economized by contracting more imperfectly on inputs, such as own time, whose day-to-day quality is hard to monitor and can be partially affected by conscious worker (and firm) behavior. In these cases, firms have interests in their workers' consumption habits because it directly affects labor costs and firm productivity. Paternalistic interests by firms in their workers' welfare can arise solely on considerations of self-interest, without any altruism whatsoever. Many U.S. firms provide athletic facilities, meals, and health services partly for these reasons.

This idea has many potential applications. Consider, for instance, the provision to workers of complementary inputs into the production process. One could imagine a system in which professors were required to purchase their own chalk for classroom lectures, instead of the system we have, where educational institutions typically provide it "free of charge." If professors were paid directly by their students and their fees varied directly with the demand for participation in specific classes, teachers would carefully calculate the costs and benefits of using chalk for enhancing their net revenues and would choose to use the socially efficient amount.

However, in the system we have, professors aren't paid directly by students. Most teachers are paid on an annual salary basis, and pay is only imperfectly geared to specific classroom performance, so having the professor buy the chalk probably would lead to inefficient decisions that would imperfectly serve the interests of students and schools. A teacher could decide to use no chalk whatsoever, saving these personal expenses while receiving, at least in the short run, more or less the same pay from the school. Under these conditions, it's just easier for the school to freely distribute chalk on each chalkboard each day and let the professor use all that is desired. Using chalk excessively at the margin may be better than not using enough.

There is no need to belabor the triviality of this example. It was chosen for its possible (mild) amusement value and familiarity to some readers, but there are many more important examples. A production worker in a large manufacturing establishment today is paid to work with capital and machines that are almost always owned by third-party shareholders in the firm and looked after by managers hired for that purpose. Yet, in the early days of the factory system, it was common for workers to rent machinery directly from the factory owner and market their own output themselves. "Compensation" would look much different under these two circumstances.

Corporate executives could be given no complementary resources, such as offices, secretaries or assistants, to work with. Instead, they might rent their own office (if indeed they wanted one) or hire additional help at their own expense. Such expenses would be worthwhile and incurred voluntarily if they improved the person's productivity enough. Yet, for most executives, decentralized arrangement such as these hardly ever arise because it is so difficult to pay executives on the basis of their specific "outputs." It is more economical for the firm to provide productivity-enhancing complementary resources as part of the work environment and pay managers mostly on the basis of their own time inputs.[2]

Worker-Firm Commitment

A particular form of these kinds of interactions has been extensively analyzed in economics over the years. When it is expensive to use and to closely control implicit markets for internal transactions within the firm, it can be efficient to substitute cooperative, sharing solutions between workers and management instead. The concept of firm-specific human capital has been an important development in labor economics and essentially this is what lies behind it. If many internal transactions are not explicitly priced or are priced incorrectly, there is potential for unproductive conflict among various agents in an organization. In making their individual production and investment decisions, some conflict is avoided by providing incentives to encourage workers to weigh the interests of the organization as a whole in addition to their self-interests. It's as if workers were brought into the enterprise as implicit partners. All parties bear some of the costs and some of the returns in mutual investments in worker-worker and worker-management knowledge and relationships. Issues of paternalism arise within the organization from the joint interests of all parties to protect their shared investments and stakes in the firm. This is not entirely unrelated to the ways in which interpersonal relationships develop in families.

Probably the most important benefit that results from these shared investments is employment security and enduring employment relationships. In reality, employment contracts always are of random duration, with future (implicit) promises guaranteed only up to the external fortunes of the firm, the state of demand for its products, the economic conditions of its suppliers, and the quality of its managers. Nevertheless, the fact is that there is an enormous amount of job continuity over the working lives of most people. The typical pattern is for job turnover to be largest at younger ages, a time when learning and information gathering about both the talents of young workers and their prospects in firms is most important. Job turnover falls sharply with work experience in the firm. Within 6 or 7 years of entry into the labor force, the typical worker has found a permanent job that will last for 20 years or more.

It is a bit unusual to think of employment security as a fringe benefit, perhaps because, with few exceptions in some trade union contracts, these terms are not explicitly written down anywhere. Nonetheless, the ties that are built up through mutual specific human capital investments serve as the equivalent of financial bonds and act to discourage costly quits and layoffs under many circumstances. They affect employment variability and the incidence and duration of unemployment in the economy (Rosen 1985).

A great deal of empirical work has established that the payment of normal fringe benefits and other fixed costs of employment in the firm, such as hiring and training costs that are not closely related to work intensity, insulate workers from short-term product market fluctuations (Hamermesh 1993; Hart 1984). For instance, if demand falls but the decline is expected to be temporary, the firm has something to lose by laying off workers. It has incentives to retain them because some valued employees will never return if they are laid off, and the fixed costs associated with their initial employment must be incurred again on subsequent replacements. Similar considerations apply to workers and serve to deter them from quitting in response to attractive short-term outside opportunities. All of this acts as a kind of self-insurance that supplements explicit unemployment insurance programs mandated by the government.

Intertemporal Consistency

Finally, there is a related concept of externalities that cuts across a different spectrum of consumption activities and personal behavior. For the problem at hand, the most important of these are "social insurance" types of activities involving transfers of resources among individuals and over time. Perhaps the main growth of the State in otherwise decentralized market economies throughout the world is attributable to mandatory, tax-financed provision of activities such as health care, unemployment insurance, retirement plans, and the like. The subject is too vast to be discussed in any detail here, except to point out the tendency for centralized government decisions to increasingly substitute for private planning and individual decisions throughout this century. The fact is that governments have increasingly undertaken these paternalistic functions, often administrated through employment records and financed by payroll and income taxes. Few, if any, compelling explanations for this most important social and economic trend have been offered, and no attempt will be made to do so here.

With the possible exception of unemployment compensation, most of these activities are best thought of as essentially private acts of consumption or investment, that is, the government supplying or regulating private goods. How much a person wishes to set aside for future retirement or to spend on a personal medical condition is inherently a private decision, so the classical economic case for the possibility of public policy does not immediately apply. However, a case can be made that external social interests arise if the financing of these private decisions turns out to concern others. Choices may then not be time-consistent in the following sense. Some individuals may make earnest but erroneous decisions, and others may not be willing to let them suffer the poor *ex post* consequences of unfortunate choices. If this outcome comes to be anticipated, however, and individuals think they can be bailed out by throwing themselves at the mercy of the community, it encourages reckless, inefficient behavior that can be avoided by forcing people to set aside resources to take care of themselves.

A person who hasn't bought health insurance on the expectation of not getting sick often is cared for at public expense should the unlikely and costly illness occur. Some people who gamble away their retirement wealth or invest retirement funds unwisely find themselves in a similar situation. The community finds it difficult to completely turn its back on such people *ex post*, and it is hard to credibly commit to not doing so *ex ante*. Knowing that the community will step in, however, creates incentives for inefficient private decision making in the first instance. Many firms make participation in retirement and health insurance plans mandatory for these reasons. It protects them against paying excessively for old loyalties and "family" ties to employees. The community at large has a similar interest in mandatory participation. In practice, it often finances these programs through payroll taxes on employment.[3]

THE PRINCIPLE OF SUBSTITUTION

The basic approach to analyzing the structure of compensation was put forth by Adam Smith in his extraordinary discussion of the tendencies for labor market equilibrium to equalize the net advantages among alternative employments. If some kinds of jobs offer attractive amenities and substantial in-kind pay compared with others, their observed monetary compensation must be lower to ration eager job applicants and encourage some workers to apply to less attractive employments. This idea implies an index number approach to assessing "total advantages," imputing value for all in-kind and other components and adding them to nominal wages to assess the total. In equilibrium, all components additively substitute for each other at the margin. Otherwise net advantages would not be equalized.

The compelling simplicity of the logic of equalizing differences is not always matched by simplicity of application, especially in the realm of public policy. As has been stressed throughout this essay, the many alternative ways of providing consumption to people makes it important to keep substitution possibilities and private incentives in mind when analyzing public programs. In many cases there are important offsets. Direct effects of policies are not always as large as they might appear on the surface. The important consequences of many programs are as likely to arise from hidden subsidies built into many of them, as to the programs themselves.

Examples are easy to find. Indeed, analysis of these programs has provided plenty of work for analysts over the years, something like a works-project-administration relief bill for applied economists in the past few decades.

1) When the payroll tax was increased to finance Medicare for elderly persons in the United States in the mid 1960s, there was a significant decline in private health insurance purchases by the aged. To be sure, Medicare increased health insurance coverage among the elderly population, but the subsequent run-up in expenditures was caused as much by the enormous subsidy in Medicare prices as by increased coverage.

2) Private pension plans in the U.S. labor market invariably coordinate their benefits and provisions with a worker's expected claims on Social Security pensions. From a firm's point of view, it is a matter of indifference whether a dollar is paid into a funded private pension plan or into Social Security's unfunded pay-as-you-go system through payroll taxes. Many have argued that the decline in private saving in the United States is partly attributable to the substitution of unfunded government pensions for funded private pensions.

3) The financing of public unemployment benefits increases the propensity for many firms to increase layoffs in adverse business conditions and increase the unemployment rate (Topel 1983). These kinds of incentives are even more adverse in the Canadian system than in the U.S. system because high-risk firms do not pay actuarial fees reflecting the risk they impose on the system to the insurance fund. Furthermore, the enormous subsidies for seasonal unemployment in the maritime provinces causes inefficient tax distortions in employment decisions elsewhere in Canada and encourages many workers to remain employed in seasonal industries even though their productivity is much lower in them than in other locations or in nonseasonal jobs.

4) The tendency for European governments to closely regulate employment commitments of firms affects their propensity to hire young workers, thus increasing the joblessness of youth and worsening their long-term prospects (Lazear 1990).

There is compelling empirical evidence of substitution between wages and private fringe benefits and direct on-the-job consumption amenities in the form of equalizing differences (Woodbury 1983; Rosen 1986). Nonetheless, what often appears in the data seems not to be equalizing in this sense at all because it is generally the good jobs— the ones with high wages, good working conditions, and low turnover—that offer the most fringe benefits. Low wage jobs are more often associated with poor working conditions, high turnover and exposure to unemployment, as well as low fringe benefits. This, however, does not affect the logic of substitution and the necessity for analysis to proceed on such terms in contemplating new regulations and programs because these observations also are readily explained by a few simple extensions of the argument.

Focusing on the consumption aspects of pay composition reveals why higher paying jobs tend to offer more benefits and perquisites. Many consumption items tied to work are normal goods. They have positive income elasticities, so higher skilled and higher wage workers would be expected to purchase more of them, on average, than would lower skilled, lower wage workers. Were it not for greater consumption and participation in these kinds of arrangements, highly skilled workers would have even higher wage rates than are actually observed. Favorable tax treatment of some forms of fringe benefits reinforces the incentives for high wage workers to convert their pay to these forms.

Estimates of total resources spent in these forms are surprisingly hard to find, but they must be a fairly large component of total compensation. Health and retirement benefits, certainly the most easily measured components, account for about 10 percent of total monetary compensation (Smeeding 1983; Slottje et al. 2000). Assessing implicit values for such things as job security, work and location amenities, flexible work schedules, and a wide variety of other aspects of work has proven more difficult, not least because of the reasons mentioned in the paragraph above. Surely numbers on the order of another 10 percent of total pay would seem to be a reasonable minimum. If so, fringe benefits broadly defined must account for 20 percent or more of total compensation in the U.S. labor force. Adding the payroll taxes used to finance a number of other related social programs contributes a substantial amount more. These are large numbers. They are important components of the economy and can be expected to grow over time.

SOME EXAMPLES AND APPLICATIONS

Some extreme cases illustrate many issues arising in the economics of fringe benefits in a dramatic way. Perhaps the most unusual case is military compensation. A substantial amount of military compensation is in-kind. In the ancient world, plunder was a principle component of military pay—today compensation is provided by governments. Conscription in modern armies relieved the state of most direct cash payment obligations, so a very large fraction of conscript army pay was direct provision of consumption and future retirement benefits. Nonetheless, even in voluntary armies the proportion of direct monetary pay in total compensation is much smaller as compared with that of other employments.

Almost all the factors mentioned above apply in one way or another to military compensation (Rosen 1992). The nature of military production requires massing personnel in far off locations largely removed from the rest of the population, so separation of consumption from production is difficult, if not impossible. The remote areas in which military outposts are placed makes it costly for private markets to supply many consumption needs directly to soldiers. The army itself must be a major provider of many of these things. To a large extent, these expenditures are taken "off the top" and make military monetary compensation appear smaller than is truly the case.

The army has direct interests in the consumption and behavioral patterns of personnel to maintain its readiness and force-quality status. Partly, this is controlled directly in the consumption goods that are made available, a point that is reinforced by the economies of scale in providing standardized consumption and other expenditures for recruits. In addition, the army has special reasons for insisting on common consumption standards and a fair bit of equality of treatment among recruits, to maintain and invest in the esprit de corps needed to maintain an effective force. Loyalties to the organization are extremely important because of the obvious conflicts between self-interest and organizational interest in dangerous situations.

Of course, many military-specific skills also have little value in other employments. To protect its training investments in personnel from excessive depreciation through turnover, military organizations tend to back load pay to a significant extent, with vesting rights set up in ways that encourage career personnel to stay for lengthy periods. Back-loaded retirement pay also helps resolve agency and obedience problems that encourage proper teamwork. There are sound economic reasons why military organizations are so paternalistic.

Some private employments have military-like features. Work required in far flung outposts, such as the Hudson Bay Company in the 19th Century, or the Alaskan pipeline in the 20th, largely followed the military model because the market for consumption goods was too thin to make complete decentralization practical. Furthermore, in many of these circumstances, the employing firms had a direct interest in the consumption patterns of their employees because it might affect their productivity. Institutions such as the truck system and the company store arose to meet these needs (Hilton 1957).

The former Soviet Union and other countries in the Eastern Bloc provide interesting contemporary examples of how fringe benefits affect resource allocation. The examples also have implications for current economic reforms there because the change in control of enterprises and production needed now may be impeded by past obligations the State enterprises made to their employees (Lazear and Rosen 1995).

In many ways those economies followed a military-style economic organization, something that is practically inevitable in a central command and control system. In addition to their overwhelming role in total production, the state-owned enterprise typically served as the natural administrative unit through which many aspects of consumption were organized. Housing was often provided to employees at subsidized rates, as were public utilities, child care, and many direct consumption items such as food and clothing. Income in-kind and other "fringe benefits" were a much larger proportion of total pay in these economies than in most market economies, partly for ideological reasons, but also because centrally commanded systems need substitutes for market mechanisms.

The socialist structure was inherently paternalistic. It encouraged equality and common consumption standards to promote solidarity and commitment to the system. Housing, education, food, and health services were viewed as more socially productive kinds of consumption than were other goods. Conspicuous consumption was stigmatized. The practicalities of central control were important as well. The command system does not allow prices to fully allocate resources across most goods. Draconian penalties for participating in illegal markets discouraged their use. When the state determines production and consumption allocations, surpluses and shortages of both goods and jobs become a chronic condition of life. Other, far more costly, social institutions arise to fill in the gap.

Queues are a familiar manifestation of nonprice rationing allocation problems, but there are other mechanisms that serve this purpose, including clout, political connections, and barter. For example, the provision of a substantial hot meal in company lunchrooms was very common in State enterprises because alternative markets either for prepared meals or for raw ingredients were so limited. Furthermore, the central authority had to limit labor mobility in order to carry out is production plans. More goods were made available in large cities such as Moscow than in other places, and an elaborate system of passport control was needed to insure that workers remained where the central plan allocated them. State control of housing was required for these purposes, and since wage rates were not allowed to clear specific labor market shortages and surpluses, firms often supplied their own housing to get the labor they needed. Company-provided housing was itself partially allocated by internal queues within the firm rather than by prices.

The tax system that supported the state bureaucratic apparatus in these economies was hidden in total government ownership of physical capital. However, there were substantial implicit payroll taxes because state income and old-age security, and some health services, though formally administered by the central and local governments, were financed through taxes on the utilization of labor by enterprises. The absence of well-functioning private financial institutions also required extensive involvement of the state and enterprises in intertemporal allocations of consumption (saving and dissaving) of workers over their lifetimes. For example, retired workers often remained in their company-provided housing paying little for rent and utilities.

In short, Soviet workers were important stakeholders in their enterprises. These intensive ties and social commitments undoubtedly were a major force in the operation of soft-budget constraints and unattainable consumption desires that eventually brought the system down. However, they have also presented serious obstacles for reform and movement toward a market system in these countries. In the command system, the firm and the state were so intertwined that it was almost impossible to distinguish between the obligations of the two. Now that the enterprise and the state have to be so clearly separated, it is not obvious to whom these commitments to workers will be transferred and how they will honored when control of enterprises redounds to private hands. The state may sell off claims to machinery, equipment, and structures, but who will gain "title" to the security and consumption obligations these firms have built up with their workers?

No doubt, many of these obligations will merely be forgotten, and workers, left with broken promises, will have to fare on their own devices. Presently it is obvious that a system of consumer and worker "sovereignty," where workers' economic fortunes and connections were not so closely tied to specific enterprises, would make the transition to a market economy much easier. Uncertainty about previous commitments is proving to be an enormous obstacle in moving toward a rational ownership and market structure in these countries. In China, the remarkably productive rural and agricultural reforms hardly have been attempted in the large urban State enterprises. These difficulties are not confined to poor economies. In such rich countries as the new, unified Germany, the willingness of West Germans to pick up the social obligations of their Eastern relatives has been a great economic and social drag on that economy. Other formerly socialist or communist countries have no such rich relatives to lean upon. These problems are not only confined to countries attempting to reform their economic structures. In the United States, tie-ins of some fringe benefits to job holding, such as health insurance, apparently have inefficiently limited labor mobility between firms in recent years (Madrian 1994).

CONCLUSIONS

Fringe benefits are of importance to such fundamental labor market problems as the social organization of work and production, as well as to social and moral obligations between workers and firms and of governments to citizens. These issues cut deeply into core issues in labor economics and, indeed, of economic systems more generally. They deserve more attention than they have generally received from the economic research community.

Notes

1. Some jobs embody negative attributes and disutility. In principle, these should be subtracted from total income to arrive at final consumption.
2. No doubt the individual income tax is a factor here as well. However, it is not decisive because offices, secretaries, and other complementary inputs usually were provided to managers free of charge before the income tax was important. The income tax encourages excessive use of these things—plusher offices on higher floors and more secretaries and assistants.
3. This logic helps one to understand why there is a community interest in "social" programs, but it cannot explain either the form it takes or the magnitude of the interest. It cannot explain why governments have often gone into these businesses directly rather than regulating participation in private programs; nor can it account for the great growth of these programs in this century.

References

Hamermesh, Daniel S. 1993. *Labor Demand.* Princeton: Princeton University Press.

Hart, Robert A. 1984. *The Economics of Non-Wage Labour Costs.* London: George Allen and Unwin.

Hilton, George W. 1957. "The British Truck System in the Nineteenth Century." *Journal of Political Economy* 65(June): 237–256.

Lazear, Edward. 1990. "Job Security Provisions and Employment." *Quarterly Journal of Economics* 105(June): 699–726.

Lazear, Edward, and Sherwin Rosen. 1995. "Publicly Provided Goods and Services in a Transition Economy." In *Economic Transition in Eastern Europe and Russia: Realities of Reform*, E. Lazear ed. Palo Alto, California: Hoover Press.

Madrian, Brigitte.   1994.   "Employment-Based Health Insurance and Job Mobility: Is their Evidence of Job Lock?" *Quarterly Journal of Economics* 109(February): 27–54.

Rosen, Sherwin. 1985. "Implicit Contracts: A Survey." *Journal of Economic Literature* 23(3): 1144–1175.

Rosen, Sherwin. 1986. "The Theory of Equalizing Differences." In *Handbook of Labor Economics,* Vol. 1, O. Ashenfelter and R. Layard eds. Amsterdam: North Holland.

Rosen, Sherwin. 1992. "The Military as an Internal Labor Market: Some Allocation, Productivity, and Incentive Problems." *Social Science Quarterly* 73(June): 227–237.

Slottje, Daniel J., Stephen Woodbury and Rod W. Anderson. 2000. "Employee Benefits and the Distribution of Income and Wealth." Chapter 9 of this volume.

Smeeding, Timothy. 1983. "The Size Distribution of Wage and Nonwage Compensation." In *The Measurement of Labor Cost*, J. Triplett ed. Chicago: University of Chicago Press.

Topel, Robert. 1983. "On Layoffs and Unemployment Insurance." *American Economic Review* 73(September): 541–559.

Woodbury, Stephen A., and Wei-Jang Huang. 1991. *The Tax Treatment of Fringe Benefits*. Kalamazoo, Michigan: W.E. Upjohn Institute for Employment Research.

Woodbury, Stephen A. 1983. "Substitution between Wage and Nonwage Benefits." *American Economic Review* 73(March): 166–182.

Part I

Worker Availability and Labor Supply

1 Child Care and the Supply of Labor in Canada and the United States

Charles Michalopoulos
Manpower Demonstration Research Corporation

Philip K. Robins
University of Miami

Increases in the employment of married women over the past few decades have been accompanied by changes in child-care choices. Today, more than one-half of all preschool children receive care during part of the day by someone other than their parents. Among children of employed parents, there has been an increasing trend toward the use of formal types of child-care arrangements, such as day-care centers and group day-care homes. Because the child-care market has become so important, economists have intensified their efforts to understand the market. Economists in both the United States and Canada have studied the effects of child-care prices on women's employment (Blau and Robins 1988; Connelly 1992; Kimmel 1995a; Cleveland, Gunderson, and Hyatt 1994), the effects of child-care prices on receipt of welfare (Connelly 1990; Kimmel 1995b), the effects of child-care costs on fertility (Blau and Robins, 1989), and the effects of child-care subsidies on employment and child-care costs (Heckman 1974; Hofferth and Wissoker 1992; Michalopoulos, Robins, and Garfinkel 1992; Ribar 1992, 1995; Cleveland and Hyatt 1994). All of these studies examine choices using data from a single country, either the United States or Canada. In contrast, this paper examines child-care choices in both countries, using a pooled data set based on national surveys in each country. Our objective is to exploit variation between the two countries to obtain better estimates of the factors that affect child-care and employment decisions.

Several recent papers have examined the effects of child-care subsidies in the United States on child-care choices and employment of mothers of young children. Hofferth and Wissoker (1992) predicted that subsidies would have a substantial effect on the mode of care chosen. According to their estimates, if states were to increase subsidies to nonparental care by 10 percent, there would be an 11 to 30 percent increase in the use of center-based care, a 6 to 10 percent increase in care by relatives, and a 12 to 18 percent reduction in parental care. Michalopoulos, Robins, and Garfinkel (1992) find that increases in child-care subsidies would increase child-care expenditures, but such subsidies might have little impact on either the quality of care or the employment of mothers of young children. According to their estimates, making the U.S. child-care tax credit considerably more progressive would more than triple child-care expenditures and increase child-care subsidies by a factor of eight. Even with such massive changes, however, they predict that the quality of child care would increase by only 30 percent and that hours worked by mothers of young children would increase by only 6 percent.[1]

A potential problem with estimating the effects of child-care subsidies using data from only one country is that parents are eligible for many of the same subsidies. For example, both countries have subsidies through the federal income tax, which depend on a family's taxable income and child-care expenses. In principle, all families within a country have the same incentives because all are subject to the same income tax system. Previous studies have examined the effects of subsidies within a particular country using instruments to predict potential subsidies. Michalopoulos, Robins, and Garfinkel, for example, used nonlabor income and predicted wage rates to determine potential subsidies.

Previous research has also found that higher child-care prices reduce the use of market care and lower the likelihood of employment of mothers of young children. However, the magnitude of this effect is still being debated in the literature (See Blau [1995], for example). Ribar (1992) found relatively large effects of prices, while Michalopoulos, Robins, and Garfinkel (1992) found very small effects. Chaplin et al. (1996) found that the effect of price is quite sensitive to the definition of price. As with subsidies, child-care prices are not given solely by providers but depend on a family's choices. Due to economies of scale, parents who work full time can expect to pay less per hour of care than those who work part time, if the care is of the same type and quality (Folk and Beller 1993). Parents can also choose from a variety of types of care, each with a different quality and price.

In this chapter, we follow previous studies in examining the effects of economic factors on child-care and employment choices. However, we add to previous studies by using pooled data from Canada and the United States in examining choices. Because there is a natural separation of markets between the two countries, and because the citizens of the two countries are subject to different systems of subsidies and regulations, we should be able to exploit exogenous differences in prices, wages, and subsidies to obtain more precise estimates of the effects of economic factors on child-care and employment choices.

According to two national surveys of child care, about half of Canadian and U.S. mothers of preschool children work in a given week, and Canadian families are slightly less likely to use parental care and center care as the primary source of care for children under age 13. Among mothers who work full time, however, Canadian mothers are only about two-thirds as likely to use center care and correspondingly are more likely to use other non-relative care. Among mothers who do not work, Canadian mothers are much more likely than U.S. mothers to use center care and correspondingly are less likely to use parental care. After controlling for various economic and demographic factors, we find that if Canadians were to face the same economic circumstances as U.S. mothers, they would be somewhat less likely to work full time. When they do work full time, Canadian mothers are less likely to use center care; when they do not work, however, Canadian mothers are less likely to use parental care. However, we find little role for differences in prices and subsidies in affecting these child-care choices.

This chapter has two objectives. The first is to describe child-care programs and choices in the two countries. The second is to assess the importance of economic differences between the two countries in child-care and employment choices. In the following sections, we summarize the major child-care subsidy programs in the two countries and discuss their respective regulations; we use national survey data from each country to examine differences in child-care choices and child-care prices; and we provide an assessment of the role of differences in tax credits, prices, and regulations, as well as other economic and demographic factors.

CHILD-CARE POLICIES IN CANADA AND THE UNITED STATES

Federal and local child-care policies are similar in Canada and the United States, but there are some differences. Both countries provide subsidies directly to parents though their federal income tax systems, as well as through subsidies targeted toward low-income families. In both countries, state and provincial governments regulate child-care providers. In addition, the Canadian provinces and most of the United States provide additional tax relief to users of child care. One key difference between the two countries has to do with state and provincial subsidies. While state spending in the United States is dwarfed by federal spending, provincial subsidies to providers who care for children in needy families are larger than federal expenditures in Canada. While state subsidies in the United States are largely targeted toward families receiving welfare, many more families in Canada are eligible for subsidies.

Federal Subsidies

In the United States, the federal government spent nearly $10 billion in 1992 on a complicated array of at least 41 federal programs that spend money directly on child care plus five additional programs that give tax breaks for families with child-care expenditures. The largest federal government expenditures were $2.8 billion for the child-care tax credit (which works through the federal income tax code) and $2.2 billion for the Head Start program.[2] In addition, the federal government provided about $3 billion in grants to the states, including $1.1 billion on the Child Care Food Program, $300–$400 million each on child care for families receiving Aid to Families with Dependent Children (AFDC), at-risk children, and the Child Care and Development Block Grant (Committee on Ways and Means of the U.S. House of Representatives 1993), and approximately $800 million on the Title

XX Social Services Block Grant.[3] Another $3 billion in tax revenue was lost through tax exclusions for employer-provided child care.

The Canadian child-care subsidy system appears to be somewhat simpler than the U.S. system. As in the United States, the Canadian federal government subsidizes child care through the income tax code.[4] In 1989, about 600,000 families claimed the tax credit, for a tax savings of $288.5 million (Hess 1992). (Note that throughout this paper, Canadian expenditures are converted to U.S. dollars using a conversion rate of 0.75 U.S. dollars per Canadian dollar.) The Canadian government also provides grants to the provinces, which are used to subsidize child care for needy families. In contrast to the array of federal programs in the United States, the Canadian government provides funds to the provinces primarily through one program, the Canadian Assistance Plan (CAP) (Child Resource and Research Unit 1993).

The federal tax-based subsidies in the two countries are quite similar. Each limits the subsidy based on parents' taxable income, so that poor families with low tax bills have limited access to the subsidy. In the United States, the credit is nonrefundable, so that a family's maximum credit is its tax bill. In Canada, the maximum deduction is two-thirds of the income of the parent with lower earnings. Each credit has a maximum exemption per child. The U.S. credit allows a family to claim expenses of up to $2,400 for one child and $4,800 for two or more children. The maximum exemption for the Canadian deduction is more generous: in 1989, it allowed up to $3,000 for each child under age 7 and $1,500 for each child between 7 and 14.[5] In both countries, the subsidy is generally available to parents regardless of the type of child care used, with some minor restrictions. In Canada, the child-care provider cannot be a member of the immediate family or a relative under age 21, and the caregiver must provide a receipt. In addition, the taxpayer must be employed, operating her own business, or working on a research grant to receive the credit. In the United States, the credit is available only to parents who work or are looking for work and taxpayers who claim the credit must provide the name, address, and an identification number of the caregiver.

The primary difference in the two plans is the relationship between allowable expenditures and the amount of the credit. In Canada, child-care expenses up to the maximum allowable amount are deducted from a parent's taxable income, so that a taxpayer essentially receives a rebate at her marginal tax rate.[6] In the United States, the credit also depends on family income but is not directly related to the tax rate. For families with income below $10,000, the credit is 30 percent of allowable expenditures. The credit rate declines gradually to 20 percent for families earning more than $28,000. As a result, the maximum credit declines as income increases in the United States, but increases (with a parent's earnings) in Canada, along with the marginal tax rate.

To compare the tax-based subsidies in the two countries, we calculated the amount that a family would receive under a variety of circumstances: if they paid $1 for child care for each hour the mother worked, if the husband earned $50,000 per year, if the family had one child under age 7, and if they took standard deductions and filed jointly in the United States. Figure 1 summarizes these calculations. The tax-based subsidy is shown for each country for up to 2,500 hours worked per year by the mother at two wage rates—$5 per hour and $20 per hour. For the lower wage earner, the U.S. credit is more generous. A woman has to work only about 250 hours (earning $1,250) in order to be eligible for some credit and would receive more than $500 per year if she worked full time. In contrast, because a Canadian mother can claim a larger amount of nontaxable earnings, she would have to work 1,000 hours before having to pay taxes and hence be eligible for a tax subsidy and would receive about $300 per year if she worked full time. For the higher wage earner, the Canadian system appears to be more generous, providing about $700 per year for a full-time worker, while the U.S. credit provides about $400 for a full-time worker. Similar calculations for larger families and for families with higher spousal income reveal the same pattern: the Canadian system is more generous for higher-earning families, but less generous for lower-earning parents because the marginal subsidy rate in the United States is lower for families with higher income, while the marginal subsidy rate in Canada is tied directly to the marginal tax rate.

Provincial and State Subsidies

Every Canadian province has an income-tested subsidy provided directly to a family's licensed child-care provider. Table 1 summarizes key features of the provincial subsidies in 1991. As is obvious from the table, the subsidies vary in generosity and eligibility from province to

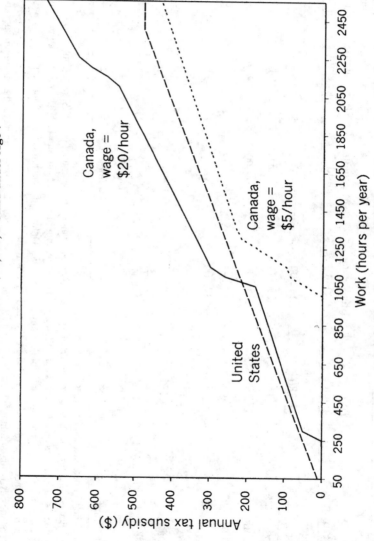

Figure 1 Federal Child-Care Tax Subsidies in Canada and the United States
Assumptions: Husband's Annual Income = $50,000, 1 Child under Age 7

Table 1 Features of the Canadian Provincial Child-Care Subsidies, 1991 ($)[a]

Province	Turning point[b]	Break-even point	Maximum subsidy[c]	Expenditure per child	Federal contribution per child
Newfoundland & Labrador	8,280	14,490	NA	10	7
Prince Edward Island	11,160	29,376	16.50/day	54	26
Nova Scotia	13,590	25,200	15.75/day	36	23
New Brunswick	10,098	19,629	10.50/day	14	6
Quebec	11,250	37,500	NA	41	28
Ontario	12,715	19,509	NA	107	25
Manitoba	14,171	30,055	3,164/year	90	52
Saskatchewan	15,651	32,571	90% of fee	36	20
Alberta	17,085	28,478	276/month	43	15
British Columbia	17,079	23,317	430/month	74	30

SOURCE: The Childcare Resource and Research Unit 1993.

[a] All Canadian expenditure numbers were converted to U.S. dollars using an exchange rate of 0.75 U.S.$ per Can$.

[b] The turning point is the income level at which a family is no longer eligible for the full subsidy. The break-even point is the income level at which the family is no longer eligible for any subsidy. For Ontario, the break-even point and turning point are not uniform across the providence. The numbers provided are the median in Toronto.

[c] Maximum subsidy is for an infant, generally less than 2 years old, in a center. For some provinces, the maximum subsidy depends on the provider's fee. These are marked "NA."

province. A family is potentially eligible for the full subsidy as long as its income is below the turning point (the income level at which the family is no longer eligible for the full subsidy).[7] As a result, in British Columbia and Alberta, a two-parent family with two children can earn more than $17,000 per year and still be potentially eligible for the full subsidy. In contrast, Newfoundland and Labrador will pay the full subsidy only to families with less than $8,250 in annual earnings. A family is potentially eligible for some subsidy until its income reaches the break-even point. As a result, a family can potentially earn more than $30,000 per year in Manitoba, Saskatchewan, and Quebec before it loses eligibility for provincial subsidies. In contrast, a family in Newfoundland is ineligible for the subsidy if it earns $14,250 or more per year.

In the United States, individual states also subsidize child care. Each of the states subsidizes child-care expenses for welfare recipients and provides funds to match federal Title XX Social Services Block Grants. In addition, many of the states provide subsidies directly to parents through state income tax child-care credits. In 1989, 28 states had such credits (Robins 1991). Like the federal income tax credit, most states' credits are nonrefundable. Only two states, New Mexico and Minnesota, had refundable credits. As a result, poor families with working parents were eligible for meager subsidies, as is the case for the federal tax credit. The maximum credit also varies considerably, from a high of $1,440 in Minnesota and $1,200 in New Mexico to a low of $39 per year in Arizona.

In general, the provinces appear to provide more generous subsidies per capita than do the states. In 1992, the provinces spent $353 million for subsidies to providers of needy children, the federal government contributed another $225 million for this subsidy through the CAP program, and the provinces spent another $226 million in other subsidies for providers (Child Resource and Research Unit 1993). Among the larger provinces, Ontario spent more than $100 per child under 12, British Columbia about $74, and Quebec about $40. In contrast, in 1985, the states spent a comparatively small $1.5 billion on child-care services (in 1992 dollars), including federal contributions, and another $350 million on income tax credits for child care (Robins 1991). California was the most generous state, spending nearly $80 per child under 12. Other large states spent much less, ranging from $16 per child under 12 in Texas to $65 in New York.[8]

Provincial and State Child-Care Regulations

While the federal governments provide funds for subsidizing child care, the states and provinces have individual regulations on both family providers and center care. These regulations take a number of forms, including background checks on providers, training requirements, and minimum education requirements. In this section, we focus on three of the regulations that are most common: the maximum number of children that a family provider can care for before being subject to regulation, the child-to-staff ratios for family providers and centers, and the maximum number of children for which a regulated family provider or center can provide care.

Figures 2 through 6 summarize and compare the percentage of children subject to several types of regulations. For example, Figure 2 shows the maximum number of children allowed in family day care. The lines in Figure 2 show the proportion of children under age 13 who live in states or provinces with a given regulation. About 25 percent of all Canadian children live in provinces which prohibit more than five children in family day care, while only about 5 percent of U.S. children live in states with such a stringent regulation.

According to all five figures, Canada appears to have more stringent child-care regulations.[9] Consider Figure 2 again. Among the states that regulate family providers, only the District of Columbia, Florida, Oklahoma, Alaska, and Massachusetts limit family providers to six or fewer children. In contrast, provinces representing about 65 percent of children (including Ontario and Quebec) have such stringent regulations. Most of the large states allow 12 or more children, including California, New York, Texas, Illinois, Michigan, and North Carolina.

All the provinces and most of the states limit the child-to-staff ratio. Figures 3 and 4 summarize the maximum number of children that the states and provinces allow in day-care centers for 18-month-old children and 4-year-old children, respectively. Again, Canada appears to have much more stringent regulations. Nearly half of all Canadian 18-month-old children live in provinces which allow no

Figure 2 Maximum Number of Children Allowed in Family Day Care (Percentage of Children Covered)

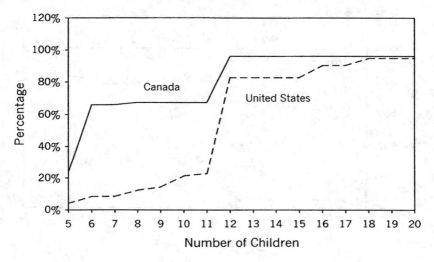

Figure 3 Child-to-Staff Ratio for 18-Month-Old Children in Center Care (Percentage of Children Covered)

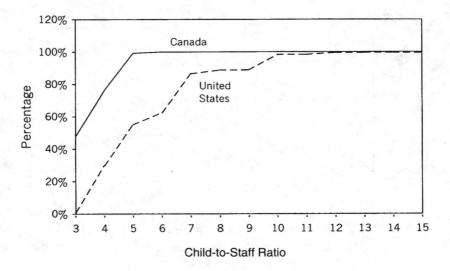

**Figure 4 Child-to-Staff Ratio for 4-Year-Old Children in Center Care
(Percentage of Children Covered)**

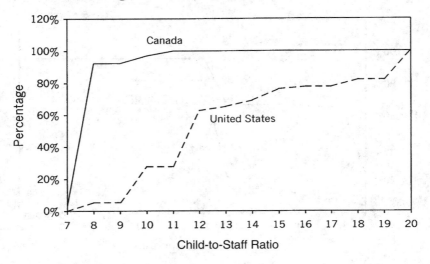

**Figure 5 Maximum Group Size for 18-Month-Old Children
in Center Care
(Percentage of Children Covered)**

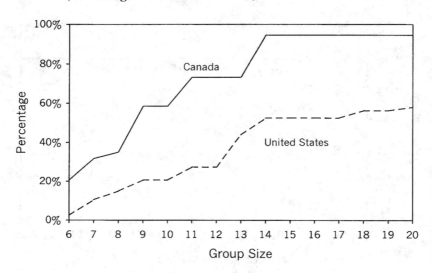

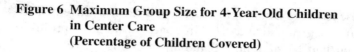

**Figure 6 Maximum Group Size for 4-Year-Old Children
in Center Care
(Percentage of Children Covered)**

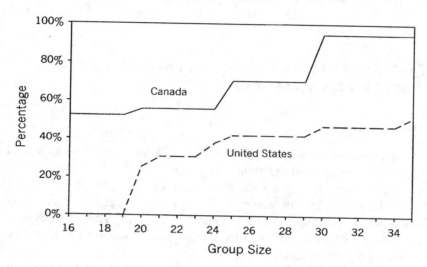

more than three children per group. In contrast, among the United States, only Maryland has such a stringent regulation. While no Canadian province allows more than six 18-month-old children per staff member, nearly 40 percent of U.S. children live in states which allow more than six children. The pattern is the same for 4-year-old children (Figure 4). While more than 90 percent of Canadian children live in provinces which prohibit more than eight children per staff member, fewer than 5 percent of U.S. children live in such states.

Most states and provinces also limit group size in center care. Figures 5 and 6 summarize these regulations for 18-month-old children and 4-year-old children, respectively. Once again, Canadian regulations appear more restrictive. Except for Prince Edward Island, New Brunswick, and Saskatchewan, which do not regulate group size, all provinces prohibit groups of 18-month-old children with more than 14 children. In contrast, nearly half of U.S. children live in states with no group-size regulations or regulations that allow more than 14 children. For 4-year-old children (Figure 6), more than 50 percent of children—

including those living in Ontario, Manitoba, and Alberta—live in provinces that cap the group size at 16. In contrast, no state prohibits groups smaller than 19, and more than half of children live in states with no group-size regulation.

CHILD-CARE CHOICES AND PRICES— A DESCRIPTIVE ANALYSIS

Data

This section describes the child-care choices made by U.S. and Canadian families and the child-care prices faced by those families. If Canadians are making different choices, then further investigation might be warranted to determine how those choices are affected by price, public policies, and other economic factors. However, even if choices are the same, differences in economic circumstances might be contributing to this similarity.

To examine these issues, we use data from two national surveys of families with children under age 13. For the United States, we use the National Child Care Survey of 1990 (USNCCS). The USNCCS contains information on a nationally representative sample of U.S. families with children under age 13. Families were chosen from phone lists in 100 counties and county groups, and interviews were conducted if the family had a child under the age of 13. To make the sample nationally representative of families with young children, the 100 counties were randomly selected, with a probability of selection proportional to the number of children under 5 in the county. Information was obtained on child-care choices and expenditures, as well as labor-market behavior, income, and demographics.[10]

For Canada, we use the National Child Care Survey of 1988 (CNCCS). The CNCCS was a supplement to the Canadian Labour Force Survey, a nationally drawn survey of labor-market activity. As with the USNCCS, the CNCCS uses a multistage stratified sampling technique to obtain information for families with children under the age of 13. Because the survey is a supplement to the Canadian Labour Force Survey, its sample is designed to be representative of the labor force, not families with young children. In addition, in order to obtain accurate information on sparsely populated areas, families from small provinces are oversampled. As with the USNCCS, information was collected on child-care choices and expenditures, labor-market behavior, income, and demographic characteristics.[11]

A drawback to the CNCCS is that it contains limited information on earnings and wages. Annual household income, as well as income for parents, is reported in ranges of $7,500, with a top range of $45,000 and higher. Hourly wages are not reported, and calculation of hourly wages based on categorical income would result in sizable measurement error. Because hourly wages are a key component in analyzing employment and child-care choices, and because annual earnings are important for determining eligibility for child-care tax subsidies, an auxiliary part of our econometric analysis uses a second Canadian sample from the Labour Market Activity Survey (LMAS).[12] The LMAS provides information on hourly wages and hours of work for a subsample of parents in the CNCCS. Powell (1997) linked the CNCCS and the LMAS.

Primary Child-Care Choices

In both child-care surveys, parents were asked for the primary, secondary, and tertiary choices of child care for each child. In this paper, we focus on the primary child-care choice. Table 2 presents the distribution of primary child-care choices in the USNCCS and the full sample of the CNCCS for children less than 13 years of age. Although U.S. families who were surveyed were given different options than Canadian families, we place choices into seven groups: care by a parent at home or at work, care by a relative in the child's home, care by a relative outside the child's home, care by someone other than a relative in the child's home, care by someone other than a relative outside the child's home, center-based care, and other.[13]

As Table 2 indicates, child-care choices are remarkably similar in the two countries.[14] Canadian parents are slightly less likely to take care of the children themselves or to use center care; they are slightly more likely to use other types of care. Although the magnitude of the differences is generally small, the sample sizes are large enough so that all but one of the differences are statistically significant.

Table 2 Distribution of Primary Child-Care Choices in Canada and the United States, Children 0–12 Years Old

Type of care	United States (%) (7,578 children)	Canada (%) (41,331 children)	t-statistic[a]
Center	13.3	11.8	3.6*
Parents	56.6	51.7	7.9*
Relative, in the child's home	7.5	9.2	9.9*
Relative, outside the child's home	7.5	7.8	0.9
Non-relative, inside the child's home	3.1	5.8	11.7*
Non-relative, outside the child's home	7.2	10.5	9.9*
Self-care and other	4.7	3.2	5.8*

SOURCE: Statistics Canada's National Child Care Survey of 1988 and The Urban Institute's National Child Care Survey of 1990.
[a] t-test that the probability is the same between countries. The chi-squared statistic for the test of the hypothesis that the distributions are the same: 261.3*.
*Difference between Canada and the United States is significant at the 5% level.

Although the primary choices are similar between the two countries, there are some important underlying differences. Tables 3 and 4 show the choices of care by the age of the child and the mother's employment status. From previous research, we know that mothers who work full time are more likely to use center care, which tends to be a more stable source of care. Mothers who do not work are generally more likely to rely on their own care. We also expect child-care arrangements to differ with the age of the child. Infants are more likely to be cared for by their parents or by relatives or non-relatives in the child's home. Older children are much more likely to be cared for in centers.

According to Table 3, the most striking differences between Canadian and U.S. children are in center care and care provided by the par-

Table 3 Distribution of Primary Child-Care Choice by Child's Age in Canada and the United States (%)

Type of care	<1 year old	1–2 years old	3–4 years old	5 years old
Center				
United States	7.4	14.6	31.9	21.6
Canada	2.2	9.2	31.8	48.6
t-statistic	4.9*	3.7*	0.0	14.6*
Parents				
United States	60.6	50.1	41.1	49.4
Canada	54.8	43.6	32.2	24.7
t-statistic	2.8*	2.1*	1.4	11.7*
Relative, inside the child's home				
United States	8.0	6.6	4.3	6.7
Canada	9.6	8.1	6.6	5.5
t-statistic	1.4	1.4	5.8*	2.5*
Relative, outside the child's home				
United States	8.1	10.3	7.7	8.2
Canada	14.2	12.6	9.4	5.3
t-statistic	5.1*	1.7	2.1*	2.5*
Non-relative, in the child's home				
United States	3.6	3.8	2.4	3.8
Canada	6.7	8.9	6.8	4.7
t-statistic	3.6*	5.6*	4.2*	1.0
Non-relative, outside the child's home				
United States	10.0	12.6	10.4	8.6
Canada	12.5	17.6	13.2	11.2
t-statistic	1.8	3.4*	2.6*	2.1*
χ^2 statistic for null hypothesis of same distributions	113.9*	61.7*	42.8*	215.7*

SOURCE: Statistics Canada's National Child Care Survey of 1988 and The Urban Institute's National Child Care Survey of 1990.

*Difference between the U.S. and Canadian percentages is significant at the 5% level.

Table 4 Distribution of Primary Child-Care Choices by Mother's Employment Status in Canada and the United States (%)

Type of care	Mothers employed full time	Mothers employed part time	Mothers not employed
Center			
United States	30.7	19.5	13.4
Canada	20.1	18.4	24.1
t-statistic	8.4*	0.6	10.5*
Parents			
United States	23.3	46.3	69.2
Canada	21.0	35.5	48.3
t-statistic	1.3	6.9*	15.1*
Relative, inside the child's home			
United States	6.6	6.2	5.4
Canada	8.8	8.9	6.2
t-statistic	3.7*	2.6*	1.2
Relative, outside the child's home			
United States	12.1	10.3	5.5
Canada	11.9	10.3	10.2
t-statistic	0.5	0.9	6.5*
Non-relative, in the child's home			
United States	3.2	3.6	2.7
Canada	9.4	8.6	5.4
t-statistic	9.5*	9.0*	5.2*
Non-relative, outside the child's home			
United States	22.2	12.3	2.5
Canada	28.8	19.1	5.6
t-statistic	4.9*	5.8*	6.1*
χ^2 statistic for null hypothesis that distributions are the same	218.8*	199.4*	294.7*

SOURCE: Statistics Canada's National Child Care Survey of 1988 and The Urban Institute's National Child Care Survey of 1990. Employment status was determined by hours worked by the mother during the survey reference week, with full time defined as 35 hours or more.
*Difference between the U.S. and Canadian percentages is significantly different at the 5% level.

ents. Canadian preschool children of all ages are less likely than corresponding U.S. children to receive parent care as their primary care. Similarly, Canadian children who are less than 3 years old are less likely to be cared for in centers than are their U.S. counterparts. However, Canadian 5-year-olds receive quite different care than U.S. 5-year-olds. About twice as many 5-year-old children in Canada are in center care as in parent care, while the proportions are reversed in the United States. For infants, the difference in parental care is made up for in Canada by use of relatives outside the child's home and non-relatives inside the child's home.

Table 4 compares the child-care choices for children who live with their mothers and the hours worked by the mother in the week prior to the interview. The differences are even more striking in this table. While Table 2 indicates that Canadian families overall are slightly less likely to use center care, Canadian mothers who work full time (30 hours or more per week) are much less likely to use center care than U.S. mothers. Only about 20 percent of Canadian mothers who work full time use center care, but more than 30 percent of U.S. mothers who work full time use center care. Equally striking is that Canadian mothers who did not work are the most likely to use center care, and they are almost twice as likely as nonworking U.S. mothers to use center care. While Canadians overall use less parental care, this masks underlying differences across employment status. Both Canadian and U.S. mothers who work full time use parental care about 22 to 23 percent of the time.[15]   In contrast, U.S. mothers who are not employed are much more likely to rely on their own care (69.2 vs. 48.3 percent).

Differences in use of center care partly reflect a difference in the surveys. In the USNCCS, school was not considered a source of care while, in the CNCCS, kindergarten was considered a source of care and grouped with center care. Therefore, 5-year-old Canadian children in kindergarten are considered to be in center care while 5-year-old U.S. children in kindergarten are assigned their secondary source of care. Likewise, Canadian children who are in kindergarten and who have unemployed mothers are considered to be in center care, while U.S. children who are in kindergarten and who have unemployed U.S. mothers are probably listed as being cared for by their parents.

Price of Child Care

Differences in regulations should affect the price of care in the two countries. In addition, the very generous provincial subsidies to providers of children in needy families should decrease the price of care paid by parents in Canada. While the subsidies are paid only to licensed providers, they might also lower prices for relative care and unregulated day-care services because parents might be unwilling to pay much for unlicensed care if licensed care is available and inexpensive.

Table 5 presents the results of tobit regressions of the price per hour of care paid for nonparental care for the youngest child under 6 in two-parent families.[16] The sample includes all families indicating that a particular type of care was used as the primary care. However, the sample is limited to the youngest child in each family since the most accurate information is collected for these children.[17]

According to these results, U.S. families paying for care paid 95 cents more per hour for center care, 72 cents more per hour for relative care, and 38 cents more per hour for non-relative care.[18] Because we use a tobit regression, these differences are most easily interpreted as the difference in hourly payments among parents who pay for care. In contrast, a simple comparison of mean hourly payments among parents paying for care (not reported) indicates that the United States pays 75 cents more per hour for center care, 63 cents more for relative care, and 6 cents less for non-relative care.

According to the estimated coefficients, more stringent regulations substantially affect the price of relative and non-relative care. Increasing the maximum children in regulated family care lowers the price of relative and non-relative care by 20 and 6 cents per hour. In addition, relative and non-relative care in states in which this maximum is not specified are substantially cheaper. For center care, the child-to-staff ratio has little effect, while allowing the group size to increase by one child leads to a 1.8 cent increase in the hourly price.

Table 5 Determinants of the Hourly Price of Child Care in Canada and the United States, Youngest Child Under 6 in Two-Parent Families (tobit estimates, standard errors in parentheses)

Variable	Relative care	Non-relative care	Center care
Intercept	0.3943	1.6427*	0.1354
	(0.6234)	(0.1193)	(0.2660)
U.S. family	0.7239	0.3848*	0.9451*
	(0.4418)	(0.0802)	(0.1662)
Child-care regulations			
Maximum children in regulated family care	−0.2067*	−0.0601*	
	(0.0457)	(0.0088)	−
Maximum children in regulated family care not specified	−2.4423*	−0.4168*	
	(0.7025)	(0.1519)	−
Maximum child-to-staff ratio			0.0090
	−	−	(0.0127)
Maximum group size in center care			0.0179*
	−	−	(0.0039)
Maximum group size not regulated			0.2020
	−	−	(0.5049)
Other variables			
Age of child is under 1 year	−1.4989*	0.1697*	0.1484
	(0.3552)	(0.0687)	(0.1858)
Age of child is 1–2 years	−0.4631	0.2044*	0.4068*
	(0.2775)	(0.0553)	(0.1269)
Number of children under age 6 years	−0.7705*	−0.3034*	−0.5055*
	(0.2394)	(0.0478)	(0.0995)
Number of children age 6–18 years	−1.0957*	−0.1300*	−0.0320
	(0.1419)	(0.0315)	(0.0530)
Lives in metropolitan area	−0.1755	0.3883*	0.1530
	(0.2490)	(0.0515)	(0.0851)
Standard error of distribution	4.5356*	1.3246*	1.9690*
	(0.1375)	(0.0188)	(0.0342)
Number of observations	3,163	3,511	2,744
Average price of care (families paying for care) ($)	1.74	1.56	1.72
Percentage of families paying for care	24.3	82.7	71.7
Log of likelihood function	−2,681	−5,100	−4,485

*Significantly different from 0 at the 5% confidence level.

THE EFFECTS OF TAX CREDITS AND PRICES ON EMPLOYMENT AND CHILD-CARE CHOICES

As discussed previously, child-care tax subsidies are different in the two countries, regulations are set by provinces and states, and provinces provide generous subsidies for children in needy families. These differences in policy have some testable implications. Greater subsidies for child care should encourage mothers of young children to work by expanding their choices of affordable child care.[19] Likewise, those subsidies should increase the likelihood of using nonparental care, which is often paid for. Stringent regulations should have the opposite effect. If licensed providers must comply with stringent regulations, they will be forced to charge more for their services. Increased prices for market child care would presumably lower the likelihood that a mother with young children would work and that she would choose market forms of care. This section attempts to test some of these hypotheses more directly.

A Model of Employment and Child-Care Choices

A common approach to estimating child-care choices is to use a multinomial logit model (see Duncan and Hill [1975] and Hofferth and Wissoker [1992], for example). We use a similar approach. Specifically, we assume that a mother chooses how much to work and which child-care type to use to maximize her utility.[20] According to this notion, the mother's decisions will be influenced by prices of various child-care opportunities, her potential earnings and other income, her preferences, and her ability to produce child care in the home. Assume that the utility of the ith individual, if she chooses employment state j and child-care mode k, is given by

$$V_{ijk} = S_{ijk} \alpha + p_{ik} \beta_j + w_i \delta_{1jk} + N_i \delta_{2jk} + X_i' \delta_{3jk} + \varepsilon_{ijk}$$

where
p_{ik} is the price per hour of child care mode k for mother i,
w_i is the mother's hourly wage rate,
N_i is her nonlabor income, which we limit to spouse's income,[21]

S_{ijk} is the potential child-care tax credit she would receive if she works at level j and chooses mode k,[22]

X_i are other characteristics of the mother, and

ε_{ijk} is random component that is i.i.d. across mothers, modes of care, and employment choices.

In this model, the explanatory variables can be classified into three types. Tax-based child-care subsidies, which depend on both income and the amount spent on care, vary by work state and child-care mode. To identify the effects of subsidies, we force the effect of subsidies to be the same across employment states and child-care modes. In other words, an extra dollar of subsidy has the same effect on utility whether the parent is considering using center care or relative care and whether the parent is considering working full time or part time. It is the *amount* of the potential subsidy that varies across these choices. The price of child care is assumed to vary only by child-care mode, so its effect is assumed to be constant within an employment state. That is, if the cost of all forms of care increased by $1 per hour, it would not affect the relative probabilities of choosing a particular type of care, but it would affect the choice of how much the mother works because working would entail higher expenses. No other variables differ by child-care mode or employment state. These variables include economic factors, such as the hourly wage rate and other sources of income, as well as demographic factors, such as the ages of the children. The contribution of these factors is assumed to vary from choice to choice. For example, the effects on utility of having a 1-year-old child will be different if the parent stays home and cares for the child than if the parent works full time and puts the child in a center.

The mother chooses employment state j and child-care mode k if $V_{ijk} > V_{ilm}$ for all l and m. If the ε_{ijk} have an extreme value distribution, the probability of working is given by the logistic distribution function. To implement this model, we let j take on three values: 0 if the mother did not work in the week prior to being interviewed, 1 if she worked part time (fewer than 35 hours) in the week prior to being interviewed, and 2 if she worked full time (35 or more hours in the week prior to being interviewed).[23] We let k take on four values: 0 for parent care, 1 for relative care, 2 for non-relative care, and 3 for center care.[24]

To identify the effects of prices, wages, and tax credits in this model, we also assume:

$$p_{ijk} = b_{0k} + b_{1k}X_i + b_{2k}Reg_{ij} + u_{ijk}$$

$$w_i = c_0 + c_1X_i + c_1Age_i + c_3Education_i + v_i$$

$$S_{ijk} = f(N_i, w_i, p_{ijk})$$

where

p_{ijk} is the price paid by family i, living in state/province j, choosing child care mode k,

Reg_{ij} are child care regulations in i's state/province, and

Age and $Education$ are used to represent the human capital of mother i.

Under this specification, we identify the effects of prices by allowing local regulations to affect prices but not to directly affect employment or child-care choices. We identify the effects of wages by allowing age and education of the mother to affect only wages but not employment or child-care choices directly.[25]

A number of calculations are necessary in order to estimate these relationships. The price a family pays for child care is endogenous: the family may choose to pay a high price in order to receive high quality care. In addition, we do not know what a family would have had to pay for types of care that it did not use. Therefore, we use the results of Table 5 to predict the price of three types of child care: relative care, non-relative care, and center care. First, we use the regression results to predict an hourly price for each type of care. For all predictions, we simulate the full distribution of prices by adding a random component to each predicted price, drawn from a normal distribution. The addition of these random components was originally suggested by Manski and Lerman (1977) as a possible means of avoiding the inconsistency of parameter estimates that results from using predicted values in a nonlinear regression. Because we use tobit analysis, there is a natural method of predicting whether a family would pay for care: if the predicted price for a family is negative, we assume the family would receive free care of that type.

We also predict wages for all women.[26] We do this for several reasons. As for child-care prices, potential wage rates are not known for mothers who do not work. In addition, we calculate wage rates in Canada from earnings and hours worked. Since this calculation introduces measurement error, an instrumental variable approach is indicated. Finally, wage rates might be endogenous to employment decisions. Women who choose to work full time are likely to receive higher wages than those who work part time simply because employers will offer higher wages to anyone who is willing to work full time. Women who are receiving higher wages are likely to be those who are more committed to the labor market, who have accumulated human capital over time, and therefore are more likely to continue working regardless of the wage they could receive.

The third calculation is of the potential tax-based subsidy for which a family would be eligible.[27] As with prices and wages, this measure is endogenous because it depends on child-care expenditures and either total family income (in the United States) or earnings of one of the parents (in Canada). Also, as with some prices and wages, the tax-based subsidy for an individual is unobserved. To calculate the tax-based subsidy, we assume that a mother will work either 0, 20, or 40 hours per week, depending on whether she does not work, works part time, or works full time; we assume that she works each week of the year; and we assume that she uses a particular child-care type for all children under 6 for each hour that she works.[28]

This model focuses on the decisions of the mother, taking the decisions of other family members as given. In particular, only the earnings of the father are considered, and it is assumed to be exogenous. This implies that the utility of other household members does not enter directly into the decision-making process, an assumption that is valid if family labor supply decisions are made sequentially, with the family first determining the work status of the father, and then determining hours supplied by the mother. In theory, the labor supply of a husband and wife are likely to be made simultaneously. Mroz (1988), however, provides some evidence that other income—primarily from the husband—is exogenous to the wife's labor supply.

Differences in Choices and Explanatory Variables by Country

Before turning to the econometric results, we present the distribution of child-care and employment choices as well as the means of explanatory factors used in the econometric analysis in Table 6. The sample used in Table 6, as well as the econometric analysis, consists of

Table 6 Sample Means of Variables Used in Econometric Analysis of Child-Care and Employment Choices, Married U.S. and Canadian Mothers of Children Under 6 Years Old

Variable	U.S. families	Canadian families
Distribution of employment and child-care choices		
Percentage employed full time	33.8	26.9
Using center care	10.8	4.8
Using relative care	6.5	5.9
Using non-relative care	8.5	10.2
Using parent care	8.0	6.0
Percentage employed part time	19.1	22.9
Using center care	3.6	3.8
Using relative care	3.5	4.2
Using non-relative care	2.8	6.7
Using parent care	9.2	8.2
Percentage not employed	47.1	50.1
Using center care	5.5	8.6
Using relative care	5.2	8.5
Using non-relative care	2.8	5.3
Using parent care	33.6	27.7
Predicted hourly price of care ($)		
Center care	1.74	1.02
Relative	0.82	0.89
Non-relative	1.70	1.76
Predicted annual subsidy ($)		
Full-time worker using center care	424	260
Full-time worker using non-relative	141	147
Full-time worker using relative	479	482
Part-time worker using center care	312	105
Part-time worker using non-relative	144	67
Part-time worker using relative	327	194

Variable	U.S. families	Canadian families
U.S. family (%)	100.0	0.0
Child is less than 1 year old (%)	24.6	23.6
Child is 1–2 years old (%)	37.4	39.4
Number of children under age 6	1.40	1.40
Number of children age 6–12	0.56	0.52
Husband's earnings (%)		
$15,001–22,500	15.7	18.3
$22,501–30,000	18.0	29.2
$30,001–37,500	17.1	24.0
$37,501–45,000	9.7	11.5
$45,001 and higher	20.9	8.3
Black (U.S.A. only, %)	9.0	0.0
Hispanic (U.S.A. only, %)	10.3	0.0
Lives in urban area (%)	41.1	79.5
Immigrant (Canada only, %)	0.0	21.6
Predicted wage ($)	10.37	9.76

two-parent families in which the youngest child is under age 6. Child-care choices are shown for the youngest child in these families, so that each family enters the calculation only once. Knowing the differences between countries will be useful in assessing the impact of various factors on differences in employment and child-care choices in the two countries.

The first part of Table 6 shows the percentage of mothers making each of the 12 possible choices. This table differs from Table 4 in two ways. First, the sample is different, consisting of choices for youngest children under 6, whereas Table 4 shows results for all children under 6. Second, the first part of Table 6 shows the overall distribution of choices, whereas Table 4 showed child-care choices given the mother's employment status. According to the first part of Table 6, U.S. mothers are more likely than Canadian mothers to work full time but less likely to work part time or to not work. Most of the difference in full-time employment is reflected in the greater use of center care by full-time working U.S. mothers (10.8 vs. 4.8 percent). Although fewer Canadian mothers work full time, more work full time and use non-relative care (10.2 vs. 8.5 percent). Likewise, while fewer U.S. mothers do not work or work part time, more U.S. mothers both do not work and use parent care (33.6 vs 27.7 percent) and work part time and use parent care (9.2 vs. 8.2 percent), indicating that Canadian mothers working less than full time are more likely to use other sources of care.

Table 6 next shows the mean predicted hourly price of care, by type of care. The means in Table 6 include both families that are predicted to pay nothing for care and those predicted to pay something. According to Table 6, center care and non-relative care for the entire sample are equally expensive, at about $1.70 per hour. Since relative care is so often free, the cost of using relative care is about $1.00 less per hour. While the means for center and non-relative care are similar in the United States, Canadians are predicted to pay just over $1.00 for center care—only about $0.10 more than for relative care—but still pay $1.76 for non-relative care. Canadians are predicted to pay less, on average, for center care because fewer Canadians are predicted to pay anything for center care (49 vs. 69 percent, numbers not shown).

Table 6 then shows the mean of predicted tax-based subsidies for six possible combinations of work (full-time and part-time) and child care (center, non-relative, and relative).[29] Differences in subsidies across countries reflect not only differences in prices but differences in the tax structures of the two countries. First, full-time working Canadian mothers are predicted to receive lower subsidies if they use center care because the price of center care is predicted to be lower in Canada. However, full-time working Canadian mothers who use either relative care or non-relative care are predicted to receive about the same tax-based subsidies as U.S. families. In contrast, Canadian mothers who work part time are predicted to receive lower average subsidies regardless of the type of care they use. This stems from the primary difference in the tax code between the two countries: U.S. couples can file jointly so that the wife's earnings in a two-earner family might be considered fully taxable, whereas Canadian couples file individually, so that a part-time working mother in Canada pays little tax (and hence receives a lower child-care tax subsidy) after the nonrefundable personal credit is deducted from her income.

The remainder of Table 6 presents differences in other explanatory factors. Several features are worth noting. The age distribution of children and the number of children is similar between countries. Roughly one-quarter of the sample have children less than 1 year old and roughly two-fifths have children between the ages of 1 and 2. Earnings of Canadian men are more equally distributed than earnings of U.S. men. Among U.S. husbands, 18.6 percent earned less than $15,000 per year, while 20.9 percent earned more than $45,000 per year. In contrast, only 8.7 percent of Canadian husbands earned less than $15,000 per year, and only 8.3 percent of Canadian husbands earned more than $45,000 per year. This finding of greater inequality in the United States corresponds with that of Blackburn and Bloom (1993), who found that the variance of male annual earnings in the United States in the late 1980s was about 10 percent higher than it was in Canada (0.32 vs. 0.29). Finally, predicted wages are similar, with U.S. women earning about 60 cents more per hour than Canadian women.[30]

Determinants of Whether a Mother Works

Table 7 presents estimates of the effects of prices, income–tax based subsidies, and demographic characteristics on the probability that a mother in the sample worked full time, worked part time, and did not work in the week prior to being interviewed.[31] The numbers in Table 7 are the product of the derivative of the probability of working times the mean difference in characteristics between women in the two countries. The numbers give a sense of the expected impact of differences in the average characteristics of the two samples and policies in the two countries. Some characteristics might be important in explaining different choices by different families (i.e., have an estimated coefficient that is significantly different from zero) but still not be important in explaining different average choices by country if families in the two countries are similar with regard to these characteristics. On the other hand, some characteristics might be quite different between countries, but not important in explaining a family's choices, and again not contribute to explaining the differences across countries. Only if a characteristic meets both criteria—significantly explains an individual

Table 7 Estimated Impact of Economic and Demographic Differences on the Distribution of Primary Child-Care Choice between Canada and the United States, Married Mothers of Children Under 6 Years Old[a]

Variable	Probability of working full time	Probability of working part time	Probability of not working
Percentage point difference in probability between U.S. and Canadian families	6.91	−3.87	−3.04
Estimated impact of			
U.S. family (%)[b]	9.06	−2.21	−6.85
Annual subsidy (000's of dollars)			
Full-time worker using center care	0.11	−0.03	−0.07
Full-time worker using non-relative	−0.01	0.00	0.01
Full-time worker using relative	−0.01	0.00	0.00
Part-time worker using center care	0.15	−0.05	−0.10
Part-time worker using non-relative	−0.002	0.06	−0.04
Part-time worker using relative	−0.06	0.19	−0.13
Hourly price of care			
Center care	−0.03	−0.01	0.05
Nonrelative	0.01	0.00	−0.01
Relative	0.01	0.00	−0.01
Child is less than 1 year old	−0.09	−0.06	0.15
Child is 1–2 years old	0.04	0.00	−0.04
Number of children under age 6	0.00	0.00	0.00
Husband's income			
$15,001–22,500	−0.13	−0.15	0.28
$22,501–30,000	0.76	0.13	−0.89
$30,001–37,500	0.35	0.18	−0.53
$37,501–40,000	0.14	0.07	−0.07
$40,001 and higher	−1.72	−1.17	2.89
Black (U.S.A. only, %)	1.23	−1.31	0.07

Variable	Probability of working full time	Probability of working part time	Probability of not working
Hispanic (U.S.A. only, %)	−0.49	−0.29	0.78
Lives in urban area (%)	−0.68	0.86	−0.18
Immigrant (Canada only, %)	−0.13	0.25−	0.11
Predicted wage ($)	0.12	0.09	−0.20

[a] Except for the first two rows, the data represent the product of the derivative of the probability of working times the mean difference in characteristics between women in the two countries. See text for a complete explanation and examples.
[b] Estimated average difference in behavior between countries from the regression (i.e., after controlling for prices, wages, etc.). See text for complete explanation.

family's choices and is substantially different between the two countries—will it help explain different employment choices.

The interpretation of the results in Table 7 can be made clearer using an example. The first row of Table 7 shows the raw differences in behavior (as implied by Table 6). Thus, it indicates that the proportion of U.S. mothers working full time is nearly 7 percentage points higher than it is for Canadian mothers, the proportion working part time is nearly 4 percentage points lower in the United States than in Canada, and the proportion of women not working in the United States is about 3 percentage points lower than it is in Canada. The second row of Table 7 shows the estimated average difference in behavior between countries from the regression (i.e., after controlling for prices, wages, and so on). As a result, the difference between the first row and the second row indicates how much these economic and demographic factors can explain different average choices in the two countries. The estimates imply that U.S. mothers are 9 percentage points more likely than Canadian mothers to work full time, nearly 7 percentage points less likely to not work, and only about 2 percentage points less likely to work part time. Thus, our model implies that if conditions and characteristics were the same in the two countries, the gap in full-time employment and not working would be even bigger than it is now.

Subsidies and prices do not help explain different employment probabilities, despite the fact that U.S. families using center care pay substantially more than Canadian families and the fact that the tax-based subsidy is more generous for part-time working mothers. Since subsidies are most different for families who use center care (because prices of center care are most different between the two countries), they have their largest effect on families who use center care. However, even this effect is small. The greater subsidy available to women employed full time and using center care would affect the difference in the proportion working full time by only 0.11 percentage points and the percentage not working by 0.07 percentage points. The greater subsidy available to women employed part time and using center care would affect the difference in the proportion working full time by 0.15 percentage points and the proportion not working by 0.10 percentage points. Likewise, differences in prices have virtually no effect, at most changing the gap in the proportion not working by only 0.05 percentage points.

Of the economic and demographic characteristics, only two have a substantial impact on employment choices: having a spouse with earnings over $40,000 and being a black U.S. resident. U.S. women are more likely to be married to men earning more than $40,000 per year. If Canadian women were just as likely as American women to be married to such men, the proportion of women working full time would decrease by 1.72 percentage points, the proportion working part time would decrease by 1.17 percentage points, and the proportion not working would increase by 2.89 percentage points. The other characteristic that has a substantial relationship to employment is race. If the U.S. population were completely non-black, then about 1.2 to 1.3 percent would shift from full-time work to part-time work.

Determinants of Child-Care Choice

Tables 8 through 10 are analogous to Table 7, but they show which factors affect the primary child care used for the youngest child in two-parent families with children under 6 years old for the various classes of workers. The three tables show the predicted effects of various factors on child-care choices of families with mothers who are employed full time (Table 8), employed part time (Table 9), and not employed (Table 10). In each table, child-care choices are placed into four categories: care by the parent, care by another relative, non-relative care, and center care.[32]

Table 8 Estimated Impact of Economic and Demographic Differences on the Distribution of Primary Child-Care Choices between Canada and the United States, Families with Mothers Working Full Time and Children under 6[a]

Variable	Probability of using center care	Probability of using relative care	Probability of using non-relative care	Probability of using parent care
Percentage point difference in probability between U.S. and Canadian families	6.01	0.64	−1.74	2.03
Estimated impact of				
U.S. family (%)[b]	7.77	−0.57	0.11	1.75
Annual subsidy (000's of dollars)				
Full-time worker using center care	0.14	−0.01	−0.01	−0.01
Full-time worker using non-reltive	0.00	−0.01	0.00	0.00
Full-time worker using relative	0.00	0.00	−0.01	0.00
Part-time worker using center care	−0.01	−0.01	−0.02	0.19
Part-time worker using non-relative	0.00	−0.01	−0.01	−0.01
Part-time worker using relative	−0.01	−0.02	−0.02	−0.02
Hourly price of care				
Center care	−0.05	0.01	0.01	0.01
Non-relative	0.00	0.01	0.00	0.00
Relative	0.00	0.00	0.01	0.00
Child is less than 1 year old	−0.03	−0.02	−0.02	−0.02
Child is 1–2 years old	0.05	0.00	−0.03	0.01
Number of children under age 6	0.00	0.00	0.00	0.00
Number of children age 6–12	−0.12	−0.17	−0.21	0.07

(continued)

Table 8 (continued)

Variable	Probability of using center care	Probability of using relative care	Probability of using non-relative care	Probability of using parent care
Husband's earnings				
$15,001–22,500	–0.01	–0.07	–0.04	–0.01
$22,501–30,000	0.03	0.07	0.23	0.44
$30,001–37,500	0.02	0.14	–0.11	0.30
$37,501–45,000	0.01	0.05	0.02	0.06
$45,001 and higher	–0.03	–0.59	–0.54	–0.57
Black (U.S.A. only, %)	0.36	1.07	–0.38	0.18
Hispanic (U.S.A. only, %)	–0.18	0.44	–0.60	–0.15
Lives in urban area (%)	–0.35	–0.27	0.34	0.40
Immigrant (Canada only, %)	0.07	–0.37	0.16	0.01
Predicted wage	0.03	–0.05	0.09	0.04

[a] See Table 7 notes and the text for explanation of values.

Table 9 Estimated Impact of Economic and Demographic Differences on the Distribution of Primary Child-Care Choice between Canada and the United States, Families with Mothers Working Part Time and Children under 6[a]

Variable	Probability of using center care	Probability of using relative care	Probability of using non-relative care	Probability of using parent care
Percentage point difference in probability between U.S. and Canadian families	–0.22	–0.73	–3.88	1.03
Estimated impact of				
U.S. family	0.84	–2.70	–3.45	3.09
Annual subsidy (000's of dollars)				
Full-time using center care	–0.01	–0.01	–0.01	–0.01
Full-time using non-relative	0.00	0.00	0.00	0.00
Full-time using relative	0.00	0.00	0.00	0.00
Part-time using center care	–0.01	–0.01	–0.01	–0.02
Part-time using non-relative	0.07	–0.01	–0.01	–0.01
Part-time using relative	–0.01	0.24	–0.02	–0.02
Hourly price of care				
Center care	–0.03	0.00	0.00	0.01
Non-relative	0.00	0.00	0.00	0.00
Relative	0.00	0.00	0.00	0.00
Child is less than 1 year old	–0.03	–0.01	0.01	–0.01
Child is 1–2 years old	0.04	0.01	–0.04	–0.01
Number of children under age 6	0.00	0.00	0.00	0.00
Number of children age 6–12	–0.02	0.00	0.00	0.01
Husband's earnings				
$15,001–22,500	–0.01	0.03	–0.06	–0.10
$22,501–30,000	0.02	0.09	–0.01	0.02
$30,001–37,500	–0.03	0.17	0.00	0.05
$37,501–40,000	–0.02	0.02	–0.05	–0.02
$40,001 and higher	–0.09	–0.57	–0.34	–0.17

Table 9 (continued)

Variable	Probability of using center care	Probability of using relative care	Probability of using non-relative care	Probability of using parent care
Black (U.S.A. only, %)	–0.20	–0.20	–0.45	–0.45
Hispanic (U.S.A. only, %)	–0.11	0.36	–0.30	–0.26
Lives in urban area (%)	–0.40	1.57	0.30	–0.62
Immigrant (Canada only, %)	0.18	–0.34	0.23	0.18
Predicted wage	0.04	–0.05	0.02	0.08

[a] See Table 7 notes and the text for explanation and examples.

Table 10   Estimated Impact of Economic and Demographic Differences on the Distribution of Primary Child-Care Choice Between Canada and the United States Families with Mothers Not Working and Children Under 6[a]

Variable	Probability of using center care	Probability of using relative care	Probability of using non-relative care	Probability of using parent care
Percentage point difference in probability between U.S. and Canadian families	−3.08	−3.32	−2.48	5.92
Estimated impact of				
U.S. family	−4.43	−6.99	−43.9	8.97
Annual subsidy (000's of dollars)				
Full-time using center care	−0.02	−0.01	−0.01	−0.03
Full-time using non-relative	0.00	0.00	0.00	0.00
Full-time using relative	0.00	0.00	0.00	0.00
Part-time using center care	−0.03	−0.02	−0.01	−0.05
Part-time using non-relative	−0.01	−0.01	0.00	−0.02
Part-time using relative	−0.02	−0.03	−0.02	−0.07
Hourly price of care				
Center care	0.02	0.01	0.00	0.02
Non-relative	0.00	0.00	0.00	0.00
Relative	0.00	0.00	0.00	0.00
Child is less than 1 year old	−0.14	0.11	0.04	0.14
Child is 1–2 years old	0.25	−0.10	−0.11	−0.08
Number of children under age 6	0.00	0.00	0.00	0.00
Number of children age 6–12	−0.07	0.10	0.06	0.34
Husband's earnings				
$15,001–22,500	0.06	0.05	0.13	0.05
$22,501–30,000	−0.02	−0.13	−0.25	−0.49
$30,001–37,500	−0.18	−0.26	−0.02	−0.07
$37,501–40,000	−0.12	0.01	0.02	0.01
$40,001 and higher	1.14	0.54	1.11	0.10

Table 10 (continued)

Variable	Probability of using center care	Probability of using relative care	Probability of using non-relative care	Probability of using parent care
Black (U.S.A. only, %)	0.10	0.40	−0.07	−0.67
Hispanic (U.S.A. only, %)	0.01	1.56	−0.42	−0.36
Lives in urban area (%)	−1.04	1.72	0.19	−1.05
Immigrant (Canada only, %)	−0.06	0.21	−0.01	−0.25
Predicted wage	0.03	−0.11	0.01	−0.14

[a] See Table 7 notes and the text for explanation and examples.

The results in Tables 8 and 9 imply that economic and demographic differences explain little of the differences between Canadian and U.S. child-care choices. For example, U.S. mothers are about 6 percentage points more likely than Canadian mothers to work full time and use center care. Economic and demographic differences alter this gap by about 1.76 percentage points; if economic and demographic characteristics were the same in the two countries, U.S. mothers would be 7.77 percentage points more likely to work full time and use center care. Among women working full time, only one factor explains even a 1-percentage-point difference in choices: if all U.S. women were non-black, then 1.07 percentage points fewer would work full time and use relative care. Likewise, among women working part time, only one factor explains even a 1-percentage-point difference in choices: the greater concentration of Canadians in urban areas lowers the difference in use of relative care by 1.57 percentage points and lowers the difference in use of parent care by 0.62 percentage points

The model does a better job at explaining differences in choices of care among women not working (Table 10). In particular, use of relative care and parent care by mothers who do not work is quite different after adjusting for demographics, prices, wages, and subsidies. The most important demographic and economic characteristics appear to be spouse's earnings, race, and urban status. If as many Canadian husbands had earnings of more than $40,000, the difference in use of center care and non-relative care would be about 1 percentage point greater. If no U.S. mother were black, the difference in use of relative care and parent care would change by about two-thirds of a percentage point. Likewise, if no U.S. mothers were Hispanic, the percentage using relative care would change by about 1.5 percentage points, while the percentage using non-relative care or parent care would change by about two-fifths of a percentage point. If Canadians and U.S. populations were equally urbanized, the difference in use of center care would change by about 1 percentage point, while the use of relative care would change by nearly 2 percentage points.

CONCLUSIONS

This chapter has used national child-care survey data in Canada and the United States to compare employment and child-care choices in the two countries. Government programs are similar in the two countries. Both countries have nonrefundable subsidies for child care that operate through the federal income tax system. In both countries, states and provinces impose regulations on child-care providers with respect to child-to-staff ratios, maximum center size, and screening procedures.

Overall, the employment and child-care choices of Canadian families are quite similar to those of U.S. families. In both countries, about 40 percent of mothers do not work and nearly 20 percent of mothers work part time. In both countries, more than 50 percent of parents provide primary care for their children, about 10 percent use center care, and about 15 percent use family care. However, Canadian families pay substantially less for center care than U.S. families. In addition, the subsidy through the federal tax system in Canada is somewhat more generous to full-time workers than the federal tax credit in the United States. We are unable to find strong evidence that subsidies and prices are important determinants of employment and child-care choices in the two countries. The factors that seem to be the most important causes of differences in employment and child-care choices are the husband's earnings (particularly in families where the husband earns more than $40,000 per year), race/ethnicity, and geographic location.

However, the bulk of the differences between the two countries are not explained by the variables included in our empirical model.

Notes

We are grateful to a number of people who have assisted us in our effort: Sandra Hofferth and Sheri Azer provided information on child-care regulations in the United States; Susanna Gurr provided information on Canadian regulations and subsidies; Paul Fronstin provided an extract of the Urban Institute's National Child Care Survey and information on the federal and state income tax credits in the United States; Michael Sivyer of Statistics Canada provided us with the Canadian National Child Care Survey of 1988; and Lisa Powell linked the CNCCS with the LMAS. We also wish to acknowledge extensive and helpful comments on an earlier version of this paper by Charles Beach, Gordon Cleveland, and Jean Kimmel.

1. To infer the effects of subsidies on quality, Michalopoulos, Robins, and Garfinkel assume that the hourly price of child care is directly proportional to quality. This is true only if child-care markets are perfectly competitive, if there are no differences in costs from place to place, if parents have full information about the care their children receive, and if quality is best measured by the parents' preferences regarding alternative sources of care. In contrast, a child-development expert might argue that quality can be measured only by looking at inputs which are known to enhance the child's development. For an excellent overview of quality and child care, see Blau (1991).
2. Because of its highly developmental nature, Head Start is not always placed in the category of child-care programs.
3. Robins (1991) estimates that the U.S. federal government spent about $550 million on the Title XX Social Serices Block Grant in 1985. The Consumer Price Index increased 34.5 percent between 1985 and 1992. If expenditures have just kept pace with inflation, Title XX grants would have totaled about $740 million in 1992.
4. These subsidies are the result of an income tax deduction, since child-care expenditures are deducted from taxable income.
5. For 1993, this was changed to a maximum deduction of $3,750 for each child under the age of 7 and for each handicapped child under the age of 15, and up to $2,250 for each child between the ages of 7 and 14.
6. The Canadian federal tax code does not allow joint returns. In a two-parent family, the parent with the lower income claims the child-care deduction. For the analysis of this paper, we assume the mother is always the parent claiming the deduction.
7. Not all families who are income eligible receive the subsidy described in Table 1. First, the subsidy is not an entitlement; each province has a limited amount of money allocated to subsidies. Second, as the table implies, each province has a maximum expenditure level that will be subsidized. Finally, each province has

social criteria for eligibility, such as requiring employment or training. As a result, there is evidence that 80 percent of child-care subsidies goes to single-parent families.

8. The source for these numbers is Robins (1991), who reports state expenditures per child under 18. since there are approximately two children under 12 for every three children under 18, we multiplied the per-child expenditures by 1.5 to make them comparable to the Canadian expenditures. In addition, the amounts have been inflated by 34.5 percent to account for the change in the Consumer Price Index between 1985 and 1992.

9. Stringent regulations are unlikely to affect the quality of child care if they are not enforced. We have no information about the relative enforcement of regulations in the two countries. In the United States, for example, Phillips and Mekos (1993) compared regulations in Georgia, Virginia, and Massachusetts. While Massachusetts had the most stringent regulations, its regulations were also most likely to be ignored. Nevertheless, child-to-staff ratios and group sizes were lower in Massachusetts than in either Georgia or Virginia.

10. See Hofferth et al. (1991) for more details on this survey.

11. See Special Services Group of Statistics Canada (1992) for more information regarding sampling techniques and information contained in the survey.

12. To be specific, we use the subsample from the LMAS only in estimating the relationship between a mother's wages and her age, education, and location. The results of this exercise are used to predict wages for the entire CNCCS sample, allowing us to use the entire sample for the primary econometric analysis in the following section on the effects of tax credits and prices.

13. Canadian families were asked to classify care as kindergarten, school program, relative inside and outside the home, non-relative inside and outside the home, center-based, respondent, respondent's spouse at work, respondent's spouse at home, older sibling, and self-care. To arrive at our definitions, we defined center care as care in a center, kindergarten, or school program; we included older siblings in relative care; and we defined parent care as care by the respondent or his or her spouse. U.S. families were given a broader range of choices. However, preprocessing of the data by the Urban Institute resulted in classifications similar to ours: center care, relatives outside the home, relatives inside the home, in-home provider, family day care, parents, and others. For comparison with the Canadian data, we equated in-home providers with non-relatives inside the home and family day care with non-relative care outside the home. The USNCCS had one type of care, lesson care, with no equivalent in the CNCCS. For children for which lesson care was the primary mode of child care, we used the secondary mode of child care. Since nearly all children in lesson care were school-age and since we focus on preschool children in this paper, this difference should not substantially affect our results.

14. In all statistical results in this paper, sample weights are used to make the results indicative of national averages.

15. This percentage might seem high, but two factors should be noted. First, parental care includes care by the father when the mother is working. Therefore, this category includes couples who stagger their work hours so that one is always available to provide care. In addition, some families with mothers who work full time have fathers who work less than full time.

16. In these regressions we make no attempt to correct for selection bias. While Ribar (1992) and Kimmel (1994) have both found that price equations are sensitive to assumptions regarding selection bias, we are not confident that the standard correction procedures provide more credible results. Note that the tobit model accounts for the fact that many users of a particular form of care report a zero price.

17. In addition, if we included all children, we would have an unbalanced panel. This would add complexity to the estimation without yielding substantially different results. In an unreported set of regressions, the sample was not limited to the youngest child but included all children under 6. Results were nearly identical to those reported.

18. By grouping Canadian kindergartners into center care but U.S. kindergartners into parent care, we are probably exaggerating the differences in cost of center care between the two countries.

19. In addition, greater subsidies might increase the gross cost of care, leaving the average net cost the same. Thus, it is possible that subsidies would have only a distributional effect in a general equilibrium setting. The model estimated in this paper does not address this issue.

20. Either parent could provide parent care. Since most parents who stay out of the labor force to care for their children are women, we focus on the mothers' decisions.

21. We limit nonlabor income to spouse's income for two reasons. First, the two primary alternative sources of income, asset income and welfare, are clearly endogenous to the mother's employment choice. Second, spouse's income is the only nonlabor income included in both surveys.

22. A number of previous studies have assumed that price of child care or the hourly subsidy affects the decision by lowering the net hourly wage rate. This is equivalent to forcing the parameter on price or the subsidy in our specification to be equal in magnitude, but opposite in sign, to the parameter on the wage rate. In contrast, our specification is more general and does not impose this restriction.

23. This procedure limits our analysis to the extensive margin, i.e., whether a mother works and, if she does work, whether she works part time or full time. An interesting question is whether child-care prices and subsidies also affect the intensive margin, i.e., how many hours a working mother works. Powell (1997), for example, finds that, for Canadian women, the elasticity of hours worked with respect to child-care prices is greater than the elasticity of participation.

24. Relative care includes relative care inside and outside the child's home. Family day care is defined as non-relative, noncenter care inside or outside the child's home.

25. In addition, our predictions of wages and prices do not correct for selection, i.e., the possibility that workers might receive higher wage offers than nonworkers and that parents using a type of care might face lower prices than other parents. Other research (Chaplin et al. 1996) has suggested that results are sensitive to variables used to identify selection equations. It is beyond the scope of this paper to test the sensitivity of estimates to alternative selection procedures. Nonetheless, our results should be suggestive of the relative effects of prices, wages, and tax subsidies on employment and child-care choices.

26. To predict wages, we use the estimated wage regression presented in Table A1 (p. 79). As in the case of prices, we add a random component to each predicted wage to simulate the full distribution of wages.

27. To measure the effects of subsidies, we focus on the federal child-care tax subsidies in both countries. In particular, we ignore the state tax credits in the United States' and Canada's provincial subsidies to providers of children in needy families. In addition, we ignore the direct effects of the many subsidies paid directly to providers. To the extent that these subsidies lower child-care prices paid by families, differences between subsidies will be reflected in differences in prices between the two countries. The effect of prices on child-care and employment choices will, therefore, include the indirect effect of subsidies paid to providers.

28. A common justification for assuming that women work either 0, 20, or 40 hours is that about three-fourths of all women either do not work or work exactly 40 hours per week. See, for example, Fraker and Moffitt (1988) or Hoynes (1993) for more discussion of the reasonableness of this assumption.

29. Predicted subsidies for nonworkers are zero since the tax-based subsidy in both countries requires recipients to work. In addition, we assume that parent care is free so that the tax-based subsidy would be zero for any family using parent care.

30. See Table A1 (p. 79) for the wage regression used to predict wages. In this regression, the effects of age and education are constrained to be the same for Canadian and U.S. women. However, an alternative specification was tried in which age and education were allowed to have different effects on wages in the two countries. This specification produced the same conclusion that U.S. women earn somewhat more than Canadian women. In addition, a specification test could not reject the simpler, constrained specification in favor of the more general specification.

31. Results of the logit regression are presented in Tables A3–A5, pp. 81–86.

32. In these tables, parent care is defined as any care by either parent, either in the home or at the place of work. Relative care is defined as care provided by a grandparent, sibling, or other nonparental relative. Informal non-relative care is care at a family day-care provider or care in the child's home. The excluded choice is parent care.

References

Blackburn, McKinley L., and David E. Bloom. 1993. "The Distribution of Family Income: Measuring and Explaining Changes in the 1980s for Canada and the United States." In *Small Differences that Matter: Labor Markets and Income Maintenance in Canada and the United States*, David Card and Richard B. Freeman, eds. Chicago: University of Chicago Press.

Blau, David M. 1991. "The Quality of Child Care: An Economic Perspective." In *The Economics of Child Care*, David Blau, ed. New York: Russell Sage Foundation.

_____. 1995. "Child Care Policy, Employment of Low Income Mothers, and Child Welfare." Paper presented at a conference on the economics of child care sponsored by Policy Analyses for California Education, University of California, Berkeley, March 8, 1995, revision, February 1996.

Blau, David M., and Philip K. Robins. 1988. "Child Care Costs and Family Labor Supply." *Review of Economics and Statistics* 70(3):374–381.

_____. 1989. "Fertility, Employment, and Child Care Costs." *Demography* 2(May):287–299.

Chaplin, Duncan D., Philip K. Robins, Sandra L. Hofferth, Douglas A. Wissoker, and Paul Fronstin. 1996. "The Price Elasticity of Child Care Demand: A Sensitivity Analysis." Unpublished manuscript.

Childcare Resource and Research Unit. 1993. *Child Care in Canada: Provinces and Territories, 1993*. Toronto: University of Toronto.

Cleveland, Gordon H., Morley Gunderson, and Douglas Hyatt. 1994. "Child Care Costs and the Employment Decision of Women: Canadian Evidence." Unpublished manuscript, University of Toronto.

Cleveland, Gordon H., and Douglas E. Hyatt. 1994. "The Effect of Price and Income on Child Care Choice: Supporting Evidence from Canada." Unpublished manuscript, University of Toronto.

Committee on Ways and Means, U.S. House of Representatives. 1993. *1993 Green Book*. Washington D.C.: U.S. Government Printing Office.

Connelly, Rachel. 1990. "The Effect of Child Care Costs on the Labor Force Participation and AFDC Recipiency of Single Mothers." Institute for Research on Poverty Discussion Paper 920-90.

Connelly, Rachel. 1992. "The Effect of Child Care Costs on Married Women's Labor Force Participation." *Review of Economics and Statistics* 75(1): 83–90.

Duncan, Greg, and C. Russell Hill. 1975. "Modal Choice in Child Care Arrangements." In *Five Thousand American Families—Patterns of Eco-*

nomic Progress, Volume III, Greg J. Duncan and James N. Morgan, eds. Ann Arbor: Institute for Social Research.

Folk, Karen Fox, and Andrea Beller. 1993. "The Relationship of Part-time and Full-time Employment Decisions to Child Care Choices." Unpublished manuscript.

Fraker, T., and R. Moffitt. 1988. "The Effect of Food Stamps on Labor Supply: A Bivariate Selection Model." *Journal of Public Economics* 35(1): 25–56.

Heckman, James J. 1974. "Effects of Child Care Programs on Women's Work Effort." *Journal of Political Economy* 82: 136–163.

Hess, Melanie. 1992. *The Canadian Fact Book on Income Security Programs*. Ottawa: Canadian Council on Social Development.

Hofferth, Sandra L., and Douglas A. Wissoker. 1992. "Price, Quality, and Income in Child Care Choice." *Journal of Human Resources* 27(1):70–111.

Hofferth, Sandra L., Duncan D. Chaplin, and Douglas A. Wissoker. 1994. "State Regulations and Child Care Choice." Unpublished manuscript, Urban Institute.

Hofferth, Sandra L., April Brayfield, Sharon Deich, and Pamela Holcomb. 1991. *National Child Care Survey, 1990*. Washington: Urban Institute Press.

Hoynes, H. W. 1993. "Welfare Transfers in Two-Parent Families: Labor Supply and Welfare Participation under AFDC-UP." National Bureau of Economic Research Working Paper No. 4407.

Kimmel, Jean. 1995a. "The Effectiveness of Child Care Subsidies in Encouraging the Welfare-to-Work Transition of Low-Income Single Mothers." *American Economic Review; Papers and Proceedings* 85(2):271–275.

————. 1995b. "Child Care Costs as a Barrier to Employment for Single and Married Mothers." Working paper, W.E. Upjohn Institute for Employment Research, Kalamazoo, Michigan.

Manski, Charles F., and Steven R. Lerman. 1977. "The Estimation of Choice Probabilities from a Choice Based Sample." *Econometrica* 45(8):1977–1988.

Michalopoulos, Charles, Philip K. Robins, and Irwin Garfinkel. 1992. "A Structural Model of Labor Supply and Child Care Demand." *Journal of Human Resources* 27(1):166–203.

Mroz, Thomas A. 1988. "The Sensitivity of an Empirical Model of Married Women's Hours of Work to Economic and Statistical Assumptions." *Econometrica* 55(4):765–799.

Phillips, Deborah A., and Debra Mekos. 1993. "The Myth of Care Regulation: Rates of Compliance in Center-Based Child Care Settings." Unpublished manuscript.

Powell, Lisa M. 1994. "The Impact of Child Care Costs on Female Labour Supply: Evidence from Canada." *Canadian Journal of Economics* 30(3): 577–597.

Ribar, David. 1992. "Child Care and the Labor Supply of Married Women: Reduced Form Evidence." *Journal of Human Resources* 27(1):134–165.

_____. 1995. "A Structural Model of Child Care and the Labor Supply of Married Women." *Journal of Human Resources* 13(3): 558–597.

Robins, Philip K. 1991. "Child Care Policy and Research: An Economist's Perspective." In *The Economics of Child Care*, David Blau, ed. New York: Russell Sage Foundation.

Special Services Group of Statistics Canada. 1992. *The National Child Care Survey Microdata User's Guide.* Ottawa: Statistics Canada.

Table A1 OLS Regression of the Log of Hourly Wage for Mothers in the United States and Canada[a]

Variable	Parameter estimate
Intercept	1.2031*
	(0.2278)
U.S.	0.1840*
	(0.1856)
Education	
High school degree	0.1360*
	(0.0537)
Some post-secondary education	0.3357*
	(0.0557)
Post-secondary education	0.6719*
	(0.0584)
University degree	1.0678*
	(0.0646)
Age	
20–24 years old	0.1749
	(0.1334)
25–34 years old	0.2700*
	(0.1267)
35–44 years old	0.3457*
	(0.1274)
45 years old and older	0.3704*
	(0.1392)
Lives in metropolitan area	0.1824*
	(0.0259)
Race/ethnicity	
French is native language	–0.0518
	(0.3254)
Neither English nor French is native language	–0.0884
	(0.4543)
Black	–0.0180
	(0.0371)
Hispanic	–0.0215
	(0.0480)
R^2	0.2091

[a] Number of observations: 2,963, standard errors in parentheses.
*Different from 0 at the 5% confidence level.

Table A2 Multinomial Logit Estimates of the Choice of Primary Child-Care and Employment Parameters Related to Child-Care Prices and Tax-Based Subsidies, Married Mothers of Children under 6 in the United States and Canada[a]

Variable	Estimate
Annual subsidy (000's of dollars)	0.3004*
	(0.0737)
Hourly price of care	
Non-relative care	0.0012
	(0.0096)
Relative care	–0.0126
	(0.0146)
Center care	–0.0259
	(0.0165)

SOURCE: Canadian National Child Care Survey of 1998, Labour Market Activity Survey of 1988, and The Urban Institute's National Child Care Survey of 1990.

[a] In the United States, if the primary care is listed as lesson, then the secondary care is used as primary care. The omitted category is parent care for nonworking mothers. The intercept includes white non-Hispanic, Canadian children 3–5 years old in families with less than 20,000 Can$ in income. Standard errors in parentheses.

*Different from 0 at the 5% confidence level.

Table A3 Multinomial Logit Estimates of the Choice of Primary Child-Care and Employment Parameters for Full-Time Employment, Married Mothers of Children under 6 in the United States and Canada[a]

Variable	Center care	Relative care	Non-relative care	Parent care
Intercept	-0.5805*	-0.3687*	-0.2507	-0.7120*
	(0.2030)	(0.1724)	(0.1470)	(0.1473)
American family	1.0308*	-0.3582*	-0.2615*	0.0194
	(0.1129)	(0.1234)	(0.0996)	(0.1093)
Age of child				
Less than 1 year	-2.3369*	-0.8933*	-0.7955*	-0.8426*
	(0.1709)	(0.1142)	(0.0940)	(0.1138)
1–2 years	-0.1661*	-0.1805	-0.0464	-0.3122
	(0.1029)	(0.0928)	(0.0752)	(0.0859)
Number of children				
Under age 6	-0.5895*	-0.2372*	0.3096*	-0.0416
	(0.1022)	(0.0761)	(0.0622)	(0.0653)
Aged 6–12	-0.8269*	-0.5886	-0.5409	-0.0447
	(0.0700)	(0.0593)	(0.0495)	(0.0477)
Husband's earnings				
$15,001–22,500	0.2646	0.4466*	0.2443*	0.1508
	(0.1589)	(0.1337)	(0.1203)	(0.1137)
$22,501–30,000	-0.2756	-0.2811*	-0.4234*	-0.9022*
	(0.1491)	(0.1314)	(0.1146)	(0.1130)
$30,001–37,500	-0.1163	-0.3914*	0.1245	-0.9159*
	(0.1547)	(0.1446)	(0.1203)	(0.1276)
$37,501–45,000	-0.1592	-0.4675*	-0.1261	-0.6818*
	(0.1850)	(0.1885))	(0.1431)	(0.1580)
More than $45,000	-0.1152	-0.1992*	-0.6815*	-1.1537*
	(0.1833)	(0.2181)	(0.1564)	(0.1846)
Black (U.S.A.)	1.2046*	1.4145*	-0.2817	0.6334
	(0.2815)	(0.3054)	(0.4567)	(0.3371)
Hispanic (U.S.A.)	-0.7588	0.6315*	-0.9469*	-0.1404
	(0.4077)	(0.2819)	(0.3531)	(0.3116)

Variable	Center care	Relative care	Non-relative care	Parent care
Immigrant (Canada)	0.2664*	0.0125	–0.1931*	0.0830
	(0.0988)	(0.0857)	(0.0685)	(0.0767)
Lives in urban area	–0.1587	0.2010	–0.1300	–0.0503
	(0.1403)	(0.1233)	(0.1094)	(0.1155)
Predicted wage	0.0286	–0.0018	0.0260*	0.0217*
	(0.0050)	(0.0055)	(0.0041)	(0.0050)

SOURCE: Canadian National Child Care Survey of 1988, Labour Market Activity Survey of 1988, and The Urban Institute's National Child Care Survey of 1990.

[a] The omitted category is parent care for nonworking mothers. The intercept includes white non-Hispanic, Canadian children 3–5 years old in families with less than $15,000 in income. All amounts are in U.S. dollars. Standard errors are in parentheses.

*Different from 0 at the 5% confidence level.

Table A4 Multinomial Logit Estimates of the Choice of Primary Child-Care and Employment Parameters for Part-Time Employment, Married Mothers of Children under 6 in the United States and Canada[a]

Variable	Center care	Relative care	Non-relative care	Parent care
Intercept	−0.9142*	−0.5023*	−0.4065*	−0.2254*
	(0.2568)	(0.1871)	(0.1862)	(0.1439)
U.S. family	−0.0196	−0.9784*	−0.0650*	0.0746
	(0.1494)	(0.1477)	(0.1434)	(0.0985)
Age of child				
Less than 1 year	−2.0560*	−0.6901*	−0.6000*	−0.6967*
	(0.2421)	(0.1259)	(0.1124)	(0.0959)
1–2 years	−0.9927*	−0.2326*	−0.0978	−0.1247
	(0.1299)	(0.1050)	(0.0894)	(0.0770)
Number of children				
Under age 6	−0.5979*	−0.1547*	0.1485*	−0.0500
	(0.1325)	(0.0784)	(0.0676)	(0.0555)
Aged 6–12	−0.2719*	−0.1801*	−0.1798*	−0.1719*
	(0.1671)	(0.0617)	(0.0536)	(0.0408)
Husband's earnings				
$15,001–22,500	0.1891	0.1072*	0.4262*	0.5396*
	(0.2124)	(0.1486)	(0.1608)	(0.1192)
$22,501–30,000	−0.2552	−0.3394*	−0.1669	−0.2031*
	(0.1943)	(0.1450)	(0.1541)	(0.1163)
$30,001–37,500	−0.1779	−0.5552*	0.0366	−0.1362*
	(0.1995)	(0.1516)	(0.1576)	(0.1207)
$37,501–45,000	−0.3939	−0.2548*	−0.3965*	−0.1944
	(0.2180)	(0.1893)	(0.1771)	(0.1463)
More than $45,000	−0.2642	−0.5098*	−0.5806*	−0.2548
	(0.2302)	(0.2120)	(0.1936)	(0.1516)
Black (U.S.A.)	−0.7657	1.1811*	−1.223	−0.7704
	(0.7528)	(0.7552)	(12.7576)	(0.5349)
Hispanic (U.S.A.)	−0.2852	0.6510*	−0.4677	−0.2971
	(0.4654)	(0.3888)	(0.6071)	(0.3026)

Variable	Center care	Relative care	Non-relative care	Parent care
Immigrant (Canada)	0.2852*	−0.7443*	−0.2205*	0.1381*
	(0.1109)	(0.0920)	(0.0814)	(0.1684)
Lives in urban area	−0.3232	0.2255	−0.2199	−0.1610
	(0.1742)	(0.1440)	(0.1224)	(0.1035)
Predicted wage	0.0301*	−0.0065	0.0150*	0.0270*
	(0.0059)	(0.0059)	(0.0051)	(0.0044)

SOURCE: Canadian National Child Care Survey of 1988, Labour Market Activity Survey of 1988, and The Urban Institute's National Child Care Survey of 1990.

[a] The omitted category is parent care for nonworking mothers. The intercept includes white non-Hispanic, Canadian children 3–5 years old in families with less than $15,000 in income. All amounts are in U.S. dollars. Standard errors are in parentheses.

*Different from 0 at the 5% confidence level.

Table A5 Multinomial Logit Estimates of the Choice of Primary Child-Care and Employment Parameters for Non-Employment, Married Mothers of Children under 6 in the United States and Canada[a]

Variable	Center care	Relative care	Non-relative care	Parent care
Intercept	-0.7914* (0.1743)	-0.5535* (0.1492)	-0.4065* (0.1862)	-1.4899* (0.1976)
U.S. family	-0.8638* (0.1328)	-1.4702* (0.1286)	-0.0650* (0.1434)	1.3608* (0.1591)
Age of child				
Less than 1 year	-3.1277* (0.2273)	0.4283* (0.0955)	-0.6000* (0.1124)	0.1206 (0.1205)
1–2 years	-0.6654* (0.1060)	-0.3516* (0.0899)	-0.0978 (0.0894)	-0.6368* (0.1039)
Number of children				
Under age 6	-0.3822* (0.0803)	-0.1452* (0.0558)	0.1485* (0.0676)	-0.1105 (0.0671)
Aged 6–12	-0.3015* (0.0465)	-0.0344 (0.0478)	-0.1798* (0.0536)	-0.0441 (0.0562)
Husband's earnings				
$15,001–22,500	-0.1649 (0.1485)	-0.1140 (0.1223)	0.4262* (0.1608)	0.9716* (0.1699)
$22,501–30,000	-0.1679 (0.1387)	-0.0456 (0.1171)	-0.1669 (0.1541)	-0.1633 (0.1549)
$30,001–37,500	0.2190 (0.1424)	0.3070* (0.1224)	0.0366 (0.1576)	-0.0271 (0.1580)
$37,501–45,000	-0.6359* (0.1615)	-0.0633 (0.1572)	-0.3965* (0.1771)	-0.1957 (0.1809)
More than $45,000	-0.6979* (0.1704)	-0.3329* (0.1588)	-0.5806* (0.1936)	0.8899* (0.1799)
Black (U.S.A.)	-0.4580 (0.4669)	0.9153* (0.3800)	-1.223 (12.7576)	-0.2223 (0.7468)
Hispanic (U.S.A.)	-0.0916 (0.3993)	1.0764* (0.2853)	-0.4677 (0.6071)	-0.7703 (0.6106)

Variable	Center care	Relative care	Non-relative care	Parent care
Immigrant (Canada)	0.2447*	−0.5125*	−0.2205*	−0.1843*
	(0.0827)	(0.0699)	(0.0814)	(0.0896)
Lives in urban area	−0.0213	0.1400	−0.2199	−0.0372
	(0.1070)	(0.1132)	(0.1224)	(0.1209)
Predicted wage	0.0163*	−0.0094	0.0150*	0.0113*
	(0.0047)	(0.0050)	(0.0051)	(0.0055)

SOURCE: Canadian National Child Care Survey of 1988, Labour Market Activity Survey of 1988, and The Urban Institute's National Child Care Survey of 1990.

[a] The omitted category is parent care for nonworking mothers. The intercept includes white non-Hispanic, Canadian children 3–5 years old in families with less than $15,000 in income. All amounts are in U.S. dollars. Standard errors are in parentheses.

*Different from 0 at the 5% confidence level.

2 An Economic Model of Employee Benefits and Labor Supply

An Application of the Almost Ideal Demand System

Paul Fronstin
Employee Benefit Research Institute

Employee benefits that are voluntarily provided by employers have become a major source of income for workers in the United States. In 1960, employee benefits accounted for 8 percent of total compensation, with pensions and health insurance accounting for 3.4 percent. By 1993, employee benefits accounted for 18 percent of total compensation, or $673.6 billion, with pensions and health insurance accounting for 10.3 percent (Employee Benefit Research Institute 1995). Among firms most likely to offer employee benefits, the percentage is even higher. The U.S. Chamber of Commerce (1995) found that the average payment for pension plans and health insurance was 17.6 percent of payroll in 1994.

Pension plans are one of the most popular employee benefits provided by employers. According to Table 1, 60 percent of all wage and salary workers in 1993 were employed by an employer that sponsored a pension plan. While 79 percent of wage and salary workers participated in the pension plan when their employer sponsored a plan, only 47 percent of all wage and salary workers participated in a pension plan because some employers did not offer a pension plan, some workers did not qualify to participate in a pension plan, and some workers voluntarily choose not to participate. Of those participating in a pension plan, 54 percent were included in a defined-benefit plan, while 62 percent were included in a defined-contribution plan. Almost 25 percent participated in both defined-benefit and defined-contribution plans.

Employer sponsorship and employee participation in a pension plan varies across demographic variables and job characteristics. Table 1 indicates that older workers are more likely to work for an employer

87

Table 1 Employer Sponsorship and Employee Participation in Pension Plans

Variable	Sponsorship rate	Participation rate	Sponsored participation rate	Of those participating		Not determinable
				Defined benefit	Defined contribution	
Total	0.60	0.47	0.79	0.54	0.62	0.14
Age						
18–24	0.43	0.16	0.38	0.37	0.59	0.18
25–34	0.59	0.44	0.73	0.49	0.65	0.14
35–44	0.64	0.55	0.86	0.57	0.62	0.13
45–54	0.65	0.59	0.90	0.57	0.61	0.13
55–64	0.59	0.52	0.88	0.59	0.58	0.14
Marital status						
Married	0.62	0.52	0.84	0.55	0.63	0.13
Widowed	0.58	0.49	0.84	0.53	0.57	0.19
Divorced	0.63	0.52	0.83	0.57	0.59	0.14
Separated	0.56	0.44	0.78	0.50	0.53	0.19
Never married	0.52	0.32	0.62	0.49	0.61	0.15
Race						
White	0.61	0.49	0.80	0.55	0.64	0.13
Black	0.62	0.47	0.75	0.51	0.50	0.20

Hispanic	0.43	0.31	0.73	0.50	0.51	0.21
Other	0.55	0.41	0.75	0.52	0.63	0.15
Education						
Some school	0.36	0.25	0.69	0.45	0.48	0.21
High school	0.58	0.45	0.77	0.53	0.59	0.15
College	0.71	0.59	0.82	0.55	0.70	0.10
Graduate school	0.79	0.70	0.88	0.63	0.66	0.10
Gender						
Male	0.59	0.49	0.83	0.55	0.64	0.13
Female	0.62	0.45	0.74	0.54	0.59	0.14
Number of children						
0	0.64	0.52	0.82	0.55	0.63	0.13
1	0.60	0.48	0.80	0.55	0.61	0.14
2	0.60	0.47	0.79	0.53	0.62	0.14
3 or more	0.52	0.38	0.73	0.53	0.60	0.15
Union contract						
Covered	0.90	0.82	0.91	0.68	0.47	0.13
Not covered	0.54	0.41	0.75	0.49	0.68	0.14
Occupation						
White collar	0.68	0.54	0.80	0.55	0.66	0.12

Table 1 (continued)

Variable	Sponsorship rate	Participation rate	Sponsored participation rate	Of those participating		
				Defined benefit	Defined contribution	Not determinable
Blue collar	0.42	0.28	0.67	0.55	0.45	0.19
Service collar	0.52	0.42	0.81	0.52	0.56	0.15
Firm size						
1–24	0.17	0.14	0.82	0.35	0.62	0.15
25–49	0.43	0.32	0.75	0.42	0.60	0.15
50–99	0.59	0.46	0.77	0.44	0.63	0.12
100–249	0.70	0.55	0.79	0.48	0.59	0.13
250 or more	0.87	0.70	0.80	0.59	0.63	0.13
Industry						
Agriculture, forestry, & fishing	0.15	0.13	0.84	0.52	0.67	0.15
Mining	0.75	0.69	0.93	0.52	0.75	0.13
Construction	0.35	0.31	0.88	0.56	0.49	0.15
Manufacturing	0.75	0.64	0.85	0.54	0.68	0.13
Transportation, communications, & utilities	0.73	0.63	0.86	0.59	0.66	0.14
Wholesale trade	0.57	0.48	0.84	0.43	0.71	0.14

Retail trade	0.41	0.25	0.61	0.37	0.63	0.17
Finance, insurance, & real estate	0.71	0.57	0.80	0.52	0.75	0.14
Personal services	0.23	0.13	0.57	0.43	0.49	0.21
Business & repair services	0.33	0.25	0.74	0.36	0.82	0.10
Entertainment services	0.38	0.24	0.62	0.55	0.63	0.14
Professional & related services	0.71	0.54	0.76	0.56	0.54	0.13
Public administration	0.93	0.85	0.91	0.71	0.51	0.13
Hours of work						
Part-time	0.41	0.15	0.37	0.48	0.54	0.15
Full-time	0.63	0.53	0.84	0.55	0.62	0.14

SOURCE: Employee Benefits Supplement to the 1993 Current Population Survey.

that sponsors a pension plan, more likely to participate in that pension plan, and more likely to have a defined-benefit plan than younger workers. Not surprisingly, differences in sponsorship and participation also occur across family type, race, education, gender, unionization, occupation, firm size, industry, and hours of work.

Health insurance is another employee benefit that many employers offer to workers. According to Table 2, 74 percent of wage and salary workers were employed by an employer that sponsored a health insurance plan in 1993, and 58 percent of all workers participated in a health insurance plan. Of the 79 percent that participated in their employer's health insurance plan, 40 percent have coverage only for themselves, while 60 percent also have coverage for a family member.[1] Table 2 also shows the probability of participating in a health insurance plan and the type of plan for various demographic variables and work-related attributes.

Theoretically, workers demand employee benefits from their employer for numerous reasons. First, preferential tax treatment of employee benefits reduces the price of the benefits to both employers and employees and is thus expected to increase the demand for employee benefits. However, the evidence regarding the effect of preferential tax treatment on employee benefits is mixed. Using cross-sectional data, Alpert (1983), Clain and Leppel (1989), and Woodbury and Bettinger (1991) found positive effects of preferential tax treatment on the demand for employee benefits. However, Turner (1987) found that employees do not demand a greater number of tax-preferred employee benefits when taxes increase. In addition, Vroman and Anderson (1984) and Alpert (1987) did not find significant positive tax effects on employee benefit growth when using time-series analysis. Second, group purchasing results in lower prices for health insurance than an individual would obtain in the marketplace. Third, the existence of economies of scale in the provision of employee benefits makes it more efficient (less costly) to provide savings vehicles for retirement and health insurance through the workplace (Mitchell and Andrews 1981).

Employers have sound reasons for providing employee benefits. Many workers have strong preferences for employee benefits. As a result, competition in the labor market will force firms to provide employee benefits. Firms that do not offer the wage/benefit packages that workers desire can experience higher turnover rates as well as dif-

Table 2 Employer Sponsorship and Employee Participation in Health Plans, by Type of Plan

Variable	Sponsorship rate	Participation rate	Sponsored participation rate	Of those participating	
				Single coverage	Family coverage
Total	0.74	0.58	0.79	0.40	0.60
Age					
18–24	0.62	0.34	0.55	0.75	0.25
25–34	0.76	0.60	0.79	0.45	0.55
35–44	0.77	0.63	0.82	0.30	0.70
45–54	0.76	0.64	0.85	0.34	0.66
55–64	0.71	0.59	0.84	0.39	0.61
Marital Status					
Married	0.75	0.59	0.79	0.20	0.80
Widowed	0.71	0.59	0.84	0.69	0.31
Divorced	0.77	0.69	0.89	0.62	0.38
Separated	0.73	0.58	0.79	0.46	0.54
Never married	0.69	0.52	0.75	0.89	0.11
Race					
White	0.75	0.59	0.79	0.39	0.61
Black	0.76	0.62	0.81	0.44	0.56

Table 2 (continued)

Variable	Sponsorship rate	Participation rate	Sponsored participation rate	Of those participating	
				Single coverage	Family coverage
Hispanic	0.60	0.47	0.77	0.41	0.59
Other	0.73	0.58	0.79	0.45	0.55
Education					
Some school	0.53	0.39	0.73	0.41	0.59
High school	0.73	0.57	0.78	0.39	0.61
College	0.82	0.68	0.82	0.43	0.57
Graduate school	0.87	0.76	0.87	0.35	0.65
Gender					
Male	0.73	0.63	0.86	0.33	0.67
Female	0.74	0.53	0.72	0.49	0.51
Number of children					
0	0.77	0.64	0.83	0.54	0.46
1	0.75	0.60	0.81	0.39	0.61
2	0.74	0.56	0.77	0.27	0.73
3 or more	0.68	0.50	0.74	0.31	0.69
Union contract					
Covered	0.95	0.86	0.90	0.31	0.69

Not covered	0.70	0.53	0.76	0.42	0.58
Occupation					
White collar	0.81	0.64	0.79	0.41	0.59
Blue collar	0.56	0.37	0.66	0.47	0.53
Service collar	0.67	0.57	0.84	0.34	0.66
Firm size					
1–24	0.35	0.27	0.76	0.45	0.55
25–49	0.76	0.55	0.72	0.47	0.53
50–99	0.84	0.64	0.77	0.44	0.56
100–249	0.87	0.68	0.78	0.44	0.56
250 or more	0.94	0.77	0.82	0.36	0.64
Industry					
Agriculture, forestry, & fishing	0.30	0.24	0.80	0.36	0.64
Mining	0.91	0.85	0.93	0.16	0.84
Construction	0.50	0.41	0.83	0.32	0.68
Manufacturing	0.89	0.79	0.89	0.33	0.67
Transportation, communications, & utilities	0.85	0.75	0.88	0.29	0.71
Wholesale trade	0.79	0.68	0.86	0.38	0.62
Retail trade	0.60	0.38	0.63	0.49	0.51

Table 2 (continued)

Variable	Sponsorship rate	Participation rate	Sponsored participation rate	Of those participating	
				Single coverage	Family coverage
Finance, insurance, & real estate	0.82	0.66	0.80	0.42	0.58
Personal services	0.36	0.25	0.70	0.54	0.46
Business & repair services	0.55	0.41	0.75	0.49	0.51
Entertainment services	0.56	0.37	0.66	0.54	0.46
Professional & related services	0.82	0.61	0.74	0.45	0.55
Public administration	0.97	0.85	0.88	0.38	0.62
Hours of work					
Part-time	0.51	0.16	0.32	0.49	0.51
Full-time	0.78	0.66	0.85	0.39	0.61

SOURCE: Employee Benefits Supplement to the 1993 Current Population Survey.

ficulties recruiting workers. Virtually all studies on labor mobility conclude that pension plans significantly reduce turnover rates (Bartel and Borjas 1977; Gustman 1990; Ippolito 1986; McCormick and Hughes 1984; Mitchell 1982; Mitchell 1983).[2] Employers also have an economic incentive to offer pension plans to reduce their hiring and training costs. If an employer's objective is to increase job tenure among workers, employers have an added incentive to increase their investment in training, which will increase the overall productivity of their work force. In addition, health insurance plans may improve the health and productivity of workers, potentially lowering the firm's rate of absenteeism. Along the same lines, the provision of child care facilities can also reduce the incidence of absenteeism.[3]

While previous research has contributed to our understanding of employee benefits, many studies have not fully utilized theoretical or econometric techniques in developing a framework for studying employee benefits and their role in the labor market. In addition, data problems have led some authors to make conclusions that conflict with economic theory. For example, Smith and Ehrenberg (1983) attempted to estimate the trade-off between wages and employee benefits but failed to find a trade-off because of data problems. In fact, most studies using micro-level data find a positive relationship between wages and employee benefits, mostly because they do not have adequate data and can not control for all of the variables that affect employee benefits. However, studies using more aggregated data have found a trade-off (Woodbury 1983; Woodbury and Huang 1991).

One reason for the various shortcomings in the employee benefits literature may be model misspecification. Traditionally, in the simple static model of labor supply, labor-force participation decisions are assumed to be a function of hourly wages, nonwage income, and personal characteristics. However, what ultimately matters to workers is the total compensation they receive per unit of time worked, along with the quality of basic working conditions. In this paper, the simple static model of labor supply is extended to include the demand for employee benefits. Unlike previous work, which has focused on specific aspects of employee benefits, the model presented in this paper is flexible enough to take into account all types of employee benefits. A unique feature of the model is that labor supply is estimated jointly with the demand for employee benefits, using Seemingly Unrelated Regression Equations with a correction for selectivity bias.

The chapter is organized into sections that develop the theoretical model, present the empirical model, describe the data set and the construction of the variables, discuss the empirical results, and provide a summary.

THEORETICAL MODEL

We assume that an individual receives earned income, Y, for time worked, and has unearned income, Y_n. Earned income and unearned income are used to purchase market goods and services, G, such that:

$$Y + Y_n = p_g G, \tag{1}$$

where p_g represents the market price of goods and services.

Earned income is equal to the individuals potential hourly wage rate[4] (p_w) (net of taxes) multiplied by the number of hours worked (H) minus the employer's and employee's contribution to employee benefits:

$$Y = p_w H - p_z B, \tag{2}$$

where Y equals $wH(1 - t)$, p_w is equal to $w(1 - t) + B/H$, t represents the marginal tax rate, p_z represents the shadow price of employee benefits,[5] and B represents the quantity of employee benefits consumed by the employee. In Eq. 2, Y represents after-tax, take-home income that the worker can freely spend to purchase market goods and services and/or employee benefits. Employee contributions to employee benefits are subtracted from potential take-home income because these contributions come out of the workers potential take-home wage in order to take advantage of lower prices via economies of scale, group purchase, and the preferential tax treatment.

Firms hire additional workers until the workers marginal revenue product is equal to the workers total compensation rate, where total compensation is equal to the sum of wages and the monetary value of employee benefits. We assume that employers are indifferent to the composition of total compensation, but adjustments are not costless. As a result, workers face a trade-off between wages and employee benefits (assuming total compensation is constant across workers with equal human capital).

Substituting Eq. 2 into Eq. 1 gives us:

$$p_w H - p_z B + Y_n = p_g G. \tag{3}$$

Individuals are also subject to a time constraint:

$$T = L + H, \tag{4}$$

where T represents total available time and L represents leisure time.[6] Solving Eq. 4 for H, and substituting into Eq. 3 yields the following full-income budget constraint:

$$p_w T + Y_n = p_w L + p_z B + p_g G. \tag{5}$$

From Eq. 5, an individual can consume leisure time (L), employee benefits (B), and other market goods and services (G).

Dual to an individual's utility maximization objective is an objective to minimize expenditures on consumption of goods and services. Formally, the individual's dual problem is to choose L, B, and G so as to minimize total expenditures (E).

$$E = p_w L + p_z B + p_g G, \tag{6}$$

subject to the constraint on utility (U_0) that

$$U_0 = U(L, B, G). \tag{7}$$

The optimal amounts of L, B, and G chosen will depend on the respective prices and required utility. Consumer behavior is summarized by the expenditure function, which shows the minimal expenditures necessary to achieve a given level of utility for a particular set of prices.

The consumers equilibrium condition is given by

$$E(p_g, p_w, p_z; U) = p_w T + Y_n \tag{8}$$

where $p_w T + Y_n$ represents full income. It is assumed that the expenditure function is linearly homogeneous and concave in prices.

ECONOMETRIC SPECIFICATION

Ever since Stone's (1954) system of demand equations, which were derived explicitly from economic theory, alternative specifications and functional forms of the consumers utility function have been proposed, the most popular being the linear model (Stone 1954), the Rotterdam model[7] (Theil 1965), and the translog model (Berndt and Christensen 1972). To avoid placing prior restrictions on the individuals utility function, a flexible approximation to the consumers' expenditure function is utilized in this study. The resulting expenditure function yields an easily estimatable system of consumer demand equations from which price and income elasticities can be derived. The consumer expenditure function is represented as follows:

$$\log E(p, u) = a(p) + ub(p), \tag{9}$$

where u lies between 0 (subsistence) and 1 (bliss) and p represents a vector of prices. The expenditure function is linearly homogeneous, concave in factor prices, and $a(p)$ and $b(p)$ can be regarded as the costs of subsistence and bliss, respectively. In order to let the consumer expenditure function be flexible, $a(p)$ and $b(p)$ are set as follows:

$$a(p) = a_0 + \sum_i a_i \log p_i + 1/2 \sum_i \sum_j c_{ij} \log p_i \log p_j \tag{10}$$

$$b(p) = b_0 \Pi_i p_i^{b_i} \tag{11}$$

Deaton and Muellbauer (1980) pointed out that the choice of functional form for the above functions is partly due to the need for a flexible functional form; however, their main justification is that the resulting system of demand equations has desirable properties. In fact, substitution of Eqs. 10 and 11 into Eq. 9 yields an expenditure function that is flexible and easily estimatable. The resulting system of demand equations is known as the Almost Ideal Demand System (AIDS). The AIDS system gives an estimate of the direct or indirect utility function yielding estimates of the structure of the workers' preferences for leisure, labor supply, employee benefits, and market goods and services. Own-price, cross-price, and income elasticities are easily derived from the AIDS model.

The expenditure function used in this study is shown as follows:

$$\log E(\boldsymbol{p}_i, U) = a_0 + \sum_i a_i \log \boldsymbol{p}_i + 1/2 \sum_i \sum_j c_{ij} \log \boldsymbol{p}_i \log \boldsymbol{p}_j \qquad (12)$$
$$+ U b_0 \prod_i \boldsymbol{p}_i^{b_i}$$

where the subscript i, j equal g, w, and z.

The expenditure function can be logarithmically differentiated, yielding the expenditure shares associated with leisure, employee benefits, and market goods and services,

$$S_w = a_w + \sum_j b_{wj} (\log \boldsymbol{p}_j) + b_w (\log m / p^*) \qquad (13a)$$

$$S_z = a_z + \sum_j b_{zj} (\log \boldsymbol{p}_j) + b_z (\log m / p^*) \qquad (13b)$$

$$S_g = a_g + \sum_j b_{gj} (\log \boldsymbol{p}_j) + b_g (\log m / p^*) \qquad (13c)$$

where $b_{ij} = \frac{1}{2}(c_{ij} + c_{ji})$, and the subscript $j = w$, z, and g. The share of total compensation spent on each good is a function of the natural log of prices and an income term, $\log(m/p^*)$, where p^* represents a price index.[8]

Economic theory requires the demand system to exhibit three properties: adding-up, homogeneity, and symmetry. Adding-up implies that the sum of the share equations equal one. We impose this condition by restricting the parameters in our system of equations as follows:

$$\sum_i a_i = 1, \sum_i b_{iw} = 0, \sum_i b_{iz} = 0, \sum_i b_{ig} = 0, \sum_i b_i = 0. \qquad (14)$$

In order for the demand system to be homogeneous of degree zero in prices and income, the following within-equation restrictions are imposed:

$$\Sigma_j b_{wj} = 0, \Sigma_j b_{zj} = 0, \Sigma_j b_{gj} = 0. \tag{15}$$

Additionally, symmetry is imposed by setting the cross-substitution effects equal, such that $b_{ij} = b_{ji}$.

After imposing the adding-up, homogeneity, and symmetry conditions, and appending a vector of demographic variables and normally distributed error terms, the system of demand equations is written as follows:

$$S_w = a_w + b_{wg}(\log p_g / p_w) + b_{wz}(\log p_z / p_w) \tag{16a}$$
$$+ b_w(\log m / p^*) + \gamma_{1i}X_i + u_{1i}$$

$$S_z = a_z + b_{zg}(\log p_g / p_z) + b_{wz}(\log p_w / p_z) \tag{16b}$$
$$+ b_z(\log m / p^*) + \gamma_{2i}Y_i + u_{2i}$$

$$S_g = a_g + b_{zg}(\log p_z / p_g) + b_{wg}(\log p_w / p_g) \tag{16c}$$
$$+ b_g(\log m / p^*) + \gamma_{3i}Z_i + u_{3i}$$

Our data allow us to estimate the system only for workers with employee benefits and, thus, needs to be adjusted for selectivity bias. The method to correct for selectivity bias when the subsample is selected based on two choices can be found in Maddala (1983, p. 368).[9]

Suppose labor supply and employee benefits are imperfectly observed such that:

$$S_w = S_w^* + u_w \tag{17a}$$

$$S_z = S_z^* + u_z \tag{17b}$$

Suppose, further, that there are latent variables:

$$y_1^* = X_1 \tau_1 + \varepsilon_1 \tag{18a}$$

$$y_2^* = X_2 \tau_2 + \varepsilon_2 \tag{18b}$$

such that the individual works if and only if $y_1^* \geq 0$ and receives employee benefits if $y_2^* \geq 0$. If the us and εs are joint normally distributed,

$$\begin{pmatrix} u \\ \varepsilon \end{pmatrix} \sim \left(\begin{pmatrix} 0 \\ 0 \end{pmatrix}, \begin{pmatrix} \Sigma_{11} & \Sigma_{12} \\ \Sigma_{21} & \Sigma_{22} \end{pmatrix} \right) \tag{19}$$

then the selectivity bias has the form

$$E\left(u \Big|_{\varepsilon_2 > -X_2\tau_2}^{\varepsilon_1 > -X_1\tau_1} \right) = \left(\sum_{11} \right)^{-1} \sum_{12} E\left(\begin{matrix} \varepsilon_1 | \varepsilon_1 > -X_1\tau_1 \\ \varepsilon_2 | \varepsilon_2 > -X_2\tau_2 \end{matrix} \right) \tag{20}$$

where

$$F(-X_1\tau_1, -X_2\tau_2) E\left(\varepsilon_1 \Big|_{\varepsilon_2 > -X_2\tau_2}^{\varepsilon_1 > -X_1\tau_1} \right) = \phi(c_i)[1 - \Phi(c_j^*)] \tag{21}$$

and $$+ \rho\phi(c_j)[1 - \Phi(c_i^*)]$$

$c_i = -x_i \tau_i,$
ρ is the correlation between e_1 and ε_2,
$c_i^* = (c_i - \rho c_j)/(1-\rho^2)(1- p^2)^{1/2}, i = 1,2$
ϕ represents the standard normal density function,
Φ represents the cumulative distribution function, and
F is the bivariate normal distribution function.

The parameters τ_1, τ_2, and part of Σ_{22} can be estimated up to scale using a bivariate probit model. The model is estimated with sample selection because only workers are assumed to receive employee benefits. The selectivity equations include a comprehensive set of economic and demographic variables likely to influence the decision to work and receive employee benefits.

Once the selectivity bias has been taken into account, the expenditure share equations can be written as follows:

$$S_w = a_w + b_{wg} (\log p_g/p_w) + b_{wz} (\log p_z/p_w) + b_w (\log m/p^*) \qquad (22a)$$
$$+ \gamma_{1i} X_i + F_w [E(u_{1i} \mid H = 1, B = 1)] + \xi_{1i}$$

$$S_z = a_z + b_{zg} (\log p_g/p_z) + b_{wz} (\log p_w/p_z) + b_z (\log m/p^*) \qquad (22b)$$
$$+ \gamma_{2i} Y_i + F_z [E(u_{2i} \mid H = 1, B = 1)] + \xi 2_i$$

$$S_g = a_g + b_{zg} (\log p_z/p_g) + b_{wg} (\log p_w/p_g) + b_g (\log m/p^*) \qquad (22c)$$
$$+ \gamma_{3i} Z_i + F_g [E(u_{3i} \mid H = 1, B = 1)] + \xi_{3i}$$

where $H = 1$ if the individual participates in the labor force, $B = 1$ if the individual receives employee benefits, F_i are parameters, and ξ_i represent error terms that have zero means conditional on both the individuals decision to work and receive employee benefits.

The system of share equations can be estimated using Zellner's two-step (or iterative) Feasible Generalized Least Squares procedure or maximum likelihood, which is suitable for constrained, singular systems. One share equation is deleted from the system of equations to avoid singularity, because the share equations sum to 1. The choice of which equation to delete is arbitrary and has no effect on the empirical results. Data limitations motivate the deletion of the market goods and services equation; however, we capture the market goods share from our estimation. Also, the price of market goods and services, p_g, is normalized to 1 to further simplify the system.

The estimates of the demand system are used to compute the own-price, cross-price, and income elasticities of demand. Confidence intervals are constructed for the elasticities by computing the large-sample variance of each elasticity (see Kmenta 1986, p. 486).

DATA

The data for this study come from the April 1993 Current Population Survey (CPS). This survey included an employee-benefits supplement in which detailed questions were asked on employer-provided pension plans and health insurance plans. With respect to employer-provided pension plans, respondents to the supplemental questions were asked if their employer or union sponsored a pension plan for anyone in their company and whether they were included in the plan. Detailed questions were also asked about the type of plan. From the survey, we can determine whether the individual was included in a defined-benefit plan or a defined-contribution plan and the type of defined-contribution plan (i.e., profit sharing, employee stock ownership plan, 401k plan, salary reduction plan, etc.). An additional set of questions was asked about any salary reduction plans (i.e. 401k, 403b, etc.), the amount the individual contributed to the plan, and the amount of the contribution that the employer matched.

Salary reduction pension plan data is highly suitable to our model because it allows individuals to make choices about their level of contributions to the pension plan. Unlike a defined-benefit plan where a worker's retirement benefit is determined by an equation, usually based on age, years of service, and final pay—an equation that the worker has little control over—a defined-contribution plan with a salary reduction component allows a worker more flexibility at the margin in determining their degree of participation in the plan. Workers are allowed to determine how much they want to contribute to the plan on a pre-tax basis, and many plans allow workers to change their level of contributions on a regular basis (i.e., once a month) so that workers are not constrained to their choice of contribution level for a long period of time. This flexibility is highly desirable when trying to model workers' preferences for pension benefits.

While the CPS also includes data on health insurance plans, the data are not detailed enough to yield information about the cost of the plan. Respondents to the survey were asked about employer sponsorship of a health insurance plan, their participation, and whether the plan also covered family members. The survey does not ask whether the worker has a choice of health insurance options or the relative cost of those options. In this survey, a worker with three options would be treated the same as a worker with only one option. In addition, the cost of health insurance is not as optimal as pension plan contributions for the model presented in this chapter because workers can not typically switch health insurance plans on a regular basis, assuming they even have a choice of health insurance plans. Open enrollment, where available, is usually limited to once per year.

The sample used in this paper is limited to the noninstitutionalized civilian population between the ages of 18 and 64. Active duty military personnel and the self-employed are not included in the sample, resulting in a sample of 37,975 working and nonworking males and 42,875 working and nonworking females. This sample is used to provide estimates of the bivariate probit model, which is used to correct the system of demand equations for selectivity bias. The system of demand equations is corrected for selectivity bias because it is only estimated with data on workers participating in a salary reduction pension plan. This results in a selected sample of 2,129 males and 1,544 females. Sample means and variable definitions are provided in Table 3.

From the CPS, the following variables are needed to estimate the system of demand equations:

1) Share of Leisure Time, S_w:
The share of leisure time is measured as the percentage of full-income spent on the consumption of leisure. This is computed as

$$S_w = (p_w L) / (p_w T + Y_n)$$

Total available time, T, is assumed to be equal to 5,840 hours, which is the total time available in a given year, given time for sleep. Nonwage income, Y_n, is measured as total personal unearned income.

2) Share of Pension Plan Contributions, S_z:
The share of pension plan contributions is computed as follows:

$$S_z = (p_z B) / (p_w T + Y_n)$$

The shadow price of pension plan contributions is measured using the workers' marginal tax rate, as discussed in the next section. The amount of pension plan contributions, B, is calculated as the annual employee contribution to the salary reduction pension plan and does not include any match provided by the employer.

3) Price of Pension Plan Contributions, P_z:

The worker's marginal tax rate is used as a proxy for the shadow price of the pension plan. As mentioned above, this variable has been used extensively in previous research. It should be noted, however, that the use of the marginal tax rate has two potential shortcomings. First, the marginal tax rate is correlated with income. Higher income workers are in higher marginal tax rates. While this may present a problem in this study because real total compensation is used as an explanatory variable, price and income should have independent effects on the share equations. Second, the possibility exists that a worker will lower their marginal tax rate by increasing their contributions to their pension plan. However, a worker's ability to contribute to a pension plan on a pre-tax basis is limited by constraints set by the Internal Revenue Service, which minimizes the severity of this problem. In 1993, workers could not contribute more than $9,200 to a 401k plan and $9,500 to a 403b plan on a pre-tax basis.

Assumptions about an individual's tax-filing status are made from the various demographic characteristics provided in the CPS. Each individual's tax-filing status is based on their marital status and the number of dependent children. It is assumed that all married and separated individuals file a joint tax return. Widowed, divorced, and never married individuals are assumed to file as heads of household if they have dependent children, otherwise they are assumed to file as single taxpayers. Standard deductions and personal exemptions from taxable income are based on the number of dependents in the family.

The marginal tax rate is computed from both federal and state income tax forms. Local taxes, where applicable, and the social security payroll tax are not included in the marginal tax rate. Given limitations on geographic region in the CPS, it is impossible to calculate local income tax rates. In addition, previous research has shown that estimates of the demand for employee benefits are commonly unaffected by the inclusion of the Social Security payroll tax (Woodbury and Hamermesh 1992; Woodbury and Bettinger 1991).

Table 3 Sample Means and Variable Definitions

Variable	Definition	Males	Females
S_w	leisure share	0.59	0.63
S_z	benefit share	0.01	0.01
S_g	goods and services share	0.40	0.37
p_w	price of leisure	16.02	11.91
p_z	price of benefits	0.21	0.21
$m/P*$	real total compensation	9827.97	6859.48
AGE	age	40.82	40.59
AGESQ	age squared	1761.98	1748.35
MARRIED	=1 if married	0.79	0.63
WIDOWED	=1 if widowed	0.01	0.03
DIVORCED	=1 if divorced	0.08	0.15
SEPARATE	=1 if separated	0.01	0.02
SINGLE	=1 if never married	0.12	0.16
OWNKIDS	number of own children under age 18	1.34	1.11
EDUC1	=1 if some school	0.02	0.02
EDUC2	=1 if high school graduate	0.51	0.62
EDUC3	=1 if college graduate	0.28	0.24
EDUC4	=1 if completed graduate school	0.18	0.12
WHITE	=1 if white, non-Hispanic	0.91	0.88
BLACK	=1 if black, non-Hispanic	0.03	0.06
HISPANIC	=1 if Hispanic	0.03	0.03
OTHRACE	=1 if other race	0.03	0.04
UNION	=1 if union worker	0.21	0.19
FULLTIME	=1 if full-time worker	0.99	0.94
WHITECOL	=1 if white collar	0.67	0.87
BLUECOL	=1 if blue collar	0.28	0.09
SERVCOL	=1 if service collar	0.05	0.04
FS1	=1 if 1–24 employees	0.06	0.08
FS2	=1 if 25–49 employees	0.03	0.03
FS3	=1 if 50–99 employees	0.06	0.04

Variable	Definition	Males	Females
FS4	=1 if 100–249 employees	0.07	0.07
FS5	=1 if 250 or more employees	0.78	0.78
MATCH	=1 if employer matches contribution	0.65	0.59
F_w	Selectivity term in leisure equation	0.20	0.15
F_z	Selectivity term in benefit equation	0.21	0.16

4) Price of Leisure Time, p_w:

The price of leisure time (the after tax hourly wage rate) is measured using observed data from the CPS. The hourly wage rate was calculated based on usual hours of work per week, weeks worked per year, and annual earnings. In some cases where weeks worked per year was missing, the mean (51.5) was substituted.

5) Real After-Tax Total Compensation, m:

The measure of real total compensation is obtained by summing after-tax annual earnings with annual pension plan contributions and dividing by the price index, p^*.

6) Price Index, p^*:

Using Stone's (1953) price index, some researchers have approximated p^* as:

$$\log p^* = S_w (\log p_w) + S_z (\log p_z) + S_g (\log p_g)$$

and have found this to be a good approximation of the price index (Anderson and Blundell 1983, 1984; Deaton and Muellbauer 1980; Kang 1983; and Woodbury and Huang 1991). We follow this approach to estimate the price index. When p_g is normalized to 1, the last term drops out.

7) Demographic Variables that Affect the Share of Leisure and the Share of Pension Plan Contributions:

A vector of demographic variables affecting both the share of leisure and the share of pension plan contributions includes controls for the following: age, marital status, number of children, race, education, union status, occupation, industry, firm size, and geographic region.

Two variables are included to control for age: age (AGE) and age-squared (AGESQ). We expect age to have a nonlinear effect on the demand for leisure with the oldest workers having a greater demand for leisure as they transition out of the labor force. With respect to pension plan contributions, we expect age to always have a positive effect. As workers age, they will have less time to take advantage of compound interest, and they will also realize the need to start saving for retirement. Thus, they will make larger contributions to their pension plans.

A set of dummy variables on marital status (WIDOWED, DIVORCED, SEPARATE, SINGLE) are also included in both the leisure demand equation and the employee benefit demand equation (MARRIED is the base group). We expect to find differences in pension plan contributions between males and females and across marital status. Unmarried women are expected to be less likely to demand leisure time and more likely to contribute to pension plans than married women. Our expectations are based on previous research, which has shown that unmarried women are less likely to intend to retire early than married women because they have access to fewer resources than married women (Holtmann et al. 1994). The marital status of men, however, has not been shown to affect their plans to retire early. We expect similar results in this study. In addition, we expect the number of children (OWNKIDS) to have an effect on both the share of leisure and the share of pension plan contributions. Workers with more children are more likely to demand leisure time than workers without children in order to spend more time with their children. With respect to pension plan contributions, workers with children are expected to contribute less to their pension plan because of the additional expenses needed to raise children, all else being equal.

Race has been shown to be correlated with the probability that an individual works, therefore, we include a set of dummy variables (BLACK, HISPANIC, OTHRACE) to determine whether race plays a role in the share of leisure demanded (given that an individual is already working) and the share of pension plan contributions demanded (given that a worker participates in a salary reduction pension plan; WHITE is the base group).

Education variables (EDUC2, EDUC3, and EDUC4) are included in the model as well (EDUC1 is the base group). We expect more educated workers to demand less leisure time because of the implicit demands of a job that are correlated with education. In addition, we expect more educated workers to demand a greater share of their total income in the form of pension plan contributions. More educated workers are more likely to be able to evaluate and understand the advantages of contributing to their pension plan than less educated workers. More educated workers may also be more comfortable directing their asset allocation decisions.

With respect to employment characteristics, variables are included to control for union membership, occupation, industry, and firm size. We expect union membership (UNION) to increase a worker's demand for leisure because the union may be better able to negotiate a fixed work schedule. Our expectations of union membership on pension plan contributions are less clear. While unions may be better able to educate their members about the advantages of contributing to a pension plan, union members are typically more likely to have an employer-funded defined-benefit plan. Therefore, there may be no need to contribute to a defined-contribution pension plan in addition to the defined-benefit plan.

The set of dummy variables to control for occupation include a variable for white collar workers (the base group), a variable to control for blue collar workers (BLUECOL), and a variable to control for service collar workers (SERVCOL).[10] With respect to firm size, we expect workers employed in large firms to have a greater demand for pension plan contributions because large firms typically have better educational programs and materials concerning the advantages of contributing to a pension plan than a small firm. Dummy variables are included to control for firms with 1–24 workers (FS1=the base group), 25–49 workers (FS2), 50–99 workers (FS3), 100–249 workers (FS4), and 250 or more workers (FS5).

8) Demographic Variables which Affect Only Pension Plan Contributions:

Two additional employment related variables are only included in the share of pension plan contributions equation. A dummy variable is include to control for whether the worker was employed part time or full time (FULLTIME), and a dummy variable was included to control for whether the employer offered a match to the workers' contributions to the pension plan (MATCH). The direction of the effect of the employer match is unclear because of two potential offsetting effects. On one hand, we expect the presence of an employer match to have a positive effect on a worker's contribution to a pension plan. If an employer offers a dollar-for-dollar match, a worker may contribute more to the plan because the opportunity cost of not contributing is higher when the match is forgone. Alternatively, the availability of an employer match may result in a worker contributing less to the plan if the match acts as a substitute for the worker's own contributions.[11]

RESULTS

Bivariate Probit Model

Table 4 contains the results from the bivariate probit model used to estimate selectivity corrected estimates of the model on leisure demand and employee benefits demand. As mentioned previously, the bivariate probit model is estimated with sample selection because we assume that only workers will receive employee benefits. The results of the bivariate probit model are worth briefly mentioning. Separate equations are estimated for males and females. A likelihood-ratio test for equality of coefficients in the male and female equations rejects the hypothesis that the two equations are the same.

With respect to the labor supply equation, we find that the probability of working is positively related to age until an individual reaches age 55, at which point the probability of working decreases as compared with the aged 18–24 base group. These results are consistent for both males and females.

The effects of marital status on the probability of working are not consistent for males and females. Married males are more likely to be working than their unmarried counterparts. Divorced, separated, and never married women, however, are more likely to be working than married or widowed women, suggesting that unmarried women have fewer resources than married women, and thus have a greater incentive to participate in the labor force.

The effect of education is consistent for males and females: there is a higher probability of participating in the labor force the more education an individual attains. Race is also generally consistent for males and females, with nonwhites less likely to be participating in the labor force than whites, with the exception of Hispanic males. In addition, the more children an individual has, the less likely they are to be participating in the labor force. This is an interesting result because most individuals with children would be expected to need the resources that can be derived from working. It is not surprising, however, that the effect is over three times larger for females than it is for males because single parent families headed by women are more likely to qualify for public assistance.

Given that an individual is working, we find the following results with respect to participation in a salary reduction pension plan. For both males and females, age effects are strongest for younger workers, implying that older workers are more likely to have a defined benefit plan or less likely to have any type of pension plan. Marital status appears to play an important role in the probability of whether a worker participates in a salary reduction pension plan, with different effects for males and females. Unmarried males are less likely than married and widowed males to be participating in a salary reduction pension plan. Divorced women, on the other hand, are more likely to be participating in a salary reduction pension plan than all other women. This result suggests that divorced women may have lost their rights to their husbands' pension benefits and must accumulate their own resources for retirement.

Education has a strong linear effect on the probability that a worker participates in a salary reduction pension plan. Race has a strong negative effect, with nonwhites having a lower probability of participating in a salary reduction pension plan than whites. Number of children also has a negative effect on the probability of participating in a salary reduction pension plan.

With respect to characteristics associated with the labor market, we find statistically significant effects for union membership, hours of work, occupation, and firm size. Union membership is found to decrease the probability that a worker participates in a salary reduction

Table 4 Bivariate Probit Model Estimates for Labor Supply Equation and Employee Benefit Equation

	Male		Female	
	Employee benefit equation	Labor supply equation	Employee benefit equation	Labor supply equation
Constant	−3.646***	−0.491***	−3.457***	−0.878***
	(0.120)	(0.031)	(0.095)	(0.031)
AGE2	0.470***	0.116***	0.445***	0.106***
	(0.059)	(0.023)	(0.056)	(0.023)
AGE3	0.520***	0.121***	0.516***	0.170***
	(0.060)	(0.026)	(0.057)	(0.025)
AGE4	0.496***	0.078***	0.532***	0.138***
	(0.062)	(0.028)	(0.059)	(0.026)
AGE5	0.284***	−0.187***	0.271***	−0.223***
	(0.068)	(0.031)	(0.067)	(0.030)
WIDOWED	−0.128	−0.326***	0.061	−0.027
	(0.157)	(0.084)	(0.076)	(0.039)
DIVORCED	−0.108***	−0.141***	0.087**	0.182***
	(0.041)	(0.026)	(0.035)	(0.021)
SEPARATE	−0.262***	−0.130***	−0.072	0.067*
	(0.091)	(0.047)	(0.076)	(0.038)
SINGLE	−0.273***	−0.168***	0.024	0.109***
	(0.035)	(0.019)	(0.034)	(0.019)
EDUC2	0.434***	0.195***	0.505***	0.364***
	(0.052)	(0.020)	(0.061)	(0.021)
EDUC3	0.681***	0.270***	0.646***	0.477***
	(0.060)	(0.025)	(0.067)	(0.026)
EDUC4	0.698***	0.316***	0.636***	0.511***
	(0.062)	(0.030)	(0.072)	(0.033)
BLACK	−0.408***	−0.140***	−0.346***	−0.085***
	(0.056)	(0.024)	(0.049)	(0.022)
HISPANIC	−0.193***	0.009	−0.265***	−0.070***
	(0.058)	(0.026)	(0.064)	(0.027)
OTHRACE	−0.238***	−0.170***	−0.074	−0.091***
	(0.059)	(0.032)	(0.061)	(0.031)
OWNKIDS	−0.025***	−0.017***	−0.093***	−0.068***
	(0.009)	(0.005)	(0.010)	(0.005)

	Male		Female	
	Employee benefit equation	Labor supply equation	Employee benefit equation	Labor supply equation
UNION	−0.152***	–	−0.145***	–
	(0.028)		(0.030)	
FULLTIME	0.672***	–	0.443***	–
	(0.088)		(0.041)	
SERVCOL	−0.299***	–	−0.431***	–
	(0.049)		(0.053)	
BLUECOL	−0.121***	–	−0.057	–
	(0.027)		(0.040)	
FS2	0.592***	–	0.373***	–
	(0.059)		(0.069)	
FS3	0.909***	–	0.626***	–
	(0.051)		(0.060)	
FS4	0.883***	–	0.669***	–
	(0.049)		(0.053)	
FS5	1.109***	–	0.900***	–
	(0.037)		(0.035)	
ρ	0.963***		0.987	
	(0.202)		(9.563)	
n	37,975		42,875	
log L	−29,179.1		−29,340.5	

NOTE: Age dummies represent the following categories: AGE1 =1 if aged 18–24 (base group), AGE2 =1 if aged 25–34, AGE3 =1 if aged 35–44, AGE4 =1 if aged 45–54, and AGE5 =1 if aged 55–64. All other variables are defined in Table 3. Standard errors in parentheses.
***significant at the 1% level.
**significant at the 5% level.
*significant at the 10% level.

pension plan. Because of collective bargaining agreements, union members are more likely to have a defined-benefit plan funded by the employer. Full-time workers are more likely than part-time workers and white collar workers are more likely than blue collar and service collar workers to participate in salary reduction plans. In addition, workers employed in large firms are more likely to participate in salary reduction pension plans than workers in small firms. These results are generally consistent for both males and females.

Finally, the correlation coefficient between the labor supply equation and the salary reduction pension plan equation, ρ, is statistically significant for males but not for females.

AIDS Model Results

Table 5 contains the estimated coefficients from the AIDS model. The adjusted R^2 for males and females is 0.89 and 0.90, respectively, for the leisure share equation, and 0.40 for both males and females for the salary reduction pension plan equation.

The parameters on the price and income variables are significant in most cases for both males and females. However, the estimated own-price, cross-price, and income elasticities presented in Table 6, give us a better understanding of the effects in the model. Therefore, we first discuss the results of the demographic and labor-market variables and then discuss the estimated elasticities.

Returning to the results in Table 5, we find consistent nonlinear effects of age on the share of leisure time for both males and females. At first, an increase in age reduces the demand for leisure time (increases time spent at work) and eventually increases the demand for leisure time. Predictions from the model indicate that males will start to increase their demand for leisure time at age 52.75, while females will increase their demand for leisure time at age 47.25. With respect to pension plan contributions, we find significant positive effects of age for males, but insignificant effects for females.

As mentioned previously, we expect marital status to have different effects for males and females on the share of leisure and the share of pension plan contributions. For males, we find that separated and never married males demand a greater share of leisure than married, widowed, and divorced males. For females, we find that all nonmarried females demand a smaller share of leisure than their married female counterparts. With respect to pension plan contributions, marital status has no effect for males (with the exception of a small negative effect for separated males). Divorced females, on the other hand, have a significantly lower share demand for pension plan contributions than all other females. This may suggest that given their budget constraints, divorced females choose to spend less on pension plan contributions than other females. While we expected unmarried women to be spending a greater share of their income on pension plan contributions, the effect of marital status appears to be working through the probability of participating in the pension plan (the bivariate probit model), as opposed to the amount contributed once participation has been determined.

The number of children exerts consistent positive effects on leisure demand for both males and females. Both males and females appear to demand a greater share of leisure the more children they have. With respect to pension plan contributions, the number of children has a negative effect on the share of pension plan contributions for males and an insignificant effect for females.

Our results for race are in large part consistent for both males and females in both the leisure share equation and the pension plan contribution share equation. We find that nonwhites demand a greater share of their income in the form of leisure than whites. For males, there is no effect of race on pension plan contributions (any difference appears in the probability of participating model), while black females demand a greater share of pension plan contributions than females of other races.

With respect to education, we find consistent effects for males and females in the leisure share equation but not in the benefits share equation. We find that increasing levels of education result in a decreased demand for the share of leisure time, indicating that higher levels of education are associated with increasing shares of work time. Higher education levels result in a greater share demand of benefits for males, while education has no effect on the share demand of benefits for females.

With respect to the variables associated with the labor market, we find the following. Hours of work do not exert a significant effect on pension plan contributions for males, but do exert a negative effect for

Table 5 Estimated Coefficients of the Leisure Share and Benefit Share Equations

	Males	Females
a_w	2.001***	2.021***
	(0.021)	(0.024)
a_z	−0.011**	−0.002
	(0.005)	(0.005)
a_g	−0.990***	−1.019***
	(0.021)	(0.025)
b_{ww}	0.079***	0.080***
	(0.002)	(0.002)
b_{wg}	−0.079***	−0.080***
	(0.002)	(0.002)
b_{wz}	0.000	0.000
	(0.000)	(0.000)
b_{zz}	−0.003***	−0.003***
	(0.001)	(0.000)
b_{zg}	0.003***	0.003***
	(0.001)	(0.001)
b_{gg}	0.076***	0.077***
	(0.002)	(0.002)
b_w	−0.175***	−0.176***
	(0.001)	(0.002)
b_z	0.003***	0.003***
	(0.000)	(0.000)
b_g	0.171***	0.173***
	(0.001)	(0.002)

	Variables in leisure equation	Variables in benefits equation	Variables in leisure equation	Variables in benefits equation
AGE	−0.00211***	0.00037**	−0.00189***	−0.00014
	(0.00069)	(0.00015)	(0.00064)	(0.00013)
AGESQ	0.00002***	0.00000**	0.00002**	0.00000
	(0.00001)	(0.00000)	(0.00001)	(0.00000)

	Males		Females	
	Variables in leisure equation	Variables in benefits equation	Variables in leisure equation	Variables in benefits equation
WIDOWED	−0.00403	−0.00301	−0.02579***	−0.00100
	(0.00915)	(0.00192)	(0.00391)	(0.00068)
DIVORCED	0.00389	−0.00084	−0.02310***	−0.00115***
	(0.00262)	(0.00056)	(0.00199)	(0.00036)
SEPARATE	0.01448**	−0.00247*	−0.01130***	−0.00102
	(0.00649)	(0.00137)	(0.00429)	(0.00074)
SINGLE	0.01155***	−0.00003	−0.00728***	−0.00027
	(0.00294)	(0.00065)	(0.00190)	(0.00033)
OWNKIDS	0.00282***	−0.00034***	0.00400***	0.00009
	(0.00057)	(0.00012)	(0.00081)	(0.00016)
BLACK	0.01321***	−0.00025	0.01865***	0.00145**
	(0.00468)	(0.00103)	(0.00336)	(0.00064)
HISPANIC	0.01065***	−0.00077	0.01020***	−0.00027
	(0.00401)	(0.00086)	(0.00412)	(0.00074)
OTHRACE	0.00974**	0.00031	0.01106***	0.00052
	(0.00442)	(0.00094)	(0.00373)	(0.00065)
EDUC2	−0.01816***	0.00180*	−0.00824*	−0.00089
	(0.00456)	(0.00099)	(0.00462)	(0.00083)
EDUC3	−0.02373***	0.00240*	−0.01340***	−0.00104
	(0.00597)	(0.00133)	(0.00520)	(0.00098)
EDUC4	−0.02240***	0.00327**	−0.01785***	−0.00087
	(0.00623)	(0.00139)	(0.00540)	(0.00102)
FULLTIME	–	0.00139	–	−0.00286***
		(0.00176)		(0.00075)
UNION	0.00621***	−0.00055	0.00521***	0.00113***
	(0.00210)	(0.00046)	(0.00198)	(0.00037)
BLUECOL	0.00608***	−0.00055	0.00264	0.00039
	(0.00205)	(0.00044)	(0.00264)	(0.00046)
SERVCOL	−0.00003	−0.00017	0.01222***	0.00062
	(0.00406)	(0.00088)	(0.00407)	(0.00074)

(continued)

Table 5 (continued)

	Males		Females	
	Variables in leisure equation	Variables in benefits equation	Variables in leisure equation	Variables in benefits equation
FS2	−0.01585***	0.00081	0.00162	−0.00021
	(0.00537)	(0.00117)	(0.00461)	(0.00080)
FS3	−0.01823***	0.00246*	−0.01401***	−0.00070
	(0.00608)	(0.00138)	(0.00439)	(0.00082)
FS4	−0.02029***	0.00274**	−0.00541	−0.00154**
	(0.00590)	(0.00135)	(0.00413)	(0.00079)
FS5	−0.02734***	0.00382**	−0.02113***	−0.00168*
	(0.00699)	(0.00162)	(0.00445)	(0.00094)
MATCH	–	0.00031	–	−0.00019
		(0.00030)		(0.00024)
Selectivity term	0.18142***	−0.02078**	0.18941***	0.01588**
	(0.03589)	(0.00821)	(0.02867)	(0.00646)
adjusted R^2	0.89	0.40	0.90	0.40
n	2,129	1,544		

NOTE: Estimation results from applying an iterative unweighted version of Zellner's seemingly unrelated regression equations. The dependent variables are the shares of total full income received as leisure consumption and employee benefit share. Asymptotic standard error shown in parentheses. Each equation includes a set of two-digit industry dummy variables, and eight region variables, in addition to the control variables shown.
Standard errors in parentheses.
***significant at the 1% level.
**significant at the 5% level.
*significant at the 10% level.

Table 6 Price and Income Elasticities

	Males		Females	
Uncompensated price elasticities				
η_{ww}	−0.691	(0.003)	−0.696	(0.003)
η_{zz}	−1.450	(0.072)	−1.547	(0.074)
η_{gg}	−0.984	(0.004)	−0.965	(0.005)
η_{wz}	0.002	(0.001)	0.002	(0.001)
η_{zw}	−0.261	(0.043)	−0.314	(0.050)
η_{wg}	0.572	(0.003)	0.555	(0.003)
η_{gw}	−0.445	(0.004)	−0.512	(0.005)
η_{zg}	0.266	(0.076)	0.334	(0.084)
η_{gz}	0.005	(0.002)	0.006	(0.002)
Compensated price elasticities				
η^*_{ww}	−0.278	(0.003)	−0.246	(0.003)
η^*_{zz}	−1.439	(0.072)	−1.538	(0.074)
η^*_{gg}	−0.409	(0.005)	−0.424	(0.005)
η^*_{wz}	0.008	(0.001)	0.006	(0.001)
η^*_{zw}	0.590	(0.048)	0.643	(0.054)
η^*_{wg}	0.270	(0.003)	0.240	(0.003)
η^*_{gw}	0.393	(0.004)	0.410	(0.005)
η^*_{zg}	0.850	(0.084)	0.895	(0.096)
η^*_{gz}	0.016	(0.002)	0.014	(0.002)
Income elasticities				
η_{wm}	0.703	(0.002)	0.718	(0.003)
η_{zm}	1.446	(0.043)	1.527	(0.059)
η_{gm}	1.424	(0.004)	1.472	(0.005)

NOTE: Elasticities computed from the parameter estimates displayed in Table 5. Standard error of each elasticity is in parentheses next to each elasticity. Standard errors are computed by taking a Taylor series approximation at the sample mean.

females. Union status significantly increases the demand for leisure for both males and females. It has no effect on pension plan contributions for males but has a positive, significant effect for females. Occupation also has no effect on pension plan contributions for both males and females. On the other hand, firm size plays an important role in pension plan contributions, but the results for males and females are mixed. We find that male workers employed in larger firms contribute a larger share of income to pension plans than workers in small firms, but the opposite is true for females. In addition, an employer match does not significantly affect a worker's pension plan contributions.

Finally, we find evidence of selectivity bias for males and females in both the leisure share equation and the pension plan contribution share equation. Note, however, that the signs on the selectivity correction term are inconsistent for males and females and may be due to the fact that the estimated correlation between the error terms in the bivariate probit model was insignificant for females.

Elasticities

The estimated coefficients shown in Table 5 are used to estimate uncompensated, compensated, and income elasticities. These elasticities, computed at the sample mean, along with each standard error (shown in parentheses next to the elasticity) are shown in Table 6. The uncompensated own-price elasticities are all statistically significant and of the correct sign. Our results suggest that a 10 percent increase in the wage rate would reduce the share of leisure by 6.91 percent for males and 6.96 percent for females. We find that a 10 percent increase in the price of a pension plan (that is, a 10 percent decrease in the marginal tax rate) results in a 14.5 percent decrease in the share of income contributed to a salary reduction pension plan for males and a 15.5 percent decrease for females, suggesting that pension plan contributions are very elastic with respect to a worker's marginal tax rate. We also find a nearly unitary own-price elasticity for other goods and services.

The uncompensated cross-price elasticities yield interesting results. We find no effect between the share of leisure time and the price of pension plans. However, we do find a negative effect between wages and pension plan contributions, suggesting that pension plan contributions and wages are gross substitutes. We find that a 10 percent decrease in the wage rate results in a 2.61 percent increase in pension plan contributions for males and a 3.14 percent decrease for females. Both males and females behave as we would expect when facing an employer's wage–benefit trade-off curve. The other uncompensated cross-price elasticities suggest that pension plan contributions and other goods and services are gross complements, while the results are mixed for the share of leisure and other goods and services.

The income elasticities are all positive and significant, indicating that all of the goods are normal goods. The results suggest that the share of leisure is income inelastic, while the share of pension plan contributions and market goods and services are income elastic.

CONCLUSION

In this chapter, the simple static model of labor supply is extended to incorporate the demand for employee benefits. Traditionally, labor-supply models have ignored employee benefits, even though they have become a significant component of total compensation during the 20th century. The model presented in this paper incorporates the demand for employee benefits by assuming that the demand for employee benefits, the demand for leisure time, and the demand for market goods and services are determined simultaneously. Previous studies assumed that labor supply decisions were exogenous to the demand for employee benefits. In addition, previous studies have only modeled the separate components of employee benefits. The model presented in this paper is flexible enough to include all employee benefits.

Our results, determined using data from the April 1993 Current Population Survey, are consistent with economic theory. We find that the income elasticity of worker contributions to a pension plan is approximately 1.5, indicating that if worker income increased by 10 percent, contributions to a pension plan would increase by 15 percent. This result is consistent with previous findings. We also find that pension plan contributions are sensitive to a worker's marginal tax rate. This result is consistent with Woodbury and Huang (1991), who found that pension plan contributions would fall between 50 and 64 percent if their tax-preferred status was removed. We also find evidence of a

trade-off between wages and employee benefits and the magnitude of
the effect is consistent with adjustments for a worker's marginal tax
rate.

While a joint model of employee benefits and labor supply is presented in this paper, data limitations allowed us to estimate the model
only for pension plan contributions. The model presented in this paper
is flexible enough to incorporate all employee benefits. As more data
on the composition and cost of employee benefits becomes available at
the micro level, future research should be able to estimate more
detailed models.

Notes

The views expressed in this paper are those of the author and should not be construed
as representing the opinions or policies of the Employee Benefit Research Institute or
any sponsoring agencies.

1. Those workers with single coverage may not need family coverage if there are no
   dependents.
2. Some of the evidence attributes the lower turnover rates to nonportability and
   backloading of pensions. Other studies present evidence that pension-covered
   jobs offer higher levels of total compensation; hence, the compensation premium
   accounts for the lower turnover rate.
3. Unionization and the role of collective bargaining have also been shown to affect
   an employer's decision to offer employee benefits (Freeman 1981; Belman and
   Heywood 1991).
4. This is the maximum wage rate that the individual would earn, based on their
   human capital and other characteristics, when no employee benefits were
   received.
5. The parameter p_z represents the rate of exchange between wages and employee
   benefits on the boundary of the employee's choice set. Competition will tend to
   bring p_z into equality both with the price at which workers would buy benefits in
   the market and with the employer's marginal cost of providing the benefits (see
   Atrostic [1982] and Triplett [1983]).
6. Leisure refers to hours not worked that are not paid for by the employer. Paid
   vacation, sick leave, and other paid time away from work are included in
   employee benefits. For the purposes of this study, time used for home production
   is included as leisure time.
7. In the Rotterdam model, the demand function is estimated in the logarithm of differentials instead of in levels of differentials.
8. The income term, $\log(m/p^*)$, can be derived using the following steps. For a utility maximizing individual, total expenditures is a function of utility and prices.

The expenditure function can be inverted to give utility as a function of income and prices. We can do this for the expenditure function given in Eq. 12 and substitute the result into the budget share Eq. 13 to get the budget share equations as a function of income and prices.

9. See Michalopoulos et al. (1992) for an application of this method to child-care demand.

10. Service collar workers include those employed as private household service workers, protective service workers, and other service workers.

11. The size of the match would be a better measure of employer contributions to the plan than whether a match is available. Unfortunately, data on the size of the employer match was missing for nearly a third of the sample.

References

Alpert, William H. 1983. "Manufacturing Workers Private Wage Supplements: A Simultaneous Equations Approach." *Applied Economics* 15(3): 363–378.

_____. 1987. "An Analysis of Fringe Benefits Using Time-Series Data." *Applied Economics* 19(1):1–16.

Anderson, Gordon, and Richard Blundell. 1983. "Testing Restrictions in a Flexible Dynamic Demand System: An Application to Consumers' Expenditure in Canada." *Review of Economics Studies* 50(July): 397–410.

_____. 1984. "Consumer Non-Durables in the U.K.: A Dynamic Demand System." *Economic Journal* 94(Supplement): 35–44.

Atrostic, B.K. 1982. "The Demand for Leisure and Nonpecuniary Job Characteristics." *American Economic Review* 72(3): 428–440.

Bartel, Ann P., and George J. Borjas. 1977. "Middle-Age Job Mobility: Its Determinants and Consequences." In *Men in Their Preretirement Years*, Seymour Wolfbein, ed. Philadelphia: Temple University.

Belman, Dale, and John S. Heywood. 1991. "Direct and Indirect Effects of Unionization and Government Employment on Fringe Benefit Provision." *Journal of Labor Research* 12(2): 111–122.

Berndt, E., and L. Christensen. 1972. "The Translog Function and the Substitution of Equipment, Structures, and Labor in U.S. Manufacturing, 1929-1968." *Journal of Econometrics* 1: 81–114.

Clain, Suzanne H., and Karen Leppel. 1989. "Fringe Benefits and the Effect of Tax Reform." *Applied Economics* 21(5):681–685.

Deaton, Angus, and John Muellbauer. 1980. "An Almost Ideal Demand System." *American Economic Review* 70(3): 312–326.

Employee Benefit Research Institute. 1995. *EBRI Databook on Employee Benefits*, third ed. Washington, D.C.: Employee Benefit Research Institute.

Freeman, Richard. 1981. "The Effect of Unionism on Fringe Benefits." *Industrial and Labor Relations Review* 34(4): 489–509.

Gustman, Alan L. 1990. "Pension Portability and Labor Mobility: Evidence from the Survey of Income and Program Participation." SIPP Working Paper Series, No. 9015, U.S. Department of Commerce, Bureau of the Census.

Holtmann, A.G., S.G. Ullmann, P. Fronstin, and C.F. Longino, Jr. 1994. "The Early Retirement Plans of Women and Men: An Empirical Application." *Applied Economics* 26(6): 591–602.

Ippolito, Richard A. 1986. *Pensions, Economics, and Public Policy*, Homewood, Illinois: Irwin.

Kang, Suk. 1983. *Estimation of An Almost Ideal Demand System from Panel Data*. Ph.D. Dissertation. University of Wisconsin-Madison.

Kmenta, Jan. 1986. *Elements of Econometrics*, Second ed. New York: MacMillan Publishing Company.

Maddala, G.S. 1983. *Limited-Dependent Variables and Qualitative Variables in Econometrics*, Cambridge, Massachusetts: Cambridge University Press.

McCormick, Barry, and Gordon Hughes. 1984. "The Influence of Pensions on Job Mobility." *Journal of Public Economics* 23(February/March): 183–206.

Michalopoulos, Charles, Philip K. Robins, and Irwin Garfinkel. 1992. "A Structural Model of Labor Supply and Child Care Demand." *Journal of Human Resources* 27(1): 166–203.

Mitchell, Olivia S. 1982. "Fringe Benefits and Labor Mobility." *Journal of Human Resources* 17(2): 286–298.

_____. 1983. "Fringe Benefits and the Cost of Changing Jobs." *Industrial and Labor Relations Review* 37(1): 70–78.

Mitchell, Olivia S., and Emily S. Andrews. 1981. "Scale Economies in Private Multi-Employer Pension Systems." *Industrial and Labor Relations Review* 34(4): 522–530.

Smith Robert S., and Ronald G. Ehrenberg. 1983. "Estimating Wage-Fringe Trade-Offs: Some Data Problems." In *The Measurement of Labor Cost*, Jack E. Triplett, ed. National Bureau of Economic Research, Conference on Research in Income and Wealth, Studies in Income and Wealth, Vol. 48, Chicago: University of Chicago Press, pp. 1–60.

Stone, J.R.N. 1953. *The Measurement of Consumers' Expenditure and Behaviour in the United Kingdom, 1920–1938, Vol. 1*, Cambridge.

_____. 1954. "Linear Expenditure Systems and Demand Analysis: An Application to the Pattern of British Demand." *Economic Journal* 64(September): 511–527.

Theil, Henri.   1965.   "The Information Approach to Demand Analysis."
    Econometrica 33(January): 67–87.
Triplett, Jack E.   1983.   "Introduction: An Essay on Labor Cost." In *The Mea-
    surement of Labor Cost*, Jack E. Triplett, ed. National Bureau of Economic
    Research, Conference on Research in Income and Wealth, Studies in Income
    and Wealth, Vol. 48, Chicago: University of Chicago Press, pp. 1–60.
Turner, Robert W.   1987.   "Taxes and the Number of Fringe Benefits
    Received." *Journal of Public Economics* 33(1): 41–57.
U.S. Chamber of Commerce. 1995. *Employee Benefits, 1995 Edition*. Wash-
    ington, D.C.: U.S. Chamber of Commerce.
Vroman, Susan, and Gerard Anderson. 1984. "The Effect of Income Taxation
    on the Demand for Employer-Provided Health Insurance." *Applied Eco-
    nomics* 16(1): 33–43.
Woodbury, Stephen A.   1983.   "Substitution Between Wage and Nonwage
    Benefits." *American Economic Review* 73(1): 166–182.
Woodbury, Stephen A., and Douglas R. Bettinger. 1991. "The Decline of
    Fringe Benefit Coverage in the 1980s." In *Structural Changes in U.S.
    Labor Markets in the 1980s: Causes and Consequences*, Randall W. Eberts
    and Erica Groshen, eds. Armonk, NY: M.E. Sharpe, pp. 101–134.
Woodbury, Stephen A., and Daniel S. Hamermesh. 1992. "Taxes, Fringe
    Benefits, and Faculty." *Review of Economics and Statistics* 74(May): 287–
    296.
Woodbury, Stephen A., and Wei-Jang Huang. 1991. *The Tax Treatment of
    Fringe Benefits*. Kalamazoo, Michigan: W.E. Upjohn Institute for Employ-
    ment Research.

3 The Economics of Family and Medical Leave in Canada and the United States

Eileen Trzcinski
Wayne State University

William T. Alpert
University of Connecticut

This chapter explores the basic premise that family and medical leave consists of two separate analytical components: the wage replacement component and the job guarantee component. In legislation and in private businesses, these two components typically are dealt with separately. In the United States, for example, the Federal Family and Medical Leave Act (FMLA) provides job-guaranteed leave but no wage replacement. Canada has legislation that compels businesses to provide job guarantees during leave and legislation that grants wage replacement administered through the unemployment insurance system. This dual system is also evident in the private practices of businesses where paid sick leave policies are separate from policies that deal with job guarantees.

The central hypothesis underlying this premise is that the factors that determine the provision of wage replacement during leave differ from the determinants of whether or not a job guarantee is provided. In general this hypothesis implies that differences exist in the factors that determine the provision of paid versus unpaid leave. It is specifically hypothesized that the determinants of paid leave are similar to those that account for other fringe benefits. Conversely, it is also hypothesized that the provision of unpaid leave will not be as fully explained by the standard reduced form demand models specifying fringe benefit determination as will the provision of paid leave. Instead, it is conjectured that the provision of unpaid leave can be explained by models that stress issues such as workplace efficiency, hours of work, and/or determinants of managerial control.

These hypotheses are tested through a combination of empirical approaches that involve 1) an examination of the incidence of leave in the United States and Canada and 2) estimation of the determinants of the incidence of leave and the conditions surrounding leave. In investigating the determinants of the incidence of leave among firms, we rely on a standard theoretical and empirical model of fringe benefit determination. This model consists of the estimation of a reduced form demand equation for fringe benefits with various proxy variables representing fringe benefit prices and other factors hypothesized to influence the incidence or levels of fringe benefits. Although this paper provides information on legislative mandates and information on the incidence of private sector policies for both Canada and the United States, the empirical analyses are limited to the United States and are based on data from the U.S. Small Business Administration Leave Survey. Overall, the findings presented below lend support to our central hypotheses that family and medical leave consists of two separate analytical components—a wage replacement component and a job guarantee component.

THE LEGAL FRAMEWORK OF FAMILY AND MEDICAL LEAVE IN CANADA AND THE UNITED STATES

Canada and the United States offer an opportunity to perform natural experiments in comparative social policies. The two countries claim common political, legal, cultural, and constitutional legacies; federal configurations; remarkably similar standards of living; and diverse societies. Both are advanced industrial countries with substantial primary and manufacturing sectors and dominant rapidly growing service sectors. Most recently, the adoption of the North American Free Trade Agreement by both countries and the passage of the Charter of Rights and Freedoms (Bill of Rights) in Canada are bound to make the two countries more similar.

Important differences between Canada and the United States do exist, however, and may grow—the melting pot versus the mosaic as metaphor for society, universal health care in one country with no equivalent system in the other, and numerous other distinctions ranging from Arctic policy to the status of urban minorities. Furthermore, Canada continues to endure a constitutional crisis while the United States faces serious racial tensions. In the area of family leave policies, Canada and the United States share the basic problems of the changing nature of the modern workforce, the altering roles of women and men in the workplace, the changing contributions of men and women to the workforce, and the shifting needs of families and businesses to be competitive in global markets (see Labour Canada, Women's Bureau [1990] for a summary of the position of women in the workforce in Canada).

Canada and the United States have a common, well-known post–World War II labor-force experience. In 1991, 53 percent of all Canadian women aged 15 and over were employed while in the United States 57 percent of women aged 16 and over were working. In both Canada and the United States, half of all new mothers enter or reenter the labor force within one year of their baby's birth. Married women accounted for nearly all the growth in female employment during the past decade in both countries. The employment rate among married women in Canada grew from 47 percent in 1981 to 56 percent in 1991. In the United States, the employment rate among married women jumped from 48 percent to an identical 56 percent during the same period. While women have historically experienced slightly higher unemployment rates than men, the unemployment rates of women and men have converged in both countries during the past several years.

In spite of progress in both countries, most women continue to work in traditionally "female dominated occupations," such as teaching, nursing or related health professions, clerical, sales, and services. Currently, however, women are entering "nontraditional" careers at rates over five times greater than 30 years ago. The number of two-career couples has increased by more than a factor of four in Canada since 1960 and by a similar amount in the United States. In the United States, more than 25 percent of all babies are now being born to single women. In Canada, where the number has risen rapidly during the past decade, the percentage is now 24.7 percent. The 1991 birth rate in Canada was 15.3 per 1,000, while the 1991 rate for the United States was 16.7 per 1,000. Birth rates have increased slightly in both countries during the past few years (Statistics Canada 1993; U.S. Department of Commerce 1993).

In Canada, family and medical leave and benefits are provided through a combination of government mandates, private policies, and union contracts. Wage replacement for medical, maternity, and parental leaves are provided under the Canadian Unemployment Insurance program. After 20 weeks of covered earnings in the year prior to a benefit application, a worker may claim 15 weeks of maternity benefits, 10 weeks of parental benefits, and 15 weeks of sickness benefits up to a maximum of 30 weeks of benefits per occurrence. Unemployment insurance covers 57 percent of insurable earnings up to a maximum amount. This figure is adjusted annually to reflect living cost changes. The maximum earnings covered in 1993 was Can$745.00 per week, yielding a maximum weekly benefit of Can$425.00. In addition, many Canadian employees are covered either by paid sick leave or a supplemental unemployment benefit plan that can pay up to 95 percent of the employee's salary, including the unemployment insurance "clawback," which is designed to limit the liability of the unemployment insurance system to highly compensated employees.[1] Additional maternity leave policies are also provided by the private sector but, as noted in the following section, private policies are less extensive for maternity leave than they are for medical reasons.

In 1992, the Canadian Unemployment Insurance system covered 10.933 million workers and had 1.148 million "regular beneficiaries." Approximately 235,000 workers received special benefits, such as sickness or maternity benefits. About 2.5 percent of the female labor force claims maternity benefits in a year, an amount equal to about 1 percent of the labor force. Tables 1 and 2 describe the growth of public payments for sickness, maternity, adoption, and parental leave in Canada. Real family-leave-type benefits have grown rapidly for the past decade and a half in Canada, keeping pace with the growth of real regular unemployment benefits. Canada has relatively low take-up rates for family-leave-type benefits. It is possible that the low Canadian rates are caused by individuals who do not meet eligibility requirements, by those who find the replacement rate too low to warrant filing for unemployment insurance, and by those who are unaware of the possibility of receiving benefits. Finally, it might be that many individuals use vacation, sick, and other paid leave time during their period of family responsibility.

Table 1 Canadian Unemployment Insurance: Nominal and Real Benefit Payments by Type of Benefit and Percentage of Regular Payments (Nominal Can$)[a]

Year	Regular	Sickness	Maternity	Adoption	Parental
1976	6,357,234 [3,019,686]	273,272 [129,804] (4.3)	293,947 [139,625] (4.6)	–[b] – –	– –
1980	5,578,202 [3,748,552]	230,164 [154,670] (4.1)	349,324 [234,746] (6.3)	– – –	– –
1984	9,551,002 [8,825,126]	221,304 [204,559] (3.4)	428,483 [395,918] (4.5)	3,324 [3,071] –	– –
1988	8,166,124 [9,309,381]	285,227 [325,159] (3.5)	488,301 [566,663] (6.1)	4,140 [4,720] –	– –
1992	13,508,947 [15,400,200]	383,596 [437,299] (2.8)	732,562 [835,121] (5.4)	4,570 [5,210] –	431,525 [491,939] (3.2)
1993	12,776,735 [14,569,478]	383,348 [437,017] (3.0)	707,604 [806,688] (5.5)	4,427 [5,047] –	432,630 [493,198] (3.3)

SOURCE: Labour Division, Unemployment Insurance Statistics Section, 1994.
[a] Values in brackets represent real Canadian dollars (CPI=100 in 1986). Percent of regular payment given in parentheses.
[b] – Not available or less than 0.1%.

Table 2 Canadian Unemployment Insurance
Number of Weeks Paid by Type of Benefit and Percentage
of Regular Benefit (in Can$)[a]

Year	Regular	Sickness	Maternity	Adoption	Parental
1976	32,419	1,345	1,399	–[b]	–
		(4.1)	(4.1)		
1980	31,262	1,210	1,806	–	–
		(3.8)	(5.8)		
1984	55,130	1,193	2,218	15	–
		(2.2)	(4.0)	–	
1988	46,696	1,498	2,590	18	–
		(3.2)	(5.5)	–	
1992	60,821	1,714	3,062	16	1,784
		(2.8)	(5.0)	–	(2.9)
1993	56,728	1,712	2,227	15	1,747
		(3.0)	(3.9)	–	(3.1)

SOURCE: Labour Division, Unemployment Insurance Statistics Section 1994.
[a] Percent of regular benefit in parentheses.
[b] – Not available or less than 0.1%.

Job guarantees in Canada are mandated in provincial and territorial legislation for most workers on maternity and parental leave. In general, Canadian women on maternity leave are guaranteed the same or comparable employment upon their return to work, their seniority is protected, and their benefits are continued. Most jurisdictions (except Alberta, Saskatchewan, and Yukon) have parental leave that allows either parent from 12 to 34 weeks of job-guaranteed leave to care for a newborn or newly adopted child. (See Labour Canada, Women's Bureau [1993, 1988, 1984]; Maldonado and McDonald [1993]; Canadian Union of Public Employees [1991]; and Schwartz [1988] for current and historical summaries of leave legislation in Canada.) Canadian law does not, however, provide specific provisions for job guarantees surrounding medical leave. Instead, Canadians must rely on interpretations of labor law regarding whether a termination of an employee by an employer on account of illness is justifiable. In Canada, a contract can be terminated as a result of "frustration when it has become impossible of performance because of a supervening event which is fortuitous and unforeseeable." In general, although there are certain exceptions, temporary incapacity by one of the parties does not result in frustration of the contract under Canadian law (Arthurs et al. 1988).

Until 1993, leave in the United States was provided either at the discretion of the employer or mandated by state statute (for surveys of state leave statutes, see Finn-Stevenson & Trzcinski [1991] and the Women's Legal Defense Fund [1990]). With the exception of five states that provide temporary disability insurance, all wage replacement during medical leave is provided through paid sick leave policies and private sickness and accident insurance. Paid leave for other family reasons is largely unavailable. The Family and Medical Leave Act was signed into law in February 1993 and became effective in August 1993. This legislation specifies that employees of companies with 50 or more workers are entitled to 12 weeks of unpaid leave per year for childbirth, adoption, or to tend to the serious illness of a child, parent, spouse, or the employee himself.

The legislation guarantees the continuation of all fringe benefits (including health insurance). Upon return from leave, the employee must be provided with the same or equivalent job, and seniority rights must also be maintained. To be eligible, the employee must have worked at the company for at least one year and have worked a minimum of 25 hours per week for that year. Under certain conditions, the company may deny leaves to "key employees," defined in the law as the highest paid 10 percent of its workforce. Finally, if the employer or the employee desires it, the person on leave must use accrued paid leave time for the leave in question. The law does not require, however, that the employer allow paid sick leave to be used for other conditions covered under the law, such as parental leave or leave to care for sick children, spouses, or parents.

An important distinction, then, between the U.S. and Canadian cases is the general availability of paid maternity, parental, and medical leave through the unemployment insurance system in Canada. A second major distinction between Canada and the United States is that Canadian workers have no mandated leave for family responsibilities other than parental leave for newborn children or newly adopted children. Only Quebec mandates five days unpaid leave for family responsibilities. Furthermore, it is also important to note that, in exempting companies with fewer than 50 employees, the Family and Medical Leave Act eliminates 95 percent of all U.S. firms as well as 61 percent of the workforce from the force of law (U.S. General Accounting Office 1989). Thus, while a mandate exists in the U.S. case, fewer than half of all U.S. workers are affected by it.

PROVISION OF LEAVE IN CANADA AND THE UNITED STATES: A DESCRIPTIVE TREATMENT

For the U.S. analysis, we use data from the U.S. Small Business Administration Employee Leave Survey commissioned in 1988 to answer several major questions facing policy makers with respect to mandated leave. An important aspect of the survey was the collection of data on the leave policies of U.S. businesses in a nationally representative sample of firms. The survey instrument for the Small Business Administration's (SBA's) Employee Leave Survey was a four-page questionnaire forwarded to 10,000 business executives. The questionnaire requested information concerning company policies on paid sick leave, sickness and accident insurance, vacation leave, unpaid leave, leave to care for sick children and ailing parents, and the handling of work during leaves. It also contained questions on costs of leaves and terminations to the firms, the benefits accruing to part-time employees, and the firm's characteristics. The survey included an instruction sheet that asked respondents to indicate whether they were the only worker in their company or if the company employed only members of the owners immediate family. In cases in which the firm employed family members only, the respondent was requested to return the blank questionnaire and the instruction sheet with an indication that the firm employed only family members.

A random sample of 10,000 firms was obtained from the SBA's Small Business Data Base (SBDB). The SBDB is a data file covering some 3.8 million businesses (enterprises) with almost 5 million establishments, representing 93 percent of private employment in the United States. The file mainly consists of firms that have paid employees and that have entered formal credit markets. It generally excludes partnerships, sole proprietorships with no paid employees, and wage and salary workers who maintain secondary businesses. The SBDB is primarily drawn from Dun and Bradstreet's Small Business and Million Dollar Directory Files. The SBDB used in this study had been last updated prior to this survey in 1986.

The SBA Employee Leave Survey was mailed in November and December of 1988. To encourage responses, the questionnaire was mailed to each potential respondent twice, approximately three weeks apart. Each mailing contained a different cover letter from the SBA underscoring the importance of the survey and urging the recipient to respond to the questionnaire. A first-class return postage paid envelope was included with each mailing to encourage responses.

Responses were received from 2,732 of the 10,000 firms for an apparent overall response rate of approximately 27 percent. However, some 2,551 of the surveys from both mailings were nondeliverable, suggesting that about 1,275 of the mailed questionnaires should not be counted as part of the 10,000 firm sample. If we discount the nondeliverable questionnaires, the sample size shrinks to 8,725 and the response rate increases to 31.3 percent. Further details on the survey design, the sample, and an analysis of nonresponse bias are presented in Trzcinski and Alpert (1990).

Policies in the United States

This section presents findings from the SBA survey on the incidence of leave as well as on benefits and guarantees surrounding leaves. Findings concerning leave for family responsibilities are also presented. Although the U.S. Bureau of Labor Statistics Employee Benefits surveys provide information on the incidence of paid sick leave, sickness and accident insurance, and maternity and paternity leave, the SBA survey remains the only national survey that collected information on the incidence of unpaid medical leave and on the conditions surrounding leave, such as health benefit continuation, seniority protection, and job guarantees.

Incidence of Leave. Table 3 presents the incidence of leave policies by firm size and differentiates among the separate categories of leave. Table 3 shows that, for businesses in the SBA survey, the incidence of paid sick leave increased as firm size increased. In companies

Table 3 Percentage of U.S. Firms with Leave, by Firm Size and Type of Leave

	Firm size[a]			
Type of leave	1–15 (N=1110)	16–49 (N=326)	50–99 (N=76)	100 or more (N=184)
Paid sick leave	31.5	48.5	61.8	75.0
Sickness and accident insurance	16.1	26.9	36.0	41.0
Unpaid leave for sickness/disability	74.1	84.7	89.5	90.2
Vacation that can be used for sickness/disability	59.9	75.6	89.5	86.5
Separate maternity leave	6.1	15.7	20.0	22.8

SOURCE: Trzcinski and Alpert 1990.
[a] Firm size is determined by number of employees.

with 1–15 employees, 31.5 percent provided paid sick leave. This percentage increased to 48.5 percent for firms with 16–49 employees and to 61.8 percent for firms with 50–99 employees. In firms with 100 or more employees, 75 percent provided job-guaranteed paid sick leave. Regardless of firm size, firms were more likely to offer unpaid leave than paid leave. Only 9.8 percent of the largest firms did not allow employees to take unpaid leave for sickness. The percentage rose to 25.9 in the smallest firms.

Table 3 also shows the percentage of firms that both provided vacation and allowed vacation days to be used for sickness. Firms sometimes place restrictions on the use of vacation because the firms want to maintain control over scheduling or are acting paternalistically. More than 50 percent of all firms allowed employees access to paid leave for sickness through reallocation of vacation days. The percentage of firms either not providing vacation or not allowing the use of vacation days for sickness ranged from 40.1 percent in the smallest firms to 11.5 percent in firms with 50–99 employees.

The 1978 U.S. Pregnancy Discrimination Act (PDA) stipulates that employers who provide sickness or disability leave must also extend this leave to women for pregnancy and childbirth-related disabilities.

Thus, prior to the enactment of the FMLA, paid sick leave, short-term temporary disability policies, and unpaid sick leave policies represented the major source of leave available for pregnancy and childbirth-related disabilities. In 1987, the Supreme Court ruled in *California Federal v. Guerra* that separate maternity leave policies do not violate the Civil Rights Act. Hence, firms may legally supplement existing sick leave policies or implement sick leave policies that apply exclusively to pregnancy and childbirth-related disabilities. The percentage of firms implementing such policies range from 6.1 in the smallest firms to 22.8 in the largest firms (Table 3). The percentages of business reporting separate maternity leave policies in the U.S. Small Business Administration survey were lower than the percentages reporting such policies in Bureau of Labor Statistics (BLS) Employee Benefits surveys, where the percentages reporting unpaid maternity leave range from 17 percent in small establishments to 37 percent in large establishments (U.S. Department of Labor, Bureau of Labor Statistics 1991). The differences between the two surveys occur because unpaid maternity leave that covers disabilities, but not care for newborn children, was usually reported under unpaid medical leave in the SBA survey. Under EEOC guidelines, maternity leave for care-giving purposes cannot be granted to women without equivalent leave also being granted to men (U.S. EEOC 1990). The BLS survey found that the incidence of unpaid paternity leave ranges from 8 percent in small establishments to 18 percent in large ones. The higher rate of maternity leave as compared with paternity leave in the BLS surveys results from the inclusion of unpaid leave for disabilities resulting from pregnancy and childbirth in the maternity leave percentages as maternity, but not paternity, leaves.

Benefits and Guarantees during Leave. All the enacted state and federal legislation provide for unpaid leave. Thus, given the relatively high incidence of unpaid leave policies in large firms and legislative exemptions for small firms, the primary role of current legislative initiatives centers on providing uniformity and certainty in leave policy to employees in firms employing 50 or more. A critical aspect of any leave legislation or firm-specific leave policy concerns how the law or firm policy deals with the conditions under which the employee may

return to work. Three major questions answered in the FMLA and in
firm-specific policy are as follows:

1) Upon returning from a leave for illness, disability, pregnancy,
    or childbirth, are employees guaranteed the same or a
    comparable job?

2) Are employees guaranteed seniority for promotion and other
    purposes during the leave?

3) Does the employer continue to pay the employer share of
    health benefits during the leave?

Information concerning guarantees and benefits during leave are
presented in Table 4. In general, the data indicate that, with the exception of unpaid sick leave and maternity leave for firms employing
between 50 and 99 workers, the incidence of all forms of leave with
health insurance continuation and job and seniority guarantees
increases with firm size. The incidence of unpaid sick leave and maternity leave (and attendant guarantees and health insurance continuation)
in firms employing between 50 and 99 workers usually is slightly
higher than it is in the largest firms. This may simply be an anomaly in
this data or it might indicate that economies of scale for these benefits
cease at a firm size of approximately 50–99 workers. The data might
also be reflecting state-level legislation mandating that such leaves be
provided by firms employing in excess of 50 people.

Between 19 and 25 percent of all firms in the smallest firm size
category (1–15 employees) provide paid sick leave with seniority and
job guarantees and health insurance continuation for both managers
and nonmanagers (Table 4). Similarly, for both occupation groups,
approximately 40 percent of small firms provide unpaid sick leave with
a job guarantee, between 30 and 32 percent with a seniority guarantee,
and about a quarter continue to pay health insurance during sick leave.
Less than 5 percent of all firms in this category provide any job, seniority, or health insurance continuation benefits while an employee is on a
maternity leave.

In the two largest firm size categories for both managers and nonmanagers, the percentage of firms providing paid sick leave with a job
guarantee increases to about 60 percent, but paid sick leave with
seniority guarantees is provided by only about 45 percent of the firms.
The same pattern is followed with both unpaid sick leave (61–70 per-

Table 4 Leaves with Benefits and Guarantees in U.S. Firms: Incidence by Type of Leave and Firm Size (%)

Type of leave	Firm size			
	1–15	16–49	50–99	100 or more
	Managers			
	(N=1025)	(N=311)	(N=75)	(N=184)
Paid sick leave				
Job guarantee	24.6	47.6	59.2	62.5
Seniority guarantee	19.4	30.2	45.3	45.3
Employer continues to pay health insurance	20.7	38.2	52.0	41.9
Unpaid sick leave				
Job guarantee	39.6	62.2	69.7	64.3
Seniority guarantee	30.1	38.7	52.6	44.8
Employer continues to pay health insurance	26.2	47.2	61.8	43.7
Separate maternity leave				
Job guarantee	4.7	12.7	19.7	16.8
Seniority guarantee	4.1	7.8	13.3	10.9
Employer continues to pay health insurance	3.8	11.2	15.8	11.4
	Nonmanagers			
	(N=1041)	(N=311)	(N=73)	(N=181)
Paid sick leave				
Job guarantee	24.6	45.1	58.9	60.2
Seniority guarantee	19.3	30.8	44.4	44.6
Employer continues to pay health insurance	20.4	36.7	51.4	40.9
Unpaid sick leave				
Job guarantee	42.3	59.6	65.8	61.3
Seniority guarantee	31.6	38.3	48.7	44.1
Employer continues to pay health insurance	25.8	42.9	57.9	39.8
Separate maternity leave				
Job guarantee	4.9	12.5	18.7	15.9
Seniority guarantee	4.2	7.8	12.2	11.0
Employer continues to pay health insurance	3.9	10.3	14.7	10.9

SOURCE: Trzcinski and Alpert 1990.
[a] Firm size determined by number of employees.

cent of firms providing this benefit with a job guarantee and 44–53 percent providing such leave with a seniority guarantee) and separate maternity leave (15–20 percent providing separate maternity leave with a job guarantee but only about 11–13 percent providing seniority guarantees). The proportion of firms with 50–99 employees providing health insurance continuation is smaller than the proportion providing job guarantees for each of the benefits listed in Table 4 but the proportion is larger for seniority guarantees. While in the largest firm size category, however, the percentage of firms providing seniority guarantees is generally larger in each benefit category than the percentage offering to pay for health insurance during an employee leave.

The data in Table 4 reveal a substantial percentage of the businesses that provided leave did so without providing a job guarantee and without providing for health benefit continuation. The major exception is separate maternity leave policies, where the incidence of leave with job guarantees quite closely matched the overall incidence of leave. Thus, prior to the enactment of the Family and Medical Leave Act, a substantial minority of firms provided neither health insurance continuation nor job or seniority guarantees with leave. While approximately 90 percent of businesses with 50–99 and with 100 or more employees provided either formal or informal unpaid medical leave, a substantial percentage of these businesses provided neither a job guarantee nor health benefit continuation.

The same basic picture is presented in Table 5, where a tabulation of the SBA survey results for questions concerning leave to care for sick children and ailing parents is presented. Specifically, the survey requested employers to note whether paid sick leave, vacation time, or any other leave could be used by managerial or nonmanagerial employees to care for their infirm children or parents. The question was phrased so that it is not known whether such leave is discretionary or whether it contains job guarantees.

As in the case of other leaves, the data in Table 5 show that, as firm size increases, the percentage of firms allowing workers to use various kinds of leave to care for sick children also increases. With the notable exception of the other leave category (in which case employers' permission for use of other leave to care for sick children increases monotonically with our firm size groupings from about 6 or 7 percent in the smallest firm size category to about 32 percent in the largest), employ-

**Table 5 Leave to Care for Sick Children and Leave to Care
for Ailing Parents in U.S. Firms, Incidence by Type of Leave
and Firm Size (%)[a]**

Type of leave	Firm size[b]			
	1–15	16–49	50–99	100 or more
	Sick children			
Managers	(N=978)	(N=281)	(N=68)	(N=168)
Sick leave	18.6	29.5	47.8	46.4
Vacation	44.2	68.7	80.6	78.6
Other leave	6.1	11.9	19.1	32.3
Sick, vacation and/or other leave	47.5	73.2	85.3	88.0
Nonmanagers	(N=988)	(N=281)	(N=67)	(N=167)
Sick leave	18.7	29.2	44.8	44.9
Vacation	45.0	68.1	79.1	78.4
Other leave	6.5	10.8	19.1	32.3
Sick, vacation and/or other leave	51.0	72.5	85.3	86.9
	Ailing parents			
Managers	(N=965)	(N=277)	(N=67)	(N=167)
Sick leave	16.6	27.4	43.3	40.1
Vacation	42.3	68.8	77.6	78.3
Other leave	5.8	11.2	15.9	30.3
Sick, vacation and/or other leave	45.2	71.5	80.0	86.2
Nonmanagers	(N=978)	(N=278)	(N=67)	(N=166)
Sick leave	16.6	26.6	40.3	38.6
Vacation	43.5	67.7	76.1	78.3
Other leave	6.0	10.9	15.9	30.3
Sick, vacation and/or other leave	50.0	71.6	82.2	85.2

SOURCE: Trzcinski and Alpert 1990.
[a] Percentages include 1) discretionary and nondiscretionary leaves and 2) leaves with and without job guarantees.
[b] Firm size determined by number of employees.

ers' permission for their employees to use either sick or vacation leaves for sick child care increases with firm size, usually reaching its maximum in the category of between 50 and 99 employees. Between 45 percent (nonmanagers) and 48 percent (managers) of all employers in this category allow sick leave to be used to care for sick offspring and 80 percent (nonmanagers) and 81 percent (managers) allow their employees to use vacation to care for sick children.

Permission to use any form of leave for the care of ailing children is granted about half the time in the smallest firm size category (approximately 48 percent for managers and 51 percent for nonmanagers) increasing (monotonically) to almost 90 percent (88 percent for managers and 87 percent for nonmanagers) in the largest firm size category.

The results for ailing parents are extremely close to those for sick children. Between 45 percent (managers) and 50 percent (nonmanagers) of employers in small firms (1–15 employees) allow their employees to use sick, vacation, or other leave to care for ailing parents. This percentage increases monotonically until, in the largest firm size category, approximately 86 percent of employers allow their managers to use sick vacation or other leave to care for infirm parents.

In summary, permission to use other leaves to care for sick children and ailing parents were approximately equally available for managers and nonmanagers. The granting of permission to use sick, vacation, and/or other leaves to care for ill children or parents is quite common, ranging from 50 percent of employers in the smallest firm size category to almost 90 percent in the largest. Firms most readily allowed the use of vacation leave for the care of sick children or infirm parents. Even in the smallest firm size category, between 40 and 45 percent of the employers surveyed allowed the use of vacation leave for this purpose. This is understandable because vacation leave is one of the most flexible benefits provided by employers. Ideally, an employer would like an employee to take the vacation to "recharge" him- or herself and to be more efficient upon return to work. However, it appears that firms recognize that they will have little control over how vacations are actually used by employees and that any attempt to monitor and control vacation use will almost certainly be counterproductive.

Private Sector Policies in Canada

Table 6, which provides results from an employer survey conducted by the Pay Research Bureau (1988), shows that the types of benefits provided in Canada mirror those provided in the United States. The incidence of paid sick leave is high in Canada among managerial and professional workers, while it is relatively low among non-office workers. On the other hand, sickness indemnity insurance coverage rate is lower among managerial and professional workers but is much higher among non-office personnel. For virtually all covered workers (non-office workers having the highest coverage rate at over 40 percent), employers pay all of the costs of sickness indemnity plans.

Most firms provide personal and parental leave; however, its length and the conditions under which it is granted vary greatly. Likewise, paid leave for an illness in the family is provided by about half of all employers of white-collar workers, but much of this leave is discretionary—that is, granted at the discretion of the employer. Most non-office workers do not have access to paid leave for family illness.

**Table 6 Incidence of Medical and Family-Related Benefits in Canada
(% employees covered)**

Benefit	Management/professional	Office	Nonoffice
Supplementary health insurance	98.3	97.3	93.2
Formal paid sick leave plans	86.6	78.8	44.7
Sickness indemnity plans	5.0	4.1	40.3
Combined formal paid sick leave and sickness indemnity plans	8.0	16.6	12.5
Long-term disability plans	97.2	85.3	76.7
Paid holidays	96.6	100.0	100.0
Paid vacations	96.6	100.0	100.0
Paid bereavement leave	81.4	86.9	98.6
Personal and parental leave	79.2	85.9	79.1
Paid leave—illness in family	51.9	50.1	19.4

SOURCE: Pay Research Bureau 1988.

The duration of paid maternity leave varies greatly in Canada, from one day to 18 weeks (Pay Research Bureau 1988). Employers are permitted to supplement unemployment insurance through formalized supplemental unemployment benefit plans. Among management and professional workers, 33.7 percent are covered by such plans. Among office workers, the percentage falls to 25.4 percent; for non-office workers, the percentage covered is only 14.6 percent. For management and professional workers, 3.3 percent of employees receive such leave through a discretionary plan. For office workers, the proportion of workers eligible for such plans is 4 percent. Among non-office workers, the percentage falls to 2.5 percent. Such plans can make up the difference between an employee's unemployment benefit and their salary, up to a maximum of 95 percent of the employee's regular salary (Pay Research Bureau 1988).

MODELING THE INCIDENCE OF LEAVE AND CONDITIONS SURROUNDING LEAVE

Theoretical Considerations

Using the data from the U.S. Small Business Administration Leave Survey, we estimate two sets of models: the first deals with leave incidence and the second with benefits and guarantees available for leave takers.

The model used to examine the provision of paid and unpaid leave is conventional since we hypothesize that leave is provided as a result of the interaction of employer supply and employee demand. The SBA survey was designed to address the question of what factors influence the incidence of leave and conditions surrounding leave. Specific questions were included in the questionnaire to measure important supply- and demand-side factors that theoretically influence whether or not leave is provided.

Fringe benefit supply varies in response to differences in relative costs of benefit provision (Rice 1966; Alpert 1982; Woodbury 1983; Vroman and Anderson 1984; and Even 1992). The supply of fringe benefits is hypothesized to vary with their costs to the firm. A principal determinate of cost is thought to be the size of the firm because fringe benefit provision is thought to be subject to economies of scale of group purchase. Measures of firm size are usually utilized to act as proxy variables for these economies of scale. We use several variables to proxy for such economies, including number of employees, sales volume, and type of firm ownership.

We also hypothesize that, in industries in which larger firms predominate, leaves will be provided more frequently as a result of competition (for comparable compensation packages), follow-the-leader relationships, and demonstration and/or learning effects among the firms in such industries. In order to proxy these effects, we include in our analysis a variable (Percentage Small in the Industry) that captures the percentage of small firms in the industry in which the firm does business. This variable measures the percentage of firms in the industry employing fewer than 100 workers. Unpublished data from the SBA was used to construct this variable.

The model also contains several demand-side variables. Recognizing that unionized workers often either demand larger quantities of fringe benefits or can express their demand for more fringe benefits through their union better than nonunionized workers, we include a variable equaling one if a majority of the firm's workforce is unionized and zero otherwise. We also include a variable reflecting the percentage of workers in the firm's industry who are unionized (reflecting the possibility of spillover effects of unionization on other union and nonunion firms in the industry). It is important to recognize that such spillover effects might operate in either direction since a heavily unionized industry would be an industry in which, all else constant, workers' tastes are better communicated to employers. If workers overall prefer other forms of compensation (for example, cash wages) to leave and insurance, a high rate of unionization might actually lower the likelihood that workers in a particular firm have such benefits (holding constant unionization in that firm). Conversely, if workers overall prefer leave and insurance to other forms of compensation, high rates of industry unionization could raise the likelihood that workers in a particular firm have such benefits.

In addition, workers' tastes (and hence their demand) for fringe benefits are likely to vary with certain demographic characteristics. Here, we hypothesize that tastes for leave can be proxied by the gender and age of a firm's workforce. We use a variable measuring the percentage of the firm's workforce that is female of childbearing age (16–44 years old) and the percentage of the firm's workforce that is over the age of 55 to measure two subgroups of workers more likely to demand leave than are other groups. Testing the hypothesis that women workers prefer leave and insurance-type benefits to other forms of compensation, we include a variable reflecting the percentage of female workers in the industry in our estimating equations. Finally, we control for the unemployment rate (at the time of the survey) in the state in which the firm is located, the percentage of the state's workforce located in rural areas, and several industry categorical variables to capture industry effects. An important variable omitted from the equations is worker income. Other variables, such as firm size and age, will act as proxies for income, but readers should be aware of the bias created in the estimated coefficients by the omission of a variable that directly measures worker income.

The following sections present bivariate logit estimates (and OLS equivalent coefficients) of the incidence of paid and unpaid medical leave and the incidence of different types of family leave.

Incidence of Medical Leave

Table 7 displays estimates of logit regressions in which employer provision of some types of medical leave are regressed on a variety of independent variables, including three measures of scale of firm: number of employees, sales volume, and ownership type. Across the different firm size measures, smaller firms are generally significantly less likely than larger firms to provide medical leave. For paid sick leave only and combined paid sick leave and sickness and accident insurance, firms with 15 or fewer employees are significantly less likely to provide these benefits than firms employing 100 or more workers. Thus, there appears to be a threshold effect for paid leave, with the threshold occurring at the smallest firm size category. It is interesting to note that no such effect is apparent for sickness and accident insurance. For formal unpaid leave, the effect suggested in the two-way analysis continues to be present. Each included firm size category variable's coefficient shows that firms within that firm size category are significantly less likely to provide this benefit than firms employing

Table 7 Logit Estimates of the Probability that a Firm Provides Medical Leave (OLS Equivalent Coefficient)[a]

Variable[b]	Paid sick leave	Sickness and accident insurance	Either paid sick & sickness & accident insurance	Unpaid leave (formal)
Firm size				
1–15 employees	−0.186 [−0.772***] (0.253)	−0.065 [−0.387] (0.274)	−0.156 [−0.626**] (0.258)	−0.266 [−1.540***] (0.310)
16–49 employees	−0.081 [−0.377] (0.265)	−0.018 [−0.105] (0.284)	−0.002 [−0.010] (0.274)	−0.157 [−0.911***] (0.316)
50–99 employees	−0.007 [−0.029] (0.338)	0.031 [0.186] (0.347)	0.068 [0.274] (0.362)	−0.144 [−0.837**] (0.412)
Sales volume				
Less than $250,000	−0.314 [−1.304***] (0.349)	−0.153 [−0.912***] (0.356)	−0.420 [−1.684***] (0.375)	−0.190 [−1.102***] (0.406)
$250,000–$1,000,000	−0.207 [−0.861***] (0.349)	−0.138 [−0.821**] (0.354)	−0.341 [−1.368***] (0.376)	−0.139 [−0.805**] (0.404)
$1,000,000–$10,000,000	−0.174 [−0.722**] (0.334)	−0.071 [−0.424] (0.324)	−0.266 [−1.068***] (0.364)	−0.087 [−0.503] (0.349)
$10,000,000–$50,000,000	−0.160 [−0.663*] (0.384)	−0.003 [−0.020] (0.361)	−0.114 [−0.457] (0.434)	−0.055 [−0.320] (0.391)
Ownership type				
Sole proprietorship	−.0131 [−0.542***] (0.197)	−0.028 [−0.165] (0.237)	−0.107 [−0.430**] (0.190)	−0.079 [−0.457] (0.332)
Partnership	−0.158 [−0.656**] (0.295)	0.005 [0.029] (0.327)	−0.150 [−0.601**] (0.284)	0.014 [0.082] (0.402)

(continued)

Table 7 (continued)

Variable[b]	Paid sick leave	Sickness and accident insurance	Either paid sick & sickness & accident insurance	Unpaid leave (formal)
Corporation	0.016 [0.066] (0.160)	0.058 [0.343*] (0.182)	0.055 [0.220] (0.160)	0.017 [0.101] (0.229)
Percentage small in industry	−0.151 [−6.255***] (1.854)	−0.046 [−3.838**] (0.1820)	−2.057 [−8.253***] (1.974)	0.309 [1.790] (2.286)
Industry Agriculture, mining, construction	−0.279 [−1.159***] (0.283)	−0.009 [−0.052] (0.303)	−0.260 [−1.043***] (0.273)	−0.108 [−0.626] (0.470)
Manufacturing	−0.159 [−0.659**] (0.307)	0.198 [1.176***] (0.329)	−0.061 [−0.244] (0.310)	−0.010 [0.058] (0.384)
Transportation	0.009 [0.037] (0.489)	0.285 [1.692***] (0.524)	0.100 [0.403] (0.490)	−0.001 [−0.003] (0.626)
Wholesale trade	0.010 [0.042] (0.212)	0.030 [0.176] (0.239)	−0.001 [−0.003] (0.216)	0.028 [0.164] (0.348)
Retail trade	−0.331 [−1.137***] (0.180)	−0.038 [−0.225] (0.210)	−0.218 [−0.873***] (0.172)	0.017 [0.096] (0.258)
Unionized	0.069 [0.285] (0.288)	0.107 [0.634**] (0.273)	0.090 [0.360] (0.301)	0.013 [0.076] (0.341)
Percent unionized in industry	−0.454 [−1.885] (1.556)	−0.872 [−5.182***] (1.652)	−0.648 [−2.602*] (1.559)	0.243 [1.410] (1.759)
Percent female age 16–44, managers	0.079 [0.328*] 0.191)	0.028 [0.167] (0.221)	0.078 [0.311*] (0.189)	0.040 [0.234] (0.286)

Variable[b]	Paid sick leave	Sickness and accident insurance	Either paid sick & sickness & accident insurance	Unpaid leave (formal)
Percent female age 16–44, nonmanagers	0.193 [0.802***] (0.173)	0.024 [0.140] (0.200)	0.143 [0.575***] (0.171)	0.034 [0.197] (0.265)
Percent female in industry	–0.191 [–0.793*] (0.456)	–0.216 [–1.286***] (0.507)	–0.391 [–1.568***] (0.454)	0.258 [1.497**] (0.679)
Percent age 55 or more, Manager	0.140 [0.581***] (0.207)	0.070 [0.419*] (0.237)	0.198 [0.796***] (0.205)	0.053 [0.307] (0.333)
Percent age 55 or more, nonmanager	–0.041 [–0.171] (0.285)	–0.019 [–0.115] (0.335)	–0.048 [–0.191] (0.274)	–0.011 [–0.063] (0.478)
State unemployment rate	–1.46 [–6.05] (3.80)	–2.346 [–13.947***] (4.339)	–2.420 [–9.710***] (3.754)	0.144 [0.833] (5.601)
Percent of state population in rural area	–0.037 [–0.152] (0.442)	–0.053 [0.316] (0.489)	–0.024 [–0.0963] (0.437)	–0.282 [–1.637**] (0.676)
N	1599	1585	1594	1564
Chi-square	367.43***	149.13***	395.94***	157.91***
–2 log L	–1790.72	–1509.19	–1812.48	–967.00
–2 log L (intercept only)	–2158.15	1658.32	–2208.43	–1124.91

[a] Original logit coefficient given in brackets and standard error of the original logit coefficient in parentheses.

[b] Excluded categories of categorical variables include: 100 or more employees, sales volume greater than $50 million annually, Subchapter S Corporations (ownership type), services (industry), and nonunion workers.

***significant at the 1% level (two-tailed test).

**significant at the 5% level (two-tailed test).

*significant at the 10% level (two-tailed test).

100 or more workers, and the likelihood that a business provides unpaid leave increases steadily as the number of the firm's employees increases.

These scale effects are quite small, however. The OLS equivalent coefficients of all forms of paid leave show that a 10 percent decrease in the size of the firm decreases the odds that a firm will offer leave by 1 or 2 percent. However, in the case of unpaid leave, a decrease in firm size decreases the odds that the firm will offer leave substantially. For example, as the size of the firm falls below 100 employees, a 10 percent reduction in firm size lowers the likelihood that a firm will provide unpaid leave by about 8.4 percent.

For both paid and unpaid leave, increases in sales volume also positively affect the likelihood that businesses provide leave. For paid leave, this effect is consistent across three of the sales volume categories and is not limited to the type of threshold effect observed for a number of employees. In the case of paid sick leave, all four sales volume categorical variables have significant and negative effects relative to the excluded category, sales volume equal to or exceeding $50 million. In this case, the lower the sales volume, the greater the negative effect on the incidence of leave relative to the excluded sales size category. For example in firms with annual sales volumes of less than $250,000 a 10 percent reduction in sales volume will result in a 3 percent reduction in the likelihood of paid leave, while in a firm with sales volume between $10 and $50 million, a 10 percent reduction in sales volume will yield a 1.6 percent lowered probability of paid sick leave provision. In the estimate of combined paid sick leave/sickness and accident insurance, the significant effects hold for the three lowest sales volume categories, while for unpaid leave, only the two lowest sales volume categories show significantly lower incidences of leave compared with businesses with higher sales volumes. Ownership type also affects the incidence of paid leave but not unpaid leave. Sole proprietorships and partnerships tend to be less likely to provide leaves than are corporations and Subchapter S Corporations. This effect is relatively large with the OLS equivalent coefficient in the paid leave equation equaling –0.66.

The variable, Percentage Small in the Industry, has significant and negative coefficients in Table 7 in the paid medical leave and combined paid sick leave and sickness and accident insurance equations, but it has no statistically significant effect in the unpaid medical leave equation.

The five dummy variables included to control for industry are agriculture, mining, and construction; manufacturing; transportation; wholesale trade; and retail trade. The excluded category is the service sector. Industry effects are limited to paid leave and sickness and accident insurance. There are large and significant differences between service and manufacturing firms in the provision of paid sick leave and sickness and accident insurance. In these cases, the OLS equivalent coefficients are −0.66 and +1.18. Firms in agriculture and in retail trade are less likely to provide paid sick leave than are firms in the service sector. Firms in transportation are more likely than service sector firms to offer sickness and accident insurance, but this difference is not observable in the joint variable of paid sick leave and/or sickness and accident insurance. No statistically significant industry effects are observed in the unpaid leave equation.

A firm-specific variable and an industry-specific variable are included in the equation to measure the effects of unionization. These two unionization variable coefficients indicate that unions tend to affect the provision of leave and insurance in opposite directions. Firms whose workers are covered by a union contract are significantly more likely to provide sickness and accident insurance compared with firms whose workers are not unionized, but this variable has no effect on the joint provision of paid leave policies (Table 7). The findings also indicate that a spillover effect may be occurring. The percentage of workers unionized in the industry depresses the likelihood that a particular firm in that industry provides sickness and accident insurance. As noted above, this result is plausible since, in spite of the fact that unionized workers are able to raise the level of a particular benefit in a given firm (industry unionization rate constant), it is also possible that even though unionization in a particular firm may raise the likelihood of the presence of leave and/or insurance-type benefits in that firm, a high rate of unionization in an industry (reflecting overall worker preferences in that industry) may lower the likelihood that a particular firm in that industry offers leave and/or insurance-type benefits. The latter result applies in this case for sickness and accident insurance. Neither the firm-specific nor the industry-specific union coefficient achieves statistical significance in the unpaid leave equation.

The firm level demographic variables (percent female aged 16–44 and percent aged 55 or more) are entered separately in the equation for both managers and nonmanagers. The empirical analyses suggest that firm-specific and industry-specific demographic variables operate on two separate and conflicting levels where the negative effects of percent female in the industry are counterbalanced by the effects of the firm-specific demographics. More specifically, the two variables, percent female of the firm's managerial and nonmanagerial workforce aged 16–44, exert positive effects on the incidence of paid sick leave. This effect carries over to the combined incidence of paid sick leave days and sickness and accident insurance. In the unpaid leave equation, no effects are observed for the firm-specific measures of percent female, but the negative industry-specific effect remains. Although both coefficients of the variables percent female of the managerial and nonmanagerial workforce achieved statistical significance, the effects of firm-specific demographics concerning older workers are limited to effects stemming from the percent of older managers. In no case does the percent of the firm's nonmanagerial workforce aged 55 or older exert a statistically significant positive effect on the dependent variable. The percent of the firm's managerial workforce, aged 55 or older affects the likelihood of paid leave in the incidence equations, but it exerts no effect on incidence of unpaid leave.

As the state unemployment rate increases, the likelihood that a firm offers sickness and accident insurance significantly declines, as does the likelihood of the firm offering either paid sick leave days and/ or sickness and accident insurance. These effects are large. For example, a 1 percent increase in the state unemployment rate reduces the likelihood that a firm will offer sickness and accident insurance by 2.35 percent. No statistically significant effect of the state unemployment rate is observed in the unpaid leave equation.

The final control variable in this analysis is the percentage of the state's population that resides in a rural area. Here, the only significant effect occurs for the provision of formal unpaid medical leave policies: the greater this percentage, the less likely is a firm to have a formal, unpaid leave policy.

Table 7 indicates that, although the unpaid leave equation does achieve statistical significance, the overall explanatory power as measured by chi-square is far below the level achieved by the paid leave equation. Several variables that consistently achieved significance in the paid leave equations do not to achieve significance in the unpaid leave equation, including ownership type, industry type, unionization (firm specific and industry), percent managers aged 55 or older, and state unemployment rate. As we noted at the beginning of this paper, we expected that a reduced form demand framework would better explain the provision of paid leave and insurance-type benefits than unpaid leave. From the results presented in Table 7, this appears to be the case.

Incidence of Family Leave

Table 8 presents logit estimates for four types of family leave: maternity leave (separate policy for disability and infant care), maternity leave (separate policy for infant care only), leave to care for sick children, and leave to care for ailing parents. In the latter two cases, the existence of such leave typically indicates that the firm permits the use of other types of leave for caring for sick children and/or ailing parents.

Only two coefficients of the categorical variables for economies of scale of group purchase are statistically significant at conventional levels in Table 8. Thus, only in the smallest firm size category do significantly fewer firms offer their workers maternity leave (either with disability and infant care or infant care only). In this set of four equations, two coefficients of the dummy variables for number of employees attain statistical significance. Firms employing 1–15 workers are less likely than other firms to have either separate maternity leave for disability and/or infant care. In no case does number of employees affect the likelihood that a firm provides leave to care for sick children or ailing parents. Sales volume, on the other hand, significantly affects the probability that a firm provides leave to care for ailing parents only in the smallest sales volume category. Sales volume has more pervasive effects on the provision of leave to care for sick children than it does for ailing parents, with the coefficient of the sick children variable achieving statistical significance in the smallest three sales size catego-

Table 8 Logit Estimates of the Probability that a Firm Provides Separate Family Leave Policies (OLS Equivalent Coefficient)[a]

	Maternity leave		Leave to care for sick children	Leave to care for ailing parents
Variable[b]	Separate policy: disability & infant care	Separate policy: infant care only		
Firm size				
1–15 employees	−0.024	−0.069	−0.053	−0.045
	[−1.259**]	[−1.295**]	[−0.245]	[−0.183]
	(0.332)	(0.567)	(0.282)	(0.305)
16–49 employees	−0.060	−0.031	−0.012	0.032
	[−0.314]	[−0.586]	[−0.058]	[0.131]
	(0.336)	(0.593)	(0.293)	(0.316)
50–99 employees	−0.062	−0.006	0.120	0.149
	[−0.100]	[−.111]	[0.559]	[0.604]
	(0.410)	(0.709)	(0.350)	(0.379)
Sales volume (annual)				
Less than $250,000	0.004	0.022	−0.279	−0.239
	[0.212]	[0.419]	[−1.295***]	[−0.970***]
	(0.435)	(0.685)	(0.361)	(0.384)
$250,000–$1,000,000	0.006	0.037	−0.144	−0.120
	[0.338]	[0.697]	[−0.669*]	[−0.489]
	(0.444)	(0.723)	(0.354)	(0.378)
$1,000,000–$10,000,000	0.005	−0.006	−0.153	−0.122
	[0.242]	[−0.119]	[−0.709**]	[−0.496]
	(0.401)	(0.668)	(0.329)	(0.351)
$10,000,000–$50,000,000	0.000	0.013	−0.097	−0.030
	[0.004]	[0.252]	[−0.452]	[−0.120]
	(0.477)	(0.783)	(0.376)	(0.402)
Ownership type				
Sole proprietorship	0.005	−0.063	−0.145	−0.179
	[0.259]	[1.186*]	[−0.675***]	[−0.729***]
	(0.327)	(0.622)	(0.243)	(0.260)
Partnership	0.003	0.001	−0.025	−0.045
	[0.177]	[0.027]	[−0.116]	[−0.181]
	(0.450)	(1.144)	(0.320)	(0.339)
Corporation	0.008	0.069	0.022	0.036
	[0.393]	[1.284**]	[0.101]	[0.147]
	(0.256)	(0.534)	(0.177)	(0.190)
Percentage small in industry	−0.051	−0.515	−0.929	−1.056
	[−2.646]	[−9.617***]	[−4.308**]	[−4.296**]
	(2.294)	(3.698)	(1.803)	(1.946)

Variable[b]	Maternity leave		Leave to care for sick children	Leave to care for ailing parents
	Separate policy: disability & infant care	Separate policy: infant care only		
Industry				
Agriculture, mining, construction	−0.008 [−0.408] (0.436)	−0.061 [−1.140] (0.908)	−0.382 [−1.774***] (0.382)	−0.477 [−1.938***] (0.411)
Manufacturing	0.000 [0.001] (0.402)	−0.041 [−0.780] (0.716)	−0.173 [−0.804**] (0.334)	−0.228 [−0.928***] (0.363)
Transportation	0.003 [0.140] (0.666)	0.015 [0.281] (1.060)	−0.152 [−0.706] (0.546)	−0.196 [−0.799] (0.605)
Wholesale trade	0.008 [0.427] (0.321)	0.014 [0.262] (0.576)	−0.079 [−0.365] (0.240)	−0.106 [−0.430*] (0.253)
Retail trade	−0.014 [−0.709**] (0.306)	0.004 [0.086] (0.459)	0.204 [−0.946***] (0.213)	−0.280 [−1.138***] (0.228)
Unionized	−0.003 [−0.134] (0.394)	−0.020 [−0.377] (0.724)	−0.055 [−0.253] (0.322)	0.043 [−0.173] (0.336)
Percent unionized in industry	−0.003 [−0.131] (1.916)	−0.013 [−0.240] (2.826)	−0.049 [−0.226] (1.604)	0.094 [0.383] (1.737)
Percent female age 16–44, Managers	0.003 [0.186] (0.284)	0.028 [0.529] (0.468)	0.085 [0.394*] (0.215)	0.125 [0.509**] (0.229)
Percent female age 16–44, Nonmanagers	0.016 [0.822***] (0.267)	0.006 [0.116] (0.461)	0.082 [0.383**] (0.197)	0.106 [0.431**] (0.210)
Percent female in industry	0.001 [0.066] (0.704)	0.038 [−0.708] (1.123)	−0.116 [−0.540] (0.513)	−0.177 [−0.727] (0.549)

(continued)

Table 8 (continued)

Variable[b]	Maternity leave			
	Separate policy: disability & infant care	Separate policy: infant care only	Leave to care for sick children	Leave to care for ailing parents
Percent age 55 or more, Managers	0.001 [0.064] (0.340)	−0.025 [−0.469] (0.685)	0.073 [0.341] (0.243)	0.140 [0.571**] (0.257)
Percent age 55 or more, Nonmanagers	0.004 [0.202] (0.469)	0.014 [0.266] (0.771)	−0.101 [−0.470] (0.367)	−0.099 [−0.402] (0.390)
State unemployment rate	−0.029 [−1.495] (5.492)	−0.395 [−7.386] (9.324)	0.531 [2.467] (4.243)	0.646 [2.629] (4.488)
Percent of state population in rural area	0.012 [0.631] 0(.651)	0.165 [3.096***] (1.110)]	−0.038 [−0.176] (0.505)	0.049 [0.201] (0.534)
N	1601	1574	1601	1399
Chi-square	86.62***	47.78***	209.76***	194.15***
−2 log L	−962.62	−388.99	−1464.09	−1280.69
−2 log L (intercept only)	−1049.24	−436.47	−1673.85	−1474.85

[a] Original logit coefficient in brackets and standard error of original logit coefficient in parentheses.

[b] Excluded categories of categorical variables include: 100 or more employees, sales volume greater than $50 million annually, Subchapter S Corporations (ownership type), services (industry), and nonunion workers.

***significant at the 1% level (two-tailed test).

**significant at the 5% level (two-tailed test).

*significant at the 10% level (two-tailed test).

ries. The statistically significant effects of ownership type also vary across the four equations. Corporations are more likely than other types of firms to provide separate maternity leave policies for infant care only, while sole proprietorships are less likely than other firms to provide separate parental leave policies and policies to care for sick children and ailing parents. As the percentage of small firms in the industry increases, the likelihood that a firm offers these same three types of leave also decreases significantly. Significant industry effects are more pronounced for leave to care for sick children and ailing parents, with firms in agriculture, manufacturing, and retail trade less likely to provide these policies than firms in the service industry.

Neither of the coefficients of the unionization variables achieve statistical significance in any of the four cases examined here. In contrast to the effect of the percent female in the industry variable on medical leave, the percent female in the industry variable exerts no effect on the incidence of different types of family leave. However, the likelihood that a firm provides leave to care for sick children and for ailing parents increases significantly as the variable percent female aged 16–44 increases for both the managerial and nonmanagerial workforce. These effects are quite small, however. The OLS equivalent coefficients indicate that a 10 percent increase in any of these variables will lead to about a 1 percent increase in the likelihood that the firm in question will provide leave to care for sick children or ailing parents. The percent female, aged 16–44 of nonmanagers variable (but not the percent of managers variable), also affects the provision of separate policies for maternity leave. The percent of the firm's managerial workforce aged 55 or more has statistically significant effects on the incidence of leave to care for ailing parents.

In contrast to its negative effect on the provision of unpaid medical leave, the percent of the state population that resides in rural areas variable shows a positive and significant relationship to the incidence of separate maternity leave policies for infant care only. The state unemployment rate has no significant effects in any of the equations.

Many of the predictions of the model are demonstrated to be accurate. The results in Table 8 show that limited economies of scale of group purchase exist for maternity leave for firms with more than 15 employees, but no scale effects (as measured by numbers of employees) are present in the provision of leaves to care for sick children or

ailing parents. Firms with less than $10 million in annual sales are sig-
nificantly less likely to provide leave to care for sick children than are
firms with annual sales in excess of $50 million and very small firms
(annual sales of less than $250,000) are significantly less likely to pro-
vide leave to care for ailing parents than are firms in the largest firm
category. Few industry effects exist for these benefits; however, in general, there is a significantly lower incidence of leave to care for sick
children in all industries (except transportation and wholesale trade)
than in services. Similarly, leave to care for sick children and ailing
parents is significantly positively related to the percent of females
(both managers and nonmanagers) variables. Only in the case of the
leave to care for ailing parents equation does the percent of the firm's
managerial workforce aged 55 or more have statistically significant
effects. Thus, the most important determinants of maternity leave and
leave to care for sick children and ailing parents are scale of firm (as
measured by annual sales) and the percentage of small firms in the
firm's industry. In the case of the latter variable, several industry
effects and the percentage of managerial and nonmanagerial female
employees between the ages of 16 and 44 are also important. The only
other coefficient achieving statistical significance in any equation is
that the larger the percent of a state's population that resides in rural
areas the more maternity leave for infant care is provided.

Benefits and Guarantees Surrounding Medical Leave

Since most large firms provide both paid and unpaid medical leave,
the major impact of the FMLA and state leave legislation centers on
the mandating of conditions surrounding leave. As Table 4 indicates, a
substantial percentage of firms, including large firms, provide leave
without providing health benefit continuation or job guarantees.
Although the lack of a job guarantee does not necessarily imply that an
employee will be terminated, analysis of the SBA survey concerning
terminations in businesses with and without job guarantees did find a
significantly higher rate of terminations on account of illness and disability in businesses without job guarantees in their plans as compared
to businesses with such job guarantees. Conversely, the analysis also
found a correspondingly higher rate of leave-taking in businesses with

job guarantees than in businesses without job guarantees (Trzcinski 1994).

We provide multinomial logit estimates of the incidence of paid and unpaid leave with and without health benefit continuation (Tables 9 and 10) and with and without job guarantees (Tables 11 and 12). The equations are estimated separately for managers (Tables 9 and 11) and nonmanagers (Tables 10 and 12).

In general, we hypothesize that the same variables that have significant effects in Table 7 for paid medical leave also have significant effects in Tables 9–12. Minor variations may occur, however, because a firm was designated as having paid or unpaid medical leave if either managerial and/or nonmanagerial employees had access to leave in Table 7. In a small percentage of cases, managers had access to leave, while nonmanagers did not (or the converse). Hence, the exact percentages reporting leave may vary slightly across the equations. The unpaid medical leave variable used in Table 7 refers to formal unpaid leave plans, while Tables 9–12 classify a firm's unpaid leave policy into three categories of unpaid leave: formal leave with a job guarantee, leave with no guarantee (including informal plans and formal plans without job guarantees), and no unpaid leave.

The major issue in examining Tables 9–12 centers on determining when a variable operates differently in its effect on whether a leave is provided with or without the benefit continuation or a job guarantee. The most potentially interesting cases are 1) those in which the variable's coefficient achieves statistical significance for one of the options but not the other, and 2) those in which the variable's coefficient achieves significance for the two options, but the effect is different in magnitude or operates in a different direction or both. In this set of four equations, there is no instance in which a variable significantly affects health benefit continuation and job guarantees and where these effects are statistically significant and in different directions.

Health Benefit Continuation. The only significant economies of scale of group purchase effects occur in firms employing more than 15 workers (Tables 9 and 10). Firms in the smallest employment size category provide significantly fewer paid leaves with and without benefit continuation for managers and nonmanagers. They also provide significantly fewer unpaid leaves with benefit continuation for managers and nonmanagers than do firms with more than 100 employees. These effects are generally small, as shown by the OLS equivalent coefficients, which indicate that a 10 percent increase in the independent variable will result in about a 1 percent increase in the probability that a firm will provide paid medical leave (with or without benefit continuation).

Other measurers of firm size have significant coefficients in the paid medical leave (managers and nonmanagers) equations. Firms with less than $50 million in sales provide significantly fewer paid medical leaves for managers and nonmanagers than do other firms. The only similar scale effects for unpaid medical leave occur for nonmanagers' unpaid medical leave without benefit continuation for workers in firms with annual sales volumes of less than $250,000, with significantly fewer firms providing such leaves.

Sole proprietorships offer significantly fewer formal unpaid medical leaves for managers (not surprisingly, since the proprietor is often the only manager in a sole proprietorship). The likelihood of firms in industries with a higher percentage of businesses employing fewer than 100 workers providing paid medical leaves (with or without benefit continuation) for either managers or nonmanagers is significantly lower than for firms in industries where the percentage of small firms in those industries is higher. The OLS equivalent coefficients show that the effect of the sole proprietorship form of business organization on the provision of paid leave with and without benefit continuation is small.

Tables 9 and 10 show few industry effects on leave for managers and nonmanagers. There is only a significantly negative coefficient on the retail trade dummy variable, indicating that firms in retail trade provide significantly fewer paid medical leaves (with or without benefit continuation) for either managers or nonmanagers than do firms in services. In the case of paid leaves (with or without benefit continuation), firms in agriculture, mining, and construction are significantly less likely to provide such leave than are service sector firms.

Other variables that significantly affect the provision of paid and unpaid medical leave are the percentage of female managers in a firm, which positively affects the likelihood that a firm will provide both types of medical leave for managers and nonmanagers with or without benefit continuation. Across the board, the higher the percentage of

Table 9 Multinomial Logit Estimates of the Probability that a Firm Provides Paid and Unpaid Medical Leave With and Without Health Benefit Continuation, for Managers (OLS Equivalent Coefficient)[a]

Variable[b]	Paid medical leave		Unpaid medical leave	
	Without benefit continuation	With benefit continuation	Without benefit continuation	With benefit continuation and formal plan
Firm Size				
1–15 employees	−0.104	−0.095	0.028	0.279
	[−0.746**]	[−0.528*]	[0.129]	[−0.125**]
	(0.332)	(0.305)	(0.304)	(0.489)
16–49 employees	−0.005	0.021	0.115	−0.098
	[−0.033]	[0.119]	[0.523]	[−0.393]
	(0.348)	(0.318)	(0.331)	(0.511)
50–99 employees	−0.003	0.111	0.155	0.151
	[−0.023]	[0.619]	[0.701]	[0.608]
	(0.466)	(0.398)	(0.475)	(0.636)
Sales volume (annual)				
Less than $250,000	−0.281	−0.413	−0.122	−0.432
	[−2.01***]	[−2.302***]	[−0.555]	[−1.739**]
	(0.455)	(0.438)	(0.406)	(0.683)
$250,000–$1,000,000	−0.248	−0.251	0.017	−0.223
	[−1.773***]	[−1.401***]	[0.077]	[−.0900]
	(0.461)	(.422)	(0.416)	(0.642)
$1,000,000–$10,000,000	−0.191	−0.192	−0.069	−0.189
	[−1.366***]	[−1.071***]	[−0.315]	[−0.761]
	(0.428)	(.403)	(0.398)	(0.566)
$10,000,000–$50,000,000	−0.039	−0.110	0.120	−0.144
	[−0.276]	[−.611]	[0.892]	[−0.581]
	(0.491)	(0.477)	(0.568)	(0.794)
Ownership type				
Sole proprietorship	−0.066	−0.169	−0.017	−0.307
	[−0.473*]	[−0.940***]	[0.078]	[−1.236**]
	(0.286)	(0.249)	(0.203)	(0.616)
Partnership	−0.081	−0.147	−0.083	−0.117
	[−0.582]	[−0.820**]	[−0.376]	[−0.471]
	(0.414)	(0.360)	(0.292)	(0.648)
Corporation	0.025	0.045	0.019	0.110
	[0.178]	[0.248]	[0.084]	[0.445]
	(0.223)	(0.184)	(0.183)	(0.354)

(continued)

Table 9 (continued)

Variable[b]	Paid medical leave		Unpaid medical leave	
	Without benefit continuation	With benefit continuation	Without benefit continuation	With benefit continuation and formal plan
Percentage small in industry	−1.143	−1.305	−0.736	1.236
	[−10.163***]	[−7.268***]	[−3.337]	[4.978]
	(2.450)	(2.285)	(2.142)	3.936)
Industry				
Agriculture, mining, construction	−0.121	−0.259	−0.075	−0.285
	[−0.868**]	[−1.442***]	[−0.340]	[−1.148]
	(0.395)	(0.352)	(0.282)	(0.718)
Manufacturing	−0.037	−0.062	−0.052	0.056
	[−0.265]	[−0.344]	[−0.235]	[0.224]
	(0.405)	(0.375)	(0.341)	(0.634)
Transportation	−0.002	0.015	−0.117	−0.046
	[0.011]	[0.083]	[−0.531]	[−0.187]
	(0.671)	(0.596)	(0.521)	(1.003)
Wholesale trade	0.019	−0.010	−0.047	0.035
	[−0.138]	[0.056]	[−0.213]	[0.139]
	(0.324)	(0.249)	(0.249)	(0.473)
Retail trade	−0.132	−0.139	−0.022	0.002
	[−0.945***]	[−0.773***]	[−0.099]	[0.010]
	(0.271)	(0.207)	(0.185)	(0.375)
Unionized	0.076	0.091	0.009	0.096
	[0.543]	[0.506]	[0.041]	[0.386]
	(0.377)	(0.346)	(0.324)	(0.526)
Percent unionized in industry	0.327	−0.0390	0.207	0.402
	[−2.340]	[−2.174]	[0.940]	[1.620]
	(1.958)	(1.885)	(1.605)	(3.149)
Percent female age 16–44, Managers	0.120	0.044	0.080	0.130
	[0.855***]	[0.244]	[0.366*]	[0.525]
	(0.261)	(0.232)	(0.221)	(0.435)
Percent female age 16–44, Nonmanagers	0.076	0.103	0.202	0.234
	[0.544**]	[0.572***]	[0.915***]	[0.941**]
	(0.247)	(0.209)	(0.200)	(0.399)
Percent female in industry	−0.150	−0.317	−0.151	0.173
	[−1.069]	[−1.768***]	[−0.683]	[0.698]
	(0.656)	(0.542)	(0.484)	(0.999)

Variable[b]	Paid medical leave		Unpaid medical leave	
	Without benefit continuation	With benefit continuation	Without benefit continuation	With benefit continuation and formal plan
Percent age 55 or more, Managers	0.133 [0.953***] (0.307)	0.136 [0.756***] (0.248)	−0.017 [0.077] (0.229)	0.088 [0.355] (0.468)
Percent age 55 or more, Nonmanagers	−0.089 [−0.637] (0.465)	−0.027 [−0.152] (0.342)	−0.016 [0.074] (0.280)	0.044 [0.178] (0.638)
State unemployment rate	−1.108 [−7.917] (5.509)	−2.204 [−12.279***] (4.540)	−0.896 [−4.062] (4.130)	−1.750 [−7.050] (8.250)
Percent of state population in rural area	−0.224 [−1.598**] (0.653)	0.087 [0.482] (0.514)	0.109 [0.494] (0.489)	0.125 [−0.503] (0.977)
N	1485		1590	
Chi-square	513.162		164.233	
−2 log L	−1201.739		−1065.228	
−2 log L (intercept only)	−1458.320		−1147.344	

[a] Original logit coefficient in brackets and standard error of original logit coefficient in parentheses.

[b] Excluded categories of categorical variables include: 100 or more employees, sales volume greater than $50 million annually, Subchapter S Corporations (ownership type), services (industry), and nonunion workers.

***significant at the 1% level (two-tailed test).

**significant at the 5% level (two-tailed test).

*significant at the 10% level (two-tailed test).

Table 10   Multinomial Logit Estimates of the Probability that a Firm Provides Paid and Unpaid Medical Leave with and without Health Benefit continuation for Nonmanagers (OLS Equivalent Coefficient)[a]

| | Paid medical leave | | Unpaid medical leave | |
| | Without benefit continuation | With benefit continuation | Without benefit continuation | Benefit continuation and formal plan |
Variable[b]				
Firm size				
1–15 employees	−0.113	−0.079	0.025	−0.240
	[−0.760**]	[−0.468]	[0.107]	[−0.982**]
	(0.324)	(0.306)	(0.303)	(0.496)
16–49 employees	0.007	0.026	0.115	−0.062
	[0.045]	[0.154]	[0.502]	[−0.254]
	(0.339)	(0.320)	(0.330)	(0.520)
50–99 employees	−0.015	0.122	0.161	0.165
	[−0.098]	[0.662*]	[0.699]	[0.674]
	(0.462)	(0.401)	(0.474)	(0.647)
Sales volume				
Less than $250,000	−0.285	−0.355	−0.141	−0.276
	[−1.922***]	[−2.093***]	[−0.614]	[−1.128*]
	(0.446)	(0.436)	(0.405)	(0.662)
$250,000–$1,000,000	−0.266	−0.237	−0.028	0.175
	[−1.790***]	[−1.399***]	[−0.123]	[−0.717]
	(0.454)	(0.426)	(0.415)	(0.663)
$1,000,000–$10,000,000	−0.052	−0.187	−0.082	0.152
	[−1.348***]	[−1.103***]	[−0.356]	[−0.621]
	(0.422)	(0.406)	(0.397)	(0.589)
$10,000,000–$50,000,000	−0.057	−0.091	0.187	−0.015
	[−0.381]	[−0.536]	[0.813]	[−0.061]
	(0.491)	(0.479)	(0.567)	(0.775)
Ownership type				
Sole proprietorship	−0.060	−0.150	−0.020	−0.178
	[−0.404]	[−0.886***]	[0.088]	[−0.726]
	(0.274)	(0.250)	(0.203)	(0.555)
Partnership	−0.095	−0.118	−0.089	−0.073
	[−0.639]	[−0.697b]	[−0.386]	[−0.298]
	(0.408)	(0.353)	(0.292)	(0.654)

Variable[b]	Paid medical leave		Unpaid medical leave	
	Without benefit continuation	With benefit continuation	Without benefit continuation	Benefit continuation and formal plan
Corporation	0.020	0.043	0.0188	0.135
	[0.137]	[0.255]	[0.082]	[0.550]
	(0.218)	(0.186)	(0.183)	(0.370)
Percentage small in industry	−1.429	−1.129	−0.747	1.113
	[−9.626***]	[−6.659***]	[−3.251]	[4.548]
	(2.388)	(2.277)	(2.142)	(4.021)
Industry				
Agri., mining, const.	−0.090	−0.218	−0.076	−0.313
	[−0.605]	[−1.283***]	[−0.330]	[−1.279*]
	(0.371)	(0.345)	(0.282)	(0.724)
Manufacturing	−0.024	−0.044	−0.053	0.031
	[−0.164]	[−0.262]	[−0.229]	[0.126]
	(0.388)	(0.368)	(0.341)	(0.638)
Transportation	0.036	0.074	−0.121	−0.076
	[0.241]	[0.438]	[−0.525]	[−0.312]
	(0.637)	(0.576)	(0.522)	(1.011)
Wholesale trade	0.006	−0.011	−0.047	−0.003
	[0.039]	[−0.064]	−0.047	[−0.014]
	(0.310)	(0.251)	(0.249)	(0.479)
Retail trade	−0.168	−0.146	−0.020	−0.062
	[−1.129***]	[−0.859***]	[−0.085]	[−0.254]
	(0.276)	(0.211)	(0.185)	(0.389)
Unionized	0.068	0.095	0.005	0.130
	[0.458]	[0.560*]	[0.023]	[0.533]
	(0.364)	(0.337)	(0.324)	(0.521)
Percent unionized in industry	−0.380	−0.392	0.213	0.461
	[−2.557]	[−2.310]	[0.928]	[1.882]
	(1.869)	(1.844)	(1.608)	[1.882]
Percent female age 16–44, Managers	0.097	0.021	0.086	0.083
	[0.652**]	[0.125]	[0.375*]	[0.339]
	(0.255)	(0.233)	(0.221)	(0.444)
Percent female age 16–44, Nonmanagers	0.086	0.119	0.209	0.252
	[0.580**]	[0.702***]	[0.910***]	[1.028***]
	(0.241)	(0.209)	(0.200)	(0.399)

(continued)

Table 10 (continued)

	Paid medical leave		Unpaid medical leave	
Variable[b]	Without benefit continuation	With benefit continuation	Without benefit continuation	Benefit continuation and formal plan
Percent female in industry	−0.121 [−0.813] (0.642)	−0.290 [−1.709***] (0.543)	−0.153 [−0.666] (0.484)	0.097 [0.398] (1.013)
Percent age 55 or more, Managers	0.114 [0.769**] (0.301)	0.102 [0.600**] (0.253)	−0.015 [−0.066] (0.228)	−0.043 [0.176] (0.480)
Percent age 55 or more, Nonmanagers	−0.019 [−0.133] (0.412)	−0.007 [−0.040] (0.343)	−0.142 [−0.620] (0.279)	−0.020 [−0.084] (0.685)
State unemployment rate	−0.812 [−5.469] (5.292)	−2.298 [−13.552***] (4.564)	−0.965 [−4.198] (4.131)	−1.088 [−4.448] (8.312)
Percent of state population in rural area	−0.234 [−1.573**] (0.634)	0.056 [0.330] (0.517)	0.116 [0.506] (0.489)	−0.184 [−0.751] (1.007)
N	1485		1590	
Chi-square	485.347		141.402	
−2 log L	−1227.464		−1063.651	
−2 log L (intercept only)	−1470.138		−1134.353	

[a] Original logit coefficient in brackets and standard error of original logit coefficient in parentheses.

[b] Excluded categories of categorical variables include: 100 or more employees, sales volume greater than $50 million annually, Subchapter S Corporations (ownership type), services (industry), and nonunion workers.

***significant at the 1% level (two-tailed test).

**significant at the 5% level (two-tailed test).

*significant at the 10% level (two-tailed test).

Table 11 Multinomial Logit Estimates of the Probability that a Firm Provides Paid and Unpaid Medical Leave with and without Job Guarantee, for Managers (OLS Equivalent Coefficient)[a]

Variable[b]	Paid medical leave		Unpaid medical leave	
	Without guarantee	With guarantee	Without guarantee	With guarantee and formal plan
Firm size				
1–15 employees	–0.046	0.137	0.035	–0.288
	[–0.515]	[–0.631**]	[0.225]	[–1.361***]
	(0.393)	(0.284)	(0.306)	(0.428)
16–49 employees	–0.009	0.027	0.092	0.080
	[–0.098]	[0.126]	[0.589*]	[–0.378]
	(0.410)	(0.298)	(0.333)	(0.447)
50–99 employees	0.013	0.106	0.137	–0.041
	[0.140]	[0.487]	[0.877*]	[–0.195]
	(0.527)	(0.382)	(0.476)	(0.627)
Sales volume				
Less than $250,000	–0.174	–0.456	–0.073	–0.351
	[–1.937***]	[–2.099***]	[–0.469]	[–1.661***]
	(0.543)	(0.402)	(0.409)	(0.582)
$250,000–$1,000,000	–0.126	–0.336	–0.002	–0.139
	[–1.411***]	[–1.544***]	[–0.013]	[–0.657]
	(0.536)	(0.399)	(0.418)	(0.564)
$1,000,000–$10,000,000	–0.102	–0.255	–0.039	–0.128
	[–1.141**]	[–1.175***]	[–0.249]	[–0.606]
	(0.501)	(0.381)	(0.401)	(0.501)
$10,000,000–$50,000,000	–0.005	–0.129	0.141	0.055
	[–0.051]	[0.594]	[0.904]	[0.262]
	(0.550)	(0.455)	(0.572)	(0.670)
Ownership type				
Sole proprietorship	–0.098	–0.103	–0.018	–0.013
	[–1.093***]	[–0.473**]	[–0.081]	[–0.531]
	(0.369)	(0.221)	(0.204)	(0.420)
Partnership	–0.091	–0.135	–0.065	–0.005
	[–1.015*]	[–0.621*]	[–0.414]	[–0.022]
	(0.535)	(0.329)	(0.295)	(0.492)
Corporation	0.018	0.062	0.018	0.024
	[0.202)	[0.286]	[0.112]	[0.113]
	(0.247)	(0.178)	(0.184)	(0.298)

Table 11 (continued)

Variable[b]	Paid medical leave		Unpaid medical leave	
	Without guarantee	With guarantee	Without guarantee	With guarantee and formal plan
Percentage small in industry	−0.593	−1.75	−0.432	−0.449
	[−6.615**]	[−8.074**]	[−2.765]	[−2.125]
	(2.828)	(2.136)	(2.152)	(3.102)
Industry				
Agri., mining, const.	−0.224	−0.204	−0.059	−0.068
	[−2.498***]	[−0.937***]	[−0.379]	[−0.322]
	(0.577)	(0.312)	(0.284)	(0.569)
Manufacturing	−0.060	−0.065	−0.035	−0.035
	[−0.672]	[−0.299]	[−0.222]	[0.164]
	(0.461)	(0.351)	(0.342)	(0.527)
Transportation	−0.093	0.043	−0.901	0.083
	[−1.032]	[0.199]	[−0.582]	[0.394]
	(0.780)	(0.559)	(0.524)	(0.806)
Wholesale trade	−0.040	0.021	−0.039	0.108
	[−0.442]	[−0.097]	[−0.248]	[−0.513]
	(0.357)	(0.239)	(0.250)	(0.435)
Retail trade	−0.083	−0.177	−0.017	0.026
	[−0.927***]	[−0.814***]	[−0.109]	[0.125]
	(0.300)	(0.196)	(0.186)	(0.339)
Unionized	0.022	0.126	0.008	0.009
	[0.249]	[0.578*]	[0.050]	[0.042]
	(0.460)	(0.320)	(0.326)	(0.464)
Percent unionized in industry	0.116	−0.585	0.157	0.102
	[1.297]	[−2.692]	[1.005]	[0.484]
	(2.314)	(1.744)	(1.610)	(2.391)
Percent female age 16–44, Managers	0.038	0.117	0.056	0.103
	[.426]	[.536**]	[.360]	[0.485]
	(0.317)	(0.210)	(0.221)	(0.379)
Percent female age 16–44, Nonmanagers	0.074	0.103	0.146	0.163
	[0.826***]	[0.474**]	[0.930***]	[0.771**]
	(0.285)	(0.194)	(0.200)	(0.348)

Variable[b]	Paid medical leave		Unpaid medical leave	
	Without guarantee	With guarantee	Without guarantee	With guarantee and formal plan
Percent female in industry	0.158	−0.278	−0.119	0.278
	[−1.766**]	[−1.279**]	[−0.758]	[1.315]
	(0.735)	(0.513)	(0.486)	(0.879)
Percent age 55 or more,	0.092	0.184	−0.014	0.094
Managers	[1.023***]	[0.848***]	[−0.091]	[0.446]
	(0.335)	(0.232)	(0.229)	(0.415)
Percent age 55 or more,	0.078	−0.047	−0.009	−0.017
Nonmanagers	[−0.867]	[−0.215]	[0.050]	[−0.078]
	(0.581)	(0.315)	(0.280)	(0.579)
State unemployment rate	−0.728	−0.624	−0.671	−0.920
	[−8.122]	[−12.076***]	[−4.292]	[−4.354]
	(6.311)	(4.256)	(4.147)	(7.151)
Percent of state population				
in rural area	−0.149	0.082	0.082	−0.114
	[−1.664**]	[0.378]	[0.521]	[−0.537]
	(0.752)	(0.485)	(0.491)	(0.856)
N	1505		1590	
Chi–square	480.657		190.557	
−2 log L	−1167.943		−1144.188	
−2 log L (intercept only)	−1408.271		−1241.466	

[a] Original logit coefficient in brackets and standard error of original logit coefficient in parentheses.

[b] Excluded categories of categorical variables include: 100 or more employees, sales volume greater than $50 million annually, Subchapter S Corporations (ownership type), services (industry), and nonunion workers.

***significant at the 1% level (two-tailed test).

**significant at the 5% level (two-tailed test).

*significant at the 10% level (two-tailed test).

Table 12 Multinomial Logit Estimates of the Probability that a Firm Provides Paid and Unpaid Medical Leave with and without Job Guarantee for Nonmanagers (OLS Equivalent Coefficient)[a]

Variable[b]	Paid medical leave		Unpaid medical leave	
	Without guarantee	With guarantee	Without guarantee	With guarantee and formal plan
Firm Size				
1–15 employees	−0.051	−0.120	−0.032	−0.293
	[−0.552]	[−0.566**]	[0.198]	[−1.203***]
	(0.381)	(0.283)	(0.306)	(0.428)
16–49 employees	−0.006	0.027	0.093	−0.076
	[−0.061]	[0.128]	[0.571*]	[−0.314]
	(0.397)	(0.297)	(0.332)	(0.451)
50–99 employees	−0.007	0.110	0.141	−0.042
	[−0.073]	[0.519]	[0.866*]	[−0.173]
	(0.532)	(0.381)	(0.475)	(0.641)
Sales volume				
Less than $250,000	−0.177	−0.406	−0.084	−0.311
	[−1.908***]	[−1.921***]	[−0.520]	[−1.277**]
	(0.528)	(0.400)	(0.408)	(0.559)
$250,000–$1,000,000	−0.120	−0.326	−0.007	−0.159
	[−1.295**]	[−1.541***]	[−0.044]	[−0.653]
	(0.518)	(0.399)	(0.418)	(0.566)
$1,000,000–$10,000,000	−0.102	−0.250	−0.045	−0.159
	[−1.103**]	[−1.185***]	[−0.275]	[−0.653]
	(0.487)	(0.381)	(0.400)	(0.507)
$10,000,000–$50,000,000	−0.011	−0.117	0.140	0.078
	[−0.121]	[−0.553]	[0.861]	[0.320]
	(0.546)	(0.456)	(0.571)	(0.672)
Ownership type				
Sole proprietorship	−0.070	−0.099	−0.015	−0.075
	[−0.754**]	[−0.468**]	[−0.092]	[−0.308]
	(0.339)	(0.217)	(0.204)	(0.402)
Partnership	−0.061	−0.114	−0.066	−0.020
	[−0.654]	[−0.541*]	[−0.409]	[−0.082]
	(0.477)	(0.317)	(0.294)	(0.506)
Corporation	0.025	0.042	0.017	0.042
	[0.270]	[0.198]	[0.107]	[0.171]
	(0.245)	(0.176)	(0.183)	(0.302)

Variable[b]	Paid medical leave		Unpaid medical leave	
	Without guarantee	With guarantee	Without guarantee	With guarantee and formal plan
Percentage small in industry	−0.556	−1.769	−0.458	−0.411
	[−5.998**]	[−8.370***]	[−2.821]	[−1.687]
	(2.774)	(2.115)	(2.151)	(3.143)
Industry				
Agriculture, mining, construction	−0.160	−0.182	−0.056	−0.183
	[−1.728***]	[−0.860***]	[−0.346]	[−0.753]
	(0.487)	(0.302)	(0.284)	(0.590)
Manufacturing	−0.053	−0.034	−0.035	−0.020
	[−0.575]	[−0.163]	[−0.213]	[−0.083]
	(0.438)	(0.341)	(0.342)	(0.527)
Transportation	−0.085	0.134	−0.094	0.062
	[−0.919]	[0.636]	[−0.567]	[0.256]
	(0.755)	(0.535)	(0.525)	(0.804)
Wholesale Trade	0.022	0.010	−0.041	0.105
	[−0.238]	[0.046]	[−0.250]	[0.432]
	(0.343)	(0.239)	(0.250)	(0.424)
Retail Trade	−0.101	−0.176	−0.017	0.014
	[−1.086***]	[−0.834***]	[−0.107]	[0.057]
	(0.301)	(0.196)	(0.186)	(0.336)
Unionized	0.018	0.123	0.002	0.076
	[0.194]	[0.582*]	[0.010]	[0.314]
	(0.434)	(0.315)	(0.326)	(0.453)
Percent unionized in industry	0.105	−0.697	0.154	0.175
	[1.133]	[−3.298*]	[0.951]	[0.717]
	(2.177)	(1.685)	(1.614)	(2.399)
Percent female age 16–44, Managers	0.018	0.086	0.059	0.118
	[0.198]	[0.409*]	[0.361]	[0.486]
	(0.307)	(0.209)	(0.222)	(0.376)
Percent female age 16–44, Nonmanagers	0.090	0.128	0.151	0.193
	[0.975***]	[0.606***]	[0.928***]	[0.792**]
	(0.271)	(0.192)	(0.200)	0(.345)
Percent female in industry	−0.119	−0.315	−0.116	0.176
	[−1.283*]	[−1.490***]	[−0.716]	[0.722]
	(0.723)	(0.507)	(0.486)	(0.867)

(continued)

Table 12 (continued)

	Paid medical leave		Unpaid medical leave	
Variable[b]	Without guarantee	With guarantee	Without guarantee	With guarantee and formal plan
Percent age 55 or more,	0.082	0.146	−0.014	0.092
Managers	[0.880***]	[0.692***]	[−0.089]	[0.377]
	(0.323)	(0.233)	(0.229)	(0.412)
Percent age 55 or more,	−0.041	−0.005	−0.009	−0.036
Nonmanagers	[−0.437]	[−0.022]	[−0.052]	[−0.147]
	(0.515)	(0.308)	(0.280)	(0.580)
State unemployment rate	−1.147	−2.351	−0.696	−0.991
	[−12.378**]	[−11.124***]	[−4.283]	[−4.073]
	(6.178)	(4.208)	(4.148)	(7.120)
Percent of state population				
in rural area	−0.181	0.037	0.084	−0.103
	[−1.959***]	[0.175]	[0.514]	[−0.425]
	(0.723)	(0.485)	(0.491)	(0.857)
N	1512		1590	
Chi-square	442.006		169.102	
−2 log L	−1211.842		−1150.392	
−2 log L (intercept only)	−1432.845		−1234.943	

[a] Original logit coefficient in brackets and standard error of original logit coefficient in parentheses.

[b] Excluded categories of categorical variables include: 100 or more employees, sales volume greater than $50 million annually, Subchapter S Corporations (ownership type), services (industry), and nonunion workers.

***significant at the 1% level (two-tailed test).

**significant at the 5% level (two-tailed test).

*significant at the 10% level (two-tailed test).

women nonmanagers or the larger the percentage of managers aged 55 or more in a firm, the more likely a firm will provide paid or unpaid medical leave (with or without benefit continuation).

The higher percentage of female managers (aged 16–44) in a firm, the more likely that firm will provide unpaid medical leave without benefit continuation for both managers and nonmanagers. The percentage of women in the industry has significant negative impacts on the likelihood that a firm will provide either paid or unpaid medical leave to its workers with benefit continuation to its workers.

Finally, the higher the unemployment rate in the state in which the firm does business, the less likely it will be to provide paid or unpaid medical leave with benefit continuation. The effect of the unemployment rate on the likelihood that a firm provides paid medical leave with benefit continuation is relatively large according to the OLS equivalent coefficients—a 1 percent increase in the state unemployment rate variable results in a lowering of the probability that a firm will provide paid medical leave for its managers or nonmanagers by more than 2 percent. The larger the percentage of a state's population that resides in rural areas, the less likely a firm will be to provide paid or unpaid medical leave without benefit continuation. Again the OLS equivalent coefficients indicate that these effects are relatively small.

The story here appears to be that, for paid leave, the reduced form demand model fits the data well. Thus, in the paid medical leave with benefit and without benefit guarantee equations for managers, the chi-square statistics are 513 for managers and 485 for nonmanagers and 25 coefficients attain statistical significance. In the unpaid medical leave equations for managers and nonmanagers, however, the chi-square statistics are only 164 and 141, respectively, and only six coefficients attain significance at conventional levels. The latter chi-square statistic (for nonmanagers) is not significant at the 10 percent level. Thus, the model performs much better in describing the provision of paid rather than unpaid leave. We speculate that the reason for this superior performance is that unpaid leave is a benefit that whose value is difficult for both employers (suppliers) and employees (demanders) to assess and therefore the "market" for such leave does not fulfill the assumptions necessary for the existence of a well functioning market and a model of behavior that assumes the existence of such conditions will not perform well in describing behavior.

Job Guarantees. The overall pattern of relationships observed in Tables 9 and 10 for health benefit continuation are also observed in Tables 11 and 12, which provide the multinomial logit estimates that differentiate between the three choices: no leave, leave without a job guarantee, and leave with a job guarantee. This section will focus on the small number of variables where differences do occur.

The most noticeable difference in the set firm size variables occurs for unpaid leave without a job guarantee in terms of the effects of the variables for 16–49 and 50–99 workers. The results suggest that such firms are significantly more likely than firms employing 100 or more workers to provide the option of leave without a job guarantee for both managers and nonmanagers. It may be that the costs of such an option are lower in midsize firms than in larger or smaller firms. Simply put, smaller and larger firms might be required to formally replace the leave-taker for different reasons. This is necessitated because there is no one available to do the leave-takers work in smaller firms, and jobs in larger firms are so specialized that such a replacement is required. It is only in medium-sized firms where there are enough other workers to "cover for" the absent worker and full job specialization has not become so pronounced as to make substitutions within the firm's own workforce possible. This is consistent with Trzcinski and Alpert (1990), in which they found that large firms were more likely than small ones to use formal temporary workers.

The second difference occurs in the effects of demographic variables. In the job guarantee equations, as the percent female of the firm's managerial workforce increases, the likelihood also increases of leave with a job guarantee relative to the other two options. The percent female of the firm's nonmanagerial workforce has significant effects for the two categories of leave with and without a job guarantee, but the magnitude of the coefficient is larger for the category, leave with no guarantee. This pattern is also observed for the percent of the firm's managerial workforce, aged 55 or older. The third and final difference occurs in the effects of the percent female in the industry variable. In the job guarantee equations, the variable's coefficient is significant and negative for leave with and without a job guarantee, with the absolute magnitude greater in the case of leave with no guarantee.

Summary

Overall, the variables included in the models tend to predict the provision or nonprovision of leave better than they predict the provision or nonprovision of health benefit continuation or job guarantees. What is particularly striking in comparing the results in Table 7 with the set of results in Tables 9–12 are the effects of the firm-specific demand-side variables. Although Table 7 suggests that unionized firms are no more likely than nonunionized firms to provide paid sick leave, Tables 9–12 indicate that unionized firms are more likely to provide health benefit continuation and job guarantees than are other firms. In Table 7, the significant effects of demographic variables are all consistent with the predictions of the model in terms of their effects on influencing the incidence of leave. In the conditions of leave equations, however, these variables either did not predict whether leave was provided with or without health benefit continuation or job guarantees, or they tended to have signs that were inconsistent with our expectations. As an additional caveat, the reader should bear in mind that several of the variables may be acting as proxy variables for income and, hence, their coefficients may be biased.

GENERAL CONCLUSIONS AND POLICY IMPLICATIONS

This chapter explored two aspects of family and medical leave with the basic premise that family and medical leave consists of two separable analytical components—a wage replacement component and a job guarantee component. We found that these components are dealt with separately in both Canada and the United States. We examined the incidence of leave to verify our hypothesis for both countries. We further investigated the correlates of two types of family and medical leave for two types of family and medical leave provision in the United States.

The central hypothesis is that the factors determining the provision of wage replacement during leave differ from the determinants of whether or not a job guarantee is provided. In general, this hypothesis implies that differences exist in the factors that determine the provision of paid versus unpaid leave. Specifically, it is hypothesized that the determinants of paid leave are similar to those which account for other fringe benefits. It is further hypothesized that the provision of unpaid leave will not be as fully explained by the standard reduced form demand models specifying fringe benefit determination as will the provision of paid leave.

Our findings indicate that the standard reduced form demand model provides a strong basis from which to predict the provision of paid leave, but it is considerably weaker in explaining the incidence of unpaid leave and conditions surrounding leave. Our findings thus suggest that different theoretical approaches need to be developed if we are to understand the provision of unpaid leave with job guarantees in the private sector and if we are to analyze actual effects of exiting legislation and potential effects of future legislative initiates.

Note

1. The clawback operates as follows:

Net income = $80,000	
UI clawback level	$58,110
Difference	$21,890
30% of difference	$6,657
UI benefits	$6,375
30% of benefits	$1,913
Amount to be repaid to UI	$1,913

    (UI clawback is the lesser of $1,913 and $6,657)

References

Alpert, W.T. 1982. "Unions and Private Wages Supplements." *Journal of Labor Research* 3: 179–199.

Arthurs, H.W., D.D. Carter, H.J. Glasbeek, and J. Fudge. 1988. *Canada, International Encyclopedia of Labor Law and Industrial Relations.* The Netherlands: Kluwer Law and Taxation Publishers.

Canadian Union of Public Employees. 1991. "UI Parental Benefits." *The Facts* 13(1): 41–44.

Even, W.E. 1992. "Determinants of Parental Leave Policies." *Applied Economics* 24: 35–43.

Finn-Stevenson, M., and E. Trzcinski. 1991. "Mandated Leave: An Analysis of Federal and State Legislation." *American Journal of Orthopsychiatry* 61(4): 567–575.

Labour Canada, Women's Bureau. 1984. *Maternity and Child Care Leave in Canada.* Ottawa: Publications Distribution Centre, Labour Canada.

_____. 1988. *Leave for Employees with Family Responsibilities.* Ottawa: Publications Distribution Centre, Labour Canada.

_____. 1990. *Women in the Labour Force: 1990–91 Edition.* Ottawa: Publications Distribution Centre, Labour Canada.

_____. 1993. *Family-Related Leave and Benefits.* Ottawa: Publications Distribution Centre, Labour Canada.

Labour Division, Unemployment Insurance Statistics Section. 1994. *Unemployment Insurance Statistics, Annual Supplement to 73-001 Monthly.* Ottawa: Statistics Canada.

Maldonado, L., and J. McDonald. 1993. "Pregnancy and Parental Leave." Seminar Handout, November 25, 1993, Peat Marwick Thorne Actuarial & Benefits Inc.

Pay Research Bureau. 1988. *Employee Benefits and Working Conditions, Canada 1988: Prevalence and Characteristics Highlights.* Ottawa: Pay Research Bureau.

Rice, R. G. 1966. *An Analysis of Private Wage Supplements.* Unpublished Ph.D. Dissertation, Columbia University.

Schwartz, L. 1988. "Parental and Maternity Leave Policies in Canada and Sweden," *School of Industrial Relations Research Essay Series No. 18.* Kingston: Industrial Relations Centre, Queen's University at Kingston.

Statistics Canada. 1993. *Canada Year Book 1993.* Ottawa: Statistics Canada.

Trzcinski, E. 1994. "Family and Medical Leave, Contingent Employment, and Flexibility: A Feminist Critique of the U.S. Approach to Work and Family Policy." *Journal of Applied Social Sciences* 18(1): 71–88.

Trzcinski, E., and W.T. Alpert. 1990. "Leave Policies in Small Business: Findings from the U.S. Small Business Administration Employee Leave Survey." Final Report Submitted to the U.S. Small Business Administration, Office of Advocacy.

U.S. Department of Commerce. 1993. *The Statistical Abstract of the United States 1993.* Washington, D.C.: U.S. Department of Commerce.

U.S. Department of Labor, Bureau of Labor Statistics. 1991. "BLS Reports on Its First Survey of Employee Benefits in Small Private Establishments." News. Bulletin Released June 10, 1991.

U.S. Equal Employment Opportunity Commission. 1990. *Policy Guidance on Parental Leave.* EEOC Notice, Title VII/EPA Division, Office of Legal Counsel, Number N-915-058, August 27, 1990.

U.S. General Accounting Office. 1989. *Report to Congressional Requester, Parental Leave: Revised Coats Estimate Reflecting the Impact of Spousal Leave, April 1989.* GAO/HRD-89-68.

Women's Legal Defense Fund. 1990. *State Laws and Regulations Guaranteeing Employees Their Jobs After Family and Medical Leaves.* Washington, D.C.: Women's Legal Defense Fund.

Woodbury, S.A. 1983. "Substitution Between Wage and Nonwage Benefits." *American Economic Review* 73: 162–182.

Vroman, S., and G. Anderson. 1984. "The Effects of Income Taxation on Demand for Employer-Provided Health Insurance." *Applied Economics* 16: 33–44.

Part II

Labor Demand

4 Payroll Taxation, Employer Mandates, and the Labor Market

Theory, Evidence, and Unanswered Questions

Jonathan Gruber
Massachusetts Institute of Technology
and
National Bureau of Economic Research

The past 30 years has been marked by rapid growth in mandated employer contributions for social insurance programs in both the United States and abroad. Payroll taxation is a large and growing source of public finance in the United States: 38 percent of federal revenues in 1993 were raised by payroll taxation while this figure was only 12.4 percent percent in 1960 (*Economic Report of the President 1992*). This corresponds to a similar growth in the reliance on payroll taxation in other developed countries. For example, the payroll tax rate in Sweden grew from 6 percent in 1950 to 40 percent by the late 1970s (Holmlund 1983). At the same time, employer-mandated provision of insurance benefits to workers has risen as well, through programs such as Workers' Compensation in the United States and maternity leave in both the United States and many other nations.

The growth in employer-financed social insurance programs has been criticized along a number of dimensions. Perhaps the most important criticism has been that payroll taxation and other mandates raise labor costs, thereby reducing competitiveness and leading to disemployment. This argument has found casual support in the high level of unemployment in Europe, where employer mandates have grown rapidly since 1960. Furthermore, payroll taxation and, in particular, lump-sum employer mandates have been labeled inequitable relative to broad-based income taxation.

The purpose of this chapter is to assess these criticisms of mandated employer contributions in the United States. This type of analysis is particularly important now given the recent proposal to finance the largest social welfare program of the last 60 years, National Health

Insurance, through an employer mandate. In the debate over the wisdom of employer-mandate-financed health reform, the criticisms noted above have taken center stage. Furthermore, as I show below, payroll taxes represent the majority of the tax burden for over 80 percent of taxpayers in the United States, highlighting the importance of assessing the efficacy of this particular mode of raising revenue.

I analyze payroll taxation and employer mandates in the United States in four steps. First, I present a brief overview of payroll tax financed and employer-mandated social insurance programs in the United States. Second, I discuss the basic theory and evidence on the labor-market effects of payroll taxes and employer mandates, highlighting the similarity between the two types of interventions. I note that while there is a growing body of reduced form literature, suggesting that the costs of mandated benefits and payroll taxes can be shifted to wages, we still have not resolved the critical structural question of whether this shifting is due to full valuation of these benefits or inelastic labor supply.

I then extend this basic analysis to consider a number of real world complications in analyzing the labor-market effects of these interventions: minimum wage constraints on wage shifting; group-specific mandates which cause employer costs to rise significantly more for some types of workers than for others; and the fact that many mandates are a fixed cost of employment which may distort the margin of hours choice. Finally, I consider the efficiency and equity implications of shifting the financing of federal social insurance programs from the payroll tax to the income tax and of removing the current cap on earnings subject to federal payroll taxation.

I conclude with two points. First, while we have learned much in recent years about the effects of payroll taxation and mandates on the labor market, there remain a number of important unanswered questions. Second, there is a critical gap in the empirical literature which makes it difficult to draw firm conclusions as to the overall efficacy of government interventions financed by payroll taxes and mandates: information on the benefits of these interventions for the affected parties.

BACKGROUND ON PAYROLL TAX FINANCED AND MANDATED PROGRAMS IN THE UNITED STATES[1]

Payroll Tax Financed Programs

At the federal level, there are three major payroll tax financed programs. The first is Social Security (SS), which provides income support to workers upon their retirement (at age 62 or greater).[2] The program is "unfunded;" that is, the benefits paid to current retirees are financed by taxation of current workers. Social Security benefit levels are not a direct function of the taxes paid by a worker but rather of his or her earnings history; earnings in the highest 35 of the 40 earnings years from age 21 to age 60, relative to average earnings in the economy, are used to determine benefits levels. Earnings histories are then translated to benefits through a formula that, in effect, favors low wage workers.[3] Benefits are paid as an annuity, yielding a fixed amount (in real terms) from the point of retirement until death.

Benefits to retirees are financed by equal payroll taxation of workers and firms. Wages, salaries, and self-employment income are taxable; other forms of capital income, such as dividends, are not. Both sides of the payroll tax are capped at the "Social Security Taxable Maximum" earnings, so that the average tax burden is actually decreasing with wages above this maximum. In recent years, payroll tax collections have greatly exceeded benefit expenditures, with the difference being used to create a trust fund for financing the retirement of the baby boomers. This trust fund is projected to be insufficient to meet the needs of future cohorts, however, leading to recent proposals to slow the growth of Social Security benefits and/or raise tax rates. This highlights the importance of reconsidering the fundamental structure of social insurance financing.

The second federal payroll tax financed program is Disability Insurance (DI), which provides income benefits to workers who have become so disabled that they must leave the labor force. The structure and financing of DI is very similar to Social Security along a number of dimensions: individuals must have worked a minimum number of quarters, and benefits are based on past earning history. Unlike Social Security, however, there is no age restriction on the receipt of benefits.

The major restriction, instead, is that individuals be physically or mentally incapable of gainful employment. Disability is assessed in a complicated (and highly imperfect) process, which begins with state examination boards and which can be ultimately appealed to the federal level.[4]

The third program is Medicare, public health insurance for all persons age 65 and above. Medicare consists of two parts. Part A finances the hospital expenditures of the elderly (along with some copayment by the elderly themselves). This part of Medicare is financed by a payroll tax similar to that of Social Security, levied equally on workers and firms. The Medicare payroll tax differs in two important respects from the Social Security payroll tax, however: it is much lower and, in recent years, the taxable maximum has greatly exceeded that for Social Security and the cap was removed altogether in 1994. The second part of Medicare, Part B, finances physician expenditures of the elderly. This portion of Medicare is financed by premium payments by elders and from general revenues.

Table 1 presents the history of the tax rates and taxable maxima for the major federal payroll tax financed programs. There was a dramatic rise in both the tax rate and the taxable maximum from 1950 to 1980. Thereafter, both have continued to rise, but at a much slower pace (except for the Medicare taxable maximum, which again rose rapidly in recent years). The fraction of workers under the taxable maximum has remained relatively constant in recent years. The growth in the size of these programs is documented in Table 2. Each program has grown very rapidly over time, although the growth of Medicare has recently been the fastest.

At the state level, the major payroll tax financed program is Unemployment Insurance (UI), which provides limited income support to workers who lose their jobs. Qualification for UI is a function of state-specific minimum work requirements. Benefits are then paid to individuals who are laid off, but not (in most states) those who quit or are fired for cause. Benefits are a redistributive function of previous earnings, with a minimum and maximum benefit and less than one for one conversion of wages to benefits in between, and are generally paid for 26 weeks. UI is financed by payroll taxation of employers, up to a taxable maximum of earnings.[5] Employers tax rates are partially experi-

Table 1 History of the Payroll Tax[a]

Year	SS rate (%)	DI rate (%)	Medicare rate (%)	Total rate (%)	SS & DI maximum ($)[b]	Medicare maximum ($)[b]	% Below maximum
1960	2.75	0.25		3.00	4,800	4,800	72.0
1970	3.65	0.55	0.60	4.80	7,800	7,800	74.0
1975	4.38	0.58	0.90	5.85	14,100	14,100	84.9
1980	4.52	0.56	1.05	6.13	25,900	25,900	91.2
1981	4.70	0.65	1.30	6.65	29,700	29,700	92.4
1982	4.58	0.83	1.30	6.70	32,400	32,400	92.9
1983	4.78	0.63	1.30	6.70	35,700	35,700	93.7
1984	5.20	0.50	1.30	7.00	37,800	37,800	93.6
1985	5.20	0.50	1.35	7.05	39,600	39,600	93.5
1986	5.20	0.50	1.45	7.15	42,000	42,000	93.8
1987	5.20	0.50	1.45	7.15	43,800	43,800	93.9
1988	5.53	0.53	1.45	7.51	45,000	45,000	93.9
1989	5.53	0.53	1.45	7.51	48,000	48,000	
1990	5.60	0.60	1.45	7.65	51,300	51,300	
1991	5.60	0.60	1.45	7.65	53,400	125,000	
1992	5.60	0.60	1.45	7.65	55,500	130,200	
1993	5.60	0.60	1.45	7.65	58,000	135,000	

SOURCE: EBRI (1992).

[a] Figures in first four columns are tax rates, levied equally on employees and employers. SS: Social Security; DI: Disability Insurance.
[b] Nominal dollars.

Table 2 History of Program Size (in millions of dollars)

Year	SS benefit payments	DI benefit payments	Medicare benefit payments
1950	961	NA	NA
1960	10,677	568	NA
1970	28,798	3,085	1,975
1975	58,517	8,505	4,273
1980	105,083	15,515	10,635
1981	123,803	17,192	13,113
1982	138,806	17,376	15,455
1983	149,221	17,524	18,106
1984	157,841	17,898	19,661
1985	167,248	18,827	22,947
1986	176,813	19,853	26,239
1987	183,587	20,519	30,820
1988	195,454	21,695	33,970
1989	207,791	22,911	38,294
1990	222,987	24,829	42,468

SOURCE: U.S. Department of Health and Human Services (1991).
NA = Program did not exist in these years.

ence rated as a function of previous layoff histories; see Anderson and Meyer (1993) for details.

Table 3 presents details of UI payroll taxation in 1993 and historically. UI payroll tax rates, as measured by the maximum rate, are fairly high, reaching 10 percent in some states. The tax base, however, is fairly small. In 1993, many states had taxable maxima below $10,000 of earnings; for the federal FUTA tax, the base was only $7,000. The striking historical trend, particularly in comparison to Table 1, is the falling coverage of the UI taxable wage base. In 1947, over 90 percent of wages were covered in most states; by 1990, many states' bases extended to less than 30 percent of payroll.

Employer Mandates for Employee Workplace Benefits[6]

Along with the payroll tax financed programs discussed above, employers in the United States also are mandated to provide a wide

Table 3 The UI Payroll Tax

State	1993 Taxable maximum ($)	1993 Maximum tax rate (%)	1990 Max. over avg. earnings	1960 Max. over avg. earnings	1947 Max. over avg. earnings
United States	7,000	NA	0.31	0.61	0.84
Alabama	8,000	6.74	0.34	0.67	0.91
Alaska	23,200	6.5	0.48	0.87	0.91
Arizona	7,000	5.4	0.29	0.62	0.89
Arkansas	8,000	6.0	0.36	0.74	0.92
California	7,000	5.4	0.25	0.65	0.83
Colorada	10,000	5.4	0.36	0.62	0.86
Connecticut	7,100	6.4	0.22	0.59	0.85
Delaware	8,500	8.0	0.29	0.61	0.80
Dist. of Columbia	9,000	5.4	0.21	0.60	0.82
Florida	7,000	5.4	0.31	0.67	0.88
Georgia	8,500	8.64	0.33	0.69	0.88
Hawaii	23,900	5.4	0.55	0.69	0.89
Idaho	19,200	6.8	0.54	0.67	0.90
Illinois	9,000	6.4	0.30	0.56	0.81
Indiana	7,000	5.7	0.28	0.59	0.86
Iowa	13,100	9.0	0.41	0.63	0.88
Kansas	8,000	5.4	0.42	0.63	0.88
Kentucky	8,000	10.0	0.33	0.65	0.90
Louisiana	8,500	6.0	0.33	0.64	0.87
Maine	7,000	6.5	0.29	0.70	0.91
Maryland	8,500	8.1	0.25	0.63	0.87
Massachusetts	10,800	9.3	0.27	0.62	0.85
Michigan	9,500	10.0	0.29	0.54	0.83
Minnesota	14,300	9.0	0.39	0.59	0.85
Mississippi	7,000	6.4	0.34	0.74	0.92
Missouri	7,500	7.8	0.27	0.60	0.84
Montana	14,500	6.4	0.65	0.67	0.90
Nebraska	7,000	5.4	0.29	0.65	0.86
Nevada	14,800	5.4	0.50	0.71	0.87
New Hampshire	7,000	6.5	0.27	0.70	0.91

Table 3 (continued)

State	1993 Taxable maximum ($)	1993 Maximum tax rate (%)	1990 Max. over avg. earnings	1960 Max. over avg. earnings	1947 Max. over avg. earnings
New Jersey	16,100	6.47	0.38	0.57	0.84
New Mexico	12,600	5.4	0.41	0.65	0.91
New York	7,000	6.4	0.20	0.57	0.79
North Carolina	12,500	5.7	0.42	0.73	0.91
North Dakota	12,600	5.4	0.39	0.68	0.88
Ohio	8,500	6.5	0.29	0.56	0.84
Oklahoma	10,400	6.2	0.37	0.64	0.86
Oregon	18,000	5.4	0.49	0.73	0.87
Pennsylvania	8,000	9.2	0.28	0.60	0.86
Rhode Island	15,600	8.4	0.42	0.74	0.87
South Carolina	7,000	5.4	0.31	0.74	0.92
South Dakota	7,000	9.5	0.33	0.67	0.89
Tennessee	7,000	10.0	0.31	0.68	0.89
Texas	9,000	6.0	0.33	0.63	0.86
Utah	15,700	8.0	0.45	0.62	0.88
Vermont	8,000	8.4	0.31	0.69	0.91
Virginia	8,000	6.2	0.28	0.67	0.89
Washington	18,500	5.4	0.48	0.60	0.87
West Virginia	8,000	7.5	0.31	0.60	0.87
Wisconsin	10,500	8.9	0.37	0.58	0.85
Wyoming	11,100	8.5	0.36	0.66	0.89

SOURCE: Committee on Ways and Means (1993).

variety of benefits for their workers. Federal law explicitly mandates the provision of maternity leave to most employees in firms with more than 50 employees (under the Family and Medical Leave Act). While not requiring employers to offer health insurance, federal law regulates the structure of insurance for those firms that do offer coverage, mandating the inclusion of comprehensive maternity health insurance coverage (under the 1978 Pregnancy Discrimination Act) and continuation of coverage benefits (under the 1986 Consolidated Omnibus Reconciliation Act) in health insurance packages.[7]

State law in 48 states mandates that employers purchase workers' compensation (WC) insurance against workplace injuries.[8] Workers' compensation is the oldest and largest mandated benefit in the United States, with benefit payments amounting to $37 billion in 1990. This program pays both the medical bills of the injured worker and an indemnity benefit, which is a redistributive function of their pre-injury wage (the benefits structure is similar to that of UI). States legislate the level of benefits that must be paid to workers for a variety of different types of injuries. Firms can then purchase insurance from either the state or private firms to cover these costs or (in most states) they can self-insure. Workers' compensation insurance costs averaged 2.1 percent of payroll in 1987, but there was a high variance. Table 4, from Gruber and Krueger (1991), shows the level and change in workers' compensation costs for the trucking industry from 1978 to 1987.[9] These costs grew dramatically during the 1980s, due both to rising medical costs and to changes in state benefits legislation, and costs were over 25 percent of payroll in some states in 1987.

States also mandate that employers include a number of particular benefits in their health insurance packages. There are over 1,000 such "state mandated benefits," covering benefits ranging from alcoholism treatment to in vitro fertilization (see Gruber [1994b] for details). In addition, several states mandate the provision of insurance to temporarily disabled workers. There are also a variety of mandates for minimal levels of workplace safety at both the federal and state levels, in addition to the compensation for workplace accidents provided by WC.

Table 4 Workers' Compensation Costs as a Percentage of Payroll

State	1978	1987	Change[a] 1978–87	State	1978	1987	Change 1978–87
Alabama	4.49	10.07	5.58	Mississippi	6.27	7.98	1.71
Alaska	10.55	17.41	6.86	Missouri	NA	5.16	NA
Arizona	11.68	11.22	-0.46	Montana	8.27	25.40	17.13
Arkansas	15.94	10.86	-5.08	Nebraska	5.04	6.47	1.43
California	10.04	17.26	7.22	New Hampshire	4.16	12.55	8.39
Colorado	5.88	11.91	6.03	New Jersey	7.36	7.89	0.53
Connecticut	6.78	12.91	6.13	New Mexico	8.60	12.23	3.63
Delaware	10.45	9.79	-0.66	New York	9.62	5.97	-3.65
Dist. of Columbia	15.04	16.04	1.00	North Carolina	2.42	5.16	2.74
Florida	17.71	15.12	-2.59	Ohio	5.32	12.20	6.88
Georgia	4.70	7.73	3.03	Oklahoma	7.81	11.55	3.74
Hawaii	9.71	20.29	10.58	Oregon	14.68	23.46	8.78
Idaho	6.39	15.50	9.11	Pennsylvania	NA	15.97	NA
Illinois	6.01	11.45	5.44	Rhode Island	5.15	7.27	2.12
Indiana	2.39	3.01	0.62	South Carolina	3.68	8.12	4.44
Iowa	5.89	8.77	2.88	South Dakota	5.87	8.22	2.35
Kansas	4.59	6.85	2.26	Tennessee	2.88	4.37	1.49
Kentucky	7.04	8.05	1.01	Texas	6.83	9.98	3.15
Louisiana	10.66	10.65	-0.01	Utah	4.92	9.23	4.31

Maine	7.05	9.16	2.11
Maryland	5.85	11.09	5.24
Massachusetts	5.50	8.48	2.98
Michigan	9.24	15.05	5.81
Minnesota	11.50	20.93	9.43
Vermont	3.11	6.53	3.42
Virginia	4.28	6.51	2.23
West Virginia	NA	5.67	NA
Wisconsin	3.41	8.86	5.45

SOURCE: Gruber and Krueger (1991).

[a] Change is in percentage points.

THE INCIDENCE OF PAYROLL TAXATION AND EMPLOYER MANDATES

Basic Model

Figure 1 displays the standard diagrammatic analysis of the labor-market effects of payroll taxation levied on the firm. The market is initially in equilibrium at the intersection of the labor supply (S_0) and demand (D_0) curves, at the employment and wage package (L_0, W_0). Payroll taxation of an amount τ lowers the amount that the firm can pay for a given level of employment, shifting labor demand inward to D_1. This reduces the wage that workers are paid to W_1, and employment falls to L_1; the tax has a deadweight loss equal to the area ABC. The difference $L_0 - L_1$ represents the disemployment effect of payroll taxation highlighted by critics of this form of revenue raising. This analysis applies equally well to a mandate that costs the employer a fraction τ of wages (such as workers' compensation); this mandate raises the cost of hiring workers, shifting demand inward and leading to disemployment.

Figure 1 Labor-Market Effects of Payroll Taxation

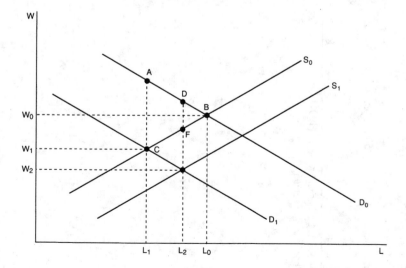

However, this basic tax incidence diagram misses an important feature of payroll taxes and mandates: tax/benefit linkages. Most of the payroll taxes described above, such as those for Social Security, disability insurance, and unemployment insurance, are financing benefits to the workers who are taxed. Similarly, mandates such as that for maternity leave or workers' compensation are providing (potentially) valuable benefits to workers in the firms that are affected by the mandate. This tax/benefit linkage is not perfect; for many workers, one more dollar of taxation does not represent one more dollar of benefits. The fact that such a linkage exists, however, affects this analysis. The key point is that, since some of taxes paid come back to the worker in the form of future benefits, the disemployment effects of payroll taxes will be reduced because workers will be more willing to accept lower wages.

This point is illustrated in Figure 1. In the presence of tax/benefit linkages, workers are now receiving higher net compensation than in the pure tax case, because the tax is buying them some benefits. Workers are therefore more willing to work for a given wage, shifting labor supply outward to S_1. As a result, employment falls only to L_2. That is, due to this tax/benefit linkage, there is a much smaller distortion from payroll taxation: the deadweight loss from taxation has been reduced from ABC to DBF.

The extent of the tax/benefit linkage will depend on the extent to which workers perceive that the taxes are returned to them as benefits. If every dollar of taxes paid were perceived by the worker to be returning in benefits, this would not be viewed as a tax at all, and there would be no distortion.[10] This can be readily seen in the simple model used by Gruber and Krueger (1991), for the case of a lump sum mandate. Suppose that labor demand (L_d) is given by:

$$L_d = f_d(W + C) \tag{1}$$

and that labor supply (L_s) is given by:

$$L_s = f_s(W + \alpha C) \tag{2}$$

where C is the cost of the mandate, W is the wage rate, and αC is the employee valuation of the mandated benefit. In equilibrium, the effect of the mandate on wages will be:

$$dW / dC = - (\eta^D - \alpha\eta^S) / (\eta^D - \eta^S) \tag{3}$$

where η^D and η^S are the elasticities of demand for and supply of labor, respectively. It is clear from this equation that, if $\alpha = 1$, there will be full shifting of the cost of the mandate to wages, and no effect on employment as a result. On the other hand, for $\alpha = 0$, this expression simplifies to that for the incidence of a payroll tax in the absence of tax benefit linkages. The analysis would be similar for a marginal payroll tax rather than a lump sum mandate; in that case, α would measure the employee's valuation on the margin.

There are two key points that must be noted in reference to this analysis and that of Summers (1989). First, the general distinction between payroll taxes and mandates is a false one. The salient feature is not the form of revenue raising but the extent of tax/benefit linkages. In both cases, employers are paying some cost and employees are receiving some benefit. This point is made most starkly by contrasting Unemployment Insurance, a payroll tax financed benefit, with Workers' Compensation, a mandated employer-provided benefit: in both cases, employers pay some fixed portion of their payroll to insure their workers. If the perceived benefits of working an additional hour under each program is the same, and the payroll cost to the employer for that hour is the same, these programs will have exactly the same effect on the labor market. Of course, in practice there are some important differences, such as the fact that mandates are often lump sum while payroll taxes are not (a point I return to below), but as a matter of general principle the two can be analyzed in a parallel manner.

Second, a key determinant of tax/benefit linkages for both mandates and payroll taxes will be the extent to which benefits are provided to both workers and nonworkers. If equal benefits are provided to nonworkers, then there is no linkage between taxes paid and benefits received, because individuals could have not worked and received the same benefit. This point is especially important when assessing the efficiency implications of financing National Health Insurance through an employer mandate. If, as seems politically likely, coverage is extended to the unemployed for free, or at least at a highly subsidized rate, it will mitigate any tax-benefit linkages for workers and may increase the efficiency cost of financing.

Evidence

Research on the incidence of payroll taxation has a long history. Early incidence research involved time-series studies of changes in payroll taxes in the United States and abroad. This research produced mixed results. Brittain (1972) reported that the payroll tax was fully shifted to wages, but his finding was criticized by Feldstein (1972). Vroman (1974) found that 1/4 to 1/2 of the payroll tax was shifted to wages in United States manufacturing. Holmlund (1983) used the time-series data on payroll taxes in Sweden to study a period when the payroll tax increased from 14 to 40 percent and found that roughly 50 percent of the tax was shifted to wages in the short run. A different approach was pursued by Hamermesh (1979), who used the variation in payroll tax rates due to the Social Security payroll tax limit to estimate wage offsets. His estimates indicated that from 0 to 35 percent of the Social Security tax is shifted to wages.

This "first generation" of studies, however, generally suffered from being unable to control for important potential omitted variables. In the time-series studies, for example, there may have been unobserved economic trends that affected both wages and tax-setting institutions. What is needed to overcome these problems is variation in employer costs within arguably homogenous locations over time, so that both time and location omitted variables can be controlled for in the analysis.

More recent research has attempted to follow this approach, using variation across U.S. states in the cost of employer mandates and payroll taxes. Gruber and Krueger (1991) studied the incidence of workers' compensation; as noted previously, even though a mandated benefit in name, workers' compensation is similar to a payroll tax for the purposes of incidence analysis. We model wage incidence by exploiting the large change in workers' compensation costs over time and across states in several high cost industries during the 1980s. Table 4 shows that this variation is quite sizeable in the trucking industry. Using a large sample of workers in these industries from the Current Population Survey, we find that 85 percent of this cost increase was shifted to wages. We are able to exactly replicate our micro-data findings using aggregate industry/state/year data on wages. Furthermore, using this source of data on employment, we find no significant employment decrease from these increases in workers' compensation cost.

Anderson and Meyer (1997) focused on the incidence of the Unemployment Insurance payroll tax at both the market and firm level, using a very large dataset of individual UI wage records from several states. UI tax costs differ systematically across markets due to differences across states in the structure of the experience rating schedule. The costs also differ across firms due to different firm locations on that schedule (which imperfectly ties a firm's current tax rate to its past layoff experience). These tax costs have changed over time at both the state and firm level due to legislated changes in experience rating schedules. Anderson and Meyer found that there is full shifting of market level differences in UI costs but not full shifting of firm level differences. Thus, the more recent evidence, which uses legislative variation in payroll costs across states, seems to suggest that payroll taxes and mandates are fully shifted to wages.

What Can We Learn from the Empirical Work?

This new reduced form evidence, however, leaves an important structural question unanswered. In the simple labor-market framework above, there are two reasons why increased costs might be shifted to wages: because individuals value the benefits that they are getting fully or because labor supply is perfectly inelastic.[11] Disentangling these alternatives is very important for future policy analysis. Consider the example of national health insurance, which is financed by a mandate and an additional payroll tax to cover nonworkers. If full shifting is due to full employee valuation with a somewhat elastic labor supply, then national health insurance will have important disemployment effects because supply will not shift for a policy not restricted to workers. If full shifting is driven by inelastic supply, however, then the population receiving benefits is irrelevant. In either case, the costs will be passed onto workers' wages, so national health insurance will not cause disemployment.

There is no evidence which bears on this question in Gruber and Krueger (1991). Anderson and Meyer (1997) provided some information in their firm/market level distinction, but it is not enough to distinguish the two structural hypotheses. It seems likely that both the elasticity of labor supply between firms is higher than that between markets and that employees may not value the extra marginal cost to the firm from experience rating. Both of these structural interpretations would therefore be consistent with their finding. Evidence from elsewhere in the empirical labor economics literature suggests that the labor supply of prime age males is fairly inelastic, while the labor supply of secondary earners is somewhat more elastic, but there is considerable uncertainty about the reliability of previous attempts to measure this crucial parameter (Heckman 1993).

What is needed to convincingly disentangle these views is some variation in one or the other of these dimensions only. For example, is the incidence of employer mandates/payroll taxes significantly different across groups with plausibly different elasticities of labor supply, such as married men and married women? Is there differential incidence with respect to elements of a policy that are likely to be valuable, such as cash benefits for work injury, as opposed to elements that are less likely to be valued, such as insurance administrative loading factors?

There are two additional limitations in applying the reduced form results from past research to modeling the incidence of future government interventions, or even the incidence of other programs. The first is that this research has examined the medium to long run incidence of the cost of mandates and payroll taxes.[12] The short run incidence is much more uncertain. It is often assumed that shifting to wages does not occur through nominal pay cuts but, rather, due to worker money illusion, through inflation erosion of the real wage.[13] There is little work addressing the important questions of whether incidence significantly differs in the short and long run or whether it varies according to differences in the inflationary environment when the mandate is enacted.

Second, the extent of tax/benefit linkages may vary substantially across different interventions. National health insurance provided to nonworkers is one example of a program with no tax/benefit linkages so that the existing incidence studies may not be relevant; this is also true for Medicare. For Social Security, the extent of tax/benefit linkage varies along a number of dimensions: it is lower for high wage earners due to the progressive manner in which earnings are converted to benefits; it is lower (and often zero) for secondary earners because they receive the higher of their accrued benefit and 50 percent of their spouse's benefit so that often their earnings record is irrelevant; and it is zero for workers in the five lowest earning "dropout years," which are not used in benefits computation. Furthermore, the perceived tax/benefit linkage may be weaker still because workers may not understand that the "FICA" contribution on their pay stub is actually a form of retirement savings. The recently announced policy of informing workers as to their retirement savings entitlement under SS might serve to improve the efficiency of SS financing, to the extent that it increases perceived tax/benefit links. Future work which could cleverly incorporate these different kinds of linkages could ideally answer the structural question posed previously.

Equity

In interpreting the empirical work in this area, it is important to understand the goal of government policy. If the government is intervening to correct a market failure and the payroll tax/mandate is simply a means of financing that intervention, then shifting to wages can be viewed as the "price" that is being paid for government provision of insurance. In the case of full valuation, perhaps due to adverse selection in the private insurance market, government mandates will be an efficient and equitable policy; the mandate is a perfect "benefits tax."

If the goal of a mandate is not to correct a market failure, however, but rather to provide benefits to some deprived group in society, then full shifting to wages may not be viewed as a desirable outcome. Rather, this may be viewed as the mandate being "undone" by the adjustment of wages. In this case, the additional deadweight loss from broad-based financing that does not have tax/benefit linkages may be a price that society is willing to pay in order to direct more resources towards one group. Thus, it is important to understand the goal of government mandate policy: is it to correct a market failure or to redirect resources across groups?[14]

THE MINIMUM WAGE

The analysis above assumed that firms could readily pass on their costs of taxation to workers in the form of lower wages. However, if workers are already earning the minimum wage, such "shifting to wages" is not possible. This is illustrated in Figure 2, for the case where the minimum wage is equal to the equilibrium wage pre-tax. In this case, a tax on firms causes a much larger fall in employment because worker wages cannot be reduced, so that the net compensation cost to the firm has risen. Employment now falls to L_2 and the presence of the minimum has increased the disemployment effects of taxes levied on firms. This disemployment effect is independent of the valuation of the benefit by workers since equilibrium is determined on the demand side of the market; the shift in the supply curve to S_1 has no effect on employment or wages.

How important is this effect quantitatively? Recent research (Card 1992a,b; Katz and Krueger 1992; Card and Krueger 1994) has shown that changes in the minimum wage cause no significant decrease in employment and may actually cause increases.[15] There are two possible interpretations of these findings, both of which suggest that the minimum is a less important consideration for the incidence of employer taxation than is implied by Figure 2.

The first, which takes the employment increase estimates seriously, is that the neoclassical model is not appropriate and that low-wage labor markets are more precisely described by a monopsony model. The effect of payroll taxation or mandates in such a model is shown in Figure 3. Demand is described by curve D_0, supply is curve S_0, and the marginal factor cost is curve MFC_0. The competitive wage is W_c, and the competitive employment level is L_c; the monopsony wage is W_m and the monopsony employment level is L_m. When a minimum wage is imposed at W_{min}, employment rises for the monopsonist to L_{min}. This is the positive employment effect estimated by some of these studies.

In such a model, a small mandate or payroll tax shifts demand to D_1. There is no effect on employment from this change; it is paid out of employer profits. Thus, a small mandate or payroll tax acts as a pure profits tax in this model. A larger policy change, however, can have real effects. If demand falls all the way to D_2 (if the increased cost to

Figure 2 Labor-Market Effects of Payroll Taxation, with an Effective Minimum Wage

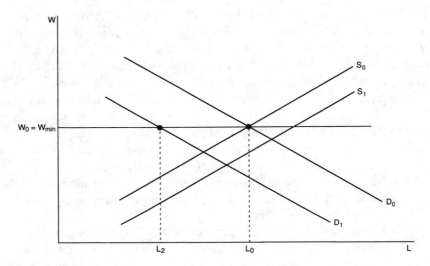

Figure 3 Labor-Market Effects of Payroll Taxation, with an Effective Minimum Wage under Monopsony

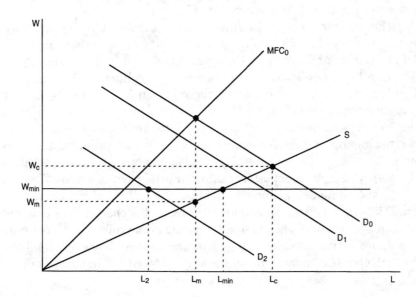

the employer is larger than the difference between the competitive wage and the minimum wage), then employment will fall to the same level as in the competitive case (L_2). The employment change, however, will still be smaller than in the competitive case because some of the cost of the mandate has still been absorbed in profits.

The second interpretation of the new minimum wage research is that it provides evidence of fairly inelastic labor demand in the low wage labor market. Indeed, even the traditional time series studies of the effects of the minimum wage suggested elasticities of demand as low as 0.1 (Brown, Gilroy, and Kohen 1982). In this case, once again, the minimum will not cause mandates to have significant disemployment effects, as the cost primarily is paid from profits or prices. So, under either interpretation, the "new" minimum wage research suggests that the minimum wage may not be an important impediment to the shifting of mandate costs to wages.

GROUP-SPECIFIC MANDATES

Analytical Framework

The previous analysis has highlighted the parallels between employer mandates and payroll taxation. However, there are many important differences between these two forms of regulation in practice. The first is that, unlike payroll taxes, which are generally uniform across all workers, mandates may cause employer costs to rise significantly more for one group of workers than for another. This can arise, for example, because the mandate is explicitly group specific, as in the case of maternity leave legislation. Alternatively, it can arise due to experience rating in private insurance markets, which raises the costs of insuring some workers above the costs of others. For example, mandated workers' compensation insurance in an experience-rated firm costs much more for a very accident-prone worker than for a safe one. Similarly, mandated health insurance costs significantly more for sicker workers, as well as for married workers and those with large families. Such problems could arise with payroll taxation in theory, but payroll tax costs rarely vary by worker characteristic.[16]

Group-specific differences in costs may complicate the analysis of a mandate's effects. If the group that benefits from the mandate (group A) fully values the intervention at the cost to the employer *and* if employers are able to shift those costs to group-specific wages, then there will be no effect of the mandate on either that group or on other groups (group B). That is, for group A, the analysis will be the same as above; since the employer costs have not changed for group A, there is no spillover onto other segments of the market.[17]

There may, however, be a number of barriers to full group-specific shifting not present in this simple model. Most obviously, there are antidiscrimination regulations that prohibit differential pay for the same job across groups or that prevent differential promotion decisions by demographic characteristic.[18] Furthermore, workplace "norms," which prohibit different pay across groups, or union rules about equality of relative pay may have similar effects as antidiscrimination rules. These will not be important considerations for workplace-wide mandates or payroll taxation.

Barriers to group-specific adjustment operate in exactly the same fashion as the previously discussed minimum wage effects for the group benefiting from the mandate. Returning to the competitive model, there will be disemployment of group A if there are such barriers because wages cannot adjust to offset the new employer costs. As a result, if there is some substitutability between groups A and B, employers will substitute towards group B. Fears of group-specific disemployment were at the heart of the debate over mandated maternity leave—since the cost of employing women of child-bearing age would rise, opponents claimed that employers would discriminate against this group in hiring. Thus, even with full valuation and no explicit regulatory barrier such as the minimum wage, there can be a distortion from a group-specific mandate.

Previous Evidence

Evidence on the incidence of a group-specific mandate is provided in Gruber (1994a). In that paper, I studied the effects of state and federal mandates that employers include comprehensive coverage for maternity in their health insurance plans. A commonly accepted feature of health insurance benefits before the mid 1970s was limited coverage for childbirth. Maternity coverage was sometimes excluded from basic health benefits; if included, it was often subject to flat rate cash amount limits, regardless of the cost of delivery. This differential coverage was widely perceived as discriminatory (Leshin 1981; Alan Guttmacher Institute 1987). Many states responded to this perception in the 1975–1978 period by passing laws prohibiting treating pregnancy differently from "comparable illnesses" in health insurance benefits. Then, in October 1978, the Federal Government passed the Pregnancy Discrimination Act (PDA), which prohibited any differential treatment of pregnancy in the employment relationship.

These laws affected a readily identifiable group, women of childbearing age and their husbands (under whose insurance these women may have been covered), so that I was able to study the impact of these laws based on observable characteristics. They were also fairly costly for these individuals, due both to the widespread existence of differential maternity benefits before 1978 and the large fraction of health insurance costs which are accounted for by maternity benefits for women of child-bearing age. I found that there was full group-specific shifting: the wages of the affected groups fell by enough to offset the cost of the mandate to their employers. As a result, there was no effect on their net labor supply. Since women are generally modeled as having much more elastic labor supply than men, the fact that there was full shifting for this group is suggestive that such shifting arose from movements in the supply curve and not from demand shifts along an inelastic supply curve.

Further evidence on this point is provided by Olson (1993), who examined the wages and health insurance coverage of single men, relative to single women and married males, during the era that saw increased incidence of AIDS. Olson did find a significant narrowing of the positive wage gap between single men and single women over this era, although he found no effect on the relative wages of single and married men. He also found that there was a drop in employer-provided health insurance for single men relative to both control groups.[19]

This work suggests that employers can shift mandated costs to the wages of demographically identifiable groups within the workplace. However, it leaves unanswered the important question of how finely employers can shift mandated increases in benefits costs. Did the shifting estimated in Gruber (1994a) arise from reduced average wages in firms with a high proportion of women of child-bearing age or from shifts in the wage structure within the workplace? In the latter case, how finely can the wage structure be manipulated to shift group-specific costs? The extent to which within-workplace shifting is possible is an important question for analyzing employer-mandated national health insurance. In a small firm with one very sick worker and, as a result, very high medical costs, it will almost certainly be impossible to shift these high costs to the wages of that single worker. As a result, it will be in the firm's interest to discriminate in the hiring of sick workers. On the other hand, an entire workplace of sick workers could presumably be paid less to compensate for employer insurance costs differences. How large does the group of sick workers have to be before employers are able to shift their excess costs of health insurance to them? It would be useful to understand the trade-off made by firms between shifting costs to very small groups in the workplace and discriminating in their hiring.

One means of addressing the first of these questions is to return to my earlier analysis and model the effect of the mandates on both individual and firm average wages. If the earlier findings are driven by lower average wages in firms with many women of child-bearing age, then including the fraction of firm employment that is in this demographic group, or the average cost to the firm, should explain all of the drop in wages for this group. If there is within-workplace shifting, however, then the individual measure will still enter the model significantly because there will be some explanatory power for the deviation of individual from firm average costs.

New Evidence—Individual or Workplace-Specific Shifting?

The data used for this analysis is the May Current Population Survey (1978) for the years 1974, 1975, 1977, and 1978. I focus on 3 of the 23 states that passed "maternity mandates" in the 1975–1979 period: Illinois, New Jersey, and New York (the "experimental" states).[20] I also use a set of "non-experimental" states designed to capture any regional shocks to the experimental states. For Illinois, the control states used are Ohio and Indiana; for New Jersey and New York, the controls are Connecticut, Massachusetts, and North Carolina. The data consist of observations on all individuals in these set of experimental and non-experimental locations, for two years before the legislation (1974, 1975), and two years after the legislation (1977, 1978).

The goal of the empirical work is to identify the effect of laws passed by certain states ("experimental states") which affected particular groups of individuals ("treatment group"). Identifying this effect requires controlling for any systematic shocks to the labor-market outcomes of the treatment group correlated with, but not due to, the law. I do so in three ways in the estimation. First, I include year effects, to capture any national trends in the earnings of the treatment group. Second, I include state effects, to control for secular earnings differences in the states that passed the laws and those that did not. Finally, I include state-by-year effects to control for state-specific shocks correlated with the passage of these laws over this period; that is, I compare the treatment individuals in the experimental states to a set of control individuals in those same states and measure the change in *relative* outcomes. This change is then compared to the change in relative outcomes in states that did not pass maternity mandates to control for national shocks to the relative earnings of these groups. The identifying assumption of this "differences-in-differences-in-differences" (DDD) estimator are fairly weak: it simply requires that there be no contemporaneous shock that affects the relative outcomes of the treatment group in the same state-years as the law.

The treatment group here are those insured workers who are "at risk" for having a child, or whose health insurance covers someone who is at risk of having a child. The controls are other individuals who were directly unaffected by the law. However, the CPS (before May 1979) contained no information on health insurance coverage. I am thus unable to exactly identify the employees for whom this was a costly mandate.

I address this problem in two ways in the empirical work. First, I use women aged 20–40 as the treatment group. This group will contain the individuals for whom the mandate was most costly. My control group is all individuals over 40 and single males aged 20–40. I exclude 20–40-year- old married males, who may also be affected by the laws if their insurance covers their wives. This "treatment dummy" approach has the virtue that it is relatively "nonparametric."

Second, I use data on insurance coverage from other datasets to model the likelihood that individuals were covered by insurance and the type of insurance coverage that they receive, and I assign each individual a cost of the mandate based on these predictions and outside data on the cost of maternity health insurance. This approach has the advantage that I use individual variation, rather than differences across broad demographic groups, to identify the impact of the law. However, it has the disadvantage that it imposes strong parametric assumptions. If the functional form for the expected cost of the mandate is incorrect, then the demographic group dummy may be a more effective means of capturing the law's impact. Thus, in the empirical work, I rely on both the treatment group dummy and the individually parameterized cost measure.

I estimate regressions of the form:

$$W_{ijt} = \alpha + \beta_1 X_{ijt} + \beta_2 \tau_t + \beta_3 \delta_j + \beta_4 TREAT_i + \beta_5 \delta_j \bullet \tau_t \qquad (4)$$
$$+ \beta_6 \tau_t \bullet TREAT_i + \beta_7 \delta_j \bullet TREAT_i + \beta_8 \delta_j \bullet \tau_t \bullet TREAT_i$$

where i indexes individuals
$\quad j$ indexes states (1 if experimental state, 0 if non-experimental)
$\quad t$ indexes years (1 if after the law, 0 if before)
$\quad W$ is the log real hourly wage
$\quad X$ is a vector of observable characteristics
$\quad \delta_j$ is a fixed state effect
$\quad \tau_t$ is a fixed year effect
$\quad TREAT$ is a dummy for treatment group (1 if treatment, 0 if control), and
$\quad \bullet$ denotes interaction between effects

In this regression, the fixed effects control for time-series changes in wages (β_2), the time-invariant characteristics of the experimental states (β_3), and the time-invariant characteristics of the treatment group (β_4). The second-level interactions control for changes over time in the experimental states (β_5), changes over time for the treatment group nationwide (b_6), and time-invariant characteristics of the treatment group in the experimental states (β_7). The third-level interaction (β_8) captures all variation in wages specific to the treatments (relative to controls), in the experimental states (relative to the non-experimentals), and in the years after the law (relative to before the law). This is the DDD estimate of the extent of shifting of the cost of the mandate to group-specific wages. The set of demographic covariates used includes years of education, experience and its square, sex, marital status, a marital status by sex interaction, a dummy for nonwhite, a control for union status, dummies for 15 major industries, and separate year dummies for 1974 and 1978.

Table 5 presents the estimates from Eq. 4. In the first column, I show that there is a significant fall in the wages of women of child-bearing age in the state that passed the mandate, relative to the control groups of single men and older workers, of 4.4 percent. This is somewhat larger than the average cost of the mandate for this group; I interpret these magnitudes in more detail below. The coefficients on the demographic covariates (not reported) are of their expected signs and magnitudes. There is a 1.2 percent fall in wages for the within-state control group (the coefficient on "After•Experimental," the state-by-year effect). This finding has one of two implications: either the experimental states, on average, saw a negative shock over this period or the effect of the mandates are "spilling over" onto the control group. These two interpretations cannot be fully distinguished within this framework, although the latter seems unlikely given the finding of full shifting to group-specific wages.

This regression is unable to disentangle whether this shifting to wages is the result of within-workplace wage adjustments or drops in average wages in firms with a high proportion of women of child-bearing age. Unfortunately, I cannot precisely distinguish these alternatives either because I do not have information on the firms in which these women work. However, I can use information on their occupation and industry to create "synthetic firms" of individuals with the same occupation/industry type. I do so by dividing the data into 15 major industries and 10 major occupations, and then calculating the fraction of workers in each cell who are 20–40-year-old women.[21] I then use this in place of the individual treatment dummy in the DDD regression framework of Eq. 4.

The results of doing so are reported in the second column of Table 5. In fact, there is a negative coefficient on the third level interaction in this regression although it is only significant at the 13 percent level.

Table 5 New Evidence on the Incidence of Maternity Mandates[a]

	(1) Treat dummy	(2) Treat dummy	(3) Treat dummy	(4) Mandate cost	(5) Mandate cost	(6) Mandate cost
After	0.009 (0.009)	0.018 (0.013	0.019 (0.013)	–0.003 (0.008)	–0.007 (0.023)	–0.005 (0.023)
Experimental state	0.101 (0.007)	0.090 (0.012)	0.091 (0.012)	0.094 (0.007)	0.120 (0.022)	0.120 (0.022)
After• experimental	–0.012 (0.011)	–0.003 (0.017)	–0.005 (0.017)	–0.006 (0.010)	–0.006 (0.031)	–0.007 (0.031)
Treatment/cost	0.077 (0.012)		0.078 (0.013)	2.321 (0.428)		2.048 (0.433)
Treatment/cost• after	0.003 (0.013)		0.009 (0.014)	0.341 (0.511)		0.253 (0.523)
Treatment/cost• experimental	0.040 (0.013)		0.033 (0.015)	3.052 (0.529)		3.148 (0.540)
Treat/cost•after •experimental	–0.044 (0.018)		–0.041 (0.020)	–2.476 (0.756)		–2.393 (0.772)
Firm treatment/ cost		–0.147 (0.027)	–0.138 (0.029)		16.15 (2.067)	16.24 (2.096)
Firm treat/cost •after		–0.022 (0.034)	–0.037 (0.037)		1.542 (2.598)	1.111 (2.660)
Firm treat/cost •experimental	0.075 (0.033)	0.040 (0.036)			–0.530 (2.530)	–3.098 (2.584)
Firm T/C •after •experimental		–0.069 (0.046)	–0.023 (0.050)		–2.126 (3.551)	0.143 (3.626)
N	30,862	30,862	30,862	40,895	40,895	40,895

[a] Standard errors in parentheses. All regressions also include years of education, experience and its square, sex, marital status, a marital status by sex interaction, a dummy for nonwhite, a control for union status, dummies for 15 major industries, and separate year dummies for 1974 and 1978. "After" is dummy for being after mandate; "Experimental" is dummy for being in a state that passed a mandate. In columns 1–3, "Treatment" is a dummy for being a woman between 20 and 40 years old, and "Firm treatment" is the percentage of 20–40-year-old females in the worker's industry/occupation cell; regressions exclude married men. In columns 4–6, "cost" is the predicted cost of mandate for the worker, and "Firm cost" is the average predicted cost in the worker's industry/occupation cell.

The coefficient is actually more sizeable than that from the individual treatment regression; it implies that a workplace entirely made up of 20–40-year-old females would see wages fall by almost 7 percent. In the individual regression, such a workplace would see wages fall by only 4 percent. Once again, however, this regression is unable to disentangle whether workplace-wide shifting or within-workplace shifting is the driving force behind this fall in wages.

In order to distinguish these views, I include both the individual and industry/occupation measure in column 3. If the results are a result of workplace-wide shifting, the inclusion of the average "firm" cost should significantly weaken the individual cost coefficient. In fact, the individual DDD coefficient is roughly unchanged, while the industry/occupation DDD coefficient falls to –0.023. Thus, the results imply that it is not just drops in average wages at workplaces with many women that is driving the basic finding. The latter estimate, however, is very imprecise, and one could not reject that it was either zero or much larger than the individual DDD coefficient.

The second empirical approach discussed above was to individually parameterize the cost of the mandate. Gruber (1992) described the methodology for generating individual-specific predicted increases in insurance costs from the mandate. The cost averages 2 percent of wages for the treatment individuals, but it ranges up to 28 percent of wages. The cost is normalized by hours per week and by predicted wages to yield a cost as a percentage of hourly wages, which is readily interpretable in this log wage framework.[22] The individually parameterized cost measure can be introduced in place of the treatment dummy in Eq. 4; to the extent that my estimate of the cost of the mandate is correct, a coefficient of –1 on the third-level interaction would indicate full shifting to wages.

The results using this individual parameterization at both the individual and the industry/occupation level are presented in columns 4–6 of Table 5. For the individual cost regressions, there is a sizeable and negative coefficient that is significantly different from zero and not significantly different from one. For the industry/occupation level cost measures, the coefficient is similar. When the two measures are entered together, the individual-level cost coefficient is essentially unchanged, while the industry/occupation-level cost coefficient is zero.

Once again, however, there is a very large standard error on the industry/occupation-level cost.

Thus, this work provides some evidence that the shifting to wages uncovered in my earlier paper arises from within-workplace changes in the wage structure. This evidence is only preliminary, however, due both to my very rough proxy for "firms" (industry/occupation cells) and the large resulting standard errors on the estimates. In particular, these findings may only be demonstrating that the individual is a better proxy for their own firm than is their industry/occupation cell. Future work, perhaps with true firm data, could fruitfully refine these estimates.

COMPOSITION OF LABOR SUPPLY

Another important difference between mandates and payroll taxes in practice is that mandates are often lump-sum benefits, such as with mandated health insurance, whereas payroll taxes are paid as a fraction of wages. Since mandates represent an increase in the fixed costs of employment, they will be more costly for employees working fewer hours. If employers are able to shift the cost to wages in a lump-sum fashion and if the benefit is fully valued by employees, then there will be no effect on desired hours for either employees or employers. But, if such lump-sum shifting is impossible, then a natural employer reaction to fixed cost mandates would be to increase hours and reduce employment. This would enable the employer to reduce the cost per hour of the mandate while leaving total labor input unchanged.

There may be forces, however, working in the opposite direction. Consider the case of a health insurance mandate. Since part-time workers may be readily excluded from health insurance coverage, employers would like to replace full-time employees with their (relatively less expensive) part-time counterparts.[23] In this case, hours would fall and employment would rise, and total labor input would remain unchanged. Furthermore, the desired supply response to these mandates from the individual perspective is for increased employment among those out of the labor force and for part-time workers to increases their hours in order to qualify for health insurance, so that both employment and hours rise. Thus, the effect on hours and employment are uncertain, even if the cost of the mandate is able to be shifted to wages on average.

Evidence on this question is provided in Gruber (1994a) and Cutler and Madrian (1996). Gruber found that, while the cost of the "maternity mandates" of the 1970s was fully shifted to wages on average with no effect on total labor supply, there was some compositional effect on labor supply: employment fell and hours of work rose, as would be expected under the first scenario above. This suggests that employers could not shift the cost of the mandates in a perfect lump sum manner so they adjusted on the margin using the composition of the work schedule. Cutler and Madrian showed that hours rose in those industries which saw the greatest rise in health care costs during the past decade, once again suggesting that employers are adjusting to these increased fixed costs using the hours margin.

Even this difference between mandates and payroll taxes, however, is not as large as it appears because payroll taxes are generally capped. For UI taxes, as noted previously, these caps can be quite low; with very low caps, payroll taxes essentially operate as lump-sum mandates. If employers can shift the proportional payroll tax cost to wages below the cap only and not to wages above the cap, then there will be no incentive to change hours for either the employer or employee. But if employers cannot, they may have to reduce wages proportionately for all workers, regardless of their position relative to the cap. In this case, there will be opposite hours of work incentives for employers and employees. Employers will see higher costs below the cap and would therefore like to increase work above the cap and reduce employment; employees will see net benefits below the cap (once again assuming full valuation) and only net taxes above it, so they would like to reduce hours and increase (below cap) employment. It would be fruitful to investigate the effect of payroll tax caps on the choice of hours vs. employment, as has been done for health insurance.

REFORMING PAYROLL TAXATION

In this section, I consider two reforms to the current system of pay-roll taxation. I do not discuss alternatives to mandates because the alternative generally is simply to not have the policy. In the final section, I return to the overall question of whether such policies should exist and be financed through employers.

Financing Social Security and Disability Insurance Through the Income Tax

A natural alternative to financing social insurance programs through payroll taxation is to finance them through general revenues. In this section, I contrast the economic effects of payroll taxes with those of one form of general revenue raising, the individual income tax.[24] In doing so, I hold the benefits side of these programs constant. For example, I assume that the Social Security benefits paid to retired workers remain a function of their lifetime work experience in the same way that they are under earmarked payroll taxation. In terms of efficiency, this implies that the tax/benefit linkage-induced shift in labor supply previously discussed will remain under income taxation—that is, so long as benefits are calculated based on past earnings histories, regardless of the source of financing, tax/benefit linkages will operate. Once again, the key in Summers' (1989) analysis is not the form of revenue raising, but that benefits are restricted to be a function of work effort.

In terms of equity, this approach means that I am not considering the net equity implication of these programs as a whole, but rather only the differential impact of alternative sources of finance. For example, the SS program as a whole may be progressive, even as the tax that finances this program is regressive. In this case, moving to more equitable income taxation would be a further increase in progressivity.

Efficiency. The deadweight loss from financing a social insurance program from two alternative revenue sources is a function of two factors: the breadth and the elasticity of the relative tax bases. The distortion of raising a given amount of revenue will be smaller as the tax base is more inelastic. At the same time, if a tax base is small, the tax rate must be higher to raise the requisite funds; because the deadweight loss from a tax rises as the square of the tax rate, a higher rate will lead to a higher distortion. Thus, for a given level of elasticity, the deadweight loss will also fall as the tax base is more broad.

Income taxes offer a potentially much larger tax base than payroll taxation because of the inclusion of unearned income and the fact that payroll taxes are capped while income taxes include all wage and salary income. However, this simple intuition is rendered incorrect by the nature of the income tax system in the United States. The income tax base has a large number of exclusions (such as those for dependents, charitable giving, and mortgage payments) that make it a very incomplete measure of total income in the United States.

The base for income taxation, total taxable income, is reported by Internal Revenue Service. I use data from the Treasury Department's Individual Tax Model, along with the NBER's TAXSIM program, to measure the base of taxable payroll below the Social Security maximum. This data provides information on the tax returns for a large sample of taxpayers, and TAXSIM calculates the tax rates paid by those taxpayers.[25] I use data from 1989, the last year for which data are available.

The total taxable income base was $2.173 trillion in 1989. In contrast, the taxable base of wage and salary earnings below the taxable maximum was only $12.9 million smaller, which is trivial relative to the size of the social insurance programs under discussion. Thus, the relative sizes of these tax bases are virtually equal. Capped earnings may be a smaller base for taxation compared with a comprehensive income definition, but capped earnings provide a base of roughly the same size compared with income taxation as it is carried out in the United States.

Furthermore, the elasticity of the income tax base is almost certainly higher than the elasticity of the payroll tax base. As noted earlier, although controversial, the empirical literature on labor supply suggests that the labor supply of prime age males is fairly inelastic and that the labor supply of secondary earners is somewhat more elastic. On the other hand, other forms of income taxed under the personal income tax (e.g., capital gains) appear to be much more elastic with respect to taxation, although this evidence is also controversial (Auerbach 1988). Similarly, charitable deductions, which lower the taxable income base, are also very sensitive to tax rates (Clotfelter 1990). Recent evidence also suggests that overall taxable income is more elastic with respect to the tax rate than is labor income alone (Feldstein 1993; Navratil 1994).[26]

Thus, it seems clear that income taxation would be a more inefficient source of revenue raising than payroll taxation: the size of the tax base would be no larger, and the tax base would be more elastic.

Equity. The other important consideration for examining income versus payroll taxation is the distribution of the tax burden across taxpayers. A standard criticism of payroll taxation, relative to broader income taxation, is that it is less equitable. This criticism is true for two reasons. First, unearned income is distributed in a much more pro-rich fashion than earned income so that a tax on all income is more progressive by definition. Second, payroll taxation is capped, so that high-income individuals escape this tax burden on income above the cap. In order to contrast the equity of payroll and income taxation, I compare the effective tax rates paid by taxpayers of different income, once again using data from the Treasury model and TAXSIM. Following the evidence provided above, I assume that all of the tax is borne by workers in the form of lower wages. The base for my definition of income is "total positive income"—the sum of the positive income elements reported on tax returns, with negative elements being set to zero. This approach is taken to avoid the problem that much of the negative income reported on tax forms is tax shelter activity, rather than true economic losses.

The left side of Table 6 compares the distribution of effective tax rates across income groups under the current system for the income tax, the payroll tax, and the combination of the two. As expected, the income tax is found to be much more progressive than the payroll tax. For the bottom 5–10 percent of taxpayers, the effective income tax rate is actually negative due to the presence of the Earned Income Tax Credit, which subsidizes labor supply for low earners. The average rate then rises gradually, reaching a maximum of 17.4 percent for the top 5 percent of taxpayers.

In contrast, the effective payroll tax rate is virtually flat for the bottom 80 percent of taxpayers. Note that for this group, payroll taxation

Table 6 The Progressivity of the Income and Payroll Taxes[a]

Income group	Current system			Uncapping tax base		
	Income tax	SSDI tax	Combined	Income tax	SSDI tax	Combined
0–5%	0.3	10.6	11.0	0.3	10.6	11.0
5–10%	–0.4	12.6	12.2	–0.4	12.6	12.2
10–20%	1.3	11.3	12.7	1.3	11.3	12.7
20–30%	3.0	11.3	14.3	3.0	11.3	14.3
30–40%	3.7	11.5	15.2	3.7	11.5	15.2
40–50%	6.6	11.9	18.5	6.6	11.9	18.5
50–60%	8.4	12.3	20.7	8.4	12.3	20.7
60–70%	9.8	12.7	22.5	9.8	12.7	22.5
70–80%	10.6	12.7	23.3	10.6	12.7	23.3
80–90%	11.7	12.3	24.0	11.7	12.3	24.0
90–95%	13.9	10.1	24.0	13.9	12.5	26.4
95–100%	17.4	6.4	23.8	17.4	10.7	28.1

[a] Author's tabulations using U.S. Department of Treasury tax data and NBER TAXSIM model.

represents the majority of their tax bill. For the top 20 percent of taxpayers, payroll tax rates actually decline. Payroll taxes are therefore much less equitable than income taxes, and this becomes a key equity consideration when payroll taxes represent the majority of taxes paid for such a high fraction of taxpayers. Thus, the consideration of payroll vs. income taxation comes down to the classic trade-off between efficiency and equity.

Of course, this discussion has taken the structure of income and payroll taxes as given. If the income tax base were widened, for example, by the removal or limitation of the deduction for mortgage interest, the attractiveness of income taxation would rise for three reasons. First, the tax base would be larger, so that there would be a lower efficiency cost per dollar of revenue raised. Second, the income tax base would be less elastic. The increased elasticity of income taxation relative to payroll taxation described above derives largely from the fact that, under the income tax, there are a number of ways to protect income from taxation, such as the mortgage interest deduction. Limiting these exclusions would reduce the extent to which reported income can be lowered in response to higher taxes and thus limit the efficiency cost of income taxation. Finally, income taxes would become even more equitable in many cases. This is because any deduction from taxable income is regressive because tax rates rise with income. Thus, removing the mortgage interest deduction would make the income tax system more progressive.[27]

Raising the Taxable Maximum for Payroll Taxation

An alternative to shifting to income taxation would be to change the structure of payroll taxation to make it more equitable. A natural means for doing so would be to remove the cap on taxable earnings for SS and DI, which was removed for Medicare beginning in 1994. Under the principle of maintaining some tax/benefit linkages, if benefits are not going to be paid based on earnings above this level, then taxes must be limited as well. However, the tax/benefit linkages are likely to be small for this top group of earners because the benefits formula used by SS only converts each dollar of earnings to 15 cents of benefits at the top of the earnings distribution.

The efficiency consequences of uncapping the payroll tax are mixed. On one hand, it substantially increases the payroll tax base. If all wage and salary income were subject to the payroll tax, the tax base would rise from $2.16 trillion to $2.61 trillion (based on calculations using the Treasury data and TAXSIM), an increase in the tax base of over 20 percent. In 1989, the total tax rate used to finance SS and DI was 12.12 percent. If the same revenues were raised by an uncapped tax, this combined tax rate could have been reduced to 10.03 percent. Using the rule that the efficiency cost of a tax rises with the square of the tax rate, the efficiency cost of financing these programs could have been reduced by 32 percent by extending the tax base to all wages and salaries.

On the other hand, the wage and salary income of top earners may be more elastic than that of earners lower down the income distribution. High-income individuals receive more fringe benefits and other diverse sources of compensation, allowing for more discretion in the form in which compensation is paid. For example, if the payroll tax were uncapped, executives might switch from cash compensation to stock options. While other workers have some opportunity for this type of arbitrage using fringe benefits such as health insurance, the opportunities are more abundant for top earners. Feenberg and Poterba (1993) documented that wage and salary income for the top 1 percent of taxpayers rose dramatically after the Tax Reform Act of 1986 lowered marginal tax rates on earned income. And Navratil (1994) also found that the wage and salary income of top earners (more than $50,000 per year in 1980 dollars) is much more elastic with respect to tax changes than is that of all earners.

Furthermore, to the extent that high wage earners reduce their reported earnings in order to avoid increased payroll taxation, there is a spillover into the revenues collected under the ordinary income tax. Since the marginal income tax rate on top earners is over three times as high as the marginal payroll tax rate would be, reduced earnings by top earners could quickly mitigate any potential gains from extending the payroll tax.

Navratil (1994) estimated an elasticity of earned income with respect to payroll taxation for high-income earners of approximately one. One can use this estimate, along with information on the revenues collected from both the payroll and income taxes, to estimate the revenue effect of uncapping the payroll tax. In fact, the net revenue increase from uncapping the payroll tax would only be $11.7 billion, or 21 percent of what would be assumed based on naive application of the 12 percent payroll tax to the incremental $450 billion in revenues because the tax would raise only $43.2 billion in payroll tax revenues but would cost $31.5 billion in income tax revenues.[28] This policy could therefore have a relatively high efficiency cost per dollar of revenues raised.

Table 6 explores the equity implications of uncapping the tax base by presenting the payroll and total tax burdens, by income class, under the current system and with the tax base uncapped. There is no effect of this policy on the bottom 90 percent of the income distribution. However, there is a large net increase in taxes paid for the wealthiest taxpayers; the top 5 percent would experience and increase in their effective tax rate of approximately 20 percent. Thus, uncapping the SS tax may raise a relatively small amount of revenues, but it would substantially raise taxes on the very upper end of the distribution of earnings.

Uncapping payroll taxes for UI would have larger effects since, as documented in Table 3, the current taxable maximums are so low. It is difficult to replicate the calculation performed above for uncapping UI taxes, however, because we do not have a good estimate of the elasticity of earned income for lower wage earners, nor is there readily available data on the marginal UI tax rate faced by workers at different income levels. Undertaking this kind of calculation could be useful for assessing the implications of uncapping UI taxes as well.

CONCLUSIONS

This chapter has tried to highlight what we know and what we don't know about the labor-market effects of payroll taxation and employer mandates in the United States. While recent evidence suggests that mandates and payroll taxes are fully shifted to workers' wages with little disemployment effect, there remains important questions and complications that must be explored by future research. In addition, I discuss the benefits and costs of shifting from payroll taxation to income taxation, as well as of uncapping the payroll tax.

There is a larger question avoided by this discussion: should payroll tax financed and mandated employer benefits exist at all? There are three components to the welfare analysis of social insurance interventions: the deadweight loss from financing, other distortions to behavior from the existence of public insurance, and the benefits for the party on whose behalf the intervention is occurring. This chapter has focused on the first of these components. There is also a large literature on the second, which has explored the distortive effects of the perverse incentives inherent in a number of different social insurance programs. However, there is little work on the third area—the benefits of social insurance interventions. Without evidence on this front, we cannot conclude as to the optimal level of government intervention in private insurance markets.

Consider the case of workers' compensation. Gruber and Krueger (1991) showed that there is little deadweight loss from financing this program. Meyer (1990) and Krueger (1990, 1992) showed that there are important distortions to worker injury reports and duration of job absence, but there is little evidence on the benefits of WC. To what extent does WC reduce the deadweight loss that would otherwise be incurred through the tort system as workers and firms tried to resolve workplace injury cases? To what extent does it smooth the consumption of myopic or liquidity constrained workers who would otherwise see a large drop in their standard of living when they were truly injured on the job? Until these benefits are measured, we have no way of assessing the optimal level of government intervention in this market; how else can we assess whether the distortions measured by the earlier work are "large"?

Similar problems exist in evaluating the optimal level of the Social Security program. In this case, we don't necessarily even know the deadweight loss from financing. There are a number of reasons, noted previously, why the results from previous incidence research may not apply to Social Security. Once again, there is a long line of research on the distortive effects of the program to savings and retirement behavior by Feldstein (1974), Burtless (1986), and Diamond and Hausman (1984). In this case, however, there is also only sketchy evidence on the benefits of the program. There has been some attention paid to issues of benefit adequacy; see Diamond (1977), Kotlikoff, Spivak, and Summers (1982), and Hamermesh (1984) for somewhat different conclusions on this adequacy issue. None of these studies, however, has been able to assess convincingly the effects of varying Social Security benefits on the welfare of retirees because they have not been able to fully model the alternative consumption smoothing opportunities available to the retiree in the absence of Social Security. Feldstein (1985) conjectured on the optimal Social Security benefit level using a model where some fraction of the population is myopic and concluded that the optimal program should be quite small. This work could be usefully extended by incorporating liquidity constraints and other capital market failures into the model and, more convincingly, by providing empirical evidence on how the living standards of the elderly change as Social Security benefits vary.

Perhaps the most complete picture can be painted for unemployment insurance. The evidence in Anderson and Meyer (1997) suggests that there is little deadweight loss at the market level from the financing of UI, although there may be a distortion at the firm level. Meyer (1990) showed that there is a large distortion of generous UI benefits to unemployment durations, and Feldstein (1978), Topel (1983), and Anderson and Meyer (1994) showed that there are also distortions of imperfect experience rating to firm layoff decisions. On the other hand, there are two forms of benefit of this program for individual workers. The first is that it helps to subsidize efficient search by liquidity constrained unemployed workers. But recent research has shown that the longer search induced by more generous unemployment insurance benefits does not result in better job matches, as measured by the ultimate wage received (Meyer 1989; Woodbury and Speigelman 1987). The second is that it smooths the consumption of individuals who, due either to myopia or some capital market failure, are unable to smooth their own consumption during unemployment spells.[29] Some preliminary evidence on this front is provided by Gruber (1997, 1998), who found that the consumption of those becoming unemployed falls significantly more if there is less generous UI. In that paper, I attempted to use a simple optimal benefits model to compare the costs and benefits of UI into a simple optimal benefits model, but there is clearly room for more systematic incorporation of the costs and benefits of social insurance programs in order to assess optimal intervention levels.

Notes

I am grateful to Jeff Liebman for research assistance.

1. The description of these programs is current as of 1993. Most information is from Committee on Ways and Means (1993) and Employee Benefits Research Institute (1992).
2. The normal age of retirement under Social Security is 65. Individuals can retire as early as age 62, but benefits are then adjusted downwards to reflect the fact that they are received for a larger number of years. Similarly, individuals can retire after age 65, and benefits are adjusted upwards, through a "delayed retirement credit." If individuals wish to both continue working and receive benefits, they can do so, but benefits are taxed away at a rate of $1 of benefit for every $3 of earnings [above some minimum threshold ($10,560)]; this is known as the "earnings test."
3. Although, for past cohorts, the system actually redistributed (in total dollar terms) towards higher income workers; see Stuerle and Bakija (1994) for an overview. This trend is projected to end for future generations, as the program becomes more progressive.
4. The problems in defining disability for the purposes of Disability Insurance are well known; see Parsons (1991) for a detailed discussion of these issues.

5. While this is primarily a state-run program, employers are obligated to pay a 0.6 percent payroll tax to the federal government (FUTA tax).

6. It is difficult to decide where "mandates" end and other workplace regulations begin. The dividing line chosen here is that mandates are government regulations of the provision of employee benefits; thus, particular regulations pertaining to health insurance benefit plans are mandates, while workplace antidiscrimination rules are not. It remains unclear whether government regulations of workplace safety should be counted as a mandate in this context.

7. Continuation of coverage benefits provide that the employee can continue to purchase health insurance from the firm at the average group rate following his or her voluntary or involuntary termination. See Gruber and Madrian (1993) for more details on these laws.

8. Workers' compensation is not mandatory in New Jersey, South Carolina, and Texas. See Deere (1994) for an analysis of the implications of voluntary workers' compensation in Texas.

9. These are the "manual rates," which provide the basis for firm insurance payments. The actual cost of insurance may differ from these rates for some firms due to within-industry experience rating; see Burton et al. (1985) for details.

10. One may wonder why, if this program is fully valued by workers, a government mandate is required. As Summers (1989) discusses, a variety of different market failures (such as adverse selection in the choice to insure) may make it difficult for these type of arrangements to emerge in the free market even if there is full valuation; government intervention may improve welfare in this case.

11. A third alternative for full shifting to wages would be perfectly elastic demand, but this would imply much larger disemployment effects than those found by Gruber and Krueger (1991).

12. The variation in payroll costs in Gruber and Krueger (1991) is over a 10-year period; for Anderson and Meyer (1997), there is a 6-year window.

13. Whether this assumption of money illusion is warranted, of course, is the subject of a large macroeconomics literature not addressed here.

14. Vergara (1990) showed that, if the social welfare function values poor individuals more highly, it will in general be optimal to have some degree of public provision financed by income taxation instead of having all of the intervention financed by a mandate.

15. These findings have not been without their critics; see Neumark and Wascher (1992), and the debate between Neumark and Wascher (1994) and Card, Krueger, and Katz (1994).

16. For example, the costs of unemployment insurance are roughly equal across all workers, unless some workers are "layoff-prone."

17. Even if the costs can be shifted on average, however, if there is not perfect lump-sum shifting, there will still be a distortion to the hours margin which may spill over to other groups. This is discussed further below.

18. See Ehrenberg and Smith (1987) for a discussion of U.S. antidiscrimination legislation, which was in place well before the mid 1970s. In this discussion, I focus

only on laws prohibiting discrimination in rates of pay and/or promotion. In fact, if there are *also* binding restrictions on relative hiring practices, then employers may be forced to bear the cost of the mandate. If discrimination rules are *only* binding on the hiring side, then they will not impede group-specific shifting in the case of full valuation.

19. These findings highlight another margin of employer response not emphasized here: reducing other (nonmandated) benefits when there are increases in mandated benefits. This margin has the advantage that existing benefits are often lump sum, so that they provide a natural means of offsetting new lump-sum costs imposed on employers.

20. In Gruber (1994a), I discuss the motivation for my choice of these states as well as a large range of empirical issues that are mentioned only briefly here.

21. The results are similar if I use other methods of creating synthetic firms. This approach allows for a relatively fine division of the data without creating many cells which have just a few women.

22. The pros and cons of this approach, as well as the robustness of the results to functional form, are discussed in Gruber (1992).

23. Under the Employee Retirement and Income Security Act (ERISA), employers who offer health insurance must make that insurance available to any worker who works 1,000 hours per year or more.

24. Of course, there are other forms of revenue raising available to the government, such as corporate taxation or federal excise taxation. However, the taxation of individual incomes is the dominant source of revenue at the federal level, so it provides a natural point for comparison; this analysis could readily be extended to consider alternative forms of taxation. I only consider the Social Security and Disability Insurance payroll tax because the structure of the Medicare payroll tax is now fundamentally different (since there is no taxable maximum).

25. Earnings is defined as wage and salary earnings plus self-employment earnings plus farm income. Where these elements are reported to be negative, I replace them with zero, under the assumption that negative earnings reflects tax shelter behavior.

26. This is true for a number of reasons, including the following: a less elastic behavioral response of labor supply than of other forms of economic activity, more scope for relabeling other forms of income to avoid taxation than is possible with labor income (i.e., shifting from dividends to capital gains when the capital gains tax rate is lower), and more scope for evasion with other forms of income (i.e., claiming artificially high charitable contributions).

27. While the first two comments apply to the removal of any exclusion in the tax code, the last does not; some tax breaks, such as the earned income tax credit, are progressive.

28. This calculation is done as follows. Assume that the currently marginal tax rate on earnings in the uncapped range is 35 percent. Uncapping the payroll tax would raise that rate to 47 percent. Navratil finds that the elasticity of earnings with respect to after-tax shares is one. Since the after-tax share is reduced by 20 per-

cent, this would mean that the additional $450 billion in earnings in the uncapped range would be reduced to $360 billion. Thus, the uncapped payroll tax would raise an additional $43.2 billion, but income tax revenues would be reduced by $31.5 billion.

29. A third traditional justification for UI is that it serves as an automatic stabilizer, reducing the severity of recessions by redistributing from good times to bad. There is little direct evidence on the automatic stabilization properties of UI. A finding that UI smooths consumption at the level of the individual, discussed below, may provide indirect evidence on its success as an automatic stabilizer.

References

Alan Guttmacher Institute. 1987. "Blessed Events and the Bottom Line: Financing Maternity Care in the United States." New York: AGI.

Anderson, Patricia, and Bruce Meyer. 1993. "The Unemployment Insurance Payroll Tax and Interindustry and Interfirm Subsidies." *Tax Policy and the Economy* 7:111–144.

_____. 1994. "The Effects of Unemployment Insurance Taxes and Benefits on Layoffs Using Firm and Individual Data." National Bureau of Economic Research Working Paper No. 4960, December.

_____. 1997. "The Effect of Firm Specific Taxes and Government Mandates with an Application to the U.S. Unemployment Insurance Program." *Journal of Public Economics* 65(August): 119–145.

Auerbach, Alan. 1988. "Capital Gains Taxation in the United States: Realizations, Revenue, and Rhetoric." *Brookings Papers on Economic Activity* 2: 595–631.

Brittain, John A. 1972. *The Payroll Tax for Social Security.* Washington, D.C.: The Brookings Institution.

Brown, Charles, Curtis Gilroy, and Andrew Kohen. 1982. "The Effect of the Minimum Wage on Employment and Unemployment." *Journal of Economic Literature* 20: 487–528.

Burtless, Gary. 1986. "Social Security, Unanticipated Benefit Increases, and the Timing of Retirement." *Review of Economic Studies* 53(5): 781–805.

Burton, John F., H. Allan Hunt, and Alan B. Krueger. 1985. *Interstate Variation in the Employers' Costs of Workers' Compensation, with Particular Reference to Michigan and the Other Great Lakes States.* Ithaca, NY: Workers' Disability Income Systems, Inc.

Card, David. 1992a. "Using Regional Variation in Wages to Measure the Effects of the Federal Minimum Wage." *Industrial and Labor Relations Review* 46: 22–37.

_____. 1992b. "Do Minimum Wages Reduce Employment? A Case Study of California, 1987–89." *Industrial and Labor Relations Review* 46: 38–54.

Card, David, and Alan B. Krueger. 1994. "Minimum Wages and Employment: A Case Study of the Fast Food Industry in New Jersey and Pennsylvania." *American Economic Review* 84(4): 772–793.

Card, David, Alan B. Krueger, and Lawrence F. Katz. 1994. "Comment on David Neumark and William Wascher." *Industrial and Labor Relations Review* 47: 487–496.

Clotfelter, Charles. 1990. "The Impact of Tax Reform on Charitable Giving: A 1989 Perspective." In *Do Taxes Matter?* J. Slemrod, ed. Cambridge, MA: MIT Press, pp. 203–235.

Committee on Ways and Means. 1993. *Overview of Entitlement Programs: 1993 Green Book.* Washington, D.C.: U.S. House of Representatives.

Cutler, David, and Brigitte C. Madrian. 1996. "Labor Market Responses to Rising Health Insurance Costs: Evidence on Hours Worked." National Bureau of Economic Research Working Paper No. 5525, April.

Deere, Donald. 1994. "Optional Participation in Workers' Compensation in Texas." Unpublished paper, Texas A&M University.

Diamond, Peter. 1977. "A Framework for Social Security Analysis." *Journal of Public Economics* 8: 275–298.

Diamond, Peter, and Jerry Hausman. 1984. "Individual Retirement and Savings Behavior." *Journal of Public Economics* 23: 81–114.

Economic Report of the President 1992. Washington, D.C.: U.S. Government Printing Office.

Ehrenberg, Ronald G., and Robert S. Smith. 1987. *Modern Labor Economics: Theory and Public Policy.* New York: Harper Collins.

Employee Benefits Research Institute. 1992. *EBRI Databook on Employee Benefits.* Washington, D.C.: EBRI.

Feenberg, Daniel, and James Poterba. 1993. "Income Inequality and the Incomes of Very High Income Taxpayers." *Tax Policy and the Economy* 7: 148–177.

Feenberg, Daniel, and Lawrence Summers. 1990. "Who Benefits from Capital Gains Tax Reductions?" *Tax Policy and the Economy* 4: 1–24.

Feldstein, Martin. 1972. "Comment on Brittain." *American Economic Review* 62: 735–738.

_____. 1974. "Social Security, Induced Retirement, and Aggregate Capital Accumulation." *Journal of Political Economy* 82: 905–926.

_____. 1978. "The Impact of Unemployment Insurance on Temporary Lay-off Unemployment." *American Economic Review* 68: 191–222.

_____. 1985. "The Optimal Level of Social Security Benefits." *Quarterly Journal of Economics* 100: 303–320.

_____. 1997. "The Effect of Marginal Tax Rates on Taxable Income: A Panel Study of the 1986 Tax Reform Act." NBER Working Paper #4496, August.

Gruber, Jonathan. 1992. "The Efficiency of a Group-Specific Mandated Benefit: Evidence from Health Insurance Benefits for Maternity." NBER Working Paper #4157.

_____. 1994a. "The Incidence of Mandated Maternity Benefits." *American Economic Review* 84(3): 622–641.

_____. 1994b. "State Mandated Benefits and Employer Provided Insurance." *Journal of Public Economics* 55(3): 433–464.

_____. 1997. "The Consumption Smoothing Benefits of Unemployment Insurance." *American Economic Review* 87(March): 192–205.

_____. 1998. "Unemployment Insurance, Consumption Smoothing, and Private Insurance: Evidence from the PSID and CEX." *Research in Employment Policy* 1:3–32.

Gruber, Jonathan, and Alan B. Krueger. 1991. "The Incidence of Mandated Employer-Provided Insurance: Lessons from Worker's Compensation Insurance." *Tax Policy and the Economy* 5: 111–143.

Gruber, Jonathan, and Brigitte Madrian. 1993. "Health Insurance Availability and the Retirement Decision." NBER Working Paper #4469.

Hamermesh, Daniel S. 1984. "Consumption During Retirement: The Missing Link in the Life Cycle." *Review of Economics and Statistics* 66: 1–7.

Heckman, James J. 1993. "What Has Been Learned About Labor Supply in the Past Twenty Years?" *American Economic Association* 83(May): 116–121.

Holmlund, Bertil. 1983. "Payroll Taxes and Wage Inflation: The Swedish Experience." *Scandinavian Journal of Economics* 85: 1–15.

Katz, Lawrence F., and Alan B. Krueger. 1992. "The Effects of the Minimum Wage on the Fast Food Industry." *Industrial and Labor Relations Review* 46: 6–21.

Killingsworth, Mark. 1983. *Labor Supply.* Cambridge, MA: Cambridge University Press.

Kotlikoff, Laurence J., Avia Spivak, and Lawrence H. Summers. 1982. "The Adequacy of Savings." *American Economic Review* 72: 1056–1069.

Krueger, A. 1990a. "Incentive Effects of Workers' Compensation Insurance." *Journal of Public Economics* 41(February): 73–100.

_____. 1990b. "Workers' Compensation Insurance and the Duration of Workplace Injuries." NBER Working Paper #3253.

Leshin, Geraldine. 1981. *EEO Law: Impact on Fringe Benefits*. Los Angeles: UCLA Institute of Industrial Relations.

Meyer, Bruce D. 1989. "A Quasi-Experimental Approach to the Effects of Unemployment Insurance." NBER Working Paper #3159.

Meyer, Bruce D. 1990. "Unemployment Insurance and Unemployment Spells." *Econometrica* 58: 757–782.

Navratil, John F. 1994. "The Economic Recovery Tax Act of 1981: Evidence on Individual Taxpayer Behavior from Panel Tax Return Data." Unpublished manuscript, Harvard University.

Neumark, David, and William Wascher. 1992. "Employment Effects of Minimum and Subminimum Wages: Panel Data on State Minimum Wage Laws." *Industrial and Labor Relations Review* 46: 55–81.

_____. 1994. "Reply to Card, Katz, and Krueger." *Industrial and Labor Relations Review* 47: 497–512.

Olson, Craig A. 1993. "The Impact of AIDS/HIV on the Health Benefits and Wages of Single Men." Unpublished manuscript, University of Wisconsin-Madison.

Parsons, Donald. 1991. "The Health and Earnings of Rejected Disability Insurance Applicants: Comment." *American Economic Review* 81: 1419–1426.

Stuerle, C. Eugene, and Jon M. Bakija. 1994. *Retooling Social Security for the 21st Century*. Washington, D.C.: Urban Institute.

Summers, Lawrence. 1989. "Some Simple Economics of Mandated Benefits." *American Economic Review* 79(May): 177–184.

Topel, Robert. 1983. "On Layoffs and Unemployment Insurance." *American Economic Review* 73: 541–559.

U.S. Department of Health and Human Services. 1991. *Social Security Bulletin Annual Statistical Supplement*. Washington, D.C.: Social Security Administration.

Vergara, Rodrigo. 1990. "The Economics of Mandatory Benefits Programs." Unpublished manuscript, Harvard University.

Vroman, Wayne. 1974. "Employer Payroll Taxes and Money Wage Behavior." *Applied Economics* 6: 189–204.

Woodbury, Stephen, and Robert Spiegelman. 1987. "Bonuses to Workers and Employers to Reduce Unemployment: Randomized Trials in Illinois." *American Economic Review* 77: 513–530.

5 Fringe Benefits and Employment

Masanori Hashimoto
Ohio State University

The past few decades have witnessed dramatic growth in the fringe benefits component of total labor compensation in the United States and other countries in the Organization for Economic Cooperation Development (Hart et al. 1988). According to the conventional wisdom, an exogenous increase in nonwage labor costs adversely impacts employment. For instance, researchers have linked increases in quasi-fixed labor costs with reductions in employment.[1] Often overlooked, however, is the fact that voluntarily provided fringe benefits have grown by as much as legally required fringe benefits over the past 40 years, with the voluntary component in fact outpacing the legally required component after the early 1980s. Although legally required fringe benefits may be viewed as exogenous for the purposes of modeling, voluntarily provided fringe benefits must be treated as endogenous in any comprehensive analysis.[2] In this chapter, we undertake just such an analysis. In particular, we discuss a market level model in which wages and employment are permitted to respond to changes in the demand for and the cost of fringe benefits and in which increases in legally mandated fringe benefits are permitted to alter the market equilibrium.

Anticipating the results, the employment and wage effects of increases in nonwage payments vary with the source of the increase. We analyze the following three such sources: 1) an increase in worker demand for benefits, 2) a reduction in the cost of providing benefits, and 3) an increase in legally mandated benefits. Although these are obvious sources, the literature does not seem to have taken them into account. Our analysis is conducted primarily in a model in which no distinction is drawn between the number of workers and the hours of work or between straight-time and overtime hours. The final sections discuss how the results are altered by incorporating such distinctions and offer some concluding remarks.

BACKGROUND

Figure 1 shows that, in the United States, both legally required and voluntary fringe benefits grew significantly over the past 40 years, with the voluntary component outpacing the legally required component after the early 1980s. As Table 1 makes clear, growth in Social Security was the single most important factor behind the upsurge in legally required fringe benefits between 1951 and 1994. As for voluntary fringe benefits, growth in health and medical insurance far outpaced growth in any other component. Table 2 depicts industry differences in the changes in nonwage payments from 1966 to 1994. In general, the percentage of nonwage labor costs in total labor costs rose steadily during this period, with growth for all industries combined reaching almost 48 percent. This rate of increase varied among industries, ranging between 1.2 percent in finance to 67.9 percent in wood products. It was higher for manufacturing industries overall (over 50 percent) than for nonmanufacturing industries (39 percent).

The observed increase in the importance of nonwage labor costs most likely affected the relative attractiveness of various labor inputs, for example, part-time versus full-time workers or additional hiring of full-time workers versus additional hours worked by incumbent workers. In particular, the existing analyses predict that part-time workers should have become more attractive than full-time workers and that additional hours should have become more attractive than additional hiring.

It is unclear whether these predictions are supported by the data, at least on the aggregate correlation level. Figure 2 indicates that there is no discernible relationship across industries between changes in the ratio of full-time to total employment and changes in the importance of nonwage labor costs. Figure 3 shows that, if anything, hours worked per employee decreased in industries that experienced increases in nonwage labor costs, a finding that seems at odds with the theoretical prediction. Although a multivariate analysis using a more comprehensive data set is needed to test these predictions rigorously, the market-level theory discussed in this essay suggests that such ambiguous findings are to be expected.

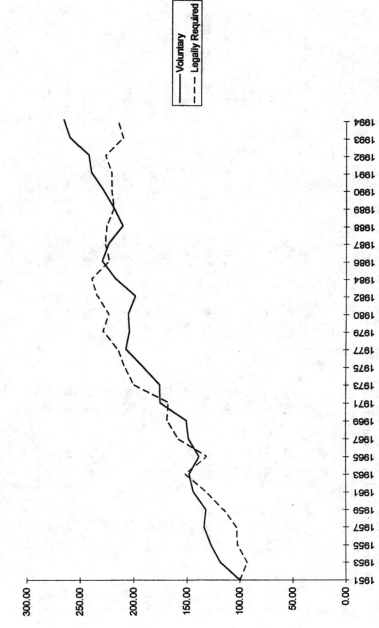

Figure 1 Fringe Benefits of Workers in Firms Surveyed by the Chamber of Commerce (Indices of Benefits as a Percent of Total Compensation, 1951=100)

232

Table 1 Components of Fringe Benefits in Firms Surveyed by the Chamber of Commerce. Indices of Benefits as a Percent of Total Compensation (1951=100)

	Legally required			Voluntary			Inside payroll	
	Social Security	Workers' comp.	Other	Retirement	Insurance	Misc.	Paid rest	Paid leave
1951	100.00	100.00	100.00	100.00	100.00	100.00	100.00	100.00
1955	174.81	87.41	58.27	102.04	174.81	145.741	16.54	104.93
1959	172.74	138.16	69.11	115.20	207.33	115.16	138.22	117.50
1963	240.98	120.49	100.44	110.50	240.98	160.65	140.60	126.55
1967	315.88	157.89	52.63	114.10	263.25	140.41	157.96	126.40
1971	360.71	160.34	40.10	126.95	360.71	146.93	173.68	144.31
1975	439.47	198.50	56.70	141.81	425.28	132.33	189.04	155.97
1979	435.71	249.06	82.83	138.36	477.16	152.13	179.82	143.18
1984	494.36	179.51	89.91	117.42	621.52	144.17	92.92	138.52
1988	522.56	166.73	43.80	126.29	711.84	46.37	117.11	160.07
1992	517.48	221.80	34.59	152.80	805.83	54.20	123.18	155.25
1993	495.39	172.18	30.33	157.98	839.94	76.50	110.03	149.35
1994	514.29	165.98	30.39	175.65	788.06	93.98	107.83	141.87

SOURCE: See Appendix A.

Table 2 Indices of Nonwage Labor Costs as a Proportion of Total Labor Compensation by Industry (1966=100)

Industry	1966 Values	1966	1971	1976	1981	1985	1988	1992	1993	1994
All	(0.198)	100.0	118.7	135.4	137.4	138.4	136.4	144.8	147.6	146.1
Manufacturing	(0.191)	100.0	122.5	142.4	144.5	148.7	139.7	152.8	150.4	153.3
Food, tobacco	(0.214)	100.0	116.4	125.2	127.6	132.7	123.4	145.5	121.4	127.4
Textiles, apparel	(0.159)	100.0	120.1	141.5	149.1	153.5	157.1	146.6	158.9	143.6
Wood products	(0.169)	100.0	130.8	150.3	157.4	154.4	149.1	164.2	167.9	161.4
Printing & publishing	(0.174)	100.0	123.6	148.9	154.6	146.6	134.0	165.7	164.2	169.1
Chemicals	(0.215)	100.0	118.6	140.5	140.9	140.0	118.5	134.8	144.1	130.7
Petroleum	(0.219)	100.0	120.1	132.4	140.6	128.3	144.1	132.3	132.5	130.2
Rubber and plastics	(0.201)	100.0	115.9	136.8	134.8	142.3	144.9	166.7	148.6	145.9
Stone, glass	(0.188)	100.0	126.6	142.0	146.3	135.1	139.1	144.5	143.9	152.8
Metals:										
Primary	(0.200)	100.0	129.0	151.0	151.0	166.0	149.9	149.6	144.6	127.4
Fabricated	(0.186)	100.0	119.9	147.3	147.8	159.1	152.2	169.1	158.5	149.2
Machinery										
Electrical	(0.192)	100.0	118.8	139.6	142.2	146.4	135.3	150.7	148.0	163.4
Other	(0.194)	100.0	119.1	140.7	143.3	147.4	137.3	149.9	144.1	154.2

(continued)

Table 2 (continued)

Industry	1966 Values	1966	1971	1976	1981	1985	1988	1992	1993	1994
Transportation equip.	(0.188)	100.0	137.8	149.5	148.9	155.9	149.0	163.3	162.0	187.6
Instruments, other	(0.192)	100.0	123.4	132.3	145.8	152.6	134.7	127.2	139.8	144.2
Nonmanufacturing	(0.212)	100.0	111.8	124.5	125.5	125.5	128.4	134.3	138.8	136.0
Utilities	(0.212)	100.0	115.6	134.0	139.2	137.7	140.2	140.0	148.6	148.4
Trade										
Department stores	(0.188)	100.0	103.7	128.7	124.5	125.0	136.4	128.9	123.4	152.2
Other	(0.194)	100.0	101.5	121.1	120.6	123.7	153.2	143.8	153.7	144.6
Finance	(0.243)	100.0	108.2	117.3	114.4	105.8	99.5	100.5	101.2	98.3
Insurance	(0.213)	100.0	113.1	99.1	130.5	128.2	120.2	132.5	136.8	134.6
Hospitals	(0.204)	–	–	100.0	116.2	125.5	121.6	123.8	134.7	131.9
Other	(0.252)	–	–	100.0	98.4	100.4	107.4	116.8	116.6	109.5

SOURCE: Calculated from Table 6 of *Employee Benefits* (Chamber of Commerce of the United States, various years) by taking $1/(1+(100/x))$, where x is employee benefits.

235

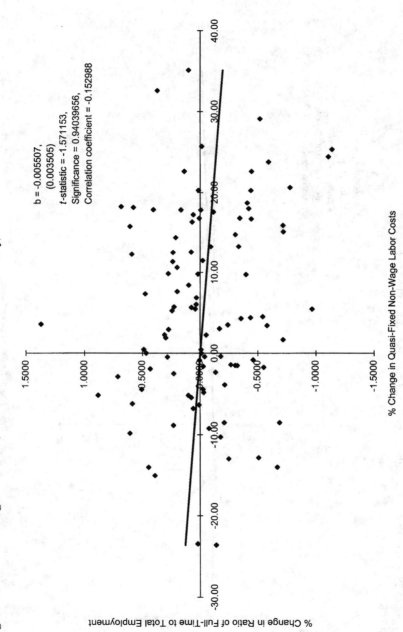

Figure 2 Manufacturing Industries (U.S. Chamber of Commerce Survey)

b = -0.005507,
(0.003505)
t-statistic = -1.571153,
Significance = 0.9403656,
Correlation coefficient = -0.152988

% Change in Ratio of Full-Time to Total Employment

% Change in Quasi-Fixed Non-Wage Labor Costs

236

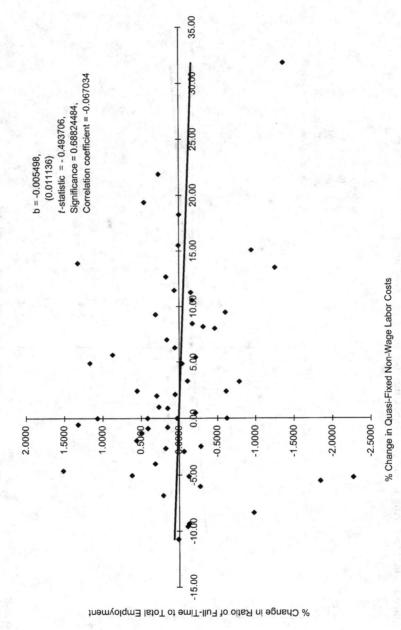

Figure 3 Nonmanufacturing Industries (U.S. Chamber of Commerce Survey)

b = -0.005498,
(0.011136)
t-statistic = -0.493706,
Significance = 0.68824484,
Correlation coefficient = -0.067034

% Change in Ratio of Full-Time to Total Employment

% Change in Quasi-Fixed Non-Wage Labor Costs

THEORY AND PREDICTIONS

In contrast to the conventional approach of analyzing a single firm's decision, we consider a model that addresses the effects of increased fringe benefits on market wages and employment. To focus on the bare essentials of the analysis, we restrict ourselves to a simple model that abstracts from the distinction between the size of the workforce and the hours of work per worker. Following this simple model, we consider the implications from an extended model that includes such a distinction.

Beginning first with a firm level analysis and then extending to the market level analysis, suppose that an industry consists of identical firms whose production functions are given by

$$Q = F(n) \tag{1}$$

where Q is output and n is a firm's level of employment. The market level of employment is then given by $E = kn$, where k is the total number of firms. Each firm faces a labor expense function,

$$\theta = \theta(n, h, G) = whn + C(G, n)n, \tag{2}$$

where w is the wage and G is the quantity of fringe benefits per worker. Equation 2 is assumed to satisfy

$$C_1 > 0, \ C_{11} > 0, \ C_2 \gtrless 0, \ C_{12} = C_{21} \gtrless 0, \ C_{22} = 0,$$

so that the marginal cost of G is positive and rising ($C_1 > 0$, $C_{11} > 0$). Equation 2 allows for the existence of either internal diseconomies or economies in providing fringe benefits. Thus, as the firm expands its workforce, the cost per worker of providing fringe benefits might increase or decrease, depending upon whether scale diseconomies ($C_2 > 0$) or economies ($C_2 < 0$) exist. More importantly, the sign of $C_{12} = C_{21}$ is critical to the analysis. We interpret $C_{12} < 0$ as an indicator of cross-economies of scale and $C_{12} \geq 0$ as an indicator cross-diseconomies of scale. Cross-economies of scale (diseconomies of scale) imply that the marginal cost of G falls (rises) with the size of the workforce. For simplicity, we assume that $C_{22} = 0$.

The ith employee is assumed to view G as having a constant marginal value of λ_i dollars, making her indifferent between receiving λ_i dollars in w or in G. To simplify, we assume that all employees have the same marginal value, λ. As a result, $\partial w / \partial G = -\lambda$ from the employer's perspective; if G is increased by one unit, all employees are willing to work for λ dollars less in w.

An employer selects the optimum n and G by solving the following problem:

$$\underset{n,G}{\text{Max}}\ \pi(n,G) = pF(n) - [w + C(G,n)]n, \tag{3}$$

where p is the product price. The first order conditions are given by

$$\partial \pi / \partial n = pF'(n) - [w + C(G,n) + nC_2] = 0 \ \text{and} \tag{4a}$$

$$\partial \pi / \partial G = (-\lambda + C_1)n = 0. \tag{4b}$$

A firm's labor demand is traced by Eq. 4a, rewritten as:

$$w = pF'(n) - [C(G,n) + nC_2]. \tag{4a*}$$

The optimum quantity of G is given by Eq. 4b, implying that the marginal cost of G is equal to λ dollars at the optimum point.

Allowing for the product price changes that occur as all firms change outputs, the market demand curves for labor can be obtained by horizontally summing the firms' demand curves. To facilitate the analysis, we linearize the market demand curves as follows (see Appendix B for the details of this linearization).

$$w^d = \alpha - \left(\eta G + pG^2\right) + \beta(G)E, \tag{5}$$

where w^d is the employers' wage offer, w is employment, and α, η, ρ, and β are parameters. The expression represents the cost of providing G, and β depends on G if there are cross-scale effects in providing the benefits. Equations 2 and 4a* imply the following restrictions:

$$\alpha, \eta, \rho > 0, \beta < 0, d\beta / dG \lessgtr 0, \text{and } d\beta / dG^2 = 0, \tag{6}$$

where the condition $d\beta / dG \lessgtr 0$ corresponds to $C_{12} \gtrless 0$ and the condition $d^2\beta / dG^2 = 0$ corresponds to $C_{12} = 0$ (see Appendix B). Figure 4 depicts the demand curves associated with three different quantities of G. If the marginal cost of G slopes upward, the demand curves diverge as G is increased, reflecting the rising cost of fringe benefits.

The supply side of the model is straightforward. As emphasized earlier, workers are assumed to be homogeneous while w and G are assumed to be perfectly substitutable at a rate of λ dollars per unit of G. As a result, the market supply of labor depends upon $w + \lambda G$. Because workers are assumed homogeneous, the supply curve depicted as a function of w is horizontal and shifts down as G is increased according to the following equation.

$$w^s = \gamma - \lambda G, \tag{7}$$

where w^s is the asking wage and γ (>0) and λ (>0) are parameters. Figure 5 depicts the supply curves.

The competitive market equilibrium is the solution that maximizes the sum total of the surpluses for both employers and employees. The process of reaching this equilibrium involves two steps. First, the market optimizes on the E associated with various quantities of G. This optimization generates a locus of the intersections of demand and supply curves corresponding to different values of G. Second, the market chooses the optimum quantity of G by equating the marginal cost of G with its marginal value. By doing so, the market in effect selects a point on the intersection locus that maximizes the sum of the surpluses. Figure 6 depicts the demand and supply curves together for three different levels of G as well as the corresponding intersection points on the intersection locus L.

The market equilibrium—the intersection of demand and supply that maximizes the joint surplus Z—is obtained by solving the following optimization problem:

$$\text{Max}_{E, G} Z = \int_0^E \left[w^d(\varepsilon) - w^s(\varepsilon) \right] d\varepsilon \tag{8}$$

$$= \left[\alpha - \left(\eta G + \rho G^2 \right) - \gamma + \lambda G \right] E + 0.5\beta E^2 + \text{Constant}.$$

Figure 4 Demand Curves

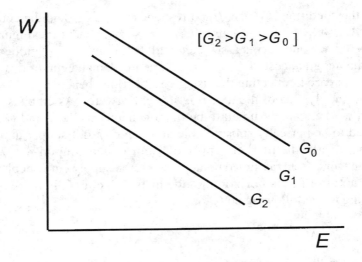

Figure 5 Supply Curves

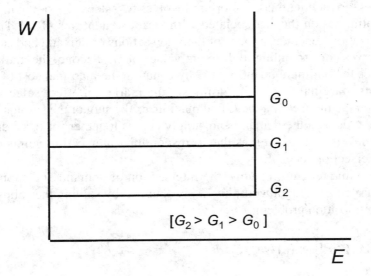

The first order conditions are given by

$$\partial Z / \partial E = \alpha - \left(\eta G + \rho G^2\right) - \gamma + \lambda G + \beta E = 0 \quad \text{and} \tag{9a}$$

$$\partial Z / \partial G = -\left[\eta + 2\rho G - 0.5(d\beta / dG)E\right]E + \lambda E = 0 \tag{9b}$$

Equation 9a optimizes Z with respect to E, resulting in a locus of intersections between the demand and supply curves for different values of G. Equation 9b optimizes on G, equating the marginal cost (the first term) with the marginal value (the second term). Equations 9a and 9b together describe the point of market equilibrium.[3]

Figure 7 portrays the market equilibrium for three cases: no cross-scale effects ($d\beta/dG = 0$) cross-economies of scale ($d\beta/dG > 0$), and cross-diseconomies of scale ($d\beta/dG < 0$). The L curve is the locus of the intersections of the demand and supply curves for the different levels of G. There is a unique L curve associated with each of these three values of $d\beta/dG$; however, in Figure 7, only one L curve is depicted to conserve space. Moving downward along this locus, G is increased and w is decreased. We should point out that the market equilibrium level of employment is not necessarily at its maximum attainable level. In particular, Figure 7 shows that if there are cross-scale effects ($d\beta/dG \neq 0$), equilibrium employment is less than the maximum feasible level of employment on the relevant L curve.[4] Only in the absence of cross-scale effects ($d\beta/dG = 0$) is equilibrium employment at its maximum feasible level (see Appendix C for a proof).

We are now in a position to evaluate the effects of nonwage payments on employment. Since G is endogenous in our model, changes in its magnitude must be traced to changes in worker demand for, and the cost of, G. These exogenous factors are represented by λ and η, respectively. In addition, we evaluate the effects of changes in legally required fringe benefits on employment and wages.

Changes in the Demand for G

A secular increase in nonwage payments can arise as a result of an increase in the demand for fringe benefits. Such an increase in demand occurs if, for example, a new law taxes nonwage benefits less heavily than wage earnings or if real income grows and fringe benefits are

Figure 6 Intersection Locus

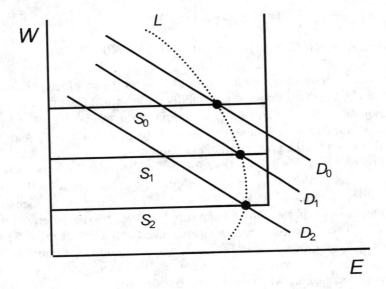

Figure 7 Market Equilibria

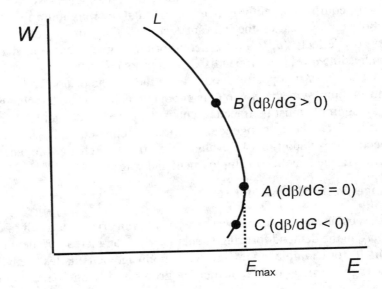

superior goods. An increased demand for G is represented by an increase in λ, yielding the following comparative statics results:

$$dG/d\lambda = (1/|H|)[-\beta + 0.5G(d\beta/dG)]E \qquad (10a)$$

$$dE/d\lambda = (1/|H|)[2\rho G + 0.5E(d\beta/dG)]E, \qquad (10b)$$

Clearly, if there are no cross-scale effects ($d\beta/dG = 0$)or if there are cross-economies of scale ($d\beta/dG > 0$), both equations are positive so that both G and E increase with λ. In other words, an increase in worker demand for fringe benefits increases both the amount of benefits provided and the level of employment. If a secular increase in non-wage payments is the result of an increased demand for these payments, such an increase in benefits should have the effect of stimulating employment.

If there are cross-diseconomies of scale ($d\beta/dG < 0$), conditions 10a and 10b seem to suggest that either G or E or both could decrease when λ increases. Such an outcome seems implausible, however, because it would imply that, as employers expand G in response to the increased demand for it, cross-diseconomies cause the cost of providing fringe benefits to rise, forcing employers to reduce the quantities of both G and E. For cross-diseconomies to remain operative, however, the aggregate amount of G must rise. On the basis of this argument, we conjecture that G, and possibly E, increase even in this case.

Because $w^d = w^s = w$ at the point of equilibrium, the effect on the wage is ascertained by evaluating the effect of a change in λ on w^s, or

$$dw/d\lambda = -\lambda(dG/d\lambda) - G \qquad (10c)$$

Equation 10 implies that, if G and E increase in response to an increase in the demand for G, then $dw/d\lambda$ is negative and the wage falls. Employees, in effect, trade their wages for larger benefits.

Changes in the Cost of G

Nonwage payments may also increase as a result of a decrease in the cost of providing fringe benefits. A change in the cost of G is represented here by a change in η. Not surprisingly, the comparative statics analysis reveals that cost effects are mirror images of demand effects. In other words,

$$dG / d\eta = -(1/|H|)[-\beta + 0.5G(d\beta / dG)]E = -dG / d\lambda \text{ and} \qquad (11a)$$

$$dE / d\eta = -(1/|H|)[2\rho G + 0.5G(d\beta / dG)]E = -dE / d\lambda. \qquad (11b)$$

If $(d\beta/dG \geq 0)$ both G and E increase when η falls. Thus, if the observed increase in nonwage benefits is the result of a decrease in the cost of providing benefits, employment as well as benefits should rise. As in the case of increased demand for fringe benefits, even if there are cross-diseconomies $(d\beta/dG < 0)$, we conjecture that G, and possibly E, increase when costs fall.

The wage effect is evaluated from the following equation:

$$dw / d\eta = \lambda(dG\ d\eta). \qquad (11c)$$

The term $dw / d\eta$ is positive when $(d\beta/dG \geq 0)$. If a decrease in η is the cause of the observed increase in nonwage payments, then, as G and E increase in response, w should decrease.

Effects of Government Control of G

As Figure 1 demonstrates, legally required benefits have risen over time. If a government regulates the quantity of employer provided fringe benefits, then G in the previous analysis is replaced by the mandated quantity, $\overline{G}$. Given that $dw / d\overline{G} = -\lambda < 0$, it is clear that the wage will fall unambiguously when $\overline{G}$ is increased. The effect on employment is not clear-cut, however.

To begin, E is now the only endogenous variable, making $\partial Z / \partial E = 0$ the only first-order condition. This first-order condition yields the following optimum level of employment:[5]

$$(d\beta / dG < 0),$$

$$E^* = \left[\alpha - \left(\eta\overline{G} + \rho\overline{G}^2\right) - \gamma + \lambda\overline{G}\right]/(-\beta). \tag{12}$$

The effect of an increased $\overline{G}$ on employment is given by

$$dE^*/d\overline{G} = \left(\eta + 2\rho\overline{G} - \lambda\right)/\beta \tag{13}$$
$$+ \left(d\beta/dG\right) \times (\text{a positive term}).$$

Suppose the market is initially at its competitive equilibrium so that $\overline{G} = G^*$, where G^* is the competitive equilibrium level of the benefits. In this case, the term $\left(\eta + 2\rho\overline{G} - \lambda\right)/\beta\gamma$ is zero because $\left(\eta + 2\rho\overline{G}\right)$ and λ are, respectively, the marginal cost and marginal value of G. We already know that in the absence of cross-scale effects $(d\beta/dG = 0)$, the competitive equilibrium corresponds to the maximum feasible level of employment.[6] It is clear, therefore, that the introduction of legally required benefits lowers employment regardless of whether the mandated $\overline{G}$ is larger or smaller than G^*. In other words, there is little that the government can do to increase employment by regulating G.

If there are cross-economies of scale $\left(d\beta/dG > 0\right)$, employment increases because $dE^*/d\overline{G} = (d\beta/dG) \times (\text{a positive term}) > 0$. The government in effect forces the market to experience cross-economies of scale beyond what is efficient. If there are cross-diseconomies of scale $(d\beta/dG < 0)$, employment decreases because $dE^*/d\overline{G} = (d\beta/dG) \times (\text{a positive term}) < 0$. In this case, the government in effect forces the market to experience cross-diseconomies beyond what is efficient.

Now assume that legally required fringe benefits already exist. What happens to employment if $\overline{G}$ is increased? Consider the case of no cross-scale effects $(d\beta/dG = 0)$. If $\overline{G}$ is already set above the market equilibrium level, then the marginal cost is above the marginal revenue so that $(\eta + 2\rho\overline{G}) > \lambda$. As a result, $dE^*/d\overline{G} < 0$, implying that employment decreases when $\overline{G}$ is increased. On the other hand, if $\overline{G}$ is initially set below the market equilibrium level, then the marginal cost is lower than the marginal revenue so that $(\eta + 2\rho G) < \lambda$. As a result, $dE^*/d\overline{G} > 0$, implying that employment increases when $\overline{G}$ is increased. With respect to the latter of these policy moves, the government forces G to move closer to the market equilibrium level.

Allowing cross-scale effects to exist complicates the analysis. Suppose there are cross-economies of scale ($d\beta/dG > 0$). If $\overline{G}$ is initially set above the competitive market level, then the effect of changes in employment of changes in $\overline{G}$ is ambiguous given that $dE*/dG$ cannot be signed. In this case, there are opposing forces at work. On one hand, the government forces $\overline{G}$ to increase beyond its already inefficiently high level, thereby adversely affecting employment. On the other hand, an increase in $\overline{G}$ forces the market to enjoy cross-economies of scale, thereby positively affecting employment. The net outcome depends upon the relative strength of the opposing forces. If $\overline{G}$ is initially below the competitive market level, then employment unambiguously increases because $dE*/d\overline{G} < 0$. In this case, the government forces the market to move towards the competitive level of G, thereby reinforcing the stimulating effect on employment originating from cross-economies of scale.

Turning to the case of cross-diseconomies of scale ($d\beta/dG < 0$), if $\overline{G}$ is initially above the competitive market level, then employment declines unambiguously when $\overline{G}$ is increased because ($d\beta/dG < 0$). In this case, the government forces $\overline{G}$ to move further away from the competitive equilibrium, thereby reinforcing the disemployment effect caused by cross-diseconomies of scale. If $\overline{G}$ is initially below the competitive market level, then employment effects are ambiguous given that $dE*/d\overline{G}$ cannot be signed. The government forces $\overline{G}$ closer to the market equilibrium level, causing employment to expand, but cross-diseconomies of scale cause employment to decline. The net effect is uncertain.

To summarize, if an increase in nonwage payments is caused by an increase in the legally required benefits, wages fall unambiguously; however, employment effects are ambiguous. An important result is that, even in the case of an exogenous increase in legally required fringe benefits, employment can increase rather than decrease as conventionally thought. Whatever happens to employment, an increase in legally mandated fringe benefits tends to be inefficient. An exception is when the fringe benefits level is initially set below the competitive equilibrium level. In this case, it is obvious that an increase in fringe benefits increases efficiency so long as the increase does not overshoot the competitive equilibrium level.

AN EXTENSION: A MODEL WITH OVERTIME HOURS

Previous analyses assume that the relevant range of hours of work includes only the standard hours, omitting consideration of overtime hours and the potential ramifications of the overtime wage premium. Our model may be extended by assuming that the equilibrium number of hours of work incorporates overtime hours. Such an extension is important if exogenous changes in nonwage payments affect the marginal cost of increasing the labor input via increases in the hours of work beyond the standard hours. We are also interested in the effects of changes in the standard hours (or in the overtime wage premium) on employment and fringe benefits. For a fuller exposition on the technical aspects of such an extended model, the reader is referred to a companion paper (Hashimoto and Zhao 1996). Here, we simply outline some of the key predictions that emerge from this extended analysis.

The predictions discussed in the preceding section are generally unchanged in the extended model. We do, however, obtain additional predictions. First, suppose the government increases the standard hours of work. If there are no cross-scale effects, neither fringe benefits nor hours of work are affected by the changes in standard hours. Employment increases if the positive effect of the increased standard hours on labor demand dominates the negative effect on labor supply; it decreases otherwise. The effects on hours of work and fringe benefits depend on how the slope of the labor demand curve, β, changes. The straight-time wage rate rises as a result of an upward shift of the worker supply curve. The effects of an increase in the overtime wage rate are opposite of the effects of an increase in standard hours.

CONCLUSION

The importance of nonwage payments has risen noticeably in the United States over the past 40 years. Contributing to this trend are increases in both voluntarily provided and legally required fringe benefits. Furthermore, since the early 1980s, the growth of the voluntary component has outpaced that of legally required component. These developments suggest the importance of evaluating how employment and wages are affected by the demand and supply forces that lead to increases in voluntarily provided fringe benefits. This chapter has addressed this issue. We find that predictions based upon the conventional firm-level analysis in which nonwage payments are assumed to be exogenous are misleading. In particular, contrary to the conventional wisdom, an increase in nonwage payments does not necessarily imply any adverse effects on employment and wages.

This outcome depends jointly on the source of the increase and the existence of cross-scale effects in the cost of providing fringe benefits. If the increase in nonwage payments is the result of either an increase in employee demand for fringe benefits or a decrease in the cost of providing benefits, employment may increase and the wage rate may decrease. More importantly, employment effects are ambiguous even when legally mandated fringe benefits are involved. To be sure, wages always fall when legally required fringe benefits are increased; however, employment may fall or rise depending on the initial condition and the existence and the nature of cross-scale effects.

In the special case in which there are no cross-diseconomies of scale, there is no presumption that an increase in nonwage benefits reduces employment so long as competitive market forces are responsible for such an increase. If new legally required fringe benefits are introduced into a labor market that is already at a competitive equilibrium, employment decreases regardless of whether the mandate is to increase or decrease such benefits. In this case, a government cannot increase employment by manipulating the levels of legally required fringe benefits.

Incorporating the distinction between standard hours of work and overtime hours of work does not change these results. Not surprisingly, we find that there is a symmetry of effects with respect to the standard hours and the overtime premium. In particular, the effects of increased standard hours of work on employment, wages, and fringe benefits are opposite of the effects of an increased overtime premium.

We end with a discussion of some of the restrictions and limitations imposed on the analysis of this paper. Relaxing these would undoubtedly make the model more complete. Given, however, that our objective is to demonstrate that making nonwage payments endogenous changes some of the conventional results, we have chosen to use a simplified model here. In any event, four limitations warrant mention.

First, we abstract from the worker's choice of the number of hours to work. Incorporating such a decision, while making the model more complete, would greatly complicate our analysis. The same may be said with respect to the second limitation of our analysis—namely, our treatment of all nonwage labor as quasi-fixed benefits that are independent of the number of hours of work. Thus, we are talking about a quasi-fixed wage component that is approximately 20 percent of total labor compensation. Third, we abstract from higher order terms in the linearly specified demand and supply functions. More complicated specifications of the demand and supply curves may be desirable, although such extensions are likely to make the predictions ambiguous. Fourth, we assume that all employees are homogeneous with respect to the marginal value of fringe benefits. If they were made heterogeneous, the supply specification would need to incorporate distribution parameters determining the taste for fringe benefits. Relaxing these four restrictions is the subject of future research. In this chapter, however, our goal is simply to demonstrate that some of the conventional predictions are modified once analysis is conducted in a more general equilibrium framework.

Notes

I thank Ronald G. Ehrenberg, Susan N. Houseman, Todd Idson, Jacob Mincer, Hajime Miyazaki, James Peck, Sherwin Rosen, Jingang Zhao, and participants at the Labor Economics Seminar at Columbia University and the 1995 Seventh World Congress of the Econometric Society for useful comments and suggestions. I also thank Tracy Foertsch for research assistance.

1. When models of employment-hours decisions are expanded to allow for changes in capital, many of the results concerning hours become ambiguous; however, the fixed-cost effect on employment remains intact (Hamermesh 1993; Hart 1984).
2. Almost all existing analyses focus on the behavior of firms for which it is reasonable to assume that fringe benefits are strictly exogenous. For example, see Rosen (1968), Ehrenberg (1971), Hamermesh (1993), and Hart (1984).

3. The second order conditions are given by $\partial^2 Z / \partial G^2 = -2\rho E < 0$ and $|H| = -2\beta\rho E - \left[0.5E(d\beta / dG)\right]^2 > 0,$ and where $|H|$ is the determinant of the Hessian matrix. It is straightforward to show that if the demand curves are all parallel to one another, i.e., $d\beta / dG = 0$, the above conditions are implied by the assumptions made with regard to the demand and supply curves. If they are not parallel, these conditions must be imposed on the model.

4. Since the L curve is unique to the value of dB/dG, the maximum employment level is different for each case.

5. The equilibrium point corresponds to the intersection of the respective demand and supply curves. The second order condition is satisfied because $\partial^2 Z^* / \partial E^2 = \beta < 0$.

6. This can be seen from $d^2 E / \left(d\overline{G}\right)^2 = 2\rho / \beta < 0$ when $\overline{G} = G^*$.

References

Chamber of Commerce of the United States. Various years. *Employee Benefits*. Washington D.C.: Chamber of Commerce of the United States.

_____. 1981. *Employee Benefits Historical Data, 1951–1979*. Washington, D.C.: Chamber of Commerce of the United States.

Ehrenberg, Ronald G. 1971. *Fringe Benefits and Overtime Behavior*. Lexington: Lexington Books.

Hamermesh, Daniel S. 1993. *Labor Demand*. Princeton: Princeton University Press.

Hart, Robert A. 1984. *The Economics of Non-Wage Labor Costs*. London: George Allen and Unwin.

Hart, Robert A., David N.F. Bell, Rudolf Frees, Seichi Kawsaki, and Stephen A. Woodbury. 1988. *Trends in Non-Wage Labor Costs and Their Effects on Employment*. Brussels-Luxembourg: Commission of the European Communities.

Hashimoto, Masanori and Jingang Zhao. 1996. "Non-Wage Compensation, Employment and Hours." Unpublished manuscript, Ohio State University.

Nathan, Felicia. 1987. "Analyzing Employers' Costs for Wages, Salaries, and Benefits." *Monthly Labor Review* 110(October)3–11.

Rosen, Sherwin. 1968. "Short-Employment Variation on Class-I Railroads in the US, 1947–1963." *Econometrica* 36: 511–529.

Woodbury, Stephen A. 1983. "Substitution between Wage and Nonwage Benefits." *American Economic Review* 73(1): 166–182.

United States Department of Labor, Bureau of Labor Statistics. Employment Cost Indexes, 1975–1993. Bulletins 2319, 2413, 2434. Washington, D.C.: U.S. Government Printing Office.

_____. BLS Handbook of Methods. Bulletin 2414. Washington, D.C.:
U.S. Government Printing Office.

_____. Employee Compensation in the Private, Nonfarm Economy, 1974.
Bulletin 1963. Washington, D.C.: U.S. Government Printing Office.

Appendix A

Table A, an extension of Table 1 in Woodbury (1983), gives the data on which Figure 1 is based. This appendix describes the procedures used to compute the entries in Table A and in Table 1 of the text. To simplify our exposition, we begin with a discussion of the construction of Table A.

Woodbury used two sources in demonstrating the growth of employee benefits from 1965 to 1978: the U.S. Chamber of Commerce publication *Employee Benefits* (various years) and the Bureau of Labor Statistics (BLS) bulletin *Employee Compensation in the Private, Nonfarm Economy* (1974). It is helpful to discuss each of these sources individually.

The data available in *Employee Compensation in the Private, Nonfarm Economy* is the product of the Employer Expenditures for Employee Compensation survey (EEEC). This survey was discontinued in 1977; however, beginning in March of 1987, the BLS started publication of *Employment Cost Indexes and Levels* (ECI), which includes a measure of "Employer Costs for Employee Compensation."[1] The data provided under this heading appears to be comparable to that provided in the older publication, from which Table 1 in Woodbury (1983) is derived. The one significant difference stressed in Nathan (1987) concerns its means of measuring these costs. In particular, the EEEC focuses upon *past expenditures*—or, the actual money an employer spends on compensation during a specified time. The compensation levels given in the new BLS publication rely upon *current costs*—or, the annual costs based upon the current price of benefits under current plan provisions. Aside from this measurement difference, however, the ECI and EEEC appear quite similar, with both covering virtually the same benefits and, more importantly, reporting costs on the same per hour basis.[2] In addition, the ECI preserves the scope of the EEEC by reporting survey coverage of the private, nonfarm workforce.

Derivation of the entries given in the last three columns of Table A simply entails the application of the per hour costs reported in the ECI to the definitions utilized by Woodbury in his calculations. These per hour costs are subsequently expressed as a percent of total compensation per hour and indexed to equal 100 in 1966.

With respect to the Chamber of Commerce data, a comparison of this table with that of Woodbury shows that the pre-1983 entries have been recalculated. This is done for reasons of data availability. In particular, the Table 19 that Woodbury used to construct his numbers is no longer included in *Employee Benefits*. To construct similar numbers for this table, it is necessary to use other sources within the publication. Two of these are selected. The first is a table giving wage data by industry (Table 17 in 1967 and 1969, Table 18 through

Table A Trends in Wage and Nonwage Compensation, 1951–1995
(benefits expressed as indices of % total compensation)

	Compensation (Chamber of Commerce, 1951=100)			Compensation (BLS, 1966=100)		
	Total comp. per hr. ($)[a]	Benefits		Total comp. per hr. ($)[a]	Benefits	
		Legally required	Voluntary[b]		Legally required	Voluntary[b]
1951	1.88	100.00	100.00			
1953	2.02	93.10	118.46			
1955	2.15	102.19	127.18			
1957	2.43	103.13	133.68			
1959	2.72	115.36	131.97			
1961	2.85	131.97	143.93			
1963	3.12	150.78	147.86			
1965	3.33	131.66	138.63			
1966				3.43	100.00	100.00
1967	3.57	157.99	148.38			
1968				3.90	92.76	115.45
1969	4.09	168.65	150.43			
1970				4.54	96.57	127.68
1971	4.69	167.08	174.87			
1972				5.23	105.52	139.48
1973	5.65	199.69	175.56			
1974				6.32	120.57	156.22
1975[c]	6.63	208.15	190.77			
1977	7.60	214.42	207.01			
1979	9.06	228.53	203.76			
1980	9.85	222.88	204.79			
1982	12.08	233.54	198.12			
1984	13.00	238.87	216.92			
1986	15.89	222.38	229.06			

	Compensation (Chamber of Commerce, 1951=100)			Compensation (BLS, 1966=100)		
	Total comp. per hr, ($)[a]	Benefits		Total comp. per hr. ($)[a]	Benefits	
		Legally required	Voluntary[b]		Legally required	Voluntary[b]
1987	16.49	226.33	222.91	13.40	157.71	195.28
1988	17.44	224.76	209.74	13.77	165.90	194.85
1989	18.41	217.87	218.29	14.26	167.05	194.21
1990	19.64	220.38	228.03	14.93	168.38	197.00
1991	20.51	220.06	239.15	15.37	169.71	203.86
1992	20.81	226.02	241.54	16.11	171.43	213.09
1993	22.67	209.09	259.32	16.68	173.52	221.24
1994	22.66	214.42	264.79	17.09	177.14	225.97
1995				17.07	174.10	212.45

[a] Total Compensation includes legally required contributions to Social Security, federal and state unemployment insurance, and Workers' Compensation.

[b] Benefits provided voluntarily by the employer include private insurance (life, health, and accidental), privately sponsored retirement and savings plans (pensions, savings and thrift plans), as well as other items (severance pay, supplemental unemployment benefits, and other miscellaneous benefits).

[c] Comparable BLS benefits data are unavailable for the period extending from 1975–1986.

1984, Table 16 after 1988); the second is a chart detailing average annual employee benefits and earnings (Chart 2 in all publications). The first of these, Table 16, gives average gross payroll for all private industries included in the survey not only on an annual basis but also on an hourly basis. That gross payroll is expressed on a per hour basis is important because such a frequency makes it possible to construct entries that are compatible with those provided by Woodbury (1983). Chart 2 categorizes employee benefits and earnings in the following manner: 1) benefits are the sum of outside payroll and inside payroll. Inside payroll encompasses paid vacations and holidays, employee rest periods, and lunch breaks; outside payroll is made up of legally required payments, pensions, insurance, and other agreed upon items, and other benefits; and 2) earnings include total pay for all time worked; they comprise straight-time and premium-time pay, a shift differential, production bonuses, and other agreed upon items.

It should be noted that Woodbury could easily make comparisons among his entries for the various years because the Table 19 he used in their construction was a summary of employee benefits for only those companies submitting data over the entire interval of 1957–1977. The entries given in Table A are constructed for all companies reporting data in the various years listed. Because of changes in the number and composition of companies reporting benefits between 1951 and 1992 ($N = 736$ and $N = 1194$, respectively), these entries are not strictly comparable. They do, however, indicate the trend in benefits over time. In addition, Woodbury's calculations for supplements (% of total) in 1967 through 1977 are larger because the average benefits of the few companies included in the old Table 19 are somewhat higher than those for the full sample. The reason for this lies in the fact that those companies reporting over the entire period have larger, more established benefits programs than those companies included in the full sample but excluded from the Table 19 sample.

A two-step procedure is utilized to construct the entries shown in the first three columns of Table A. To begin, the information in Table 16 regarding average annual and average hourly gross payroll is used to determine the average number of hours for which an employee is paid. Given this information, Chart 2 is employed to determine the average benefits received per hour per employee.[3] After calculating such benefits on per hour basis, these are applied to Woodbury's definitions of the three entries; the results reported in Table A are expressed as a percent of total compensation per hour and are indexed to equal 100 in 1951.

The entries given in Table 1 of the text are derived in a similar manner. In this case, however, we take from Table 7 of the *Employee Benefits* publications estimates of the average hourly employer contributions to the following components of legally required, voluntary, and inside payroll labor costs:[4] 1) Social Security, workers' compensation, and other legally required benefits (unemployment insurance, state sickness benefits, etc.); 2) pension plan premiums and retirement savings plan contributions; contributions to employee life, death, and medical (and medically related) insurance, as well as miscellaneous voluntary benefits (supplemental unemployment insurance, employee discounts on company goods and services, employee meals, childcare, and other benefits payments); and 3) paid rest (coffee and meal breaks, setup and wash up time, travel time, etc.) and paid leave (paid vacations and holidays, sick leave, parental leave, etc.). These benefit costs per hour are in turn expressed as a percent of total compensation per hour using data from the first column of Table A; the results are subsequently indexed to equal 100 in 1951.

Notes

1. The ECI was only implemented in stages. Beginning in 1976, published statistics covered only quarterly changes in wages and salaries of private, nonfarm workers. In 1978, the BLS expanded the survey to include 13 additional statistical series (e.g., union/nonunion, manufacturing/nonmanufacturing); by 1980, it had incorporated into the survey the publication of quarterly changes in total employee compensation. What the *BLS Handbook of Methods* (Chapter 8, p. 56) terms the third stage in the development of the ECI involved the expansion of the survey to state and local (not federal) government employees. Finally, the most recent development in the ECI involves the inclusion of actual compensation costs on a per hour basis; the BLS has included these measures in the ECI since March of 1987.

2. These benefits include paid leave (vacations, holidays, sick leave, and other), supplemental pay (premium pay for overtime and for work on weekends and holidays, nonproduction bonuses), insurance benefits (life, health, sickness and accident insurance), retirement and savings benefits (pension and other retirement plans, savings and thrift plans), legally required benefits (Social Security, Workers' Compensation, Unemployment Insurance, and other), and other benefits (severance pay, supplemental unemployment plans, and employee merchandise discounts in department stores).

3. In other words, average benefits received per hour equal the ratio of average annual benefits to average hours for which the employee is paid per year.

4. All entries after 1979 are computed from Table 7 of the *Employee Benefits* publication (Chamber of Commerce of the United States, various years) for the corresponding year; all pre-1980 entries are computed from Table 7 of *Employee Benefits Historical Data, 1951–1979* (Chamber of Commerce of the United States 1981).

Appendix B

Derivation of Market Labor Demand Function

Assume that F and C are both quadratic as follows:

$$F(n) = 1/2\, F_{11}n^2 + \theta_1 n + \theta_0,$$

$$C(G,n) = 1/2\, C_{11}G^2 + C_{12}Gn + \phi_1 G + \phi_2 n + \phi_0.$$

We first show that the individual labor demand functions have the following form:

$$n = \frac{1}{\Delta}(w - \Omega), \tag{B1}$$

where

$$\Delta = pF_{11} - 2(C_{12}G + \phi_2),$$

$$\Omega = p(F_n - F_{11} \cdot n) - \left(1/2\, C_{11}G^2 + \phi_1 G + \phi_0\right).$$

To prove the above, note that we have the following expressions:

$$F_n = \frac{\partial F}{\partial n} = F_{11}n + \theta_1 > 0,$$

$$C_1 = \frac{\partial C}{\partial G} = C_{11}G + C_{12}n + \phi_1 > 0,$$

$$C_2 = \frac{\partial C}{\partial n} = C_{12}G + \phi_2 \gtrless 0.$$

Now, the firm's labor demand function given by Eq. 4a* is expanded so that

$$w = pF_n - (C + nC_2)$$
$$= \left\{ pF_n - \left[1/2\,C_{11}G^2 + C_{12}Gn + \phi_1 G + \phi_2 n + \phi_0 + n(C_{12}G + \phi_2) \right] \right\}$$
$$= \left\{ pF_n - \left(1/2\,C_{11}G^2 + \phi_1 G + \phi_0 \right) - 2(C_{12}G + \phi_2)n \right\}$$
$$= \left\{ p(F_n - F_{11}n) - \left(1/2\,C_{11}G^2 + \phi_1 G + \phi_0 \right) + [p \cdot F_{11} - 2(C_{12}G + \phi_2)]n \right\}$$
$$= (\Omega + \Delta n).$$

As a result,

$$n = \frac{1}{\Delta}(w - \Omega) \tag{B2}$$
$$= \frac{w - p(F_n - F_{11} \cdot n) + \left(1/2\,C_{11}G^2 + \phi_1 G + \phi_0 \right)}{pF_{11} - 2(C_{12}G + \phi_2)}$$

is the firm's new labor demand function. Note that

$$F_n - F_{11}n = \theta_1,$$

so that the right hand side of Eq. B2 is a function of w, parameterized by G and p.

Next, we show that if all K firms are identical and if the price feedback is given by $p = p(E)$, $p' < 0$, , where $E = Kn$, then the inverse market labor demand function has the form

$$w = \tau(G) + \beta(G)E + \varepsilon(G, E), \tag{B3}$$

where

$$\tau(G) = \left[const. - 1/2\,C_{11}G^2 - \phi_1 G \right], \tag{B4}$$

$$\beta(G) = [const. - 2C_{12}G + Kp'\theta_1], \tag{B5}$$

and $\varepsilon(G,E)$ is an error term.

To prove the above, note that since $p = p(E)$ is a function of E, the right-hand side of Eq. B2 contains the term E. This implies that the market labor demand function cannot be obtained by simply multiplying Eq. B2 by K. Instead, one must first gather all the E terms on the left-hand side as follows:

Multiplying Eq. B2 by K, we have

$$E = n \cdot K = \frac{K}{\Delta}(w - \Omega).$$

As such,

$$Kw = \Delta E + K\Omega$$

$$= E[pF_{11} - 2(C_{12}G + \phi_2)] + K\left[p(F_n - F_{11}n) - \left(1/2\, C_{11}G^2 + \phi_1 G + \phi_0\right)\right]$$

$$= -\left(1/2\, C_{11}G^2 + \phi_1 G + \phi_0\right)K - 2(C_{12}G + \phi_2)E + KF_n \cdot p(E).$$

Substituting $F_n = F_{11}n + \theta_1$, and $p(E) = p_0 + p'E + \ldots$ into the above expression, we obtain

$$w = const. - 1/2\, C_{11}G^2 - \phi_1 G$$

$$+ \frac{(const. - 2C_{12}G + K \cdot p'\theta_1)E}{K} + \varepsilon(G, E)$$

$$= \tau(G) + \beta(G)E + \varepsilon(G, E),$$

where $\varepsilon(G,E)$ is an error term containing all higher order terms of E. Letting $\tau(G) = a_0 + a(G)$, we have $a(G) = (const. - 1/2\, C_{11}G^2 - \phi_1 G)$. Thus

$$\frac{\partial \tau}{\partial G} = -(C_{11}G + \phi_1), \frac{\partial \tau^2}{\partial G^2} = -C_{11} < 0, \tag{B6}$$

$$\frac{\partial \beta}{\partial G} = \frac{-2C_{12}}{K} \tag{B7}$$

Note that Eq. B3 is approximated by Eq. 5 as $w^d = \alpha - (\eta G + \rho G^2) + \beta(G)E$.

Appendix C

This appendix describes the logic behind Figure 7. Let us first prove the proposition that the competitive equilibrium occurs at the maximum feasible level of employment on the L curve only when $d\beta/dG = 0$. By solving Eq. 9a for E and computing $dE/dG = 0$ to select the maximum employment point, we obtain

$$(\eta + 2\rho G - \lambda) - E(d\beta/dG) = 0. \tag{C1}$$

Now, the competitive equilibrium point on the L curve is now obtained by combining Equations 9a and 9b to obtain

$$(\eta + 2\rho G - \lambda) - 0.5E(d\beta/dG) = 0. \tag{C2}$$

Clearly, Equations C1 and C2 are equivalent only when $d\beta/dG = 0$; therefore, the competitive equilibrium employment level is the maximum employment level only when $d\beta/dG = 0$.

We now demonstrate the locations of points A, B, and C in Figure 7. Rearranging Eq. 9b, we obtain

$$(\eta + 2\rho G - \lambda) = 0.5E(d\beta/dG) = 0. \tag{C3}$$

Assuming that $d^2\beta/dG^2 = 0$, an increase in G increases the left-hand side of Eq. C3; as a result, the right-hand side must also increase. If $d\beta/dG > 0$, the right-hand side will increase only when E rises. This result implies that, in this case, we are at point B in Figure 7. Similarly, if $d\beta/dG < 0$, E must decrease when G increases; in this case, we must be at point C in Figure 7.

Part III

Labor Market Adjustment
and Equity

6 Family Health Benefits and Worker Turnover

Dan A. Black
Syracuse University

One of the major differences between the labor markets in the United States and Canada lies in the treatment of health benefits. While Canada relies on government provision of health care, employers in the United States provide health insurance to most of the employed. The U.S. government's role is primarily to provide health insurance to those over 64 years of age through the Medicare system and to the poor through the Medicaid system. Despite the recent calls for health care reform in the United States, the reliance on employer-provided benefits appears to be a feature of the U.S. system for some time to come. The Clinton health care proposal of 1994 and the numerous Congressional alternatives rely on employer-provided health benefits.

In this chapter, I examine the impact of employer-provided health benefits on job turnover. I focus on a peculiar aspect of employer-provided health benefits: because many employer-provided plans extend coverage to a worker's entire family, the value of an employer's employment offer to a worker depends on whether the worker's spouse provides the family with health benefits. If a worker's spouse has employer-provided health insurance for his family, the worker will value employment offers with and without health insurance benefits differently than a worker whose spouse does not have employer-provided health benefits. Importantly, this distortion arises from the reliance on employer-provided benefits and is independent of any preexisting conditions clauses or issues concerning the portability of health plans. As I show in a later section (p. 273), this is potentially a large distortion. According to the April 1993 Supplement of the Current Population Survey (CPS), among full-time workers, at least 23 percent of the women and 12 percent of the men have coverage from their spouses.

REVIEW OF THE LITERATURE

There is no obvious reason why employers should provide health benefits. While health insurance is less expensive in groups, there is no particular reason the groups should be based on place of employment. Indeed, the initial growth in employer-provided health was the result of firms offering health insurance to their workers during World War II to avoid wage controls. As Long and Scott (1982) and Woodbury (1983) emphasized, the U.S. tax codes provide the major impetus for the employer provision of health and other benefits. The magnitudes of the tax savings are surprising. Consider a university in the Common-wealth of Kentucky that offers an insurance policy whose market value is $131 a month to a college professor who has a 28 percent marginal tax rate for the federal income tax (family income between $36,900 and $89,150 for married couples filing jointly). How much would it cost to increase the professor's after-tax income by $131 per month in 1993? Assuming the professor's wages are not over the social security cap of $57,600 and taking into account Kentucky's 6 percent state income tax and the deductibility of state income taxes from the federal tax bill, the university would have to pay more than $250 a month.

As a result of the substantial tax savings associated with the exemption of health benefits from federal and state taxation, employers have become the major providers of health benefits in the United States. The tax expenditures for the tax deductibility of employer health care premiums now exceed tax expenditures on the home mort-gage deduction.[1]

Economists have long recognized that the association of fringe benefits and employment may affect the employment relationship. Lazear (1979, 1981) argued that firms use defined-benefit pensions to defer compensation in jobs with agency problems or in jobs with large investments in specific human capital. In jobs with agency problems, the deferred compensation deters the worker from shirking; while, in jobs with specific human capital, the deferred compensation reduces job turnover.[2] Thus, employers in the United States may use their pension plans to improve the efficiency of labor contracts, an option that many Canadian employers do not have. Lazear and the literature that his papers generate (e.g., Ippolito 1985; Hutchens 1987; Dorsey 1987) recognized that deferred compensation is not without its costs and may have to be implemented with other policies such as restrictions on hours and mandatory retirement to mitigate those costs.[3]

Firms are not, however, perfectly able to tailor the parameters of their pension plans to meet contracting needs of individual employees. As Scott, Berger, and Black (1989) and Scott, Berger, and Garen (1995) emphasized, the U.S. Internal Revenue Service (IRS) requires firms to offer fringe benefits in a manner that does not discriminate against the firm's low-wage employees. If the firm wishes to offer an executive a defined-benefit pension plan that defers compensation, the firm must offer her secretary a similar plan. Thus, firms are not able to structure fringe benefit packages to match perfectly the optimal contract for each employee.

The requirement that fringe benefits be offered in a nondiscriminatory manner has a special bite in the provision of health benefits.[4] While firms may tie pension benefits to the earnings of the worker, the firm must offer all full-time workers the same health benefits, which has the predictable consequence that high-wage firms will avoid hiring low-wage workers (Scott, Berger, and Black 1989). Madrian (1994) identified another possible distortion that employer-provided health benefits create: the possibility that workers will be locked into their jobs because they or family members have preexisting conditions and would lose their medical coverage if they changed employers. Using the 1987 National Medical Expenditure Survey, she estimated that job lock reduces voluntary job turnover by 25 percent as compared with a system of perfectly portable health insurance. Madrian's results are controversial. Holtz-Eakin (1994) found no evidence of job lock.[5] If her results are correct, however, Madrian has identified a potentially important distortion in the U.S. labor market that employer-provided health insurance creates. Obviously, labor markets in Canada, with its perfectly portable health insurance, are free from such distortions.

Madrian argued that job lock arises from coverage gaps that preexisting conditions clauses and length-of-service provisions create. If a worker must wait, say, six months before being covered by a new employer's plan, then the worker may choose not to switch employers. Because this coverage gap is unrelated to the efficient allocation of labor, such a reduction in mobility is inefficient. She suggested that eliminating preexisting condition clauses and increasing the portability of health insurance would largely eliminate the inefficient reduction in job turnover. In the next section, I offer a theoretical model that challenges this suggestion. I show that when dual-earning couples consider employment offers, the value placed on a job offer will depend on the coverage of the spouse's health plan. As I demonstrate in the next section, this difference in valuation may explain the turnover pattern that Madrian uncovered.

JOB SEARCH WITH THE POTENTIAL FOR DOUBLE COVERAGE OF HEALTH BENEFITS

In this section, I construct a simple model to examine the impact of the double coverage of health benefits on labor turnover. To abstract from other issues, I will assume that there are no preexisting conditions provisions and no length-of-service provisions. If a worker finds employment at an alternative employer who is offering health insurance, the coverage begins immediately.

To begin, first consider a worker who has no spouse. The worker is currently employed at a firm paying wage w_0 and a health plan indexed by the value h_0. I assume that all health plans may be indexed by a single value, h, and that workers always strictly prefer plans with a greater h. Workers without health coverage have a plan with the value of $h_0 = 0$. Let the worker have a utility function $u(\bullet)$ that depends on the level of wages, w_0, and the level of health benefits, h_0, or

$$V^0 = u(w_0, h_0). \tag{1}$$

The value of current employment, V^0, forms the reservation utility for all subsequent employment offers. The worker has worked for the current employer for one period and will work, at most, one additional period for the employer. In Figure 1, I depict an indifference curve for

Figure 1 Indifference Curve for Worker's Utility Function

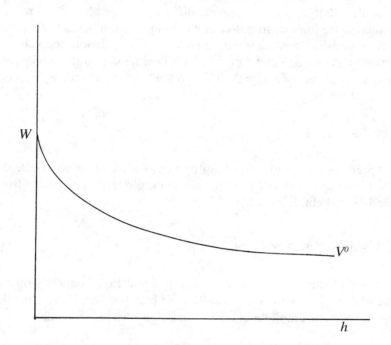

the worker's utility function as a convex function. If firms could individually tailor their fringe benefit packages to the needs of a worker, the worker would simply pick the amount of health benefits he desires. If the worker had adequate coverage from another source, he could simply elect to take all compensation as wages. Unfortunately, IRS regulations preclude such a design.

Before beginning employment in the second period, the worker entertains employment offers from other employers, which I assume are exogenously determined. The worker's utility in the second-period is

$$V = \max[u(w_a, h_a), V^0]. \tag{2}$$

where $u(w_a, h_a)$ is the utility associated with the best alternative offer. In Eq. 2, the set of acceptable offers is simply all combinations of (w, h)

that are above the indifference curve V^0 depicted in Figure 1. The probability that a worker leaves his current employer, therefore, depends on the joint distribution of wages and health benefits offered.

Now consider a worker with a spouse. Let h_s denote the value of the worker's coverage under his spouse's health plan. If the worker has no such coverage, then $h_s = 0$. The worker's utility from employment in the first period is

$$V^0 = u[w_0, \max(h_0, h_s)]. \tag{3}$$

Again, before beginning employment in the second period, the worker entertains offers from alternative employers. The utility from second-period employment is

$$V = \max\{u[w_a, \max(h_a, h_s)], V^0\}. \tag{4}$$

The value of the right-hand sides of Eq. 3 and Eq. 4 depends on the value of h_s. Spouse-provided health care benefits, therefore, alter the value of current employment and thus alter the value of alternative offers.

Figure 2 illustrates how the coverage by a spouse's plan affects the worker's job mobility decision. In Figure 2A, I consider the case where $h_s < h_0$, or the worker's own plan is more generous than his spouse's plan. The indifference curve V^0 denotes a worker's indifference curve if $h_s = 0$, with the point (w_0, h_0) denoting the worker's current contract. From Eq. 3, spouse-provided coverage $(h_0 > h_s > 0)$ clearly does not alter the value of current employment, but it may affect the value of alternative offers. To see why, consider the point (w_s, h_s), where w_s is implicitly defined as

$$V^0 = u(w_s, h_s). \tag{5}$$

The wage w_s leaves the worker indifferent to his current position and the job offering w_s and consuming his spouse's health insurance. Any job that pays a wage greater than w_s will be strictly preferred to his current position. Thus, the area under the indifference curve V^0 and above

**Figure 2 Indifference Curves for Worker's Utility Function When
(A) Worker's Own Benefits are More Generous ($h_s < h_0$)
and (B) Spouse's Benefits are More Generous ($h_s > h_0$)**

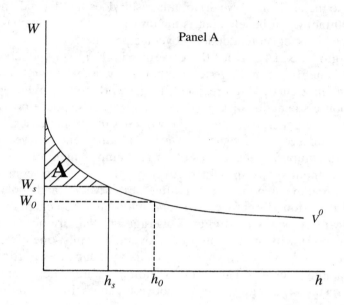

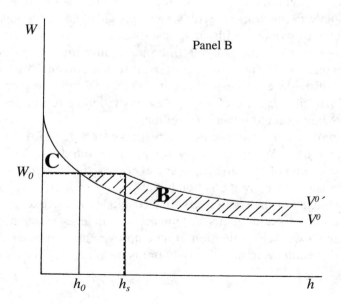

the wage w_s, denoted as A in Figure 2A, becomes a part of the set of acceptable offers. For workers with spouse-provided coverage, therefore, the likelihood of turnover unambiguously increases whenever $h_s < h_0$. Unlike the analysis of Madrian, this result does not depend on the lack of portability of benefits but is the direct result of the increase in the acceptable offer set that double coverage provides.

In Figure 2B, I consider the case in which $h_s > h_0$, where the spouse's benefits are more generous than the worker's own. Again, the indifference curve $V^{0'}$ corresponds to the worker without coverage by his spouse's benefits, or $h_s = 0$. When a worker's spouse provides access to more generous benefits, the worker's utility increases. The indifference curve $V^{0'}$, depicts the worker's indifference curve when $h_s > h_0$. In comparing the values of current employment of workers with and without spouse-provided coverage, there are two regions of interest. First, the area under the indifference curve $V^{0'}$ and above V^0, denoted as region B, represents offers that would be acceptable to workers without spouse-provided coverage but that are not acceptable to workers with spouse-provided coverage. Thus, one effect of spouse-provided coverage, when $h_s > h_0$, is to reduce this portion of the acceptable offer set. The second region of interest, however, offsets this result. The region that lies above w_0 and below the indifference curve V^0, denoted as region C, represents an area of offers that are acceptable to the workers with spouse-provided coverage but are unacceptable to workers without spouse-provided coverage. As the worker does not use his own health benefits, any job that offers a wage greater than w_0 is strictly preferred to his current situation, regardless of the level of health benefits associated with the job. For workers with $h_s > h_0$, therefore, spouse-provided coverage has an ambiguous impact on turnover probabilities.

My analysis has abstracted from the search decision of the worker's spouse. When allowing for joint search decisions, the worker's valuation of his current job and alternative offers depends not only on his spouse's current position but also her best alternative offer. While the impact of the spouse-provided coverage on a worker's turnover probabilities is ambiguous, the impact on efficiency is unambiguous—having a worker's valuation of an employment offer depend on his spouse's health insurance plan only limits the efficient allocation of labor.[6]

Of course, my analysis has not considered the possible responses of firms. One obvious response to double coverage is to offer employees the ability to select other benefits or cash in the place of health care benefits. The Revenue Act of 1978 permitted establishment of such cafeteria plans. The economic rationale for offering such plans is obvious: by allowing employees who already have other sources of coverage to select from other benefits or cash payments, firms may reduce their turnover.

Another way in which firms may counter the problem of dual coverage is to attempt to specialize in the hiring of workers of one type of coverage or another. For instance, a firm may seek to hire only workers with access to alternative forms of health care coverage by offering jobs with higher wages and no health benefits. Another firm may seek to specialize in the hiring of workers who wish to provide coverage to their entire families by offering low wages but a generous health plan with family coverage. See Dye and Antle (1984) for a model of such a separating equilibrium applied to fringe benefits.

COVERAGE, DOUBLE COVERAGE, AND REFUSAL OF EMPLOYER-PROVIDED HEALTH BENEFITS

In this section, I present an overview of employer-provided health benefits from the April 1993 Supplement to the CPS. The supplement provides detailed information about employee benefits. I limit my sample to workers between the ages of 18 and 64 for all of the tables. In addition, I report most statistics for full-time workers, which I define to be those who usually work at least 35 hours a week and those who work at least 47 weeks a year. I demonstrate that neither the use of cafeteria plans nor sorting strategies on the part of firms have solved the problem of double coverage. I show that a significant portion of the population has double coverage, that a surprising number of people turn down coverage, and that among those who turn down coverage, most do so without explicit compensation.

Nearly 90 percent of the male workers and 90 percent of the female workers have health insurance from some source (Table 1). For female workers, 88.0 percent reported that they are at a firm that offers

Table 1 Mean Coverage Rates for Employer-Provided Health Benefits for Full-Time Workers

Benefit situation	Female (%)	Male (%)
Covered by some form of health insurance	90.7	89.6
Employed at firm that offers health insurance	88.0	88.5
Eligible for employer-provided health insurance	83.7	85.0
Covered by employer-provided health insurance	72.5	79.5
Refused employer-provided health insurance	11.2	5.6
Covered by spouse's health insurance	22.0	10.7
Sample size	6,987	9,023

SOURCE: April 1993 Supplement to the CPS.

health insurance to at least some workers at the firm, and 88.5 percent of males responded similarly. Firms can place some restrictions on who may qualify for insurance. Often times, temporary, part-time, or leased employees may not be eligible for health benefits. Also, many firms require length-of-service requirements a worker must complete before qualifying for health benefits. To see who is and is not eligible for health benefits, I identify workers as eligible for health benefits if they reported that their firm offers health insurance to some of its workers and either reported that they received those benefits or explicitly stated that they declined those benefits. Using this definition, 83.7 percent of female workers and 85.0 percent of male workers reported that they are eligible for benefits.

Looking at the coverage rate of employer-provided health plans, 79.5 percent of all men but only 72.5 percent of women reported that they have employer-provided health benefits. Thus, gender differences in wages understate the true compensation difference. Nearly 8.2 percent of women and 10.1 percent of men do not receive health insurance from their employers but do receive it from another source. The differentials between the eligibility rates and the coverage rates suggest that many workers refuse health insurance coverage and, indeed, 11.2 percent of all women and 5.6 percent of all men decline coverage from their employers.[7] Among full-time workers, 22.0 percent of all women and 10.7 percent of all men reported that they have health insurance under their spouse's plan.[8]

The CPS Supplement also gives us an opportunity to examine another issue: the health insurance coverage of the self-employed. Folklore suggests that the spouses of the self-employed provide the health coverage for the family. I examine this issue in Table 2 by comparing the rate at which the spouses of the self-employed provide health insurance to their spouses as compared with the rate at which the spouses of wage and salary workers provided health insurance to their spouses. In Panel A we see no evidence supporting this folklore. The husbands' provision of health insurance to their wives is independent of their wives' self-employment status, which is surprising. In contrast, in Panel B wives are more likely to provide self-employed husbands with health insurance than are wives of wage and salary workers. Women with self-employed spouses are 66 percent more likely to provide their husbands with health insurance than are women whose spouses are not self-employed.

Table 2 Spouse's Provision of Employer-Provided Health Benefits by Self-Employment Status

Insurance provision	Spouse is not self-employed	Spouse is self-employed	n
Panel A: Husband's provision of health insurance to spouse by wife's self-employment status			
Husband does not provide spouse with employer-provided insurance	56.6%	56.3%	4006
Husband provides spouse with employer-provided insurance	43.4%	43.7%	3077
n	6387	696	7083
Panel B: Wife's provision of health insurance to spouse by husband's self-employment status			
Wife does not provide spouse with employer-provided insurance	84.5%	74.0%	7297
Wife does provides spouse with employer-provided insurance	15.5%	26.0%	1527
n	7314	1510	8824

SOURCE: April 1993 Supplement to the CPS.

The model presented in the previous section suggests that employees whose spouses also have employer-provided coverage may value job offers differently than employees whose spouses do not have such coverage. For dual coverage to have an important effect on labor-market transitions, however, there must be a sizable portion of the working population that may have double coverage. To determine what fraction of dual-earning couples have dual health coverage, I matched husbands' and wives' responses to the April Supplement for those households in which both members are full-time, full-year workers. In Table 3, I present evidence about the possibility of double coverage. For males, 80.3 percent of the men from dual-earning households are eligible for health insurance from their employers, and their spouses are also eligible for family benefits. Thus, over 80 percent of these males could be covered by their wives' plans, and 38.5 percent of these men have wives who elect to provide family benefits. Similar stories arise for men whose employers offer family coverage: 80.6 percent of men who are eligible for family coverage have wives whose employers offer family plans. Interestingly, 38.0 percent of men from dual-earning households who are eligible for family health plans have wives who provide family health plans, representing a sizable segment of the married, dual-earning families. Workers with spouses who have their own employer-provided health benefits may value family health benefits differently than workers whose spouses do not have employer-provided health benefits: 84.9 percent of these male workers have spouses who are eligible for employer-provided health benefits, and 62.4 percent have spouses who receive employer-provided health benefits.

Table 3 presents similar statistics for full-time female employees: 84.6 percent of women in dual-earning households who are offered health insurance have spouses who are eligible for family plans, and 58.6 percent have spouses who provide family health benefits. Thus, women are more likely to have access to health benefits from multiple sources than are men. Of women who are eligible to provide family health benefits, 84.9 percent of their spouses are eligible for family health benefits, and 58.0 percent provide such benefits. Finally, of women in dual-earning households who are eligible for family health benefits, 87.7 percent are married to men who are eligible for health benefits, and 76.5 percent are married to men who have employer-provided benefits.

Table 3   Dual Health Care Coverage of Married, Full-Time Couples[a]

Coverage	Percentage	n
Husband's employer offers		
Health benefits and spouse is eligible for family health benefits	80.3	2636
Health benefits and spouse provides family health benefits	38.5	2636
Family health benefits and spouse is eligible for family health benefits	80.6	2630
Family health benefits and spouse provides family health benefits	38.0	2630
Family health benefits and spouse is eligible for health benefits	84.9	2650
Family health benefits and spouse receives health benefits	62.4	2645
Wife's employer offers		
Health benefits and spouse is eligible for family health benefits	84.6	2650
Health benefits and spouse provides family health benefits	58.6	2222
Family health benefits and spouse is eligible for family health benefits	84.9	2085
Family health benefits and spouse provides family health benefits	58.0	2085
Family health benefits and spouse is eligible for health benefits	87.7	2636
Family health benefits and spouse receives health benefits	76.5	2636

SOURCE: April 1993 Supplement to the CPS.

[a] To be included in this sample, workers must be working full-time and eligible for employer-provided health benefits. Spouses may or may not be eligible for health benefits but must be full-time workers.

When employers only partially pay for health benefits, employees have an incentive not to accept health benefits when they receive coverage from their spouses' plans. The refusal of health benefits is not uncommon; 11.2 percent of all female workers and 5.6 percent of all male workers decline employer-provided health benefits (see Table 1). In Table 4, I examine the incidence of workers from dual-earning households refusing employer-provided health benefits by whether or not the workers' spouses are eligible for family health benefits. The table indicates that 3.1 percent of male workers whose spouses are not eligible for family health benefits refuse coverage, but 12.9 percent of workers whose spouses are eligible for family health benefits refuse coverage. Thus, male workers who have spouses who are eligible for family health coverage are more than four times more likely to refuse employer-provided health benefits than are men whose wives are not eligible for family health benefits. The impact for females is even more dramatic. Only 4.1 percent of women whose spouses are not eligible for family health benefits refuse employer-provided benefits, but 26.7 percent of women whose spouses are eligible for family health benefits refuse employer-provided benefits. Thus, women whose husbands have access to family health benefits are six times more likely to refuse health benefits than women whose husbands do not have access to family health benefits.

Table 4 Full-Time, Married Couple's Refusal of Employer-Provided Health Benefits[a]

Decision	Spouse is not eligible for family health coverage	Spouse is eligible for family health coverage	*n*
Panel A: Husband's decision to accept or refuse employer-provided health insurance			
Husband accepts employer-provided insurance	96.9 %	87.1%	2035
Husband refuses employer-provided insurance	3.1%	12.9%	251
n	451	1835	2286
Panel B: Wife's decision to accept or refuse employer-provided health insurance			
Wife accepts employer-provided insurance	95.9%	73.3%	1707
Wife refuses employer-provided insurance	4.1%	26.7%	515
n	343	1879	2222

SOURCE: April 1993 Supplement to the CPS.
[a] To be included in this sample, workers must be working full-time and eligible for employer-provided health benefits. Spouses may or may not be eligible for health benefits but must be full-time workers.

When husband and wife search for employment and employers offer health insurance coverage for the whole family, my theory predicts that the husband's and wife's health care coverage decision should be negatively correlated. Thus, controlling for other factors that affect the demand for health insurance coverage, we should see the likelihood of a worker choosing employer-provided health insurance declining when his spouse has selected employer-provided health insurance. To test this hypothesis, I estimate a bivariate probit model that allows for correlation between the husband's and wife's decisions. I limit the sample to couples where both are full-time, full-year workers.[9] For covariates, I use a vector of race dummies (whites are the excluded category), a vector of education variables (high school graduates are the excluded category), the number of children in the household less than 18 years old, a quadratic in the worker's age, a quadratic in the worker's tenure at the firm, and a dummy variable indicating that the worker's tenure is less than a year. The method of estimation is full information, maximum likelihood. The starting values were taken from probits on the individual equations, and the starting value for the correlation coefficient, ρ, is zero.

The estimated coefficients on the covariates provide few surprises (Table 5). Workers of both genders have strong tenure effects. It seems unlikely that length-of-service requirements would account for the strong tenure-health benefits relationship, so the strong relationship may simply reflect the fact that matches that offer health benefits tend to survive while those that do not offer health insurance do not survive, a point that Mortensen (1989) and Garen (1988) made in examining the wage-tenure relationship. Workers with at least a BA degree are more likely to have health insurance than less educated workers. A larger number of children reduces the likelihood of having employer-provided health insurance for women, while the relationship is not statistically significant for men. Interestingly, hispanic wives are more likely but hispanic husbands are less likely to have employer-provided health insurance than similar whites. Similarly, black wives are more likely to have employer-provided health insurance than are white wives.

Controlling for the worker's own characteristics, there is a strong, negative correlation between husbands' and wives' health care decisions. The estimated correlation coefficient is –0.35 and the z-statistic

Table 5 Health Insurance Coverage for Dual Earning Couples, Estimated Coefficients from a Bivariate Probit Model

	Female	Male
Worker is Hispanic	0.273	−0.289
	(2.06)	(2.29)
Worker is Black	0.230	0.090
	(2.03)	(0.77)
Worker is Asian	−0.011	0.246
	(0.08)	(1.32)
Worker is Native American	0.716	0.020
	(1.52)	(0.04)
Worker's age	−0.028	0.019
	(1.27)	(0.84)
Age squared /100	0.018	−0.031
	(0.63)	(1.13)
Worker has less than one year of tenure	−0.231	−0.271
	(2.40)	(2.69)
Worker's tenure	0.090	0.092
	(7.29)	(7.80)
Tenure squared / 100	−0.194	−0.180
	(4.13)	(4.75)
Number of children	−0.069	−0.025
	(2.54)	(0.82)
Worker did not begin high school	0.058	−0.226
	(0.27)	(1.26)
Worker did not complete high school	0.067	−0.209
	(0.56)	(1.78)
Worker attended college but has no degree	0.069	0.137
	(0.96)	(1.68)
Worker has a vocational degree from junior college	0.038	−0.067
	(0.34)	(0.56)
Worker has an associate's degree	0.272	0.020
	(1.97)	(0.12)
Worker has a bachelor's degree	0.289	0.154
	(3.84)	(1.87)
Worker has a master's degree	0.300	0.265
	(2.68)	(2.04)

	Female	Male
Worker has a Ph.D. degree	0.161	0.623
	(0.39)	(2.31)
Worker has a professional degree	0.431	0.542
	(1.46)	(1.95)
Constant	0.681	0.001
	(1.70)	(0.00)
ρ	−0.350	
	(9.03)	
Likelihood function	−2798.59	
Number of observations	2600	

NOTE: Mean of the dependent variable for females 0.6465 and for males is 0.7727. Absolute values of z-statistics are given in parentheses.

is −9.03. Thus, the data overwhelmingly reject the hypothesis that the health care decisions of dual-earning couples are independent and accept the hypothesis, which my theory implies, that the decisions are negatively correlated. Husbands and wives appear to coordinate their search activities, presumably looking for other forms of compensation when their spouses provide health benefits. Thus, within households, there is some evidence that workers do indeed trade off health benefits for other forms of compensation.

DOES SPOUSE-PROVIDED HEALTH INSURANCE AFFECT TURNOVER PROBABILITIES?

The analysis earlier suggested that coverage under a spouse's health insurance plan alters the worker's likelihood of accepting an offer. If the spouse's plan is less generous than the worker's own health insurance plan, then coverage by the spouse unambiguously increases the likelihood that a worker will accept another offer. In equilibrium, therefore, we should see such workers more likely to change jobs than workers without spouse-provided coverage. When the spouse's plan is more generous than the worker's own plan, there is an ambiguity, but it remains possible that spouse-provided coverage would result in higher turnover rates.

Unfortunately, the CPS is a less than ideal data set to use to examine job transitions. Because the CPS is a short panel and provides few details about a worker's employers, it is often impossible to spot job-to-job transitions. In the April 1993 Supplement, however, workers were asked directly if they have less than one-year tenure, and answers to this question allow me to identify those individuals who have changed jobs in the last year. It is not possible, however, to determine whether the transition was a result of a quit, layoff, or dismissal.

The CPS provides only workers' current health insurance and not their coverage at the time of their job transitions, which causes a potentially serious problem. If workers who have recently had an involuntary job transition (layoff or dismissal) are likely to enroll in their spouses' health care plans, then there is a correlation between current health care coverage under a spouse's plan and turnover that is unrelated to any search story. In addition, the CPS provides no information about the generosity of workers', or their spouses', health care plans. As the generosity of the two plans affects the likelihood of turnover in my model, this data limitation is particularly serious. Finally, the CPS provides no information about tenure on the previous job. As virtually all research has found that hazard functions for employment spells exhibit duration dependence (e.g., Farber 1994), the failure to include tenure in a turnover equation may cause a specification bias.[10]

With these caveats in mind, I can examine the relationship between job transitions and health insurance coverage provided by a worker's spouse with the equation:

$$\Pr(job\ change) = F(X_i\beta + S_i\delta + u_i). \qquad (6)$$

where X_i is a vector of controls, β is the corresponding vector of parameters, S_i is an indicator variable that is equal to one if the worker is covered by his spouse's plan and zero otherwise, δ is the corresponding parameter, u_i is the error term that I assume is identically and independently distributed, and $F(\bullet)$ is a logistic distribution function.

Because males and females may have much different patterns of turnover, I run separate equations for male and female workers. In addition to controls for whether the spouse is employed or self-employed, I use the same control variables as those I use in Table 5 except, of course, I use no controls for tenure. In column 1 of Tables 6 and 7, I present the estimates for Eq. 6 for male and female workers. I limit my sample to workers who are married, full-time, full-year workers who have at least two years of potential experience, where potential experience is defined to be age minus years of schooling minus six. This restriction should exclude most school-to-work transitions, which presumably occur regardless of the spouse's provision of health benefits.[11]

A common feature of the results from both samples is that having an employed spouse substantially reduces the likelihood of workers changing jobs. (This result remains regardless of whether I control for coverage by the spouse's health insurance plan.) Spouse-provided coverage has a large impact on the likelihood of turnover for male workers; evaluated at the mean, spouse-provided coverage increases the likelihood of a male worker changing jobs from about 0.10 to 0.16.[12] For females, the impact is smaller but still large; evaluated at the mean, spouse-provided coverage increases the likelihood of a female worker changing jobs from about 0.10 to 0.14.

My estimates for males are somewhat higher than those of Madrian (1994), who found that not having other health insurance coverage lowered male job transitions by about 26 percent.[13] Importantly, Madrian was able to control for whether the job transition was voluntary, and I am unable to do so.[14] To guard against the possibility that spouse-provided coverage is somehow indicative of an involuntary transition from the last job, I reestimate the equation, limiting my sample to those workers who report that they are eligible for employer-provided health insurance (see column 2 of Tables 6 and 7). For this sample, workers who made job transitions at least have the option of taking their employer-provided plan. While clearly this does not preclude a worker from having been laid-off or dismissed from his past position, this does eliminate any workers who have spouse-provided benefits because they have no alternative source of health care. With this sample restriction, the coefficients on the spouse-provided coverage are reasonably stable. Evaluated at the means, spouse-provided coverage increases the likelihood of a male worker changing jobs from 0.07 to 0.11 and the likelihood of a female worker changing jobs from 0.07 to 0.12.[15]

Table 6 Turnover Propensities and Health Insurance Coverage Status, Married Males

		All workers (1)		Workers eligible for health insurance (2)
	Means		Means	
Worker is Hispanic	0.066	0.336 (2.03)	0.051	0.407 (1.83)
Worker is Black	0.054	0.417 (2.38)	0.051	0.527 (2.48)
Worker is Asian	0.028	0.178 (0.68)	0.027	0.361 (1.23)
Worker is Native American	0.006	−0.089 (0.16)	0.005	−1.045 (1.01)
Worker's age	40.9	−0.157 (4.52)	41.3	−0.125 (2.83)
Age squared /100	1772	0.123 (2.86)	1804	0.089 (1.63)
Worker did not begin high school	0.034	0.162 (0.62)	0.026	0.037 (0.09)
Worker did not complete high school	0.069	0.382 (2.29)	0.057	0.286 (1.21)
Worker attended college but has no degree	0.187	0.150 (1.18)	0.0188	0.156 (0.97)
Worker has a vocational degree from junior college	0.052	0.119 (0.59)	0.053	0.222 (0.90)

Worker has an associate's degree	0.0300	0.082 (0.30)	0.031	0.506 (1.76)
Worker has a bachelor's degree	0.186	0.088 (0.67)	0.198	0.202 (1.28)
Worker has a master's degree	0.075	0.192 (1.00)	0.082	0.492 (2.35)
Worker has a Ph.D. degree	0.017	-0.104 (0.24)	0.020	0.199 (0.45)
Worker has a professional degree	0.018	0.065 (0.19)	0.019	0.540 (1.52)
Number of children	1.152	-0.047 (1.12)	1.152	-0.062 (1.18)
Spouse is employed	0.629	-0.487 (5.68)	0.635	-0.430 (3.44)
Spouse is self-employed	0.045	-0.177 (0.77)	0.046	-0.023 (0.09)
Worker is covered by spouse's plan	0.149	0.762 (6.28)	0.129	0.697 (4.58)
Worker is covered by other plan	0.070	1.045 (7.33)	0.051	1.095 (5.63)
Constant	–	1.818 (2.83)	–	0.775 (0.93)
Likelihood function		-1839.97		-1304.81
Number of observations		6235		5457

NOTE: Mean of the dependent variable for column (1) is 0.096 and for column (2) is 0.069. Absolute values of z-statistics are given in parentheses.

Table 7 Turnover Propensities and Health Insurance Coverage Status, Married Females

	Means	All workers (1)	Means	Workers eligible for health insurance (2)
Worker is Hispanic	0.055	-0.234 (0.89)	0.048	-0.029 (0.09)
Worker is Black	0.065	-0.329 (1.31)	0.065	-0.563 (1.66)
Worker is Asian	0.032	0.248 (0.85)	0.031	-0.135 (0.33)
Worker is Native American	0.008	0.366 (0.72)	0.007	-0.043 (0.06)
Worker's age	39.4	-0.029 (0.58)	39.5	-0.044 (0.70)
Age squared /100	1652	-0.041 (0.63)	1656	-0.033 (0.39)
Worker did not begin high school	0.021	-0.172 (0.58)	0.015	-0.091 (0.12)
Worker did not complete high school	0.054	0.688 (3.25)	0.046	0.567 (1.87)
Worker attended college but has no degree	0.194	-0.302 (1.85)	0.197	0.008 (0.04)
Worker has a vocational degree from junior college	0.054	-0.190 (0.75)	0.057	0.120 (0.41)

		(1)		(2)
Worker has an associate's degree	0.039	0.122 (0.46)	0.038	0.346 (1.08)
Worker has a bachelor's degree	0.174	-0.062 (0.40)	0.184	0.179 (0.94)
Worker has a master's degree	0.066	-0.194 (0.74)	0.072	0.187 (0.63)
Worker has a Ph.D. degree	0.006	0.422 (0.67)	0.008	0.929 (1.45)
Worker has a professional degree	0.009	-1.277 (1.25)	0.009	-0.693 (0.67)
Number of children	0.885	0.014 (0.25)	0.866	0.002 (0.03)
Spouse is employed	0.980	-0.834 (2.75)	0.983	-0.284 (0.63)
Worker is covered by spouse's plan	0.365	0.527 (4.55)	0.339	0.693 (4.92)
Worker is covered by other plan	0.058	0.471 (1.98)	0.040	0.792 (2.42)
Constant	–	0.049 (0.05)		-0.547 (1.18)
Likelihood function		-1179.74		-820.36
Number of observations		3940		3320

NOTE: Mean of the dependent variable for column (1) is 0.097 and for column (2) is 0.074. Absolute values of z-statistics are given in parentheses.

Thus, the CPS data seem to support the conclusion that spouse-provided coverage does encourage job transitions, and the results are largely consistent with those of Madrian (1994) for workers with dual coverage. Her interpretation, however, is that workers without dual coverage are possibly "locked-out" of jobs that offer insurance with preexisting conditions clauses or length-of-service requirements. Health care reform that eliminates preexisting conditions clauses and length-of-service requirements and requires employers to offer health insurance would virtually eliminate job-lock. Unless the employer mandate also eliminates variations in the type of employer-provided coverage, my analysis suggests that the turnover that spouse-provided coverage creates is likely to persist. Ideally, therefore, we would like to be able to distinguish my search explanation from her job-lock explanation and be able to decompose the turnover effect into a search component and a job-lock component.

That is likely to prove a difficult task. Gruber and Madrian (1994) and Holtz-Eakin (1994) contended that most job-lock appears to be a short-run problem, presumably arising more from the length-of-service requirements than from preexisting conditions.[16] Individuals without a preexisting condition, however, have the option of purchasing insurance from the private market, or, as Gruber and Madrian emphasized, some workers may purchase health care from their previous employers to bridge the gap in coverage that length-of-service provisions create. This solution to a coverage gap is expensive: the worker loses the tax exemption of health care insurance premiums, and, if purchasing health insurance from the private market, individual policies are often more expensive. Yet for these workers, a solution does exist, and a sufficiently generous offer will induce the worker to change jobs. Because this solution is expensive and because workers with spouse-provided coverage avoid these costs, workers differ in their valuation of offers from alternative employers, which, of course, is the essence of my search explanation for the turnover effect from spouse-provided coverage. In my view, distinguishing between these two explanations would be difficult.

POLICY IMPLICATIONS

My results support the findings of Madrian (1994) and Gruber and Madrian (1994) that employer-provided health insurance does affect the turnover propensities of workers. Indeed, the magnitude of my results for male workers is somewhat larger than Madrian's estimate, and I find that female workers are similarly affected. While I have offered no formal welfare analysis of this effect, it is difficult to believe that a policy that makes a worker's turnover propensity dependent on the health care policy of his spouse would improve the efficiency of labor markets.

Why have employer-provided health insurance? Friedman (1993) argued that many firms initially offered health care as a fringe benefit, as a means of avoiding the wage-price controls of World War II. As the IRS did not initially count fringe benefits as a part of taxable income, the tax system encouraged firms to offer health care, and Congress eventually codified the tax exemption. As health benefits are income elastic (Woodbury and Huang 1991), the tax exemption favors those with high earnings. Therefore, equity concerns suggest that a change is in order as well. When efficiency and equity concerns agree, one hopes that economists would find the course of action uncontroversial.

The political appeal of continuing the employer-provision of health benefits or the expansion of the system through mandates seems to arise because the costs remain hidden from consumers. Gruber (1994) and Gruber and Krueger (1992) suggested that most, if not all, costs of mandated benefits are passed through to the workers as lower wages, but if the mandated program is sufficiently small, these wage pass-throughs may be difficult for workers to perceive. Moreover, the tax expenditure that arises from the exemption of employer-provided health insurance is not readily apparent. Those of us who are beneficiaries of the tax expenditure probably do not appreciate the largesse of the U.S. government, at least not until the exemption is threatened.

Unfortunately, any elimination of the tax subsidy of health insurance benefits would not be invisible. Consider a reform along the lines that Diamond (1992) suggested, but one without any tax subsidy for middle-class families. In such a plan, employer-provided health insurance is replaced with a system of mandatory coverage where, at least for most middle class households, consumers pay the full cost of their health insurance. Those workers who previously had employer-provided health insurance should receive a nice increase in compensation. Under Diamond's proposal, regional "HealthFeds" negotiate several different policies with insurance companies, and consumers within the region choose among the approved policies. When consumers begin looking at the prices of the various policies, however, they will notice that, even if firms increased their compensation by the exact cost of the previously provided health insurance, the increase in their compensation is not enough to allow them to purchase an insurance plan of comparable quality to their employer-provided plan. Because the tax subsidy is eliminated, the income and substitution effects presumably would move most consumers to purchase less generous insurance plans. Woodbury and Huang's simulation results suggest that the full taxation of health benefits may result in up to a 15 percent decline in the amount of health insurance. They calculated these estimates for the 1986 U.S. tax codes, and marginal tax rates have increased since then. Forcing consumers to understand fully the costs of health care may not be good politics but, in my view, it is good economics.

Notes

I thank Susan Black and Mike Clark for research assistance. Paul Anglin, Michael Baye, William Custer, Daniel Hamermesh, and seminar participants at the University of Kentucky provided useful comments. The National Institutes for Health provided research support.

1. *Statistical Abstract of the United States 1993*, Table 515. The tax expenditure on employer-provided pension plans is the largest single tax expenditure ($70.5 billion), followed by employer contributions to health insurance ($63.2 billion), and the mortgage interest deduction ($48.1 billion).
2. See Allen, Clark, and McDermed (1993) and Luzadis and Mitchell (1991) for recent evidence.
3. The U.S. government no longer allows firms to use mandatory retirement provisions.
4. Hutchens (1986) presented evidence that pensions, when coupled with the nondiscriminatory provision of the IRS codes, causes firms not to hire older workers. Scott, Berger, and Garen (1995) argued that health benefits may dissuade firms from hiring older workers as well.
5. Monheit and Cooper (1994), who also used the National Medical Expenditure Survey, found evidence of job lock using a much different methodology than

Madrian. Using SIPP data, Gruber and Madrian (1994) found evidence that the 1985 COBRA legislation that allows workers to buy insurance from past employers as well as earlier state legislation that also allowed limited portability increased labor turnover and substantially mitigated job lock.

6. My analysis ignores many other issues that concern most search models. To name but a couple, I have not considered the distinction between unemployed and on-the-job search, nor have I considered the intensity at which workers attempt to generate new offers. Given the underlying ambiguity about the impact of double coverage on the workers' turnover decisions, these extensions would not appear too useful. Perhaps more important, for simplicity, I do not consider the joint search problem of a wife and husband. In a model with such a joint search decision, a worker may refuse a job with a higher wage and more health benefits if it will allow his spouse to take a sufficiently attractive offer.

7. Not all workers decline extra coverage: 12.1 percent of all women and 8.7 percent of all men in the sample of full-time workers reported that they have coverage from at least two sources.

8. This estimate of 10.7 percent differs considerably from Madrian's estimate of 33.5 percent using the National Medical Expenditure Survey, although it is conditional on being married. Of course, our two samples differ considerably because I am requiring males to be full-time, full-year workers to be in the sample. As a consistency check on the data, I matched the husbands and wives in the April Supplement. Among married males, 15.1 percent reported that their spouses' plans cover them; 30.8 percent of spouses of these men, however, reported that they chose a family health insurance plan, which is clearly closer to Madrian's estimate of 33.5. It is important to keep in mind, however, that offering a family plan does not imply that this coverage is free. Employers may charge the employee some or all of the additional costs for obtaining family coverage.

9. Olson (2000) looked at the labor-supply decision and how it may be affected by the spouse's health insurance coverage.

10. The CPS is not the only data set that suffers from these limitations. To my knowledge, no data set with good labor-market information provides detailed analysis of health insurance benefits. As Madrian (1994) notes, the National Medical Expenditure data lack measures of worker tenure; workers' insurance coverage can only be determined at two points in time, 7 to 15 months apart, and not at the time of job transition. As she notes, there are similar problems with the use of the PSID and NLSY. I am currently working with my colleagues Mark Berger and Frank Scott to use the SIPP data set to examine the impact of insurance coverage on worker turnover. While the SIPP does contain continuous information on health insurance coverage, it does not contain information about the generosity of workers' health care plans nor of their spouses' plans.

11. I am grateful to Daniel Hamermesh for this suggestion.

12. Recall that, in logit models, the change in the probability of the dependent variable equals one for a change in the jth independent variable is, for the ith worker,

$$\partial p_i / x_i = p_i(1 - p_i)\beta_j$$

13. In her specification, Madrian included health care coverage from any source, not simply spouse-provided coverage. As sources of coverage other than the worker's spouse include Medicaid and Champus, I was afraid that these individuals may be different from the population as a whole. For this reason, I use dual coverage arising from some source other than a spouse as a separate variable.

14. It is by no means obvious that we should exclude involuntary transitions. If spouse provision of employer-provided allows workers to accept jobs in riskier occupation, higher involuntary turnover rates may be an outcome of spouse-provided health benefits.

15. These results are robust to various other specification checks. For the male portion of the sample, I divided the sample into age categories and reestimated the equations for each category. Despite the relatively small cell size, the coefficients on spouse-provided coverage are always positive and generally statistically significant. Similarly, if I include a family income variable, undoubtedly endogenous, the coefficient remains statistically significant and of similar magnitude to that reported in Table 4. Moreover, if I included nonmarried workers, the coefficient remains statistically significant.

16. Among full-time employees who have changed jobs within the last year and have jobs with firms that offer health insurance, 14 percent report that they are ineligible for coverage because they have not completed a "probationary period," which I interpret as a length-of-service requirement. In contrast, 0.7 percent claim to be ineligible because of a preexisting condition, and another 3.0 percent report that they have a preexisting condition not covered by their health care plan.

References

Allen, Steven G., Robert L. Clark, and Ann A. McDermed. 1993. "Pensions, Bonding, and Lifetime Employment." *Journal of Human Resources* 28(Summer): 463–481.

Diamond, Peter. 1992. "Organizing the Health Insurance Market." *Econometrica* 50(November): 1233–1255.

Dorsey, Stuart. 1987. "The Economic Function of Private Pensions: An Empirical Analysis." *Journal of Labor Economics* 5: s171–s189.

Dye, Ronald A., and Rick Antle. 1984. "Self-Selection via Fringe Benefits." *Journal of Labor Economics* 2(July): 388-411.

Farber, Henry. 1994. "The Analysis of Interfirm Mobility." *Journal of Labor Economics* 12(October): 554–593.

Friedman, Milton. 1993. "The Folly of Buying Health Care at the Company Store." *The Wall Street Journal,* February 3, A20.

Garen, John E. 1988. "Empirical Studies of the Job Matching Hypothesis." *Research in Labor Economics* 9: 187–224.

Gruber, Jonathan. 1994. "The Incidence of Mandated Maternity Benefits." *American Economic Review* 84(June): 622–641.

Gruber, Jonathan, and Alan B. Krueger. 1992. "The Incidence of Mandated Employer-Provided Insurance: Lessons from Workman's Compensation Insurance." *Tax Policy and the Economy* 5: 111–143.

Gruber, Jonathan, and Brigitte Madrian. 1994. "Limited Insurance Portability and Job Mobility: The Effects of Public Policy on Job-Lock." *Industrial and Labor Relations Review* 48(October): 86–102.

Holtz-Eakin, Douglas. 1994. "Health Insurance Provision and Labor Market Efficiency in the United States and Germany." In *Protection Versus Economic Flexibility: Is There a Tradeoff?* Rebecca Blank, ed. Chicago: University of Chicago Press, pp. 157–187.

Hutchens, Robert. 1986. "Delayed Payment Contracts and the Firm's Propensity to Hire Older Workers." *Journal of Labor Economics* 4(October): 439–457.

_____. 1987. "A Test of Lazear's Theory of Delayed Payment Contracts." *Journal of Labor Economics* 5(October): s153–170.

Ippolito, Richard A. 1985. "The Labor Contract and True Economic Pension Liabilities." *American Economic Review* 75(December): 1031–1043.

Lazear, Edward P. 1979. "Why is there Mandatory Retirement?" *Journal of Political Economy* 87(6): 1261–1284.

_____. 1981. "Agency Earnings Profiles, Productivity, and Hours Restrictions." *The American Economic Review* 71(4): 606–620.

Long, James, and Frank Scott. 1982. "The Income Tax and Nonwage Compensation." *Review of Economics and Statistics* 64(May): 211–219.

Luzadis, Rebecca A., and Olivia S. Mitchell. 1991. "Explaining Pension Dynamics." *Journal of Human Resources* 26(Fall): 679–703.

Madrian, Brigitte. 1994. "Employment-Based Health Insurance and Job Mobility: Is There Evidence of Job Lock?" *Quarterly Journal of Economics* 109(February): 27–54.

Monheit, Alan C., and Philip Cooper. 1994. "Health Insurance and Job Mobility: Theory and Evidence." *Industrial and Labor Relations Review* 48(October): 68–85.

Mortensen, Dale T. 1988. "Wages, Separation and Job Tenure: On-the-Job Specific Training or Matching?" *Journal of Labor Economics* 6(October): 445–472.

Olson, Craig. 2000. "Part-time Work, Health Insurance Coverage, and the Wages of Married Women." Chapter 7 in this volume, pp. 295–324.

Scott, Frank A., Mark C. Berger, and Dan A. Black. 1989. "Effects of the Tax Treatment of Fringe Benefits on Labor Market Segmentation." *Industrial and Labor Relations Review* 42(January): 216–229.

Scott, Frank, Mark Berger, and John Garen. 1995. "Do Health Insurance Costs and Nondiscrimination Policies Reduce the Job Opportunities of Older Workers?" *Industrial and Labor Relations Review* 48(4): 775–791.

Woodbury, Stephen. 1983. "Substitution Between Wage and Nonwage Benefits." *American Economic Review* 73(March): 166–182.

Woodbury, Stephen, and Wei-Jang Huang. 1991. *The Tax Treatment of Fringe Benefits*. Kalamazoo, MI: W.E. Upjohn Institute for Employment Research.

7 Part-Time Work, Health Insurance Coverage, and the Wages of Married Women

Craig A. Olson
University of Wisconsin–Madison

One of the most significant and persistent differences between the behavior of men and women in the U.S. labor market is the greater variability in hours worked per week by women. In 1991, the median number of weekly hours worked by women in the labor force who were 18–60 years old was 40 hours, with substantial variation around this median. The first decile of the hours distribution for working women was 20 hours per week and the first quartile was 32 hours. This distribution has remained basically unchanged since at least 1979.[1]

The dominant factor thought to account for the greater variability in hours worked among women is gender specialization in household production activities, with women choosing to adjust the intensity of their labor-market activities in response to the demands placed on their time by other household members. In a simple labor-supply model, womens' wages are taken as exogenous to their labor-supply decisions, and women select hours of work based on other household income and the relative value of their market and household time. Thus, as the value of household time changes relative to market activity, the simple theory predicts that adjustments will be made in hours worked. However, research in recent years suggests that adjusting hours worked in response to changing labor-supply preferences is costly for women because of employer constraints on hours worked and incomplete information about the wage-hour combinations available in the market (e.g., Blank 1988; Altonji and Paxson 1988, 1991; Dickens and Lundberg 1993). These constraints call into question the assumption that the wage rate is exogenous to the labor-supply decision.

This chapter investigates a different demand-side constraint that may influence the labor-supply decisions of married women and that has not been previously investigated. I investigate how the correlation between hours worked per week and the structure of the compensation package offered by employers alters the labor-supply decisions of married women in the United States. This study focuses on employer-provided health insurance and investigates how the demand for health insurance by married women alters their labor-supply decisions.[2] I hypothesize the demand by a married woman for a job with health benefits is greater among those wives whose husbands do not have employer-provided health insurance as compared with households where husbands have jobs that provide health benefits. Because health insurance is typically not available to employees working less than 35 hours per week, married women without spousal health insurance coverage adjust their labor-supply decisions to obtain health benefits. To test this prediction, I use data on weekly hours worked and employer-provided health insurance (EPHI) for 1982 and 1992 as reported in the 1983 and 1993 March Current Population Survey (CPS).

The results in this paper show that in 1992, married women whose husbands lacked employer-provided health benefits worked more hours per week than wives in households where their spouses had health insurance. In contrast, the 1982 estimates show no effect of husbands health insurance coverage on the labor supply decisions of wives. The differing results for the two time periods is explained by the decline in employer provided health insurance among married males between 1982 and 1992. In 1982 some wives seeking a job with employer provided health insurance because their husbands lacked these benefits would have worked full time even if their husband had a job with EPHI. However, the decline in EPHI coverage among married males over the 1982–1992 time period from 0.67 to 0.62 caused working wives in some households in 1992 to seek full-time jobs with health benefits. By 1992 this included some households where the wife would have preferred to work part time if her husband had a job that provided health benefits. Thus, the employer constraint that full-time work is required to obtain health benefits was not binding on married women in 1982 but became binding by 1992 because of the decline in married male health insurance coverage.

Compensating wage theory predicts that women choosing to work full time to obtain health insurance receive a lower wage compared to what they could earn if they accepted a full-time job without health insurance. Using the husband's health insurance coverage as an instrument that is correlated with his wife's health insurance coverage but assumed to be uncorrelated with his wife's wage. I find the predicted negative relationship between the hourly wage of wives working full time and their estimate suggests that married women working full time accept about a 10 percent wage reduction in exchange for employer-provided health benefits.

EMPLOYER-PROVIDED HEALTH INSURANCE: THEORY AND EVIDENCE

The application of standard compensating wage theory to fringe benefits predicts that workers differ in their demand for employer-provided benefits and sort themselves across firms so the mix between wages and fringe benefits matches their preferences. Holding human capital and other variables influencing wages constant, workers that receive more generous fringe benefits receive a lower wage than comparable workers that prefer fewer fringe benefits (Rosen 1986). The standard figure illustrating this prediction is shown in Figure 1, where workers maximize their utility subject to a budget constraint that is defined by the human capital and ability levels. Worker A prefers a compensation package without any fringe benefits and Worker B accepts a job that provides both wages (W_B) and fringe benefits (FB_B).

This standard story of the relationship between wages and fringe benefits is complicated in the case of employer-provided health benefits because of the private information employees and potential employees have about their demand for health care. Private information held by individuals about their demand for health care creates an adverse selection problem for the firm if all employees are charged the same price for health insurance through an identical wage adjustment. There are several ways firms may respond to this adverse selection. Firms could individually adjust worker wages *ex post* based on the pattern of health expenditure claims observed as worker tenure increases.[3]

Figure 1 Wage–Fringe Benefit Trade-off

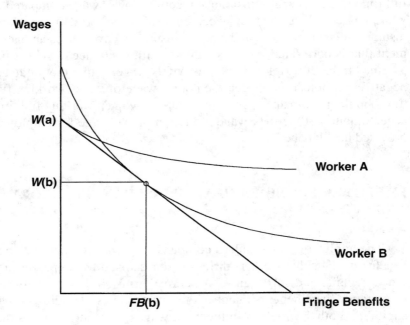

Firms could also create rate classes based on expected health care costs (e.g., younger versus older workers) and adjust wages differently for workers in the different rate classes.[4] Although it is unclear which alternative firms will select, I hypothesize that most firms simply charge all employees the same price for health benefits in the form of lower wages and, like an insurance company, screen out less healthy workers and try to create a workforce with homogenous health demands that minimizes the subsidies from healthy to less healthy workers. This approach, of course, provides less healthy workers with a strong incentive to seek employment in firms that offer health insurance so they can receive health benefits at a price that is less than their expected health care expenditures.

One strategy firms follow to screen out workers with high demand for health care is to limit health insurance coverage to full-time workers. Such a policy reduces adverse selection in two ways. First, the ability to work full time may screen out workers with costly health care problems because these same health problems may preclude full-time employment. Second, limiting health insurance to only full-time workers ensures health care benefits are a small share of total compensation. Health benefits are a relatively larger share of total compensation when they are provided to part-time workers, and this may cause some workers with very high demands for health insurance to work part time just for the health benefits.

Table 1 reports data from the health insurance questions in the 1983 and 1993 March CPSs; the data show a strong positive relationship between hours worked per week and health insurance coverage. The probability of having a job that provided health insurance increases modestly with hours worked up to 30 hours per week, increases substantially for those working 30–34 hours per week, and then increases very significantly at 35 or more hours per week (full-time employment).

Table 1 Employer Health Insurance Coverage by Hours Worked, 1982 and 1992 (%)

Usual hours per week	1982	1992
1 – 10	9.8	14.3
11 – 20	17.4	17.9
21 – 30	27.7	24.6
30 – 34	47.6	38.8
≥ 35	73.1	64.2

SOURCE: Author's tabulations from the March 1983 and 1993 CPS.

More direct evidence showing how employer policies prevent part-time workers from receiving health benefits is provided by the Fringe Benefit Supplement to the April 1993 CPS. This supplement included questions asking the reasons why respondents were not covered by employer-provided health benefits. Thirty-one percent of those working were not covered by employer-provided health benefits. Among those uncovered, 81 percent worked for an employer that did not provide health insurance to any of its employees and 19 percent were uncovered even though they worked for an employer that offered insurance to some employees. Of the 19 percent uncovered, 11.17 percent (more than half) were ineligible because of their status as part-time employees. To summarize, the data suggest firms hiring part-time workers frequently do not offer health insurance to any employee or do not extend health insurance to the part-time workers in their workforce. I hypothesize this discrimination reflects firm efforts to minimize adverse selection by part-time workers who, for reasons unobserved by the firm, have a high demand for health insurance.

THE DEMAND FOR HEALTH INSURANCE COVERAGE AMONG MARRIED FEMALES

The prediction that married women adjust their labor-supply decisions based on their husbands' health insurance coverage assumes the demand by wives for jobs with employer-provided health benefits is influenced by spousal coverage. In this section, I test this assumption and report estimates of the effect of husbands' health insurance coverage on the probability that wives have health insurance coverage through their employers. Table 2 shows the two by two table of own employer health coverage for working couples. The percentage of couples where neither individual had own employer health insurance increased slightly from 15.8 percent in 1982 to 17 percent in 1992. In 1982, 31 percent of the sample included couples where both the husband and wife were covered by their respective employers. By 1992, this percentage had dropped to 24.2 percent. Over the 10-year period,

Table 2 The Joint Distribution of Own Employer Health Insurance Coverage For Working Couples (%)[a]

| Wife's coverage from own employer | Husband's coverage from own employer | | | |
| | Uncovered | | Covered | |
	1982	1992	1982	1992
Uncovered	15.77 (2,523)	17.03 (3,170)	36.70 (5,872)	38.0 (7,086)
Covered	16.62 (2,661)	20.79 (3,870)	30.80 (4,943)	24.21 (4,491)

[a] The top number is the cell percentage. The number in parentheses shows the cell sample sizes.

there was also a slight increase in the share of couples where only the husband had coverage and a larger increase, from 16.6 to 20.8 percent, in the share of couples where only the wife had own employer coverage. This increase is consistent with data from other years (Olson 1995) and suggests coverage through the wife's employer became a more important source of family coverage over the 10-year period.

One statistical model for describing the relationship between spousal health insurance coverage is a binary probit model where the equation describing a wife's health insurance coverage from her own job includes her husband's coverage through his job as a covariate. Unfortunately, the estimates from this single equation approach are likely to be biased because of the correlation between unobservables affecting the demand for health insurance coverage for both the husband and wife. To overcome this problem, I jointly estimate the husband's and wife's coverage and include the husband's coverage on his job in her health insurance equation. This model, a bivariate probit model with a structural shift (Heckman 1978), is described by the following equations:

$$HI^*_H = X_H \beta_H + \varepsilon_H \tag{1}$$

$$HI^*_W = X_W \beta_W + \alpha HI_H + \varepsilon_W \tag{2}$$

$$HI_i = 1 \text{ if } HI^*_i > 0, \text{ otherwise } HI_i = 0 \text{ where } i = H \text{ or } W \tag{3}$$

$$\varepsilon_i \sim N(0, 1) \tag{4}$$

The subscripts in each equation refer to the husband (H) or wife (W), and HI^*_i is a latent variable indicating the propensity that a job provides health insurance. HI^*_i is a function of a set of observable exogenous factors and an unobserved, normally distributed error term. In this recursive model, a husband's health benefit status directly affects the probability that his wife has a job with health benefits, and α describes the causal effect of the husband's health benefits on the probability his wife has a job with health benefits. I hypothesize that $\alpha < 0$. In other words, own employer coverage by the husband lowers the wife's demand for coverage through her job.

This model permits a nonzero correlation between the error terms in Eqs. 1 and 2 and is identified if there is at least one variable in Eq. 1

that is excluded from Eq. 2. This exclusion restriction is satisfied by assuming the characteristics of the husband (e.g., education, age, race) that affect the probability that he has health benefits on his job do not directly affect HI^*_w. The X_i matrices include individual characteristics typically used in an earnings function: years of completed education, age, age^2, age^3, three race and ethnic variables, the number of children in the household under the age of 6, the number of children aged 6–17 years old, and three region dummies. The data for each year were constructed by creating separate data files from the 1983 and 1993 March CPSs for husbands and wives and merging these files using the household, family, and individual identification codes.

The results in Table 3 show health insurance coverage increases with age and level of education and is lower for minorities than for white workers. The coefficient on husband's health insurance coverage is in the expected negative direction in both 1982 and 1992, and the parameter estimates are virtually the same. The negative coefficients on husband's coverage imply that women married to husbands without health benefits were more likely to be working on jobs that provide health insurance than working wives whose husbands had health benefits. In 1993, the predicted probability that an "average" working wife had a job with health benefits was 0.533 if the husband did not have health benefits and 0.302 if the husband had a job with health benefits.[5]

Alternatives to the Bivariate Probit Model

The recursive structure of the bivariate model describes by Equations 1–4 is a necessary assumption of the statistical model because of the cross-sectional data and the latent variable formulation of health insurance coverage. As Heckman (1978) showed, a simultaneous latent variable model where each individual's health insurance coverage casually affects the coverage of his or her spouse is logically inconsistent. However, there is another recursive model, alternative to Equations 1–4, which reverses the recursive structure and assumes a wife's coverage is exogenous and has a causal effect on the coverage of her husband. Such a model may be appropriate for some couples, and the model reported in Table 3 is obviously misspecified for these couples. Choosing between these two alternative recursive models is difficult. The best solution is to have sample information (e.g., longitudinal data) that could be used to identify which spouse's coverage is exoge-

Table 3 Bivariate Probit Estimates of Own Employer Health Benefit Coverage For Married Couples

Variable	1982		1992	
	Wife's coverage	Husband's coverage	Wife's coverage	Husband's coverage
Constant	−3.538	0.477	−4.563	−0.934
	(0.504)	(0.392)	(0.566)	(0.394)
Kids < 6	−0.249	0.033	−0.209	−0.015
	(0.018)	(0.018)	(0.018)	(0.017)
Kids 6–17	−0.207	0.031	−0.181	0.004
	(0.012)	(0.012)	0.011)	(0.011)
North central	−0.185	−0.095	−0.067	−0.002
	(0.031)	(0.032)	(0.028)	(0.028)
South	−0.005	−0.121	0.003	−0.122
	(0.030)	(0.032)	(0.028)	(0.027)
West	−0.085	−0.158	−0.056	−0.076
	(0.032)	(0.033)	(0.029)	(0.029)
Education (years)	0.050	0.067	–	–
	(0.004)	(0.004)		
High school	–	–	0.297	0.414
			(0.038)	(0.033)
Some college	–	–	0.392	0.498
			(0.040)	(0.034)
College	–	–	0.598	0.638
			(0.044)	(0.037)
Graduate school	–	–	0.823	0.698
			(0.052)	(0.042)
Black	0.327	−0.034	0.171	−0.066
	(0.043)	(0.045)	(0.040)	(0.040)
Hispanic	0.194	0.042	0.019	−0.165
	(0.039)	(0.042)	(0.035)	(0.035)
Other race	0.024	−0.290	−0.033	−0.185
	(0.058)	(0.063)	(0.046)	(0.049)
Age	0.291	−0.100	0.359	−0.042
	(0.041)	(0.029)	(0.045)	(0.028)
Age^2/100	−0.737	0.354	−0.869	−0.042
	(0.107)	(0.067)	(0.113)	(0.062)

(continued)

Table 3 (continued)

Variable	1982		1992	
	Wife's coverage	Husband's coverage	Wife's coverage	Husband's coverage
Age^3/10,000	0.572	−0.371	0.663	−0.010
	(0.090)	(0.050)	(0.093)	(0.045)
Husband's *HI*	−0.634		−0.602	
	(0.104)	−	(0.134)	−
ρ	0.311		0.092	
	(0.065)	−	(0.085)	−
N	15,999			18,617
−Log L	20107.1			24142.9

NOTE: Standard errors are in parentheses.

nous and then estimate different recursive models for the two types of couples. Unfortunately, this sample separation information is not available in the March CPSs.

An alternative method of investigating the sensitivity of the estimates obtained from the recursive structure defined by Equations 1–4 is to use Two-Stage Least Squares (TSLS) and estimate a two equation simultaneous equation model of husbands' and wives' coverage where the coverage of each spouse affects the coverage of the other. Each equation in this two equation system is identified because the husband's (wife's) individual characteristics (age, race, and education) are assumed to be exogenous to the own employer health coverage of the wife (husband). TSLS avoids the recursive structure constraint required of the bivariate probit model because it ignores the latent variable formulation. However, like a single equation linear probability model, the TSLS does not account for the fact that health insurance coverage can only take on a value of 0 or 1. The coefficients are, however, unbiased if the exclusion restrictions are appropriate.

The TSLS model estimates in Table 4 suggest a wife's coverage does affect her husband's coverage, and the point estimate of this effect was larger in 1982 than in 1992. However, the estimated effect of the husband's coverage on the wife's coverage was much larger than the effect of wife's coverage on husband's coverage in both years—nearly twice as large in 1982 and almost three times larger in 1992. In addi-

Table 4 TSLS Estimates of Wives and Husbands Own Employer Health Insurance (HI) Coverage[a]

	Dependent variable			
	Wife's HI		Husband's HI	
Independent variable	1982	1992	1982	1992
Wife's HI			−0.1775	−0.1055
			(0.0622)	(0.0458
Husband's HI	−0.3205	−0.2953		
	(0.0461)	(0.0500)		

[a] Each model also includes the variables reported in Table 3. Standard errors are in parentheses.

tion, the coefficient of −0.295 on husband's coverage in 1992 implies an almost 30 percentage point effect of a husband's coverage on the probability that his wife is covered by health insurance from her employer. This value is close to the predicted 23.1 percentage point difference (0.533 − 0.202) previously reported from the bivariate probit estimates for an average couple.

These TSLS results suggest that there are some couples where the husband's coverage is affected by his wife's coverage. However, the more common occurrence appears to correspond to the model described by Equations 1–4, where the husband's coverage is exogenous. While the joint determination of spousal coverage deserves additional research with better data, these results support the conclusion that, for many couples, a wife's demand for employer-provided health insurance is causally affected by her husband's coverage.

Coverage Versus Eligibility for Health Insurance

The health insurance questions in the two March CPSs solicit information on whether or not household members are covered by employer-provided health insurance obtained from an employer. As previously discussed, there are two distinct subgroups among uncovered workers. An uncovered individual could be ineligible for insurance because the employer does not offer insurance or because he/she works for an employer that offered health insurance but, for various reasons, the individual was not eligible for coverage. It is also possible an uncovered individual is eligible for employer-provided health benefits but voluntarily decides not to accept the coverage, perhaps because of the cost of health insurance (e.g., substantial premium copayments) or because of spousal coverage.

The distinction between uncovered individuals who are ineligible for coverage but select out of coverage is critical for this analysis. The bivariate probit and TSLS estimates show wives whose husbands are uncovered by health benefits are more likely to be covered by own employer health benefits. I interpret this estimate to mean a husband's coverage affects a wife's demand for a job where she is eligible for insurance, and it is this demand for health insurance eligibility that leads some women to adjust their labor supply and shift from part-time to full-time employment. In the March CPS data, it is impossible to distinguish between this explanation and the alternative explanation that wives with spousal coverage choose not to accept coverage even though they are eligible because of their husbands' insurance coverage. If this latter explanation is the dominant causal explanation, then the estimates in Table 3 are biased estimates of the effect of husbands' coverage on the labor-supply decisions of wives.

While the March surveys do not identify the reasons individuals are not covered by employer health insurance, this information is available from the April 1993 CPS. Figure 2 shows a tree diagram of the distribution of coverage and eligibility for working wives included in the April survey. Of those not covered by own employer health insurance, 62.4 percent are ineligible for coverage through their employer. The remaining share of uncovered wives are eligible for coverage but have not taken advantage of the health benefits. Most (87.8 percent) of those that elect no coverage are covered by their husband's employer-provided health insurance (EPHI); overall, 29 percent of those not covered by their own EPHI are covered by their husband's EPHI.

Fully modeling the joint decisions of couples that determine both coverage and eligibility is beyond the scope of this paper. However, I did estimate the bivariate probit model described by Equations 1–4 using the April data, for which the dependent variable for the wife indicates eligibility for coverage. The coefficient on spouse's coverage in the wife's eligibility equation was −0.6975 with a standard error of 0.260, very similar to the estimates reported in Table 3. These results

Figure 2 Health Insurance Coverage and Eligibility for Wives in the Labor Force, April 1993 (EPHI=Employer-provided health insurance)

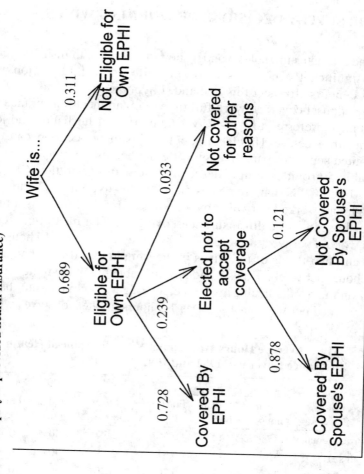

SOURCE: Author's calculations from the April 1993 CPS (n = 5077 married couples).

suggest that the effect of spousal coverage reported in Table 3 is dominated by the effect of husband's coverage on eligibility and not seriously biased by wives who are eligible through their employers for coverage but decide to decline coverage.

LABOR SUPPLY DECISIONS OF WORKING WIVES

The estimates in Tables 3 and 4 show spousal health insurance coverage significantly increases a working wife's demand for a job with health benefits. To meet this demand, I hypothesize that some wives lacking spousal coverage work full time to obtain health insurance but would have preferred to work fewer hours if their husbands had jobs with health benefits. This labor-supply adjustment occurs because of the limited supply of part-time jobs offering health insurance.

Table 5 provides simple descriptive statistics from the 1983 and 1993 March CPSs that are consistent with this hypothesis. The table shows hours worked per week by working, married women as a function of husband's health insurance coverage. The mean number of hours worked per week was 33.9 in 1982; the median was 40 hours per week and two-thirds of the wives in the sample usually worked 35 or more hours per week. Rows 2 and 3 of the table breakdown the sample based on husband's health insurance coverage. The mean number of hours worked per week in 1982 was 1.5 hours greater for wives whose

Table 5 Wives' Average Hours Worked per Week by Spousal Health Insurance Coverage, 1982 and 1992

	1982			1992		
	Mean hours	Median hours	Fraction ≥ 35 hours	Mean hours	Median hours	Fraction ≥ 35 hours
All married females	33.9	40	0.667	35.7	40	0.709
Husband's HI = 1[a]	33.4	40	0.649	34.9	40	0.678
Husband's HI = 0	34.9	40	0.703	37.0	40	0.759

SOURCE: Authors calculations from 1983 and 1993 March CPS.
[a] If HI = 1, the husband has health insurance; if HI = 0, he does not.

husbands did not have health insurance. In addition, the percentage of wives working 35 or more hours per week was 64.9 percent for households where the husband had health insurance and 70.3 percent in households where the husband lacked health insurance. The difference by spousal health benefit coverage in the fraction of married women working 35 or more hours per week had increase in 1992 to 8.1 percentage points.

While other factors correlated with labor supply and husbands health insurance coverage (e.g., husband's income) are not controlled for in Table 5, a simple difference-in-difference estimator calculated over the time period suggests spousal coverage had an effect on the labor-supply decisions of some wives. Specifically, the change over the 10 years in the fraction of married women working full time (e.g., 35 hours/week) was 0.0423 and the fraction of husbands with health insurance declined by 0.054. This implies a one point decline in the fraction of husbands without health benefits led to 0.78 point increase in the percentage of wives working full time (e.g., 0.0423 / –0.0541). The other noteworthy fact from Table 5 is the difference in the fraction of wives working full time by spousal coverage may have had a bigger effect on labor supply in 1992 than in 1982.

The inferences that can be drawn from Table 5 obviously do not control for individual and family characteristics that influence labor supply and are possibly correlated with husbands health insurance coverage or change in the status of husbands health insurance coverage.[6]

To address this concern, Table 6 reports ordinary least square (OLS) estimates of the hours worked per week in 1982 and 1992 as a function of education, three race/ethnicity dummies, age, the presence and age of children in the household, husbands income, and whether or not the husband has health insurance on his job.[7] The parameter estimates on the control variables are all in the expected direction and consistent with prior research. The estimate on husband's health insurance coverage is also in the predicted negative direction in both years. However, the estimated parameter is smaller in 1982 and is not significantly different from zero at the 0.05 level. In 1992, however, the coefficient is much larger and more precisely estimated. The 1992 estimate suggests that married women whose husbands did have health insurance worked an average of 1.5 hours less per week relative to women whose husbands did not have health insurance. I interpret this estimate as the

Table 6 OLS Estimates of Hours Worked per Week by Wives in the Labor Force

Variable	1982	1992
Constant	23.237	23.980
	(4.530)	(4.749)
Kids < 6	−3.316	−2.988
	(0.158)	(0.143)
Kids 6–17	−1.610	−1.879
	(0.103)	(0.092)
Education	0.083	−
	(0.039)	
High school	−	0.549
		(0.312)
Some college	−	0.595
		(0.324)
College	−	2.007
		(0.351)
Graduate school	−	4.517
		(0.413)
Black	2.901	2.100
	(0.389)	(0.347)
Hispanic	2.878	1.168
	(0.349)	(0.288)
Other race	3.094	2.138
	(0.525)	(0.400)
Age	1.078	1.058
	(0.374)	(0.378)
Age 2/100	−2.602	−2.126
	(0.972)	(0.961)
Age 3/10,000	0.180	0.109
	(0.081)	(0.079)
Husband's HI	−0.351	−1.458
	(0.230)	(0.182)
Husband's salary ($1,000)	−0.062	−0.036
	(0.008)	(0.004)
R^2	0.0517	0.0634
N	15,999	18,617

NOTE: Standard errors are in parentheses.

average labor-supply response of women caused by the effect of spousal coverage on the choice between a part-time job without health benefits and a full-time job with benefits.

There are several alternative explanations for the results in Table 6. First, husband's health insurance coverage may simply index "better" jobs. Thus, in households where the husband has a better job as measured by the presence of health insurance, the wife works fewer hours per week because her husband has a "good" job. This alternative explanation could conceivably explain the difference between the estimated effect of husband's health insurance coverage in 1982 and 1992 because there was a decline in health insurance coverage among men over this time period that was most pronounced among less educated men with little work experience (Olson 1995). Thus, health insurance coverage in 1992 was a better predictor of "good" jobs than health insurance coverage in 1982. While it is difficult to rule out this alternative explanation, I think it is an unlikely explanation for the results since the model also controls for husbands earned income. Therefore, this explanation requires that the distinction between "good" and "bad" jobs is correlated with health insurance coverage after conditioning on husband's income.

A second explanation for the results in Table 6 is that the effect of husband's health insurance coverage on the labor supply simply reflects the income effect of these health benefits. However, the magnitude of the coefficient on husband's health coverage in 1992 is simply too big for this explanation to be plausible. Ten thousand dollars in husband's income in 1992 produces a predicted 0.4 hour decline in the work week. If the effect of husband's health coverage was due only to the income effect, the estimate of 1.458 on the health coverage variable corresponds to an income effect equivalent to about $40,000 (e.g., 1.458 / 0.036). Since health insurance is substantially less expensive than $40,000, the estimated effect of husband's health insurance in his wife's labor supply cannot be accounted for by the income effect of the benefit. This explanation is more plausible in 1982 because the coefficient on husband's health insurance implies the income value of health benefits was about $5,600 (e.g., 0.351 / 0.062). While group health insurance in 1982 was also less expensive than this point estimate, given the standard errors around the parameter estimates, it is possible

that a husband's health insurance had an effect on his wife's labor supply in 1982 due primarily to the income effect.

What accounts for the different effect of husband's health insurance coverage on their wives' labor-supply decisions in 1982 and
1992? One explanation is that the relative increase in the cost of health
care between 1982 and 1993 increased household demand for health
insurance because the higher cost of health care raised the risk of not
having health insurance. This increase in demand caused more wives
without health insurance to work full time to obtain employer-provided
health insurance. While this explanation is intuitively appealing, it is
not consistent with the bivariate probit results reported in Table 2. If
this explanation accounted for the differing results, I would have
expected husbands health insurance coverage to have a bigger effect on
the probability a wife held a job with health benefits in 1992 than in
1982. As discussed above, this is not the case; the coefficient on husband's health insurance coverage in the wife's health insurance equation is virtually the same for the two time periods.

The differing effect of a husbands coverage on his wife's hours
worked in the two time periods is more easily explained by the decline
in health insurance coverage among married males. The probability
that husbands in the sample had employer-provided health benefits
declined from 0.67 in 1982 to 0.62 in 1992. This fact suggests that
wives who worked full time in 1982 and were married to husbands
without coverage would have worked full time even if their husbands
had held a job with health insurance. In 1992, however, the decline in
health insurance coverage among husbands meant that more households were faced with the prospect of not having any employer-provided health insurance. This new segment of potentially uninsured
households included families where the woman would have preferred
to work part time if her husband had a job with health benefits but
increased her work week to full time to obtain health benefits. This
explanation suggest the full-time hours constraint that had to be met to
obtain health insurance was not binding on wives in 1982 but was
binding on the labor-supply decision of some wives in 1992.[8]

QUANTILE REGRESSION AND MULTINOMIAL LOGIT ESTIMATES OF HOURS WORKED

The OLS estimates reported in Table 6 will not adequately capture the changes in the hours distribution resulting from differences in husband's health insurance coverage if the impact of spousal coverage varies at different values of the hours distribution. The OLS estimates for 1992 that describe a simple mean shift in the conditional hours distribution by the 1.5 hours is not sufficient to move workers from part-time to full-time status except for those workers already very close the margin between full-time and part-time employment. Moreover, it is likely that those women close to the margin between full-time and part-time work were most affected by their husbands' health insurance status because a full-time job with health insurance involves only a modest increase in hours worked.

This suggests the difference in the hours distribution between wives with and without spousal health benefits will look like Figure 3 if the employer constraint hypothesis is correct. Compared to households where the husband has health benefits, in households where the husband does not have health insurance, the distribution has less mass immediately below full-time employment and more mass at full-time employment (e.g., 35–40 hours per week). However, the tails of the two distributions are similar for two reasons. First, the lower tails of the hours distributions are similar because of the high cost of full-time employment for wives that would otherwise prefer to work substantially less than full time. The upper tails do not differ by husbands coverage because working substantially more than 35–40 hours per week has no impact in the probability a woman has a job with health benefits. The OLS estimates cannot capture the differential behavioral responses of women at different points of the hours distribution.

Quantile regression was used to test if the impact of husbands coverage on the distribution of hours worked by married women is consistent with Figure 2.[9] Separate quantile regression models were estimated for the 10th, 15th, 20th, 25th, 30th, 35th, 40th, and 90th percentiles of the conditional hours distribution, where each model included the same exogenous variables used in the OLS estimates. A comparison of the coefficients on husband's health insurance coverage

**Figure 3 Predicted Effect of Husband's HI on f(hours)
for Working Wives**

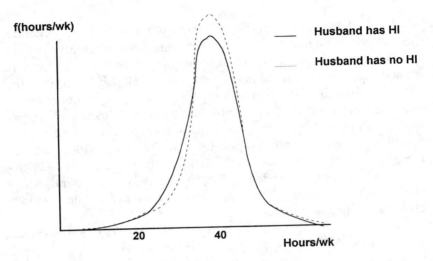

f(hours/wk)

————— Husband has HI

·············· Husband has no HI

20   40

Hours/wk

across these different quantile regressions identifies the portion of the conditional hours distribution most affected by husband's health insurance overage.

Table 7 reports the key results from the quantile regressions for each of the two years. Consistent with the OLS results, the coefficient estimates for 1982 are all insignificant and show husbands health insurance had no impact on any point of the hours distribution for married working women. In contrast, the negative and significant coefficients for 1992 show fewer women worked part time when their husbands did not have health insurance. Furthermore, the larger (in absolute value) coefficients at 21–30 hours suggest that the lack of spousal coverage had the biggest impact on women that were already working more than half time. However, at the 40th percentile (about 40 hours per week), there was only a very modest difference (0.7 of an hour) between those with and without spousal health insurance. This pattern of results is consistent with the hypothesized effect summarized in Figure 3, where the differences in the distribution become very modest once the full-time threshold is reached.

Table 7 Summary of the Quantile Regression Estimates of the Effect of Husband's HI on Hours Worked by Spouse

Estimated quantile	1982		1992	
	Hours worked per week at this quantile	Coeff. on husband's HI	Hours worked per week at this quantile	Coeff. on husband's HI
0.10	16	0.775 (0.582)	20	−1.939 (0.466)
0.15	20	0.284 (0.432)	21	−2.843 (0.364)
0.20	24	0.441 (0.513)	25	−2.738 (0.416)
0.25	27	0.049 (0.486)	30	−2.253 (0.324)
0.30	30	0.021 (0.442)	35	−2.084 (0.238)
0.35	35	0.001 (0.291)	36	−.307 (0.191)
0.40	36	0.086 (0.202)	40	−0.678 (0.125)
0.90	40	−1.587 (0.190)	45	−1.023 (0.254)

NOTE: Each quantile regression includes controls for education, race, age, children in the family, and husband's earning. Standard errors are in parentheses.

I next estimated separate quantile regressions for points of the cumulative hours distribution over two ranges—(0.01, 0.46) and (0.87, 0.95)—to more fully describe the impact of husband's health benefits on hours worked by women in 1992.[10] Models were estimated at 0.01 intervals, and the results were then used to predict and plot the estimated cumulative conditional weekly hours distribution for two working wives that were identical except for husband's health insurance benefits.[11]

Figure 4 shows that, among women with average sample characteristics, those wives most likely to increase hours from part time to full time because their husbands lack coverage were wives who would have been working close to full time even if their husbands had health benefits.[12] Figure 4 shows that about 29 percent of those without spousal health insurance would have worked 30 or fewer hours. In contrast, about 33 percent of those with spousal coverage would have worked 30 or fewer hours per week. Note, however, that the distributions are very similar up to about 15 hours per week and then converge once again at about 37 hours per week. These differences correspond to the hypothesized differences in the probability density functions shown in Figure 3. In other words, the estimates suggest that in 1992 the lack of spousal coverage caused a small fraction of wives to work full time and obtain a job with health insurance instead of working 15–35 hours per week without health benefits.

Figure 4 shows the predicted marginal effect of husband's coverage on hours worked for a wife with average sample characteristics. The position of this predicted conditional density of hours worked by spousal coverage will differ from Figure 4 for women with different characteristics. For this reason, Figure 4 cannot be interpreted as the average effect in the sample of spousal coverage on hours worked but only the marginal effect for wives with the average characteristics.

Estimates from a multinomial logit model of hours worked can be used to obtain an estimate of the average effect of husband's coverage on hours worked for the sample, which does permit husband's coverage to have a different effect on different portions of the hours distribution (e.g., Figure 3). This is accomplished by dividing the hours distribution into non-overlapping intervals and predicting the effect of spousal coverage on the probability that hours of work for wives fall in each interval.

Such a model was estimated for 1992 using the same independent variables included in the OLS and quantile regression models. The dependent variable was constructed by classifying the hours worked by wives into one of the following ranges: 1–10 hours, 11–20 hours, 21–30 hours, 31–34 hours, 35–39 hours, exactly 40 hours, and more than 40 hours.

To conserve space, I have not reported the coefficients for the multinomial model.[13] However, the hypothesis that husband's health insurance has no effect on wife's coverage was easily rejected, as was the hypothesis that husband's coverage had the same effect on the probability of being in each interval of the hours distribution.[14] Table 8 illustrates the predicted effect of husband's coverage on wife's coverage

317

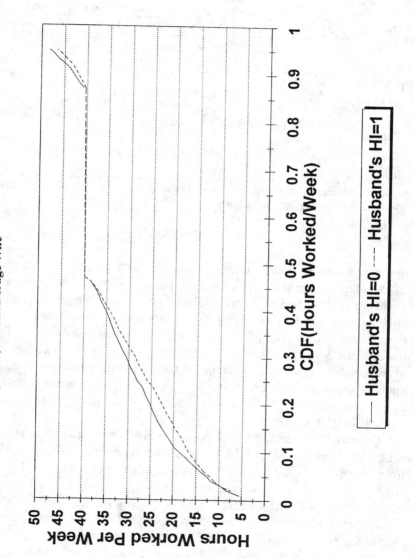

Figure 4 Predicted Conditional CDF (Hours) for an Average Wife

Table 8 Predicted Average Effect from Multinomial Logit Model of Husband's Coverage on Hours Worked by Wives, 1992

	Predicted percentage in each weekly hours range	
Hours/week range	Husband is covered	Husband is uncovered
1–10	4.70	4.36
11–20	12.42	9.33
21–30	12.75	10.31
31–34	2.79	2.48
35–39	10.23	10.85
Exactly 40	44.20	47.51
> 40	12.92	15.16
Total	100.00	100.00

NOTE: These predictions are based on a multinomial logit model that includes all of the variables reported in column 2 of Table 3.

obtained from the multinomial logit model. The estimates were used to calculate two probabilities for each person—one where husband's coverage is set equal to 0 and a second probability where husband's coverage is set equal to 1. The probabilities for each hours range were then averaged over the entire sample and are reported in Table 8. The differences between columns 1 and 2 of Table 8 show the predicted average effect of spousal coverage on the probability wives worked in each hours range. For example, the first row shows husband's coverage had a very small effect (4.7 – 4.36) on the probability wives worked 1–10 hours per week.

Overall, the results reported in Table 8 are consistent with the theoretical predictions and the OLS and Quantile regression estimates. The average effect of spousal coverage on the probability a wife works full time (35 or more hours) was 6.17 percentage points (e.g., 47.51 + 15.16 + 10.85 – 44.20 – 12.92 – 10.23). As rows 2 and 3 of the table show, this shift to full-time work was generated primarily by a reduction in the probability of working 11–30 hours per week.

The estimates reported in Table 8 were used to generate an estimate of the impact of husband's coverage on the expected number of hours worked by wives. This was obtained using the midpoints of each hours range to calculate a weighted average for hours worked using the estimates in each column as weights.[15] This exercise produced the following values:

$$E \text{ (Hours } |HI_H = 1) = 34.31$$

$$E \text{ (Hours } |HI_H = 0) = 35.74$$

The difference between these two values, 1.43 hours, is an estimate of the average effect of husbands' coverage on wives' labor supply. This is about a 4 percent effect (1.43/34.31) and very close to the 1.5 hours obtained from the OLS model.

ESTIMATES OF THE TRADE-OFF BETWEEN WAGES AND HEALTH BENEFITS

In this section I report estimates of the wage-health benefit trade-off faced by married women predicted by compensating wage theory. To estimate this trade-off, I confined the sample to married women that were in the Outgoing Rotation Group subsamples in the March 1993 CPS and that worked 35 or more hours per week. The sample was limited to wives working 35 or more hours per week because this appears to be the threshold between full-time and part-time employment (Hotchkiss 1991). Restricting the sample to the Outgoing Rotation Group allowed use of union status and usual weekly earnings questions. The latter question permits a better measure of the hourly wages than that which is available for the entire March CPS.

The usual empirical strategy for determining the magnitude (and existence) of the wage-fringe benefit trade-off is to estimate a standard earnings equation and include as one of the independent variables the presence or absence of health insurance. Frequently, however, this strategy does not provide results consistent with the theory, and the usual explanation is that the fringe benefit dummy is correlated with the error term in the wage equation because of unobserved factors (e.g., unobserved human capital) that have an impact on both wage levels and health insurance coverage (Smith and Ehrenberg 1983). The

OLS estimate reported in Table 9 suffers from this problem. The OLS coefficient on wife's coverage in a standard wage model is positive, highly significant, and implies married women with coverage receive a 17.8 percent wage premium.[16]

Table 9 OLS and IV Estimates of the Trade-Off between Wages and Health Insurance for Wives in the Labor Force, 1992

	OLS estimates	IV estimates
Constant	−0.213	−0.255
	(0.454)	(0.479)
North Central	−0.103	−0.126
	(0.022)	(0.024)
South	−0.143	−0.147
	(0.021)	(0.022)
High school	−0.037	−0.030
	(0.023)	(0.024)
Some college	0.386	0.418
	(0.031)	(0.034)
College	0.611	0.665
	(0.033)	(0.038)
Grad. school	0.742	0.801
	(0.037)	(0.043)
Black	−0.029	−0.041
	(0.030)	(0.032)
Hispanic	−0.088	−0.000
	(0.026)	(0.039)
Other race	−0.041	−0.073
	(0.036)	(0.038)
Age	0.147	0.161
	(0.036)	(0.038)
Age 2/100	−0.327	−0.364
	(0.091)	(0.097)
Age 3/20,000	0.241	0.273
	(0.075)	(0.080)
Wife's HI	0.164	−0.113
	(0.016)	(0.084)
Union	0.088	0.135
	(0.020)	(0.025)
R^2	0.327	0.252

$N = 2,790$.
NOTE: Standard errors are in parentheses.

An unbiased estimate of the health insurance/wage trade-off can be obtained using an instrument correlated with wife's coverage but uncorrelated with the error term in her wage equation. The variable I used as an instrument for her coverage is her husband's coverage through his employer.[17] As the estimates in Table 2 show, husband's health insurance coverage has a strong effect on the probability his wife has health insurance on her job. Using this variable as an instrument for HI_w, the coefficient on HI_w is negative and implies women with health insurance earn about 11 percent less than comparable women without health insurance. This estimate is consistent with the theory of compensating wage differentials.

SUMMARY

The primary purpose of this study was to investigate the relationship between employer-provided health insurance and the labor-supply decisions of married women. I argue that the demand by a married woman for a job with health insurance is heavily influenced by whether or not her husband has health insurance through his employer. Where husbands lack health insurance coverage, married working women are more likely to be found in jobs that provide health benefits. This bivariate estimates using both 1982 and 1992 data strongly support this prediction.

Employer efforts to minimize adverse selection in the provision of health benefits limits the supply of part-time jobs that provide health benefits. As a result, individuals typically have to work full time to obtain a job with health insurance. This constraint implies husbands health insurance coverage will have an effect on the labor supply decisions of working wives without spousal coverage who seek health insurance through their employer. The estimates for 1982 fail to support the hypothesis that spousal health insurance coverage changed the labor supply of women in 1982. In contrast, there was a small but significant increase in hours worked in 1992 by those women married to men without health insurance. The differing results for the two time periods is explained by the decline in employer-provided health insurance among husbands. In 1982, the requirement that wives worked full time to obtain health insurance was not binding, but the decline in coverage among husbands became binding by 1992 and caused some wives to shift from part-time to full-time employment to obtain health coverage.

The quantile regression and multinomial logit estimates for 1992 suggest that most of the shift in hours occurred among women who would have preferred to work 10–35 hours with spousal coverage but increased their work week to 35–50 hours per week to obtain health insurance. The multinomial logit estimates suggest that, on average, a change in husband's coverage alters the probability his wife works full time by about 9.2 percent.

Finally, estimates of the determinants of the hourly wage for married women working full-time in 1993 supports the trade-off between wages and health benefits that is predicted by compensating wage theory.

Notes

The author has benefited from helpful comments by Ron Ehrenberg, Jonathan Gruber, Doug Hyatt, and seminar participants at Princeton University and Columbia University.

1. This statement is based on my tabulations of the usual weekly hours from the 1979–1991 Outgoing Rotation Group (ORG) file of the Current Population Survey. The data were from the National Bureau of Employment Research CD extract of the ORG.
2. The analysis focuses on hours worked per week conditional on participation in the labor market. I do not investigate the impact of health benefits on the labor-force participation decision.
3. This approach is not without problems. First, it may take considerable time before the firm is able to distinguish between claims due to purely random health shocks and claims that reveal information about the underlying but unobserved health status of the individual and other family members. Second, if the external labor market doesn't observe the information on health status that is revealed to the firm, the firm may be unable to retain the worker because his or her total compensation net of the firm's estimate of expected health claims will fall below the worker's opportunity wage in the external market.
4. The firm may face discrimination charges if it adjusts wages based on certain predictors of health claims such as age and sex.

5. By "average" I mean a 30-year-old, white, high school-educated, working wife living in the Northeast with one child under the age of 6 and one child 6 to 17 years old.

6. For example, the difference-in-difference estimator calculated from changes of the 10-year period will substantially overstate the effect of husband's coverage on the fraction of wives working full time if, between 1982 and 1992, broader changes in the commitment of wives to full-time employment were occurring. The difference-in-difference estimator would mistakenly attribute the impact of these changes to the decline in husband's health coverage.

7. Whether or not the wife has health insurance on her job is not included in her labor-supply equation because health insurance coverage and hours worked are assumed to be jointly chosen by the wife, given the employer constraints that full-time work is required to receive health benefits. Therefore, this labor-supply equation is most appropriately thought of as a "reduced form" equation where husband's health insurance coverage influences both the wife's coverage and her labor-supply decision.

8. Another explanation for the differing results is that firms were less likely to offer health benefits to part-time workers in 1992 and, therefore, the hours constraint became binding on more households. The results in Table 1 do not support this explanation.

9. Quantile regression is most commonly used to estimate how exogenous variables influenced the median of the dependent variable.

10. Approximately 41 percent ($0.87 - 0.46$) of the sample worked exactly 40 hours per week, which was the median for virtually all groups in the sample. Thus, differences in the exogenous variables had no impact on this mass point in the hours distribution, and models for values in the $(0.47, 0.86)$ range were not "identified."

11. The predictions were based on a 30-year-old, white, high school-educated woman living in the Northeast with one child under 6 and another child between 6 and 17 years old.

12. Note that the axes in this graph are reversed from what is customary. The cumulative distribution function (CDF) of hours worked is on the horizontal axis and the vertical axis plots the predicted hours worked at each point of the CDF.

13. These coefficients are available from the author upon request.

14. A likelihood ratio test of the hypothesis that husband's coverage had no effect on wife's coverage produced an χ^2 value of 77.82, and the critical value for 6 d.f. and 0.001 significance level is 22.5. The likelihood ratio test of the hypothesis that husband's coverage has an equal effect on the chances of being in each hours interval produced an χ^2 value of 76.78, and the critical value for 5 d.f. and 0.001 significance level is 20.5.

15. For the over 40 hours per week category, I used the average number of hours worked for those working more than 40 hours per week (e.g., 50.33 hours).

16. The premium is equal to exp. $(0.1636) - 1$.

17. The estimate of ρ, the correlation between the error terms in the two health insurance equations reported in Table 2, is not different from zero in 1992. This suggests husband's health insurance coverage is a plausible instrument.

References

Altonji, Joseph G., and Christina H. Paxson. 1988. "Labor Supply Preferences, Hours Constraints, and Hours-Wage Trade-Offs." *Journal of Labor Economics* 6:254–276.

————. 1991. "Labor Supply, Hours Constraints, and Job Mobility." *Journal of Human Resources* 27(March): 256–278.

Blank, Rebecca M. 1988. "Simultaneously Modeling the Supply of Weeks and Hours of Work among Female Household Heads." *Journal of Labor Economics* 6: 177–204.

Dickens, William T., and Shelly J. Lundberg. 1993. "Hours Restrictions and Labor Supply." *International Economic Review* 34: 169–192.

Heckman, James. 1978. "Dummy Exogenous Variables in a Simultaneous Equation System." *Econometrica* 46: 931–959.

Hotchkiss, Julie L. 1991. "The Definition of Part-time Employment: A Switching Regression Model with Unknown Sample Selection." *Economic Review* 32(November): 899–917.

Olson, Craig A. 1995. "Health Benefit Coverage among Male Workers." *Monthly Labor Review* 118(March): 55–61.

Rosen, Sherwin. 1986. "The Theory of Equalizing Differences." In *Handbook of Labor Economics*, Volume 1, Orley C. Ashenfelter and Richard Layard, eds. Amsterdam: North-Holland.

Smith, Robert S., and Ronald G. Ehrenberg. 1983. "Estimating Wage-Fringe Tradeoffs: Some Data Problems." In *The Measurement of Labor Cost*, J.E. Triplett, ed. Chicago: University of Chicago Press.

8 Employer-Provided versus Publicly Provided Health Insurance

Effects on Hours Worked and Compensation

Janet Hunt-McCool
Economics Consultant

Thomas J. McCool
U.S. General Accounting Office

Avi Dor
Case Western Reserve University

In this chapter, we investigate whether alternative methods of providing health insurance have consequences for the labor market. In the United States, public policy relies heavily on incentives to enhance the ability and willingness of employers to voluntarily purchase group health insurance for workers and their families. This approach contrasts with that of Canada, where all persons are eligible for a minimum health benefit, which can be supplemented but not supplanted by additional employer-provided benefits. Effectively, the U.S. system bundles relatively high-wage full-time work with the health insurance benefits, while in Canada work and health care coverage remain largely independent. How these two disparate approaches to the provision of health care affect the labor-force decision, hours of work, and the compensation mix is a largely unexplored subject, and it is the focus of this research.

Ideally, we would like to empirically model and directly compare the Canadian and the U.S. systems of health care provision and financing to see how each affects the allocation of time between market and nonmarket activities. However, differences in institutions and social insurance provisions, along with data limitations, make such direct comparisons impossible. Instead, we use U.S. data to draw conclusions about the two systems by analyzing two groups of U.S.workers. In the first group, members are covered by health insurance whether or not they are employed ("virtual Canadians") but, in the second, members must work to obtain equivalent insurance.

Canada has a system characterized by minimum basic coverage available to everyone independent of work effort. Additional coverage can be purchased on a tax-preferred basis, either through the employer or individually. However, this additional coverage cannot compete with the minimum benefits, so the private insurance purchased represents a different set of goods and services. In the United States, a subset of the population operates under a similar system: persons who obtain health insurance coverage through the employment of their spouses. If one spouse has insurance, the other's labor supply is less conditioned on and possible independent of the insurance decision. For our purposes, such individuals will be used to simulate the Canadian experience.

Two aspects of the health insurance market are likely to affect labor-market behavior. First, because of problems of adverse risk selection, individually purchased insurance tends to be extremely expensive or to have fewer benefits relative to employer-purchased insurance. Second, employers usually require that employees work close to full-time hours on the job as a condition for health insurance eligibility. Taken together, when one spouse is not offered health insurance at work, the other must generally work full time to obtain such coverage.

The options of full-time employment with coverage and part-time employment without health benefits may create a particularly difficult choice for an individual who must provide both health insurance and home production for the family. The full-time alternative may be selected even if it results in a sub-optimal allocation of time in the household. Thus, by comparing two groups of married women—those covered by spousal insurance and those who are not—we can simulate labor-supply responses under the U.S. and Canadian systems and try to isolate the importance of this effect.

EFFECTS OF HEALTH INSURANCE PROVISION ON HOURS WORKED AND COMPENSATION

The effects of employment-based health insurance on hours of work follow from broad studies of the division of compensation between fringe benefits and earnings. In competitive markets, firms will only provide a more generous benefit, such as health insurance or pensions, at the expense of wages that are lower than usual for workers of a given skill level. Evidence on the trade-off can be found in Woodbury (1983) and Woodbury and Huang (1991).

Evidence of the effect of health insurance on labor supply has been inconclusive and has generally tried to relate health status to work effort. Women are disproportionately low-wage workers and, on average, are less likely to be offered employment-based health insurance than men.[1] Moffitt and Wolfe (1990) have examined the role of public- and employer-provided insurance on the work effort of female heads of households. They found that there would be significant entry into the labor force by women currently on Medicaid if employer benefits were expanded. They estimate that a one-third increase in insurance offers by employers would reduce Aid to Families with Dependent Children (AFDC) rolls by 6 percent and raise labor-force participation by 12 percent. While this effect is largely confined to AFDC households with relatively high demand for medical care, the pull into the workforce from employment-related insurance also shows up more generally for female household heads. Other labor-supply effects may be present for another set of female workers, namely women in dual-earner households. In related work, Wolfe and Hill (1992) simulated the effects of mandated benefits for low-wage mothers under different health states and varying hours of work. Health insurance appears to create a stronger work incentive than either a wage increase or a child care subsidy when these women or their dependents are in poor health.

Changes in labor-supply behavior are also implied by studies of job lock or immobility due to preexisting health conditions that would limit coverage or make workers ineligible for health insurance benefits in a new firm (e.g., Madrian 1994). Monheit and Vistness (1995) showed that spouses appear to take efforts to avoid problems of risk selection due to poor health. Among dual earners, if one is in poor health, the other tends to be the primary holder of employment-based health insurance. On its face, recent legislation also seems based on the assumption that labor-force effort and employment prospects are constrained in the United States by tying insurance to the job. The Kennedy–Kassenbaum Act of 1996 allows former employees to maintain their health insurance indefinitely at the full-employment-based premium, replacing COBRA legislation (Consolidated Omnibus Budget Reconciliation Act of 1985) that limited this option to about two years.

Our analysis extends this research to the general case of health risks, rather than existing health needs, and makes explicit the mechanisms that limit labor hours. Figure 1 shows the general case, based on the household production model of Grossman (1972) in which health is produced using time (h) and market-purchased medical inputs (M). Further, total time in a week is limited to 168 hours, so hours not devoted to home production (e.g., health production) must be used in market-labor supply (n). Given the shadow value of nonmarket time, (w, usually the wage rate) and the market price of medical care P_M, the budget constraint for health is illustrated by the line h_1M_1. If all available time is spent in nonmarket activity ($H_1 = 168$, $n_1 = 0$), no medical care is affordable. As we move down the budget constraint, more hours are worked so more purchasing power is available for medical care but fewer hours are available to provide health care services to the family.

Because it can reduce the problem of adverse selection, group-purchased health insurance is cheaper than that purchased by individuals. The lower price per unit of medical care paid for through employer-provided insurance rotates the budget constraint to h_1M_2, allowing greater purchases of medical care for a given amount of work. Thus, the indirect purchase of health insurance as a component of compensation effectively results in an in-kind transfer of medical care to the worker because the benefits of the price reduction accrue only if medical care is consumed.

To obtain insurance, however, the worker generally has to commit to a minimum work schedule. This convention may be imposed on small firms by insurance companies to avoid expensive family coverage that is disguised as employee coverage. Because health insurance benefit premiums are somewhat indivisible, firms may also need a

Figure 1 Wage/Benefit Trade-off: Health Insurance and Work

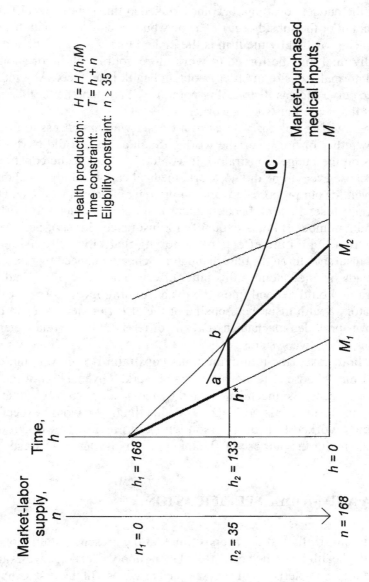

Health production: $H = H(h, M)$
Time constraint: $T = h + n$
Eligibility constraint: $n \geq 35$

large commitment of hours of work to cover the premium expenditures. In Figure 1, we set the constraint at 35 hours per week. Effectively, the budget constraint becomes kinked at this point and shifts by the amount of the subsidy (ab). The new budget constraint with health insurance provided by the firm is the kinked line h_1abM_2. Therefore, an individual may be forced to work more hours than he or should would normally desire in order to obtain health insurance. Any indifference curve such as IC touching point h^* with a slope flatter than the budget line represents such a worker.

We compare this case to that of a worker who has access to insurance whether or not he or she works. Such access would have two effects on the budget constraint. It would clearly shift the constraint out because even if one did not work, medical care would be available. However, for our purposes, the more important effect is that the budget constraint loses its kink because there is no longer a need to work a minimum number of hours to qualify for insurance. Most of our attention is focused on the effects of removing that kink. Provision of health insurance through some mandatory scheme financed by taxes, as in Canada, is equivalent to this latter effect. The slope of the budget constraint would depend upon the exact funding mechanism for the mandatory health insurance scheme or the effect on net wages in the employer-provided mechanism and any differences in the relative efficiencies of the two systems.

In both cases, the minimum hours constraint is removed and the worker may choose to reallocate hours of work. Given a high value of nonmarket time, the incentive created by the need to work full time to qualify for insurance is no longer as compelling. We would expect to see hours worked fall for a person who had previously worked too many hours for the purpose of obtaining health insurance coverage.

DATA AND MODEL SPECIFICATION

To empirically test the proposition that the presence of employer-provided health insurance can affect labor-supply decisions, we evaluate the job characteristics of two samples of wives. In the first sample, husbands hold employment-based health insurance. In the second sample, husbands are not covered by a job-related health policy. We use a two-stage process to determine if there is self-selection of wives into jobs with health insurance and whether self-selection differs according to health insurance coverage of the spouse.

In the first stage, wives face a trichotomous choice of no work, work without insurance, and work with health insurance coverage. Using a multiple logit model, we estimate probabilities of working with and without health insurance for both groups of wives (husbands with and without coverage). The estimator we use is described in Trost and Lee (1984) and Lee (1983).

We use the first-stage results to create selectivity adjustment terms for our second-stage models of labor compensation. The signs and significance of the selection terms provide information on whether self-selection differs according to the spouse's coverage. In particular, the second stage estimates hourly wages, annual earnings from the current job, and two separate indicators of the share of annualized compensation received in the form of health insurance. The shares consist of the total premium and the employer-purchased premium. We expect that the value of health insurance for wives whose husbands do not have insurance would be greater than for wives whose husbands are covered. We also expect to observe an inverse relationship between the value of health insurance and other compensation (shown as a negative sign on the selection term) if insurance is the result of deliberate selection. This latter is the well-known compensation trade-off required if labor markets are competitive.[2]

The main advantage of this two-step approach is that the estimator is consistent with theory. The hours and compensation mix are treated as jointly determined by the introduction of the trichotomous selection terms that condition the second-stage coefficients. Further, rigidities in the work schedule are implicit in the first-stage estimation of work choices.

The main disadvantage is that the estimator does not allow us to measure the magnitude of the trade-off between total compensation and health insurance, if one exists. The effects of the characteristics that affect the probability of working with insurance are highly nonlinear. Thus, measuring the unit change in compensation associated with a fixed-interval change in the selection term (or its underlying odds) is highly artificial. However, this procedure may still be preferred to attempts to estimate the trade-off without attention to self-selection of hours and jobs. Any trade-offs observed otherwise may be biased upward because only persons who choose insurance are observed, and their preferences for insurance are likely to be higher than those whose compensation consists of wages only. Additionally, the data we use have limitations for trying to estimate the magnitude of compensation trade-offs because we do not observe pension accrual benefits. Thus, we are forced to omit an important component of compensation against which health benefits could be exchanged.

Data and Sample Characteristics

Table 1 contains the variable symbols and definitions of the independent variables in the first-stage logit models, the characteristics used to develop the dependent variables in the second stage, and the independent variables of the second-stage analysis. The data on individual health insurance and labor-market characteristics were obtained from Round 4 of the 1987 National Medical Expenditure Survey (NMES) and the supplemental Health Insurance Provider Survey, 1987. The NMES household survey uses a national probability sample of the civilian, noninstitutionalized population. In the provider survey, employers reported information on the kinds of insurance offered and held by household respondents. It also contains data on total premiums and employee and employer share of total premiums. Individual data are augmented by state and county level characteristics of firms and state insurance regulations from Area Resource File, County-City Data Book (Census Bureau), and from state Medicaid and insurance regulation files. Area Resource Files contain a composite of survey results pertaining to the health care market at the county level and are produced biennially by the Bureau of Health Professions. State insurance regulations have been collected annually by Blue Cross and Blue Shield. Medicaid data by state is made available from the Health Care Financing Administration.

We included persons whose job or family status did not change during the round (the quarter year) but, within this group, we focused on married women between the ages of 19 and 62 whose husbands were employed. For empirical purposes, this group was further divided according to whether or not the husband had employment-

Table 1 Variable Definitions

Variable	Variable definition (data source)
Dependent variables	
First stage logit WORK = 1,2,3	Wife does not work outside home; works with no employer-provided insurance; works with insurance, respectively
Second stage	
HOURLY WAGE ($)	Annual earnings/annual hours of work
EARNINGS ($)	Annual earnings (actual, dependent upon wages, weeks, and hours per week)
COMP ($)	Annualized earnings plus annual insurance premium calculated as if wife worked full time and full year
PREMIUM/COMP (%)	Total annual health insurance premium as a percent of COMP
EMPLOYER CONTRIBUTION ($)	The employer portion of the premium
Independent variables	
NONEARNED INCOME ($)	All other household income reported in 1987
DEP	Number of dependents
ADL	Number of limitations of activities of daily living of the wife (health limitations such as walking, bathing, etc.)
AGE (years)	Wife's age in years
BLACK (0, 1)	Wife's race is Black
EDUCATION (years)	Wife's years of education
PROF (0, 1)	Wife is in professional occupation
TENURE (years)	Years at current job of wife
RISK POOL (0, 1)	State where wife resides has a high-risk pool to covered uninsurable persons (Blue Cross Blue Shield data)
CONVERSION (0, 1)	State has a mandate requiring conversion to private insurance if job loss occurs (Blue Cross Blue Shield data)
TAX RATE (%)	Tax rate applied to insurance premiums by state (Blue Cross Blue Shield)

(continued)

Table 1 (continued)

Variable	Variable definition (data source)
MEDICARE CHARGE ($)	Prevailing health care cost index by geographic area (HCFA data)
PER K INCOME ($)	Income per capita in state where wife resides (area resource files)
MDS PER CAPITA (ratio)	Physicians per capita in state (area resource files)
COUNTY POP	Population of county of wife (city and county data book)
MSA (0, 1)	Wife resides in metropolitan statistical area (large urban area)
SOUTH (0, 1)	Wife resides in South
LAMBDA	Selection term in second state

based health insurance from his firm or union. Employment was by far the major source of coverage for all of these households. Only 32 husbands had health insurance from other private sources.

The sample characteristics are described in Table 2. Of interest are the lower wages, earnings, and job tenure of uninsured female workers as compared with insured females. Since this table provides only the analytic variables under investigation, data on hours or type of insurance are not provided. However, such data provide additional insight about the way health insurance may influence work decisions. As expected, there were differences in hours of work based on insurance status. Within the group of women who received insurance, just over 80 percent worked more than 35 hours per week, averaging 39 hours per week. By contrast, those who worked without insurance averaged only 32 hours per week. Similarly, when dual health insurance coverage occurred, 45 percent of sample women chose an individual over a family plan. This contrasts with women who were the sole suppliers of health insurance to their families. Only 19 percent of these women chose individual coverage.

Table 2 Descriptive Statistics of the Samples of Employed Wives: Means (Standard Errors)

	Husband insured		Husband not insured	
Variable	Wife – no insurance	Wife insured	Wife – no insurance	Wife insured
Sample size	974	816	332	547
HOURLY WAGE ($)	7.32 (4.9)	9.04 (4.60)	7.8 (4.6)	8.95 (4.5)
EARNINGS ($)	4,294 (5,067)	7,208 (12,342)	4,781 (10,211)	7,047 (11,888)
COMP ($)		9,368 (13,010)		9,191 (11,955)
PREMIUM ($)		1,965 (1,573)		2,526 (1,862
EMPLOYER CONTRIBUTION ($)		1,631 (1,261)		1,941 (1,392)
NONEARNED INCOME ($)	25,200 (21,908)	35,206 (24,267)	26,672 (23,934)	27,624 (22,720)
DEP	1.6 (1.40)	1.31 (1.30)	1.56 (1.5)	1.38 (1.2)
ADL	0.01 (0.1)	0.01 (0.1)	0.01 (0.2)	0.01 (0.2)
AGE (years)	36.7 (10.1)	37.7 (10.1)	36.2 (10.3)	36.7 (9.9)
BLACK (0, 1)	0.16 (0.4)	0.21 (0.4)	1.56 (1.5)	0.17 (0.4)
EDUCATION (years)	13.0 (3.0)	13.2 (2.8)	12.7 (3.1)	13.0 (3.0)
PROF (0, 1)	0.12 (0.3)	0.12 (0.3)	0.18 (0.4)	0.15 (0.4)
MANUF (0, 1)	0.10 (0.3)	0.12 (0.3)	0.16 (0.4)	0.6 (0.2)
TENURE (years)	4.3 (6.6)	7.8 (6.8)	1.56 (1.5)	7.3 (6.6)
RISK POOL (0, 1)	0.17 4	0.16 (0.41)	0.19 (0.4)	0.19 (0.4)
CONVERSION (0, 1)	0.9 (0.3)	0.9 (0.3)	0.87(0.3)	0.87 (0.3)

(continued)

Table 2 (continued)

	Husband insured		Husband not insured	
	Wife – no insurance	Wife insured	Wife – no insurance	Wife insured
TAX RATE (%)	1.80 (0.8)	1.85 (0.8)	1.81 (0.8)	1.82 (0.8)
MEDICARE CHARGE ($)	27,600 (5,100)	28,008 (5,345)	27,289 (5,519)	27,261 (5,465)
PER K INCOME ($)	14,727 (3,540)	14,883 (3,776)	14,168 (3,327)	14,524 (3,465)
MDS PER CAPITA	0.01 (0.1)	0.01 (0.1)	0.01 (0.1)	0.01 (0.1)
COUNTY POP	776,550 (1,487,000)	798,533 (1,450,790)	885,441 (1,924,000)	868,240 (1,648,652)
MSA (0, 1)	0.25 (0.4)	0.28 (0.4)	0.25 (0.4)	0.27 (0.4)
SOUTH (0, 1)	0.34 (0.5)	0.36 (0.5)	0.40 (0.5)	0.37 (0.5)

SOURCE: Authors' tabulations of the 1987 National Medical Care Expenditure Survey and Health Insurance Provider Survey.

RESULTS

First-Stage Multinomial Logit

Separate logit models were estimated for each of the two subsamples. For brevity, we describe only the results for wives whose husbands worked with insurance.[3] Regression coefficients are reported for those who work with insurance (Table 3) and those who work without insurance (Table 4). These coefficients are calculated relative to those who do not work.[4] In multinomial logit estimation, the signs of coefficients are not necessarily those of the marginal probabilities, so marginal probabilities are calculated if the coefficients are statistically significant.

The independent variables include both person-specific characteristics and area or market characteristics. Some of these variables are excluded from the second-stage regressions so that they also fulfill the theoretical requirement of model identification. Statistical identification is insured because of the nonlinear first-stage technique in which the selection terms are created.

Table 3 shows that nonearned income, education, and per capita income significantly and positively increase the odds of working with insurance (relative to not working) and without insurance (relative to not working). The number of dependents tends to encourage working without insurance. Some area variables such as per capita income affect both working groups while others, the prevailing Medicare charge structure (a proxy for medical care costs), affect one group and not the other.

Second-Stage Results

We estimate the second state as a function of personal and area characteristics. Personal characteristics include the number of dependents, nonearned income, education, race, age, a measure of health status (the number of ADLs),[5] MSA residency, and job-related traits: industry and occupation (MANUF and PROF), job tenure, and location (South). The education and tenure variables should account for a significant part of skill formation on the job and its associated "internal

Table 3 Multinomial Logit Results of the Work Decision of Married Women: Husbands with Health Insurance on the Job

Variable	Work with insurance		Work without insurance	
	Coefficient (*t*-statistic)	Marg. prob.[a]	Coefficient (*t*-statistic)	Marg. prob.
CONSTANT	−4.65 (−8.22)		−2.56 (−49.7)	
NONEARNED INCOME	1.8E-04 (−6.38)	0.000045	−6.E-06 (−3.41)	−2.5E-05
DEP	−0.35 (−8.67)	−0.079	0.0125 (7.05)	0.048572
EDUCATION	0.21 (9.77)	0.030	0.125 (7.08)	0.002632
BLACK	0.55 (3.56)	0.143	−0.171 (−0.80)	−0.11262
MSA	−0.215 (−1.54)		−0.172 (−1.37)	
SOUTH	10.52 (1.68)	0.096	10.32 (1.25)	
COUNTY POP	−9.7E-08 (−2.30)	−2E-08	−8.2E-09 (−0.219)	1.0E-08
PER K INCOME	1.1E-04 (4.51)	1.0E-05	1.1E-04 (4.92)	1.0E-05
RISK POOL	0.153 (1.06)		0.204 (1.597)	
CONVERSION	0.69 (−0.41)		−0.23 (−1.62)	
UNEMPLOY	−2.05 (−0.79)		−0.68 (−0.29)	
TAX RATE	−0.009 (1.42)		−0.088 (−1.58)	
MEDICARE CHARGE	4.4E-05 (3.22)	9.0E-06	1.7E-06 (0.14)	
MD PER CAPITA	−30.66 (−0.61)		−56.69 (−1.24)	

[a] Marginal probabilities are calculated for statistically significant coefficients.

Dep var. = 1   *n* =   925
     = 2   *n* =   1,384
     = 3   *n* =   1,099
−2 log *L*   =   −3,110
Chi-square   =   30

Table 4 Multinomial Logit Results of the Work Decision of Married Women: Husbands Have No Health Insurance on the Job

Variable	Work with insurance		Work without insurance	
	Coefficient (t-statistic)	Marg. prob.[a]	Coefficient (t-statistic)	Marg. prob.
CONSTANT	−4.429 (−5.32)		−2.70 (−3.27)	
NONEARNED INCOME	−4.1E-06 (−1.59)		−1.9E-05 (−0.69)	
DEP	−0.207 (−3.90)	−0.041	0.03 (−0.67)	
EDUCATION	0.240 (8.35)	0.039	0.11 (4.05)	0.002
BLACK	−0.091 (−0.15)		−0.59 (−2.11)	−0.120
MSA	−0.29 (1.20)		−0.61 (−2.41)	−0.109
SOUTH	10.53 (1.23)		10.58 (1.24)	
COUNTY POP	−8.4E-08 (1.35)		1.8E-07 (2.95)	3E-07
PER K INCOME	1.7E-04 (4.11)	0.00001	1.3E-03 (3.2)	
RISK POOL	−0.19 (−0.96)		−0.13 (0.21)	
CONVERSION	−0.31 (−1.26)		−7.9E-01 (0.25)	
UNEMPLOY	−0.397 (−0.12)		0.35 (3.31)	0.112
TAX RATE	−0.095 (−0.95)		−0.18 (−1.83)	−0.030
MEDICARE CHARGE	−8.1E-06 (0.39)		−9.3E-06 (−0.43)	
MD PER CAPITA	73.30 (0.98)		17.42 (0.227)	

[a] Marginal probabilities are calculated for statistically significant coefficients.

Dep var. = 1 n =   572
       = 2 n =   462
       = 3 n =   420
−2 log L = −1,288
Chi-square   =   594

wage rate." The final variable in the regressions is the selection term that is derived from the first-stage results.

Tables 5 and 6 contain the results for the sample of women whose husbands have health insurance. The results for women whose husbands work without insurance are presented in Tables 7 and 8. Tables 5 and 7 present results for wives without insurance. In these cases, the attributes of the job that are estimated are confined to the hourly wage and the earnings on the present job. For wives with insurance, additional dependent variables include total annualized compensation and two compensation share equations. The first of the two share equation is the total annual health premium as a proportion of annualized compensation and the second is the employer contribution to the premium as a proportion of annualized compensation.

An important reason to elect nonwage compensation may be its nontaxed status. If taxes, which are unmeasured but correlated with income, influence this decision, their effect should appear in the latter measure, which considers only the tax-shielded portion of the insurance premium. Presumably, both the demand for health and the desire for a tax shield increase with income.

For wives married to husbands with insurance, no coefficient on any selection term is statistically significant in either Table 5 or 6. In the case of dual coverage, Table 6, we observe only the standard human capital effects on hourly compensation, earnings, and total compensation. MSA residency, education, tenure, and professional status enhance earnings, while women from the South have lower average hourly wages than other women. There is also a positive relationship between wages and nonearned income, which includes earnings of the husband as well as household nonwage income. Generally, this correlation occurs because of marriage between persons with similar human capital and socioeconomic backgrounds, rather than as a pure income effect.

When we evaluate the shares of annualized compensation attributed to health insurance and to the employer's contribution to insurance in Table 6, we observe an inverse relationship to tenure and a positive relationship to dependents. Earnings increase faster than premiums with tenure, but education raises the premium relative to total compensation. The former result suggests the limitations of trading benefits for wages as total compensation increases. The latter result

Table 5 Regression Results of Compensation Equations: Wives Without Insurance and Husbands With Insurance, Coefficients (t-statistics)[a]

Variable	Hourly wage	Earnings
CONSTANT	2.49	−9,390.85
	(2.67)	(−5.02)
NONEARNED INCOME	4.4E-05	0.065
	(8.07)	(5.94)
DEP	−0.139	−431.49
	(−1.32)	(−2.04)
ADL	0.37	−879.22
	(0.33)	(−0.35)
AGE	−0.007	−15.03
	(−0.49)	(−0.49)
BLACK	−0.181	8.83
	(−0.42)	(0.01)
EDUCATION	0.22	672.46
	(4.29)	(6.35)
PROF	1.92	1,712.02
	(5.13)	(2.33)
MANUF	0.37	−80.45
	(0.33)	(−0.09)
SOUTH	−0.57	800.55
	(−1.95)	(1.37)
MSA	1.42	1,693.37
	(4.65)	(2.78)
TENURE	0.132	224.24
	(4.89)	(4.40)
LAMBDA	−0.34	540.48
	(−1.37)	(1.09)
R^2	0.10	0.17
n	974	974

[a] The model contains a dummy variable for missing data on TENURE.

Table 6 Regression Results of Compensation Equations: Wives With Insurance and Husbands With Insurance, Coefficients (*t*-statistics)[a]

Variable	Hourly wage	Earnings	Comp	Employer share	Premium/ comp
CONSTANT	212	−168.62	−2,954.70	0.15	0.02
	(2.03)	(−5.79)	(−3.64)	(6.64)	(6.55)
NONEARNED	2.2E-05	0.08	0.06	−5.4E-08	3.01E-08
INCOME	(3.51)	(4.77)	(2.48)	(−0.44)	(0.21)
DEP	−0.14	−3.02.22	142.28	4.0E-03	0.02
	(−1.41)	(−0.37)	(0.31)	(1.67)	(1.70)
ADL	1.32	8,712.42	−892.58	−0.02	−0.01
	(0.95)	(0.37)	(−0.44)	(−0.37)	(−0.42)
AGE	0.01	50.92	3.98	1.0E-03	5.5E-05
	(0.47)	(1.09)	(0.37)	(0.33)	(0.13)
BLACK	0.55	1,119.67	987.53	1.0E-03	0.01
	(1.51)	(1.07)	(2.16)	(−1.82)	(0.45)
EDUCATION	0.36	1,359.11	1,285.97	−0.34	4.0E-03
	(6.12)	(8.14)	(6.34)	(−0.24)	(3.07)
PROF	1.08	−117.18	55.16	−0.002	−0.02
	(2.41)	(−0.11)	(0.64)	(−1.41)	(−1.71°
MANUF	−0.24	−1,455.08	−887.97	−0.01	(0.01
	(−0.69)	(−1.48)	(−0.74)	(−0.37)	(−0.42)
SOUTH	−0.91	−3.02	−376.89	−0.01	−0.10
	(−3.08)	(−0.37)	(−0.38)	(−0.37)	(−0.42)
MSA	0.91	1,966.65	2,208.22	−0.05	−3.04E-04
	(2.86)	(2.18)	(1.89)	(−0.54)	(−0.40)
TENURE	0.12	186.22	978.53	−0.01	−1.0E-04
	(5.09)	(2.76)	(0.72)	(−2.20)	(−1.83)
LAMBDA	−0.18	−428.36	−417.08	0.0002	0.0003
	(−0.29)	(0.29)	(−0.22)	(0.24)	(0.24)
R^2	0.19	0.23	0.24	0.22	0.06
n	816	816	584	565	634

[a] The model contains a dummy variable for missing data on TENURE.

implies more educated women may demand greater amounts of coverage on the job. We have controlled for age, the wife's disabilities (measured by ADLs), and other income sources. Thus, the link between education and selecting higher levels of coverage appears as a direct one. Such a link is consistent with research on consumption of medical services, suggesting that the higher productivity in health production caused by additional education is offset by greater demand (see, for example, Newhouse 1993).

In Tables 7 and 8, we examine the outcomes for uninsured women married to men without health insurance. Since no feasible substitute exists, household demand for insurance must be met through the wife's job. These women should be more responsive to the offer of insurance than wives whose families obtain insurance through the husband's job. First, we look at uninsured women in Table 7. Again, we do not find the selectivity term to be significant, and standard human capital factors explain hourly wages or earnings (e.g., education, tenure, MSA residency). Earnings on the current job are also positively related to other income.

The most interesting effects of employment/insurance choices are found in Table 8. They pertain to insured women married to men without health insurance. The selection terms are significant in all equations, those explaining elements of compensation and those explaining premium shares. In each case the selection term is signed depending upon the covariance of working with insurance and the continuous dependent variable in the second stage. All elements of compensation fall with greater values of LAMBDA, suggesting a willingness to trade compensation for access to health insurance. The coefficient of LAMBDA, the selection term, is negative in the equation explaining the employer share of total compensation but positive for the ratio of total premiums to compensation. Because the difference between total premiums and the employer share is paid by the employee, it appears that at least some of the net gain accruing to women who select longer hours shows up in the employee's (taxable) portion of the premium. Taken together, these results imply that wives who select jobs that are tied to insurance earn less than the would otherwise earn and receive lower annualized compensation than they would otherwise attain. Moreover, they are even willing to settle for a relatively smaller portion of compensation in the form of nontaxed employer spending on health

Table 7   Regression Results of Compensation Equations: Wives Without Insurance and Husbands Without Insurance, Coefficients (*t*-statistics)[a]

Variable	Hourly wage	Earnings
CONSTANT	3.14	−1,689.98
	(2.21)	(−1.05)
NONEARNED INCOME	1.1E-05	0.02
	(1.09)	(1.97)
DEP	−0.16	−166.29
	(−1.17)	(−1.06)
ADL	−1.09	−102.67
	(−0.28)	(−0.25)
AGE	−0.02	−7.82
	(−0.84)	(−0.32)
BLACK	−0.39	368.62
	(−0.61)	(0.51)
EDUCATION	0.23	184.83
	(3.09)	(2.17)
PROF	1.54	35.97
	(2.00)	(0.04)
MANUF	0.27	1,156.92
	(0.42)	(1.59)
SOUTH	0.43	−105.16
	(0.92)	(−0.20)
MSA	1.25	−133.80
	(2.23)	(−0.21)
TENURE	0.39	155.83
	(3.21)	(2.04)
LAMBDA	−0.46	−277.37
	(−0.42)	(−0.19)
R^2	0.06	0.18
n	323	292

[a] The model contains a dummy variable for missing data on TENURE.

Table 8 Regression Results of Compensation Equation: Wives With Insurance and Husbands Without Insurance, Coefficients (*t*-statistics)[a]

Variable	Hourly wage	Earnings	Comp	Employer share	Premium/comp
CONSTANT	−0.08	−11,283	−9,558.97	8.02	0.32
	(−0.06)	(−3.09)	(−2.11)	(7.67)	(8.37)
NONEARNED INCOME	1.9E-05	0.05	0.06	−9.8E-08	−2.3E-06
	(2.52)	(2.22)	(2.48)	(−0.97)	(−2.71)
DEP	0.15	370.09	142.28	−0.01	−3.0E-04
	(1.06)	(−0.95)	(0.31)	(−0.75)	(−0.02)
ADL	−3.17	−334.32	−892.58	−0.03	−0.85
	−(0.95)	(−0.17)	(−0.44)	(−1.57)	(−0.70)
AGE	−0.04	27.47	−17.86	−0.01	2.0E-05
	(−2.06)	(0.49)	(−0.27)	(−4.32)	(0.09)
BLACK	−0.04	−4,440.41	−3,479.51	−0.01	0.04
	(−0.08)	(−3.30)	(−3.47)	(−1.03)	(0.93)
EDUCATION	−0.08	−1,511.63	1,598.63	−0.08	−0.05
	(−0.06)	(−8.18)	(6.72)	(−7.05)	(−6.51)
PROF	0.39	−286.05	−1,515.59	−0.01	0.04
	(0.87)	(−0.23)	(−1.04)	(−0.66)	(0.93)
MANUF	0.90	2,737.21	2,621.28	9.0E-04	−0.01
	(2.08)	(2.71)	(1.69)	(0.08)	(−0.16)
SOUTH	−1.11	376.63	519.69	0.01	−0.10
	(−3.17)	(0.39)	(0.46)	(0.66)	(−0.18)
MSA	−1.25	3,025.24	3,079.95	0.01	−0.02
	(−3.16)	(2.71)	(2.30)	(0.72)	(−0.46)
TENURE	0.16	255.56	230.18	1.9E-05	−0.10
	(5.57)	(3.14)	(2.42)	(0.03)	(−0.18)
LAMBDA	−2.97	−17,013	−16,487	−0.07	0.39
	(−2.42)	(−5.01)	(−4.03)	(−1.99)	(2.12)
R^2	0.30	0.28	0.29	0.11	0.06
n	547	497	395	384	373

[a] The model contains a dummy variable for missing data on TENURE.

insurance premiums. When given the choice, women whose husbands are not covered on the job will prefer jobs tied to insurance offers, despite certain costs. It appears that at least one motivation for selecting such jobs is access to health insurance.

CONCLUSIONS: IT'S AS EASY TO FALL IN LOVE WITH A MAN WITH HEALTH INSURANCE . . .

Our findings confirm the important work of Moffitt and Wolfe and the suggestions of others that labor supply is affected by insurance offerings. Women in the United States appear to have two options to obtain covers, the "correct" marriage or full-time work. Thus, the Canadian system appears to be less intrusive than the U.S. system of health care delivery, at least in terms of labor supply and, therefore, the household's optimal division of time.

While health benefits in the United States and Canada have both suffered from rising costs, the U.S. system also leaves prominent gaps in coverage (see, for example, Levitt, Olin, and Letsch 1992; Woodbury and Bettinger 1993). We have investigated only part of this problem—the necessity to constrain hours of work to some minimum before a worker becomes eligible for health insurance. Indirect evidence about the sufficiency of full-time work as a means of obtaining insurance may be discerned by comparing wives who hold insurance with wives who do not. Part-time versus full-time work also predicts the returns to education in the form of wages. Wages range from about 22 to 23 cents per hour per year of schooling for wives working without insurance (Tables 5 and 7). In contrast, for other wives, a year of schooling generates 36 to 50 cents extra an hour (Tables 6 and 8). Arguing that obtaining insurance through full-time work is a viable option for all women may be equivalent to arguing that all women can attain high-wage jobs.

What we have been able to demonstrate is that health insurance affects the labor-supply decision and that a trade-off appears to occur between insurance and wage compensation—at least for one U.S. population subgroup, wives who are the sole source of health insurance for their families. Presumably, they represent the conditions under which the majority of U.S. workers operate.

Since their complement, wives whose husbands have health insurance, depict the Canadian case, we conclude that at least some Canadians are likely to choose to work fewer hours than their U.S. counterparts, other things equal. The equality of other things depends particularly upon whether, in which direction, and by how much the health insurance financing scheme in Canada affects labor compensation. Crude evidence suggests that U.S. workers do spend more time than Canadians in labor supply. If a part of this extra effort results from constraints of the health delivery system, social welfare is also reduced.

Notes

The views in this chapter do not necessarily reflect those of the U.S. General Accounting Office. We are indebted to William Alpert and Paul Menchik, whose careful comments and advice contributed substantially to the development of this chapter.

1. In fact, more women than men are covered by health insurance in the United States. The disproportionate coverage by women occurs through public coverage. Adult enrollers in Medicaid and Medicare are disproportionately female, and women are more often than men covered as dependents on group policies.
2. Until recently, little empirical evidence has supported its existence. High-wage workers also tend to have generous benefits, and it is difficult to disentangle all aspects of employment in secondary databases (see Ehrenberg and Smith 1983).
3. In the example we present, we do not deal with issues of joint labor supply by family members. Instead, we act as if male labor supply decision is predetermined and see how this insurance coverage affects the wife's decision to work.
4. We also tested the effect of the husband's health insurance coverage on the wife's labor supply using an alternative multinomial choice model. All wives were pooled and the choices they faced involved full-time work, part-time work, and no work. A dichotomous variable for the insurance status of the husband was included as an explanatory variable. Coverage for the husband was found to be a significant inverse predictor of female labor supply. Because we can only observe insurance premiums for those who obtain insurance, we could not use such a model to determine if trade-offs between wages and health insurance exist, as we can in the alternative approach presented here.
5. ADLs stands for Activities of Daily Living. These include maintenance activities such as bathing, dressing, and eating. The number of ADLs is the number of activities a person is unable to perform and is therefore a measure of disability.

References

Grossman, Michael. 1972. "On the Concept of Human Capital and the Demand for Health." *Journal of Political Economy* 85: 223–277.

Lee, Lung-Fei. 1983. "Generalized Econometric Models with Selectivity." *Econometrica* 51(March): 507–512.

Levit, Katharine, Gary Olin, and Suzanne Letsch. 1992. "Americans' Health Insurance Coverage, 1980–91." *HCF Review* 14(1): 31–58.

Madrian, Brigitte. 1994. "Employment-Based Health Insurance and Job Mobility: Is There Evidence of Job-Lock?" *Quarterly Journal of Economics* 109(1): 27–53.

Moffitt, Robert, and Barbara Wolfe. 1990. "The Effects of Medicaid on Welfare Dependency and Work." Special Report no. 49, Institute for Research on Poverty, University of Wisconsin–Madison.

Monheit, Alan C., and Jessica P. Vistness. 1995. "Implicit Pooling of Workers from Large and Small Firms." *Health Affairs* 3: 201–212.

Newhouse, Joseph P. 1993. *Free for All? Lessons from the RAND Health Insurance Experiment.* Cambridge, MA: Harvard University Press.

Smith, Robert S., and Ronald G. Ehrenberg. 1983. "Estimating Wage-Fringe Tradeoffs: Some Data Problems." In *Measurement of Labor Cost*, Jack E. Triplett, ed. Chicago, IL: University of Chicago Press, pp. 347–369.

Trost, Robert P., and Lung-Fei Lee. 1984. "Technical Training and Earnings: A Polychotomous Choice Model with Selectivity." *Review of Economics and Statistics* 66: 151–156.

Wolfe, Barbara, and Steven Hill. 1992. "The Effects of Health on the Work Effort of Low-Income Single Mothers." Discussion Paper 979. Institute for Research on Poverty, University of Wisconsin–Madison.

Woodbury, Stephen A. 1983. "Substitution between Wage and Nonwage Benefits." *American Economic Review* 73(1): 166–182.

Woodbury, Stephen, and Wei-Jang Huang. 1991. *The Tax Treatment of Fringe Benefits.* Kalamazoo, MI: W.E. Upjohn Institute for Employment Research.

Woodbury, S.A., and D.R. Bettinger. 1992. "The Decline of Fringe Benefit Coverage in the 1980s." In *Structural Changes in U.S. Labor Markets in the 1980s: Causes and Consequences*, Randall W. Eberts and Erica Groshen, eds. Armonk, NY: M.E. Sharpe, pp. 101–134.

9 Employee Benefits and the Distribution of Income and Wealth

Daniel J. Slottje
Southern Methodist University

Stephen A. Woodbury
Michigan State University and *W.E. Upjohn Institute*

Rod W. Anderson
W.E. Upjohn Institute

Changes in the size distribution of income during the 1980s have resulted in a proliferation of new research on the distribution of income and earnings (for a review of the work through the 1980s, see Levy and Murnane 1992). Most of the recent work has focused on explaining increased earnings inequality in the United States during the 1980s, although Raj and Slottje (1994) found that the trend of increasing inequality extends back further.

Far less is known about the size distribution once employer-provided nonwage benefits are taken into account. It is well-known, however, that employee benefits are a significant part of total compensation—voluntarily provided employee benefits such as pensions, health insurance, and life insurance accounted for 9.2 percent of all employer expenditures for employee compensation in 1994, and legally required employee benefits such as Social Security, unemployment insurance, and workers' compensation accounted for another 7.4 percent of compensation expenditures (U.S. Department of Commerce 1998). Two issues need to be explored: 1) whether the picture of income inequality would change if employee benefits were taken into account and 2) whether changes in the mix of total compensation have occurred concurrently with changes in income inequality, hence altering the picture of changes in inequality over time.

The basic difficulty faced by researchers who would like to include employee benefits in estimates of income distribution is that few existing household surveys record the employer contribution *in dollar terms* for major voluntarily provided benefits, such as health insurance and pensions. It is now relatively common for household surveys to record whether a worker is covered by an employer-provided health insurance or pension plan—for example, the Current Population Survey (CPS), National Longitudinal Surveys, and Panel Study of Income Dynamics all include questions on health insurance and pension plan coverage at least periodically. Coverage data are little help, however, in gaining an understanding of how employer provision of benefits (or changes over time in that provision) might bear on the size distribution of income (or changes over time in that distribution).

The lack of household data on employer contributions for fringe benefits explains the scarcity of research on how benefits bear on the size distribution of income. In what is, to our knowledge, the first attempt to examine the issue, Tim Smeeding (1983) linked establishment data on benefit contributions from the Survey of Employer Expenditures for Employee Compensation (EEEC) to household data from the CPS, thereby imputing the dollar benefit contributions made in behalf of individual workers. Lack of data directly linking a worker to employer contributions in that worker's name necessitated such an imputation procedure, although it is clearly a less than ideal way of understanding how benefits bear on income distribution.

In this chapter, we attempt to improve on Smeeding's work in three ways. First, we make use of two household surveys that provide data on concurrent health insurance contributions, accumulated pension contributions made by an employer in a worker's name, or the pension benefits that a worker can expect to receive from participation in the pension plan of a current or past employer. The direct link between a worker and his or her employee benefits is clearly a desirable improvement. Second, we examine inequality in both the joint distribution of total compensation and the marginal distributions of the income components. In particular, we present a decomposition of the Gini inequality coefficient that gives a rough idea of the contribution of each component of compensation to overall inequality. Third, by using more recent data, we are able to draw inferences on whether and how the role of benefits in contributing to income inequality changed over the decade of the 1980s.

Others have attempted improvements on Smeeding's work as well, although most have focused exclusively on the effect of pensions on the distribution of income and wealth. For example, Benedict and Shaw (1995) used the 1983 Survey of Consumer Finances (SCF) to examine how annual pension accruals (calculated as the annual increase in the present value of pension wealth) affect the distribution of earnings. They found that pensions increased annual income inequality slightly in 1983. (Our work using the 1983 and 1989 SCF, reported below, differs from that of Shaw and Benedict by focusing on pension wealth—and changes in pension wealth—between 1983 and 1989.) Several others, including Weicher (1997), Wolff (1994), and Kennickell and Sunden (1997), have done work yielding results that can be compared with those in our fourth section, and we draw those comparisons below.

The chapter is organized as follows. In the first section, we briefly describe the measures we use to make inferences about inequality. In particular, we develop the decomposition of the well-known Gini coefficient. We show that inequality can be decomposed by component of compensation into inequality within each component of compensation and inequality across components. We use the Gini coefficient to make these decompositions meaningful within and across components of compensation.

The second section presents results on the distribution of compensation using current contributions to health insurance and pensions from an old establishment data set—the 1977 EEEC survey. Oddly enough, the EEEC remains the most recent establishment-level data available. (The establishment-level data underlying the Employment Cost Index have never been made available to researchers.) Although dated, the 1977 EEEC do provide a useful benchmark because they are the data on which Smeeding's inferences were based.

The third section examines the distribution of personal income and employer contributions to health insurance plans using the 1977 National Medical Care Expenditure Survey (NMCES) and the 1987 National Medical Expenditure Survey (NMES). These two surveys were fielded to improve understanding of a broad array of health care issues, but they can also be used to obtain estimates of the extent to which employer contributions to health insurance plans increase or decrease the distribution of compensation.

In the fourth section, we develop estimates of wealth inequality using the 1983 and 1989 SCF. Much previous work on wealth inequality has been based on the SCF (see, for example, Kennickell and Sunden 1997; Weicher 1995, 1997; Wolff 1987, 1994, 1996), and we attempt to expand on this work by adding private pension wealth and Social Security wealth to the measurement of wealth inequality. We argue that, for two reasons, wealth holdings provide the proper context in which to examine the influence of employer-provided pensions on inequality in the distribution of compensation. First, annual pension contributions in behalf of an individual worker are frequently unobservable (as with defined-benefit plans). Second, when annual contributions are observable (as with defined-contribution plans), they may vary from year to year in ways that have little to do with the ultimate generosity of the retirement income to be derived from a pension plan. (The argument for using pension wealth and Social Security wealth in gauging the extent to which pensions contribute to inequality is similar to the argument for using Social Security wealth and pension wealth in analyzing retirement incentives; see, for example, Burkhauser and Quinn 1983; Quinn and Burkhauser 1983.)

One disclaimer needs to be made at the outset. We have not attempted to adjust the dollar contributions to health insurance or pension plans to reflect the "value" to the worker of those contributions. Since there are both tax advantages and scale advantages to receiving health insurance and pensions from an employer, dollar contributions by an employer may understate the value to workers of employer-provided nonwage benefits (see, for example, Smeeding 1983, pp. 243–245; Famulari and Manser 1989). We defer an examination of these valuation issues for the time being.

INEQUALITY MEASURES AND A DECOMPOSITION OF THE GINI COEFFICIENT

In this chapter, we use three measures of inequality: 1) the percentage of compensation (or a component of compensation) received by the top 5 percent, 10 percent, and 20 percent of the size distribution, 2) the coefficient of variation, and 3) the Gini coefficient, including a decomposition of the Gini. Although other measures of inequality could be used, all three of these measures (except for the Gini decomposition to be developed next) are well understood and should provide useful estimates of the extent of inequality of total compensation and its components. (For an accessible discussion of a variety of other inequality measures, see Cowell 1977.)

As already mentioned, a decomposition of the Gini coefficient is useful in showing how changes in the distribution of employee benefits have influenced the distribution of total compensation. Yitzhaki (1983) has shown that the Gini coefficient can be written as:

$$G(x) = 2 \operatorname{cov}[x, F(x)] / \mu_x \tag{1}$$

where $F(x)$ is the cumulative distribution of x, and μ_x is the mean of x. Note that this formulation is similar to the coefficient of variation: writing the variance as $\operatorname{cov}(x, x)$, the coefficient of variation is $\operatorname{cov}(x, x)^{1/2} \div \mu_x$.

Suppose now that total compensation (x) is composed of wage and salary earnings (w) and employee benefits (b):

$$x = w + b \tag{2}$$

Since $\operatorname{cov}(w + b, z) = \operatorname{cov}(w, z) + \operatorname{cov}(b, z)$, where z is a random variable, the Gini coefficient can be decomposed as follows:

$$G(x) = 2 \operatorname{cov}[w, F(x)] / \mu_x + 2 \operatorname{cov}[b, F(x)] / \mu_x \tag{3}$$

Now multiply the first term by the following well-chosen 1,

$$\operatorname{cov}[w, F(w)]\mu_w / \operatorname{cov}[w, F(w)]\mu_w \tag{4}$$

where μ_x is the mean of w, and multiply the second term by a similar well-chosen 1,

$$\operatorname{cov}[b, F(b)] \mu_b / \operatorname{cov}[b, F(b)] \mu_b \tag{5}$$

where μ_b is the mean of b, and rearrange terms to obtain

$$G(x) = \frac{\text{cov}[w, F(x)]}{\text{cov}[w, F(w)]} \cdot \frac{2\,\text{cov}[w, F(w)]}{\mu_w} \cdot \frac{\mu_w}{\mu_x} \\ + \frac{\text{cov}[b, F(w)]}{\text{cov}[b, F(b)]} \cdot \frac{2\,\text{cov}[b, F(b)]}{\mu_b} \cdot \frac{\mu_b}{\mu_x} \tag{6}$$

The first part of the first term $\{\text{cov}[w, F(x)] / \text{cov}[w, F(w)]\}$ is the Gini correlation coefficient of w (wage and salary earnings) with x (total compensation), which we denote R_w. This correlation has a mixture of properties of the Pearson and Spearman rank correlation coefficients. Specifically, it is Pearson in w and Spearman in x. The second part of the first term $\{2\,\text{cov}[w, F(w)] / \mu_w\}$ is the Gini coefficient of w, which we denote G_w. The third part of the first term (μ_w / μ_x) is the share of wage and salary earnings in total compensation, which we denote S_w. Defining R_b as the Gini correlation coefficient of employee benefits (b) with total compensation, G_b as the Gini coefficient of employee benefits, and S_b as the share of employee benefits in total compensation, we can rewrite Eq. 6 as follows:

$$G(x) = R_w G_w S_w + R_b G_b S_b \tag{7}$$

That is, the contribution of each component of compensation to the inequality of total compensation equals the Gini correlation between that component and total compensation (R_i), multiplied by that component's Gini coefficient (G_i), multiplied by that component's share of total compensation (S_i).

FINDINGS FROM THE SURVEY OF EMPLOYER EXPENDITURES FOR EMPLOYEE COMPENSATION (EEEC)

The EEEC was a survey of establishments conducted by the Bureau of Labor Statistics from 1966 through 1977. The 1977 EEEC sampled 3,320 establishments of all sizes in order to obtain detailed data on wages and employer contributions to employee benefit plans.

From our standpoint, the main advantage of the EEEC is that it includes data on dollar expenditures by the employer on health insurance and pension plans, as opposed to just employee benefit coverage. Hence, it allows one to examine inequality in the distribution of three components of compensation: wages and salaries (or payroll), employer contributions to health insurance (a category that includes life insurance in the EEEC), and employer contributions to pensions.

We derive inequality estimates from a sample of 5,714 groups of workers from the 1977 EEEC. It is important to understand that, although the EEEC are establishment-level data, we actually observe workers disaggregated into two groups in each establishment: blue-collar workers and white-collar workers. Hence, the unit of observation is not the establishment per se, but either a group of blue-collar workers or a group of white-collar workers observed in an establishment included in the EEEC survey.

Table 1 displays the basic results on the distribution of total compensation from the 1977 EEEC. The average payroll per worker of establishments in the survey was just over $12,500, average contributions to health and life insurance were nearly $550, and average pension contributions were just over $550. As Table 1 shows, the median level of each of the three components is lower than the mean, suggesting positively skewed distributions.

All the measures of inequality—shares of the top 5 percent, 10 percent, and 20 percent, as well as the coefficient of variation and the Gini—suggest that payroll earnings are the most equally distributed component of compensation and that pension contributions are the least equally distributed component. This finding accords with Smeeding's (1983) basic finding although, as already noted, Smeeding linked the EEEC data with individual CPS data.

The evidence suggests that health insurance and pension contributions are highly correlated with total compensation—the Gini correlation coefficient between health contributions and total compensation is 0.75, and that between pension contributions and total compensation is 0.76. The findings suggest, then, that health and pension contributions both tend to increase the overall inequality of total compensation: the Gini coefficient for payroll is 0.265, whereas the Gini for total compensation is slightly higher, 0.277.

Table 1 Distribution of Total Compensation, 1977

	Mean ($) (std. dev.)	Median ($)	% Share of			Coefficient of variation	Gini correlation	Gini coefficient	Share of total compensation (%)
			Top 5%	Top 10%	Top 20%				
Total compensation	13,658 (6,844)	12,797	11.1	19.8	35.0	0.501	–	0.277	100.0
Payroll	12,557 (6,040)	11,898	10.8	19.3	34.2	0.481	0.995	0.265	91.9
Health and life insurance contributions	544 (489)	423	17.7	29.7	48.4	0.899	0.749	0.473	4.0
Pension contributions	557 (770)	267	26.5	42.6	64.7	1.383	0.760	0.657	4.1

SOURCE: Authors' tabulations of 1977 EEEC data on 5,714 worker groups in 3,320 establishments.

FINDINGS ON HEALTH INSURANCE FROM THE MEDICAL EXPENDITURE SURVEYS

In this section, we examine two surveys that combine data on the income of individuals with data on employer contributions to health insurance that were made for an individual. The first is the 1977 National Medical Care Expenditure Survey (NMCES), and the second is the 1987 National Medical Expenditure Survey (NMES). Our goal is to understand the distribution of employer contributions to health insurance and the extent to which that distribution adds to or subtracts from overall inequality in the distribution of compensation.

Data Sources

The National Medical Care Expenditure Survey (NMCES) is a 1977–1978 survey of roughly 14,000 households. It was designed to obtain data on the health status, access to health care, and health insurance coverage of a representative sample of the civilian, noninstitutional U.S. population. The NMCES has two parts. The first part—a household survey—contains standard data on demographic characteristics and personal income, as well as the data on health status and access to health care that were the primary reasons for conducting the survey (Kasper, Walden, and Wilson 1983). The second part—the Health Insurance/Employer Survey (or HIES)—is a supplement to the NMCES that is highly unusual in that it includes data obtained from employers on premiums paid for the health insurance of each covered worker in the sample (Cantor 1986).

The National Medical Expenditure Survey (NMES) is a 1987 survey of roughly 14,000 households whose purpose was the same as the 1977 NMCES (U.S. Department of Health and Human Services 1991). Like the NMCES, the 1987 NMES includes both a household survey and a supplement—the Health Insurance Plan Survey (or HIPS)—that includes data on the characteristics of the employer-provided health insurance (if any) covering each worker in the sample. As with the NMCES, these data were collected from employers and include the premiums paid by employers for health insurance.

Data on workers' wages and salaries are nonexistent in the 1977 NMCES sample and limited in the 1987 NMES sample, a drawback when using these data sets for the purposes we have in mind. We are forced to use personal income from all sources as a proxy for wage and salary earnings. The availability of accurate data on employer contributions to health insurance is the overriding reason for using these data sets.

To examine how employer-provided health insurance contributed to inequality in the distribution of compensation, we select samples of workers aged 25 and over who were employed full-year from the 1977 NMCES and 1987 NMES. We have attempted to create samples that are as comparable as possible, but the questions on employment in the two surveys differ somewhat. Specifically, the 1977 NMCES includes a single variable indicating whether a worker was "continuously employed," whereas the 1987 NMES includes a series of questions (and variables) in each of four survey rounds on whether the worker was employed or unemployed and the number of weeks of employment. For the 1977 NMCES, we have included workers in the sample who are defined as "employed all year." (The definition of this variable is rather problematic. It appears to include both workers who were employed continuously during 1977 and workers who were employed at some time during 1977 but whose employment continuity was unknown.) In the 1987 NMES, we have included individuals who worked 48 or more weeks during 1987. It is impossible to know precisely how comparable these two sets of inclusion criteria are, but we believe that, given the survey questions, we have created two samples that are as comparable as possible. Ultimately, we have used a sample of 7,963 workers from the 1977 NMCES and a sample of 6,009 workers from the 1987 NMES. (For the 1977 NMCES, we use the WTINSP weight; for the 1987 NMES, we use the INCALPER weight.)

Findings

Table 2 shows descriptive statistics and various measures of the inequality of employer contributions to health insurance, personal income, and total compensation for 1977 (from the NMCES) and 1987 (from the NMES). As already noted, because the NMCES does not include information on wage and salary earnings, we define total compensation here as personal income plus employer contributions to health insurance.

Table 2 Distribution of Personal Income and Employer Contributions to Health Insurance, 1977 and 1987

	Mean($) (std. dev.)	Median ($)	% Share of Top 5%	Top 10%	Top 20%	Coefficient of variation	Gini correlation	Gini coefficient	Share of total compensation (%)
NMCES (1977)									
Total compensation	14,120 (13,238)	11,683	19.8	29.6	44.9	0.938	–	0.403	100.0
Personal Income	13,705 (13,141)	11,150	20.2	30.1	45.4	0.959	0.999	0.407	97.1
Employer contributions to health insurance	415 (527)	243	22.7	37.4	60.4	1.270	0.434	0.634	2.9
NMES (1987)									
Total compensation	27,547 (24,598)	23,000	17.6	27.4	42.9	0.893	–	0.375	100.0
Personal income	26,334 (24,265)	21,802	18.1	28.0	43.5	0.921	0.998	0.381	95.6
Employer contributions to health insurance	1,213 (1,321)	873	19.4	32.7	54.1	1.088	0.479	0.569	4.4

SOURCE: Authors' computations from samples of workers aged 25 or older and employed "full-year" in the 1977 National Medical Care Expenditures Survey (N=7,963) and the 1987 National Medical Expenditures Survey (N=6,009).

In 1977, the average personal income of full-year workers aged 25 and over in the NMCES was about $13,700 (in current dollars), and the average employer contribution to health insurance was slightly over $400. In 1987, the average personal income of full-year workers aged 25 and over in the NMES was about $26,300 (in current dollars), and the average employer contribution to health insurance was about $1,200. Thus, in 1977 employer contributions to health insurance made up 2.9 percent of what we are defining as total compensation (personal income plus employer contributions to health insurance), whereas in 1987 employer contributions to health insurance were 4.4 percent of total compensation. This roughly 50 percent growth in the share of compensation accounted for by health insurance closely mirrors the economy-wide growth in the share of total compensation accounted for by employer contributions to health insurance observed in the National Income and Product Accounts from 1977 to 1987 (U.S. Department of Commerce, Bureau of Economic Analysis 1998).

In both 1977 and 1987, the median personal income and the median employer contribution to health insurance are well below the means for either of these variables in both years, suggesting positively skewed distributions.

Figures on the share of personal income and of contributions to health insurance going to workers in the top 5 percent, 10 percent, and 20 percent of the size distribution clearly show that, in both 1977 and 1987, personal income was more equally distributed than employer contributions to health insurance. The coefficients of variation and the Gini coefficients for personal income and employer contributions to health insurance provide the same inference.

However, total compensation is more *equally* distributed than either personal income or employer contributions to health insurance. The Gini coefficients for personal income are 0.407 (in 1977) and 0.381 (in 1987), and the Ginis for employer contributions to health insurance are 0.634 (in 1977) and 0.569 (in 1988). The Ginis for total compensation, however, are slightly lower than the Ginis for either component—0.403 (in 1977) and 0.375 (in 1987). That is, even though employer contributions to health insurance were more unequally distributed than personal income in both 1977 and 1987, health contributions were distributed so as to slightly lower overall inequality. Similar inferences follow from an examination of the coefficients of variation and shares of total compensation going to the top 5, 10, and 20 percent of individuals. The distribution of health insurance contributions reduces the inequality of the distribution of total compensation, even though it is less equally distributed than personal income.

The finding that total compensation is more equally distributed than its components suggests both the importance of micro data in drawing inferences about compensation inequality and the usefulness of the Gini decomposition. Also, it accords with the rather low correlations between total compensation and health contributions—the Gini correlation coefficients of health contributions with total compensation are just 0.434 (in 1977) and 0.479 (in 1987).

The finding from both the NMCES and the NMES that health contributions are more unequally distributed than personal income accords (in a rough way) with the finding from the EEEC establishment data that health contributions are more unequally distributed than is payroll. But the conclusion from the NMCES and NMES that health contributions *decrease* overall inequality is counter to the analogous finding from the EEEC establishment data. The result suggests both the importance of micro data in drawing inferences about compensation inequality and the usefulness of the Gini decomposition.

In contrast to many studies of wage and income inequality in the 1980s, the NMCES and NMES suggest that the distribution of personal income became somewhat more equal between 1977 and 1987. (On the distribution of earnings, see Levy and Murnane 1992; on the distribution of personal income, see Raj and Slottje 1994.) Given the preponderance of evidence that the distribution of earnings and income became less equal during the 1980s, we are unwilling to place much weight on this interyear comparison. It seems likely that the result is due to the difficulty we had in creating comparable samples of workers from the NMCES and NMES. In other words, the finding that personal income inequality fell between 1977 and 1987 should probably be viewed as an artifact of the way we had to draw our samples.

To summarize, employer contributions to health insurance in both 1977 and 1987 were far less equally distributed than personal income among full-year workers aged 25 and older. However, although very unequal, the distribution of employer contributions to health insurance was such that it slightly lowered the distribution of total compensation (defined as the sum of personal income and employer contributions to health insurance).

FINDINGS ON RETIREMENT BENEFITS AND WEALTH DISTRIBUTION FROM THE SCF

In analyzing the EEEC data, we took the annual employer contribution to the pension plan as an accurate reflection of the pension plan's generosity. But the annual contribution may vary from year to year depending on changes in the performance of the pension plan's assets or in changes in actuarial assumptions. Hence, the annual contribution to a pension plan may be a poor reflection of the plan's generosity, understood as the stream of retirement income that the pension plan ultimately will yield. In order to obtain a more accurate picture of how pensions contribute to individual inequality, it is necessary to consider the asset value of a pension plan—that is, the present value of the promised future income stream to be derived from the pension.

In this section, we use the 1983 and 1989 Surveys of Consumer Finances (SCF) to examine the distribution of retirement and nonretirement wealth (Kennickell and Shack-Marquez 1992; Fries, Starr-McCluer, and Sunden 1998). We construct estimates of both private pension wealth and Social Security wealth and compare the distribution of these with the distribution of other more conventional forms of wealth, such as housing and business assets. Our premise is that wealth holdings provide the proper context in which to examine the influence of employer-provided pensions on inequality.

Data Sources and Variable Construction

The 1983 and 1989 SCFs are a natural choice for studies of the distribution of wealth, and they have been used in previous work on wealth inequality (Wolff 1987, 1994, 1996, 1998; Weicher 1995, 1997; Kennickell and Sunden 1997). The SCF is an extensive survey designed to estimate the wealth holdings of a representative sample of households in the United States. It includes information on pensions and retirement wealth, as well as data on conventional asset holdings such as property and financial wealth. In addition, the SCF includes retrospective data on the employment histories of both the respondent and spouse (if present).

The main strength of the SCF, from our standpoint, is its data on asset holdings and coverage by private pension plans. Although asset holdings and pension coverage are self-reported, inspection of the questionnaire and the asset and pension data themselves suggest that considerable lengths were taken to obtain a consistent picture of households' assets and pension expectations. Also, the SCF's employment data are sufficient to construct a reasonable approximation to Social Security wealth, as described below.

We draw samples of households from the 1983 and 1989 SCFs that mirror those used by Feldstein (1976) in his pioneering study of Social Security wealth. That is, we examine all households in which there was a male aged 35 to 64 present. This basic selection criterion yields samples of 1,721 households in 1983 and 1,572 in 1989.

Three forms of wealth are of main interest to us: 1) private pension wealth, 2) Social Security wealth, and 3) nonretirement wealth. The first two are the main forms of retirement wealth held by households, and the third includes all forms of conventional (or nonretirement) wealth. We discuss the construction of variables measuring each in turn.

Private Pension Wealth. The present value of expected annual pension benefits for which a household is eligible represents that household's private pension wealth. Private pension wealth must be computed separately for defined-benefit and defined-contribution pension plans.

For defined-benefit pension plans, we have calculated the present value of 1) pension benefits that are expected in the future from current employment, 2) pension benefits that are expected in the future from past employment, and 3) pension benefits currently being received from past employment.

For both men and women expecting to receive a defined-benefit pension from a current job or jobs, we use the self-reported age of expected pension receipt and the annual pension amount to calculate a present value of the flow of future pension receipts from the expected age at which benefits begin until age 100. We adjust each year's benefit amount for the probability of death based on the worker's gender and age at which the benefit would be received (National Center for Health Statistics 1984). We subtract the present value of employee contributions (also adjusted for the probability of death) from the current year until the expected retirement age. Benefits and contributions are discounted back to the present (1983 or 1989) at a rate of 9 percent (the Federal Funds rate in both 1983 and 1989).

For both men and women expecting to receive a defined-benefit pension from a past job or jobs, the procedure is similar. We again calculate a present value of the flow of future pension receipts from the age when benefits are expected to begin until age 100, adjusting for the probability of death in each year. We subtract the present value of employee contributions (again adjusted for the probability of death) and again use a discount rate of 9 percent.

For both men and women who are currently receiving pensions, we calculate a present value of the flow of future pension receipts from the current age until age 100, using a 9 percent discount rate and adjusting for the probability of death in each year.

For defined-contribution pension plans, we follow Wolff (1987), McDermed, Clark, and Allen (1989), and Kennickell and Sunden (1997) in using the current amount reported in a worker's defined-contribution account as the measure of pension wealth. The dollar amount in any profit-sharing plan held by the individual is also included as pension wealth. The 1983 SCF includes information on one defined-contribution plan from a current employer for each individual (respondent and spouse) and up to three plans (either defined-contribution or defined-benefit) for each individual from past employers. The 1989 SCF includes information on up to three defined-contribution plans from a current employer for each individual (respondent and spouse) and up to six defined-contribution plans for each individual from past employers.

To arrive at a summary measure of private pension wealth for each household, we sum the pension assets from all sources except for Individual Retirement Accounts (IRAs) and Keogh plans. We treat IRAs and Keogh account balances as a separate category of retirement wealth, using the current account balances as the measure of wealth in each.

Social Security Wealth. The present discounted value of the Social Security old-age benefits for which a household is eligible represents the household's Social Security wealth. We compute Social Security wealth in a way resembling the method Feldstein (1976) used with the 1963–1964 Survey of Financial Characteristics of Consumers, a survey that is similar to the SCF used here.

For a respondent and spouse who are not currently receiving Social Security benefits, we impute the expected annual Social Security old-age benefit by assigning a Primary Insurance Amount (PIA) based on the relative position of the individual's earnings in the earnings distribution of workers of his or her age and gender. (Five-year age cohorts of workers were used to avoid using distributions based on very small samples.) Specifically, we use the worker's current earnings unless the worker was not currently employed, in which case we use the highest earnings from past jobs and bring them forward to the current year (either 1983 or 1989) using the wage index factor used by the Social Security Administration (Social Security Administration 1984). For each respondent and spouse, we obtain the relative position in the earnings distribution that the individual occupied in his or her gender and five-year age cohort. If this relative position in the earnings distribution did not change over the working life, then the individual would be at the same relative position in the benefits distribution at the time of retirement. Each worker's Social Security benefit was imputed from the distribution of benefits paid for newly retired workers using the relative position of each worker in the earnings distribution.

Each household's Social Security benefits are then computed from individual Social Security benefits. For a single-worker household, we sum the worker's benefit amount and the spouse's benefit amount (one-half the worker's benefit). For a two-worker household, we take the larger of 1) the sum of the benefit amount of the worker with higher benefits and the corresponding spouse's benefit amount or 2) the sum of the two workers' imputed benefit amounts.

To convert each household's benefit amount into household Social Security wealth, we calculate a present value of the flow of future Social Security benefits from age 65 until age 100. We adjust each year's benefit amount for the probability of death based on the worker's gender and age. (Also, we take account of expected widow's or widower's benefits by calculating the joint probability that the worker will be deceased and the spouse will be alive and by applying this probability to the worker's benefit amount.) We assume that the annual benefit amount grows at 4 percent per year from the current year onward, and we discount benefits back to the present (1983 or 1989) at a rate of 9 percent.

For all households currently receiving Social Security old-age or disability benefits, we use current benefit amounts to calculate a present value of the flow of future Social Security benefits from the current age until age 100. We adjust for the probability of death in each year, allow benefits to grow at an annual rate of 4 percent, and discount to the present at a rate of 9 percent.

Nonretirement Wealth. Most forms of assets and wealth as conventionally defined are included in nonretirement wealth. In particular, we consider the following six types of wealth.

1) Housing wealth, which we divide into two components: a) equity in the principal residence and b) equity in other real estate, including up to four (in 1983) or three (in 1989) additional properties, plus the amount owed to the household for land contracts (less the amount owed on land contracts). For each property, we compute equity as the difference between the current market value of the property and the amount owed on that property (using up to two mortgages).

2) Business assets, or the net value of the household's share in up to two (in 1983) or three (in 1989) businesses in which someone in the household had an active management role, plus the net value of the household's share in businesses in which no one in the household had an active management role.

3) Life insurance, the value of which was calculated by taking the cash value of straight (or whole life) insurance and subtracting the amount of borrowing against the policy. (The face value of term insurance was excluded because term insurance is not a financial asset, in that it cannot be borrowed against.)

4) Liquid assets, or the sum of the average balance in all checking accounts, all money market accounts, and all saving accounts, plus the dollar value of short-term certificates and certificates of deposit.

5) Stocks and bonds, or the sum of a) the market value of all stocks, call money accounts, and stock and other mutual funds held, b)

the face value of U.S. savings bonds, government bonds and Treasury bills, state and municipal bonds, and corporate or foreign bonds held; and c) the value of trust accounts and managed investment accounts held.

6) Other assets, comprising cars (net of outstanding car loans) and tangible assets (such as gold, jewelry, and other objects).

Our results leave out debt that is not part of any of the other wealth category; that is, consumer loans, home improvement loans, credit card debt, and other lines of credit are not taken into account in any way.

Findings

Tables 3 and 4 report descriptive statistics and various measures of the inequality of wealth distribution from the 1983 and 1989 Surveys of Consumer Finance. It is useful to first examine the shares of the individual components of total wealth. The largest single component of wealth is housing (27 percent in 1983, 30 percent in 1989), followed by business assets (19 percent in both 1983 and 1989), private pension wealth (17 percent in 1983, 14 percent in 1989), Social Security wealth (17 percent in 1983, 15 percent in 1989), and stocks and bonds (9 percent in 1983, 8 percent in 1989). The other main forms of wealth—liquid assets, life insurance, IRA/Keogh plans, and other assets—each account for 5 percent or less of total wealth. In aggregate, retirement wealth made up 35 percent of total wealth in 1983, 32 percent of total wealth in 1989, and was split roughly evenly between private pension wealth and Social Security wealth in both years.

The computed Gini coefficients suggest that all forms of assets are distributed highly unequally, except for Social Security wealth, which has Ginis of 0.334 in 1983 and 0.352 in 1989. Principal residence housing is next most equally distributed, with Ginis of 0.561 in 1983 and 0.615 in 1989. Private pensions are the third most equally distributed form of wealth, with Ginis of 0.739 in 1983 and 0.765 in 1989. The distributions of business assets, stocks and bonds, and other real estate appear to be most unequal, with Gini coefficients of 0.90 or higher. Life insurance, liquid assets, and other assets have Ginis that are in the middle of the pack. Substantially the same inferences can be drawn from the share figures and the coefficients of variation.

Table 3 Distribution of Wealth by Component, 1983

	Mean ($) (std. dev.)	Median ($)	% Share of Top 5%	% Share of Top 10%	% Share of Top 20%	Coefficient of variation	Gini correlation	Gini coefficient	Share of total wealth (%)
Total wealth	262,643 (916,406)	147,273	36.3	47.0	61.4	3.489	–	0.578	100.0
Retirement wealth	92,786 (107,363)	60,469	22.3	35.2	53.2	1.157	0.796	0.489	35.3
Private pension wealth	45,790 (91,122)	10,644	35.6	53.4	75.8	1.990	0.726	0.739	17.4
Social security wealth	43,628 (27,346)	36,666	13.5	23.5	40.2	0.627	0.632	0.334	16.6
IRA/Keogh plans	3,369 (23,421)	0	70.5	83.1	95.5	6.953	0.768	0.910	1.3
Nonretirement wealth	169,857 (891,456)	64,072	49.5	61.0	73.8	5.248	0.955	0.713	64.7
Housing	71,830 (190,049)	42,082	35.0	47.0	63.0	2.646	0.873	0.619	27.4
Principal residence	49,584 (74,409)	37,098	26.2	38.4	55.7	1.500	0.800	0.561	18.9
Other real estate	22,246 (158,257)	0	67.6	83.4	97.4	7.114	0.819	0.910	8.5
Business assets	49,128 (553,086)	0	82.6	93.8	99.8	11.258	0.916	0.948	18.7

Life insurance	4,626 (19,103)	0	55.2	72.5	89.2	4.130	0.503	0.852	1.8
Liquid asset	12,881 (43,906)	3,009	45.4	61.2	78.9	3.409	0.730	0.761	4.9
Stocks/bonds	24,533 (490,904)	0	88.2	95.3	99.0	20.010	0.930	0.963	9.3
Other assets	6,859 (28,831)	3,650	43.4	54.9	69.3	4.204	0.621	0.719	2.6

SOURCE: Authors' tabulations of 1983 SCF data on 1,722 households with a male aged 35 to 64 present. See text for variable definitions.

Table 4 Distribution of Wealth by Component, 1989

	Mean ($) (std. dev.)	Median ($)	% Share of			Coefficient of variation	Gini correlation	Gini coefficient	Share of total wealth (%)
			Top 5%	Top 10%	Top 20%				
Total wealth	362,183 (1,643,389)	185,571	42.4	52.7	65.7	4.537	–	0.622	100.0
Retirement wealth	114,887 (149,094)	72,646	24.2	36.9	54.2	1.298	0.824	0.500	31.7
Private pension wealth	51,519 (123,461)	10,000	41.3	59.1	78.3	2.396	0.751	0.765	14.2
Social security wealth	53,558 (35,312)	44,329	13.9	23.9	41.0	0.659	0.594	0.352	14.8
IRA/Keogh plans	9,809 (40,350)	0	58.2	73.9	91.5	4.114	0.773	0.869	2.7
Nonretirement wealth	247,297 (1,611,928)	89,809	55.0	65.6	76.6	6.518	0.969	0.743	68.3
Housing	107,766 (512,182)	52,409	41.9	53.6	68.1	4.753	0.894	0.676	29.8
Principal residence	68,825 (133,577)	41,000	30.0	43.3	59.8	1.941	0.796	0.615	19.0
Other real estate	38,941 (459,591)	1,409	75.8	88.3	96.6	11.802	0.869	0.928	10.8
Business assets	69,280 (1,203,050)	0	91.4	98.1	100.0	17.365	0.928	0.972	19.1

Life insurance	5,886 (39,619)	0	59.8	74.1	91.8	6.731	0.546	0.886	1.6
Liquid asset	17,865 (116,921)	2,800	58.8	72.7	85.5	6.545	0.799	0.824	4.9
Stocks/bonds	28,351 (383,716)	0	85.5	94.1	98.7	13.534	0.915	0.954	7.8
Other assets	18,148 (180,269)	6,000	56.4	67.2	78.4	9.933	0.786	0.774	5.1

SOURCE: Authors' tabulations of 1983 SCF data on 1,722 households with a male aged 35 to 64 present. See text for variable definitions.

Comparison of the Gini coefficients for overall retirement wealth (0.489 in 1983 and 0.500 in 1989) with the Ginis for overall nonretirement wealth (0.718 in 1983 and 0.753 in 1989) suggests that retirement wealth is considerably more evenly distributed than is nonretirement wealth. The relatively equal distribution of Social Security wealth is mainly responsible for this result. The Ginis for private pension wealth (0.739 in 1983 and 0.765 in 1989) are similar to those for nonretirement wealth overall (0.713 in 1983 and 0.743 in 1989). Social Security wealth (with Ginis of 0.334 in 1983 and 0.352 in 1989) clearly reduces inequality in the distribution of total retirement wealth. Again, the share figures and coefficients of variation are consistent with the Ginis.

However, the influence of private pension wealth on overall inequality is not simple. Substantially less private pension wealth is concentrated in the top 5 and 10 percent of private pension holders than is the case for nonretirement wealth overall. Also, the coefficient of variation of private pension wealth is lower than that of nonretirement wealth overall. But, as already noted, the Gini coefficients of private pension wealth are slightly higher than those of nonretirement wealth overall. It follows that private pension wealth tends to even out the high end of the wealth distribution, but increases inequality below the 20th percentile or so of the wealth distribution.

A comparison of Tables 3 and 4 suggests that, overall, the distribution of wealth grew more unequal between 1983 and 1989. With the exception of IRA/Keogh plans and stocks and bonds, the Gini coefficient of every category of wealth increased between 1983 and 1989. The Ginis of principal residence housing, liquid assets, and other assets increased especially sharply. The Ginis for both Social Security wealth and private pension wealth increased moderately during the 1980s, and the share figures suggest that much of the increased inequality of private pension wealth occurred because of greater concentration of pension wealth at the very high end of the distribution (that is, above the 10th percentile).

It is useful to compare the findings in Tables 3 and 4 with other empirical findings on the distribution of wealth. Kennickell and Sunden (1997), Weicher (1995, 1997), and Wolff (1994) used the 1983 and 1989 SCF to examine nonretirement wealth and all found slight increases (comparable to that which we displayed in Tables 3 and 4) in the Gini coefficients of nonretirement wealth between 1983 and 1989. Kennickell and Sunden, Weicher, and Wolff all used more heterogeneous samples that we do—we restrict our sample to households with a male aged 35 to 64 present—and hence obtained higher Gini coefficients than we do. The changes in the Ginis from 1983 to 1989 are similar, however.

Other researchers have used the 1992 interview of the Retirement History Survey (RHS) to examine the impact of Social Security and private pensions on wealth inequality. Gustman et al. (1997) found that Social Security reduces overall wealth inequality, whereas private pensions increase overall wealth inequality. Gustman et al. found that pensions account for 23 percent and Social Security about 27 percent of total wealth—figures that are far higher than ours using the SCF. McGarry and Davenport (1997) concluded that private pensions have only slightly increased overall wealth inequality. Apart from the relatively high proportion of wealth that is accounted for by Social Security and private pensions (Gustman et al. 1997), the findings from the RHS studies are broadly similar to those from our work with the SCF.

To summarize our results, Tables 3 and 4 show that there are five major forms of wealth holding in the United States: housing (both principal residence and other real estate, which account for 27–30 percent of all wealth), business assets (19 percent of all wealth), private pensions (14–17 percent), Social Security (15–17 percent), and stocks and bonds (8–9 percent). The figures show clearly that business assets, stocks and bonds, and real estate other than the principal residence are the strongest contributors to overall wealth inequality (all have Gini coefficients of at least 0.9), whereas Social Security wealth is the main contributor to greater equality in the distribution of wealth (with a Gini of 0.33 to 0.35).

Principal residence housing plays an intermediate role in the distribution of wealth. Principal residence housing has a Gini coefficient (around 0.6) that is close to that of the total wealth distribution (when Social Security wealth is included), although inspection of the wealth share figures suggests that the distribution of principal residence housing is equalizing at the high end of the total wealth distribution and disequalizing at the low end.

This leaves private pension wealth, which results essentially from employer contributions to pension plans. The Gini coefficients associated with private pension wealth (around 0.75) suggest that private pensions do increase inequality in the total wealth distribution, when total wealth is defined to include the present value of future expected Social Security benefits. However, the Gini correlation of private pension wealth with total wealth is relatively low: only the Gini correlations of life insurance and (in 1989) other assets with total wealth are lower. Also, as noted above, the distribution of private pension wealth tends to smooth out the high end of the wealth distribution. That is, although the Gini coefficients of private pension wealth are slightly higher than for nonretirement wealth overall, the coefficients of variation of private pension wealth and the shares of private pension wealth going to the top 5 and 10 percent of the distribution are lower than for nonretirement wealth overall. This finding suggests that private pensions play an intermediate role in determining the distribution of wealth. Although they clearly fail to help equalize the overall distribution (as Social Security does), neither are private pensions a driving force behind increased wealth inequality, as are business assets, stocks and bonds, and real estate other than the principal residence.

SUMMARY AND DISCUSSION

We have attempted to address a rather simple question: do employer contributions to health insurance and pensions increase or decrease inequalities in the distribution of compensation, income, and wealth? Most existing evidence—and intuition informed by the observation that highly paid workers tend to receive more generous nonwage benefits—suggests that employee benefits tend to increase inequality, but the answers we found are a bit more complicated.

First, we find that employer contributions to health insurance are far more unequally distributed than is personal income (most of which is earnings). Nevertheless, health insurance contributions are distributed in such a way that they slightly reduce inequality in the overall distribution of income (defined as the sum of personal income and employer contributions to health insurance). We would not make too much of this finding because the reduction of inequality accounted for by health insurance contributions is small. It is clear, however, that health insurance contributions made by employers, despite their highly unequal distribution, do not exacerbate inequalities of compensation and income. This is an unexpected result but one that is robust in both the 1977 NMCES and the 1987 NMES (see the third section above).

Second, we find that employer contributions to pension plans are a major form of wealth holding, about equal to Social Security wealth as a proportion of total wealth, and surpassed only by housing wealth and business assets. Stocks and bonds, the other major form of wealth holding, are less significant than private pensions or Social Security. Our main conclusion on the role of private pensions in the distribution of wealth can be summarized in two parts. First, private pensions are not one of the driving forces behind increased wealth inequality. Rather, business assets, stocks and bonds, and real estate other than the principal residence are the main contributors to wealth inequality. Second, it is clear that, when total wealth is defined to include Social Security wealth, private pensions do increase overall inequality in the total wealth distribution. However, the distribution of private pension wealth is quite different from that of overall nonretirement wealth. Private pension wealth clearly smooths the high end of the wealth distribution, increasing wealth inequality only below the 20th percentile of the wealth distribution. Private pensions, then, seem to play an intermediate role in determining the distribution of wealth. Although they do not help to equalize the overall distribution of wealth (as does Social Security), they are not one of the driving forces behind increased wealth inequality, and they reduce inequality at the high end of the wealth distribution.

What are the implications of these findings? Employer contributions to both health insurance and pension plans receive favorable treatment under existing tax law, and the continued favorable tax treatment of each is a key part of the ongoing debate over fundamental tax reform (see, for example, Woodbury 1997 and the references cited there). The main finding from the medical expenditure surveys—that health insurance contributions have a slightly equalizing effect on the distribution of income—tends to argue for continued favorable tax treatment of employer-provided health insurance. It is not a strong argument because the equalizing effect of employer contributions to health insurance is not great. Moreover, the argument must be weighed against the various arguments for taxing employer contributions to health insurance, most of which are based on efficiency considerations.

There were two main findings from the Surveys of Consumer Finances: Social Security is the great equalizer of wealth and private pensions are not a major force behind increasing wealth inequality. There are two implications. First, Social Security's central role in decreasing wealth inequality could well be an overriding reason to avoid full privatization of Social Security because full privatization would almost surely reduce the tendency of Social Security to equalize the wealth distribution. Second, in that private pensions are not a major force behind increasing wealth inequality, taxing employer contributions to pension plans would be a less effective wealth equalizer than policies directed toward business assets, stocks and bonds, and real estate other than the principal residence. Also, any increases in wealth equality that might be achieved by taxing pension contributions would need to be weighed against the decline in savings that would likely result (Gale 1995).

Note

We are grateful to the William H. Donner Foundation and the W.E. Upjohn Institute for support.

References

Benedict, Mary Ellen, and Kathryn Shaw. 1995. "The Impact of Pension Benefits on the Distribution of Earned Income." *Industrial and Labor Relations Review* 48 (July): 740–757.

Burkhauser, Richard V., and Joseph F. Quinn. 1983. "The Effect of Pension Plans on the Pattern of Life-Cycle Compensation." In *The Measurement of Labor Cost*, Jack Triplett, ed. Chicago: University of Chicago Press, pp. 395–415.

Cantor, J.C. 1986. *National Medical Care Expenditure Survey Health Insurance/Employer Survey Data: Person Record Public Use Tape Documentation for Premium Data and Benefit Data.* Rockville, MD: National Center for Health Services Research and Health Care Technology Assessment.

Cowell, F.A. 1977. *Measuring Inequality.* New York: John Wiley and Sons.

Famulari, Melissa, and Marilyn E. Manser. 1989. "Employer-Provided Benefits: Employer Cost versus Employee Value." *Monthly Labor Review* 112 (December): 24–32.

Feldstein, Martin. 1976. "Social Security and the Distribution of Wealth." *Journal of the American Statistical Association* 71 (December): 800–807.

Fries, Gerhard, Martha Starr-McCluer, and Annika Sunden. 1998. "The Measurement of Household Wealth Using Survey Data: An Overview of the Survey of Consumer Finances." Working paper, Federal Reserve Board of Governors, Washington, D.C.

Gale, William. 1995. "The Effects of Pensions on Wealth: A Re-Evaluation of Theory and Evidence." Working paper, The Brookings Institution, Washington, D.C.

Gustman, Alan L., Olivia S. Mitchell, Andrew A. Samwick, and Thomas L. Steinmeier. 1997. "Pension and Social Security Wealth in the Health and Retirement Study." National Bureau of Economic Research Working Paper No. 5912.

Kasper, J.A., D.C. Walden, and R. Wilson. 1983. *National Medical Care Expenditure Survey Household Data: Person Records Documentation and Codebook.* Rockville, MD: National Center for Health Services Research.

Kennickell, Arthur B., and Janice Shack-Marquez. 1992. "Changes in Family Finances from 1983 to 1989: Evidence from the Survey of Consumer Finances." *Federal Reserve Bulletin* (January): 1–18.

Kennickell, Arthur B., and Annika Sunden. 1997. "Pensions, Social Security, and the Distribution of Wealth." Working paper, Federal Reserve Board of Governors, Washington, D.C.

Levy, Frank, and Richard J. Murnane. 1992. "U.S. Earnings Levels and Earnings Inequality: A Review of Recent Trends and Proposed Explanations." *Journal of Economic Literature* 30 (September): 1333–1381.

McDermed, Ann A., Robert L. Clark, and Steven G. Allen. 1989. "Pension Wealth, Age-Wealth Profiles, and the Distribution of Net Worth." In *The Measurement of Saving, Investment, and Wealth*, Robert E. Lipsey and Helen Stone Tile, eds. Chicago: University of Chicago Press, pp. 689–736.

McGarry, Kathleen, and Andrew Davenport. 1997. "Pensions and the Distribution of Wealth." National Bureau of Economic Research Working Paper No. 6171.

National Center for Health Statistics. 1984. *Vital Statistics of the United States, 1980*, Volume II, section 6, Life Tables. Washington, D.C.: U.S. Government Printing Office.

Quinn, Joseph F., and Richard V. Burkhauser. 1983. "Influencing Retirement Behavior: A Key Issue for Social Security." *Journal of Policy Analysis and Management* 3 (Fall): 1–13.

Raj, Baldev, and Daniel J. Slottje. 1994. "The Trend Behavior of Alternative Income Inequality Measures in the United States from 1947–1990 and the Structural Break." *Journal of Business and Economic Statistics* 12 (October): 479–487.

Smeeding, Timothy. 1983. "The Size Distribution of Wage and Nonwage Compensation: Employer Cost vs. Employee Value." In *The Measurement of Labor Cost*, Jack Triplett, ed. Chicago: University of Chicago Press.

Social Security Administration. 1984. *Social Security Bulletin Annual Statistical Supplement*, 1983. Washington, D.C.: U.S. Government Printing Office.

U.S. Department of Commerce, Bureau of Economic Analysis. 1998. *National Income and Product Accounts of the United States: Statistical Supplement, 1929–1994*. Washington, D.C.: U.S. Government Printing Office.

U.S. Department of Health and Human Services, Agency for Health Care Policy and Research. 1991. *National Medical Expenditure Survey, 1987: Household Survey, Population Characteristics, and Person Level Utilization, Rounds 1-4 [Public use Tape 13]*. Rockville, MD: U.S. Department of Health and Human Services, Agency for Health Care Policy and Research.

Weicher, John C. 1995. "Changes in the Distribution of Wealth: Increasing Inequality?" *Federal Reserve Bank of St. Louis Review* 77(January/February): 5–23.

_____. 1997. "Wealth and Its Distribution, 1983–1992: Secular Growth, Cyclical Stability." *Federal Reserve Bank of St. Louis Review* 79(January/February): 3–23.

Wolff, Edward N. 1987. "Estimates of Household Wealth Inequality in the U.S., 1962–1983." *Review of Income and Wealth* 33 (September): 231–256.

_____. 1994. "Trends in Household Wealth in the United States, 1962–83 and 1983–89." *Review of Income and Wealth* 40(June): 143–174.

_____. 1996. *Top Heavy*. New York: The New Press.

_____. 1998. "Recent Trends in the Size Distribution of Wealth." *Journal of Economic Perspectives* 12(Summer): 131–150.

Woodbury, Stephen A. 1997. "Employee Benefits and Tax Reform." In *Tax Reform: Implications for Economic Security and Employee Benefits*, Dallas L. Salisbury, ed. Washington, D.C.: Employee Benefit Research Institute, pp. 27–34.

Yitzhaki, Shlomo. 1983. "On an Extension of the Gini Inequality Index." *International Economic Review* 24(October): 617–623.

Part IV

Pensions

10 Public Pension Plans in the United States and Canada

Morley Gunderson
University of Toronto

Douglas Hyatt
University of Toronto

James E. Pesando
University of Toronto

Increased attention is being paid to the similarities and differences between Canada and the United States in a variety of areas of social policy. The similarities provide elements of a natural experiment to facilitate controlling for the myriad of observable and unobservable factors that can affect behavior. They also make it more likely that the experiences in one country have relevance for the other country. The differences provide variation in a number of factors that are of interest for their possible impact on behavior. The differences are especially of interest when they involve variables that are subject to a degree of policy control.

These similarities and differences have been exploited in a number of areas of social policy. Card and Freeman (1993) analyzed the impact of differences in labor-market and social policies on various outcomes, including wage and income inequality, poverty, union density, unemployment, and immigration. Chiswick (1992) looked at the impact of differences in immigration and language policies on such factors as immigrant assimilation, fertility, domestic earnings, language fluency, and the economic returns to that fluency.

The purpose of this chapter is to outline important similarities and differences between Canada and the United States in public pension plans. While the focus is on public pension plans, brief mention is made of private pensions, so as to put the public plans in perspective. Particular attention is paid to the potential redistributive and incentive effects of the public plans, especially as they may shed light on the trend towards earlier retirement.

The chapter begins with a description of the different components of the Canadian public pension system, emphasizing features that have potential redistributive and incentive effects. Private employer-sponsored occupational pension plans are briefly discussed, and the importance of both public and private pension plans are documented as sources of retirement income. The extent to which public pension plans serve to replace preretirement earnings is documented, as are their potential redistributive effects. Intergenerational transfers implied by the "pay-as-you-go" financing are then analyzed as is the shift in policy emphasis from public to private pensions. A similar but briefer description of the U.S. public pension system is provided, and the similarities and differences are used to shed light on the trend in both countries to reward earlier retirement. The paper concludes with a brief summary of the salient points.

PUBLIC PENSION PROGRAMS IN CANADA

The public pension programs provided by the Government of Canada consist of three components: 1) Old Age Security (OAS) payable to all Canadians aged 65 and over regardless of means; 2) an income-tested supplement (the Guaranteed Income Supplement or GIS) payable, upon application, to recipients of the basic OAS pension who have little or no other income; and 3) an earnings-related component (the Canada Pension Plan or CPP) linked to an individual's average lifetime earnings.[1] The basic features of these public pension programs are summarized in Table 1. Unlike the situation in the United States, health insurance is provided under the universal public programs in each of the provinces, and coverage is unaffected by retirement status.

Old Age Security (OAS)

Old Age Security is a demogrant, financed out of general tax revenues and payable to those aged 65 and older and with 40 years of residence. It is a flat-rate, universal benefit unrelated to work history. It

Table 1 Public Pension Programs: Government of Canada

Program	Nature	Benefit	Financing
Old Age Security (OAS)	Demogrant payable to those over 65 subject to residency requirement; benefits reduced for Canadians with incomes over $39,911	Maximum annual pension is $3,472; fully indexed to CPI	General tax revenues
Guaranteed Income Supplement (GIS)	Income-tested benefit; recipient must be over age 65 and in receipt of OAS pension	Maximum annual pension is $4,127; reduced by 50% of recipient's income in excess of OAS benefits; not taxable and fully indexed to CPI	General tax revenues
Canada Pension Plan (CPP)	Earnings-related; designed to replace 25% of average lifetime earnings, up to the average industrial wage	Maximum annual pension is $6,250; fully indexed to CPI	Equal employer/employee contributions, set at 2.6% of earnings between $3,300 and $33,400

NOTE: All amounts are expressed in U.S. dollars, at an exchange rate of 75 cents (U.S.) for each Canadian dollar, and pertain to January 1, 1994. The provinces of Alberta, British Columbia, Nova Scotia, Manitoba, Ontario, and Saskatchewan provide income-tested supplements, thereby raising the guaranteed annual income of those aged 65 in excess of OAS/GIS benefits.

began as a means-tested pension, introduced in 1927, payable to qualifying individuals at the age of 70. By 1951, it had become a universal
flat-rate pension payable at age 70, and the age of eligibility was subsequently reduced to 65 in concert with the introduction of the Canada
Pension Plan. The full OAS benefit is equal to $3,472 per year as of
1994.[2] (All dollar amounts hereafter are expressed in U.S. dollars, at
an exchange rate of 75 cents [U.S.] for each Canadian dollar.) Beginning in 1989, the OAS pensions of higher income Canadians have been
"clawed-back" at the rate of 15 percent after net income of $39,911 in
1993.

Guaranteed Income Supplement (GIS)

The Guaranteed Income Supplement is an income-tested transfer
payment given to residents of Canada who are in receipt of the basic
OAS pension and who have little or no other income. The GIS was
introduced in 1966. Like OAS, GIS is financed from general tax revenues. At the beginning of 1994, the maximum GIS pension was $4,127
for singles and $5,376 for married couples. The GIS places a floor on
the minimum income of those aged 65 and over. Unlike OAS and CPP
pensions, GIS benefits are not subject to income tax. The implicit tax-
back rate for GIS benefits is 50 percent; that is, for each dollar of
income (including CPP benefits) in excess of the basic OAS pension,
GIS benefits are reduced by 50 percent.[3]

Canada Pension Plan (CPP)

The Canada Pension Plan (like Social Security in the United
States) is a mandatory, contributory, earnings-based pension that provides coverage for the majority of workers. It was established in
(largely) its present form in 1965. The CPP is designed to replace 25
percent of a worker's average lifetime earnings for persons whose
earnings are equal to or less than the average industrial wage. For persons whose earnings are higher than the average industrial wage, the
CPP is designed to replace a smaller portion of their average lifetime
earnings. At the beginning of 1994, the maximum CPP benefit was
$6,248 per year, or approximately 25 percent of the average industrial
wage of $25,800. The maximum CPP benefit is paid to workers whose

earnings equal or exceed the ceiling on contributions (the Year's Maximum Pensionable Earnings, or YMPE) for each year during their work lives.

The CPP is financed out of a payroll tax, with equal contributions from employers and employees. In 1994, the contribution rate for employers and employees was set for both at 2.6 percent of earnings between the Year's Basic Exemption ($2,550) and the YMPE ($25,800).[4] The average contribution was $680 in 1991. The contribution rate is scheduled to rise steadily over the next 25 years, from 5.2 percent (combined rate) in 1994 to 10.10 percent in 2016 and to 12.73 percent in 2030.

Prior to 1987, CPP benefits were payable at age 65 (or later, at the worker's option). Since 1987, CPP benefits have been payable at age 60, on an actuarially reduced basis and subject to the requirement that the recipient is not working.[5] The actuarially fair reduction is designed to exactly compensate for the fact that the pension is received earlier and for a longer expected period of time. In January 1992, the majority of males who commenced receipt of CPP retirement benefits were aged 60 to 64. Indeed, the number of males commencing receipt of benefits at age 60 was only modestly less than the number commencing receipt at age 65. For females, the early receipt of benefits is more pronounced, with the number commencing receipt of CPP benefits at age 60 exceeding the number commencing receipt at age 65 (Health and Welfare Canada 1992, Table 8).

CPP benefits can be delayed until age 70, in which case annual benefits are actuarially increased to compensate for the fact that they will be received later and for a shorter expected period of time. After the age of 70, there is no actuarial adjustment so that there is in effect a penalty for delaying receipt after that age.

CPP benefits are fully taxable as a normal source of income. However, there is no clawback if the person does not retire (after attaining age 65) but continues to work and earn income. The only clawbacks are indirect: CPP income is subject to income tax and if the person continues to work, the person would presumably be in a higher marginal tax bracket. As well, if the person continues to work, the person is more likely to exceed the threshold level of income of $39,111 that would subject their OAS income to the 15 percent clawback. More importantly, if the person is eligible for the GIS supplement, the person's GIS benefits would be reduced by the 50 percent "tax-back" that applies to income (including CPP income) beyond the OAS demogrant.

Private Pension Plans (RPPs and RRSPs)

Canada's public and private pension system is generally described as involving three tiers: 1) the universal Old Age Security component consisting of the OAS demogrant and the possible GIS income-tested supplement; 2) the Social Insurance component involving the mandatory, earnings-based CPP which covers most workers; and 3) and employer-sponsored, occupational Registered Pension Plans (RPPs). The first two tiers are the public pension system, and the third is the private pension system.

Private, employer-sponsored RPPs are financed by employers, usually with employee contributions.[6] In 1992, 38.4 percent of the labor force were covered by such occupational pension plans, the coverage being slightly higher for males than for females (Statistics Canada 1994, p.16). In 1992, 90 percent of plan members were in defined-benefit plans, with 18 percent being in flat-benefit plans (predominantly in the unionized sector) and 72 percent being in earnings-based plans (usually dependent upon the individual's final years of earnings). Only 9 percent of plan members were in defined-contribution plans. Although membership in both defined-benefit and defined-contribution plans has been growing, membership in defined-contribution plans has been growing at a faster rate.

Private, earnings-based pensions also exist in the form of personal savings through Registered Retirement Savings Plans (RRSPs) that basically involve a deferral of taxes until the pension is withdrawn upon retirement. These are earnings-based in the sense that (as of 1991) individuals are allowed to contribute up to 18 percent of their earned income in the previous year. The maximum contribution for 1991 was $8,625 for individuals who did not have an RPP, or $8625 less what is known as the "Pension Adjustment" for those who belong to an RPP. (The pension adjustment seeks to underscore the value of the pension benefit carried during the year by a member of a defined-benefit pension plan. Technically, it equals nine times the benefit entitlement less $1,000). In 1991, 24 percent of all tax filers made RRSP contributions, averaging $2,172 .

Contributions and Benefits from Pension Plans

As indicated in Table 2, among the different contributory pension plans, the CPP has the greatest number of contributors, given the mandatory nature of such contributions. Private RPPs and tax-advantaged RRSPs have considerably fewer contributors. The number of contributors has grown most rapidly, however, for RRSPs. Although the CPP involves the greatest number of contributors, it also involves the lowest average contribution ($680) compared to average contributions of over $2,000 for both RPPs and RRSPs. This smaller average contribution for CPPs leads to lower total contributions for CPPs than for RRSPs, which—in turn—are less than contributions for RPPs. From 1981 to 1991, the growth of total contributions has been greatest for RRSPs, followed by the CPP and then RPPs.[7]

With respect to benefits paid under the different pension plans, Table 3 indicates that the CPP and the OAS/GIS have the greatest number of beneficiaries. Beneficiaries of the CPP have grown the most, reflecting the aging of the workforce and the tendency to retire early and receive the actuarially adjusted benefits after age 60. Average benefits are greatest for RPPs, followed by OAS/GIS, with CPP benefits being the smallest. Total benefits, however, have grown the most under CPP, reflecting the highest growth in both the number of recipients and the average benefit per recipient.

Pension Income as Component of Retirement Income: Canada

The importance of the three public pension plans in contributing to retirement income is shown in Table 4. In 1988, they accounted for 38 percent of retirement income for men and 50 percent for women. The earnings-based CPP, however, constitutes a smaller component for women than for men, reflecting the fact that women tend to have lower earnings (and less continuous work histories) than do men. The OAS and GIS benefits are not linked to labor-market earnings; hence, their fixed nature means that, in combination, they constitute a larger portion of the retirement income for women (40.0 percent) than for men (22.5

Table 2 Contributors and Contributions of the CPP Relative to Employer Private Registered Pension Plans (RPP) and Earnings-Based Registered Retirement Savings Plans (RRSPs) in Canada, in 1991

Contributors/contributions	Public (CPP)	Employer-based private pension (RPP)	Tax advantaged savings (RRSP)
Contributors			
Number (millions)	12.0	5.3	4.6
Growth 1981–91	9%	14%	136%
Average contribution			
Average ($US)	680	2,411	2,172
Growth 1981–91	151%	47%	46%
Total contributions			
Total (million $US)	8,135	12,822	10,028
Growth 1981–91	173%	68%	245%

Working age population growth 1981–91,   14.5%

Labor force growth 1981–91,   16.8%

Nominal GDP growth 1981–91,   86.7%

Consumer price growth 1981–91,   67.2%

SOURCE: Calculations based on data from Statistics Canada (1994, p. 9). Growth rates calculated using the following data series from the Statistics Canada CANSIM Main base: working age population, D767867; labor force, D767870; nominal GDP, I28026; and, consumer price index, P490000.

NOTE: All dollar amounts are converted to U.S. dollars, at an exchange rate of 75 cents (U.S.) for each Canadian dollar.

Table 3 Benefits Paid Under Public Pension Plans (OAS, GIS, CPP) and Employer-Registered Pension Plans (RPP) in Canada, in 1991

Beneficiaries and benefits	OAS/GIS	CPP	RPP
Beneficiaries			
Number (millions)	3.3	3.7	1.8
Growth 1981–91	34%	108%	98%
Average benefit			
Average ($US)	4,136	3,020	7,328
Growth 1981–91	63%	128%	99%
Total benefits			
Total (millions $US)	13,571	11,171	13,083
Growth 1981–91	118%	375%	294%

SOURCE: Calculations based on data from Statistics Canada (1994, p. 14).
NOTE: All dollar amounts are converted to U.S. dollars, at an exchange rate of 75 cents (U.S.) for each Canadian dollar.

Table 4 Public Pension Income as a Percentage of Total Retirement Income Males and Females Age 65 and Over in Canada, in 1978 and 1988

% Income derived from	1978		1988	
	Men	Women	Men	Women
OAS demogrant	20.8	36.2	17.2	29.1
GIS supplement	5.6	11.0	5.3	10.9
CPP public pension[a]	8.5	4.3	15.9	10.5
(Total public pensions)	(34.9)	(51.5)	(38.4)	(50.5)
Private pensions (RRP, RRSP)[b]	16.7	8.4	23.1	11.6
Investment income	25.4	32.6	21.9	31.4
Employment income	19.5	5.3	14.0	4.2
Other income	3.5	2.1	2.7	2.4
Total retirement income	100.0	100.0	100.0	100.0

SOURCE: Based on data presented in Galarneau (1991, p. 29).
[a] The CPP benefits include payments to surviving spouses, which amount to 32 percent of total CPP payments in 1988.
[b] Private pension income includes income from employer-sponsored Registered Pension Plans (RPP) and tax-advantaged private Registered Retirement Savings Plans (RRSP).

percent). This larger portion more than offsets the lower portion from CPP income for women, so that overall pension income from the three pension programs comprises 50.5 percent of the retirement income for women, compared to 38.4 percent for men in 1988.

Because of their higher earnings and greater labor force attachment, the earnings-based occupational pension plans (RPPs) and earnings-based RRSPs also constitute a larger portion of retirement income for men than for women. The same applies to employment income. Table 5, based on more current and comprehensive data from the 1991 census, presents a similar picture.

Figure 1 illustrates that, between 1981 and 1991, there was a relative decrease in the importance of the OAS demogrant and GIS supplement as a source of pension income, in contrast to the increased importance of employer-sponsored RPPs and especially the public CPP.

Table 5 Public Pension Income as a Percentage of Total Retirement Income Persons Age 65 and Over in Canada in 1991

% Income derived from	Males	Females	Both sexes
OAS demogrant/GIS supplement	20.0	36.0	27.3
CPP public pension	15.3	12.6	14.0
(Total public pension)	(35.3)	(48.6)	(41.3)
Private pension (RRP, RRSP)	22.3	11.6	17.4
Investment income	19.1	25.9	22.2
Employment income	17.1	7.6	12.8
Other income	6.2	6.3	6.3
Total retirement income	100.0	100.0	100.0
Average income ($US)	17,699	11,255	14,018

SOURCE: Calculated from the individual files of the Public Use Sample Tapes of the 1991 Census of Canada, weighted by the Statistics Canada sample weights.

Figure 1 Components of Pension Income in Canada, 1981 and 1991

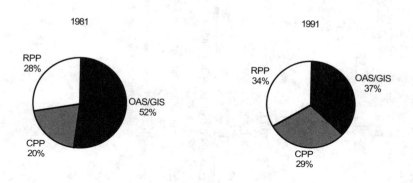

The Income Replacement of Public Pension Programs in Canada

The income replacement rate (i.e., the ratio of postretirement to preretirement annual income) is a standard measure of the adequacy of pension benefits. As indicated previously, the benefits delivered by the CPP, the earnings-related component of Canada's public retirement system, are modest. The CPP is designed to replace 25 percent of the worker's average annual lifetime earnings, with a lower replacement rate for persons beyond the average industrial wage. As well, there is a maximum on the CPP benefit, equal to $6,248 per year in 1994. The target replacement rate of 25 percent for the CPP indicates that the CPP is to serve as only one component of the overall replacement rate of 70 percent that is widely used in Canada as the goal for retirement planning.

This fact, together with the flat pension provided through OAS and the income-tested benefit provided by the GIS, implies that income replacement rates from public pension programs will be high for low-income Canadians, and low for high-income Canadians. This result is readily confirmed by examining the income replaced through Canada's public pension programs for individuals whose lifetime earnings equal different fractions (or multiples) of the average industrial wage (Table 6).[8]

Table 6 Income Replaced by Public Pension Programs in Canada

Individual's earnings, preretirement[a]	OAS benefits ($)[b]	GIS benefits ($)[c]	CPP benefits ($)	Total benefits ($)	Replacement rate (%)
Nil	3,472	4,127	Nil	7,599	NA
$6,450 (25%)	3,472	3,346	1,562	8,380	129.9
$12,900 (50%)	3,472	2,565	3,124	9,161	71.0
$19,350 (75%)	3,472	1,784	4,686	9,942	51.4
$25,800 (100%)	3,472	1,003	6,248	10,723	41.6
$51,600 (200%)	3,472	1,003	6,248	10,723	20.8
$129,000 (500%)	3,472	1,003	6,248	10,723	8.3

[a] The different levels of preretirement earnings represent the indicated fraction (enclosed in parentheses) of the average industrial wage in Canada.

[b] All amounts are expressed in U.S. dollars, at an exchange rate of 75 cents (U.S.) for each Canadian dollar, and pertain to January 1, 1994.

[c] GIS benefits are income-tested and reduced by 50 percent of income in excess of OAS benefits. In these illustrations, the recipient is assumed to receive income *only* from the public pension programs. For the purpose of these illustrations, additional income-tested pensions provided by some provinces are ignored

For an individual who earns the average industrial wage (i.e., with preretirement earnings of $25,800 per year), 42 percent of their preretirement earnings would be replaced by Canada's public pension programs. This ratio rises to 71 percent for those who earn half the industrial wage and falls sharply to 21 percent for those who earn twice the average industrial wage. The modest role of the earnings-based CPP is further illustrated by the fact that an individual who qualifies for the maximum CPP pension will also qualify for (partial) income-tested GIS benefits, if the individual has no other source of retirement income.

The OAS benefits shown in Table 6 are constant at the maximum amount of $3,472 because the individuals are assumed to have no post-retirement income other than public pension income and hence are not subject to the 15 percent clawback. However, GIS benefits fall as pre-retirement earnings increase, because higher preretirement earnings lead to higher CPP benefits and CPP benefits are included in the income that is subject to the 50 percent GIS "tax-back." Therefore, GIS benefits fall by 50 percent of the increase in CPP benefits. When CPP benefits reach their maximum of $6,248, there is no further reduction of the GIS supplement and it bottoms out at $1,003 as long as the person has no source of income other than public pension income.

As a result of these opposing forces, total public pension benefits are relatively flat and do not increase much for persons with higher pre-retirement earnings. Only earnings-based CPP benefits increase as preretirement earnings increase, but these are capped at a fairly modest level. The increase up to the cap is subject to the 50 percent "tax-back" of the GIS supplement. The fact that OAS benefits are flat and that CPP benefits are modest, capped, and effectively subject to the GIS "tax-back," means that total public pension benefits do not change substantially as the individual's preretirement earnings change. This means that the income replacement rate is very high for persons with low preretirement earnings and very low for persons with high preretirement earnings.

Clearly, the public pension system is very "progressive," yielding relatively constant total benefits and hence high income replacement rates for low-income individuals. Furthermore, the earnings-based CPP component is relatively modest as evidenced by the fact that even when the full maximum CPP benefits are received, individuals are still eligible for the income-tested GIS supplement if they have no other source of income.

Intergenerational Transfers: Canada

The tax rates, explicit or implicit, to finance Canada's public pension programs will rise sharply in the years ahead, to offset the aging of the population and the increasing ratio of pensioners to active workers. In 1966, when the CPP was introduced, the total contribution rate was set at 3.6 percent, to be shared equally by employers and their employees. This rate remained in effect until 1986. Since then, the CPP contribution rate has gradually increased, to 5.2 percent in 1994. This rate is somewhat higher than the contribution rate that would have been forecast for 1993 in 1966, the year that the CPP was introduced. This result is due to subsequent benefit enrichments and "unfavorable" demographic developments.

The CPP contribution rate is scheduled to rise to 10.10 percent in 2016, 12.73 percent in 2030, and 13.18 percent in 2040.[9] These increases presume there will be no change to the CPP benefit formula. However, two points merit attention. First, future generations of workers will be required to pay higher CPP contribution rates than does the current generation of workers, with no increase in the benefit formula. Second, there are no published forecasts of the implicit tax or contribution rates for OAS, GIS, and the various provincial "top-ups." Since these programs are also financed on a "pay-as-you-go" basis, however, it is clear that the implicit tax or contribution rates necessary to finance these programmes will rise as well.

With "pay-as-you-go" financing, each generation of workers pays for the pensions of the previous generation. The security of CPP (and other public pension) benefits is linked, ultimately, to the willingness of the next generation of workers to pay the tax or contribution rates necessary to finance the level of benefits promised to the current generation.

Canadians born in 1920—who reached age 65 in 1985—will receive far more in benefits from the CPP than they paid in contributions. Canadians who were born in 1960—who will attain age 65 in 2025 —will also receive more in benefits than they paid in contributions but on a more modest scale. For Canadians born after 1980, however, lifetime CPP contributions are likely to equal or exceed CPP benefits. The "pension crisis" thus reflects the concern that the next generation of workers may choose not to honor the rules of the game established by the current generation because the next generation will be treated less favorably.

This likelihood of younger generations "breaking" an implicit social contract established by older generations who will benefit by such a contract is enhanced by a number of other factors. The younger generations will also be experiencing greater pressure for health and elder-care expenditures, associated with the aging population that is also in receipt of the pension income. Pressure may be enhanced by the possibility both of inheriting a large government deficit and assuming responsibility for substantial deferred wage obligations being paid to public sector workers in the form of generous occupational pensions and seniority-based wage increases and job security. Concern that labor markets may not be able to absorb traditional immigrant flows may lead to reductions in that source of labor-force growth that could otherwise sustain pension obligations. The likelihood that the implicit pension contract is not adhered to is also enhanced by the fact that the "pension crisis" is not an exogenous unforseen event that leaves the older generation no time to adjust.

Because of these and related considerations, there has been a profound shift in the past 15 years in the nature of the policy debate regarding public pensions in Canada. In the late 1970s, the major issue was whether or not to double the size of the CPP, as advocated by the Canadian Labour Congress and other groups. This potential initiative was debated at length in a National Pension Conference convened by the federal government in 1980. In 1991, in sharp contrast, the Organization for Economic Cooperation and Development (OECD) held a major conference on "Private Pensions and Public Policy." The first sentence in the "Foreword" to the conference volume (OECD 1992) sets the tone for the current policy debate in Canada:

> Government interest in relying more on private arrangements and less on public pensions for income in retirement appears to be increasing across OECD countries. Old-age pensions currently are the largest social policy expenditure in public budgets, and their share of public costs is expected to grow in the years ahead.

Clearly, the potential financial problems and the intergenerational transfers associated with public pension plans has redirected attention from public to private pensions.

PUBLIC PENSION BENEFITS IN THE UNITED STATES

A brief treatment of the U.S. public pension system is given here, highlighting the main similarities and differences with the Canadian system.

Social Security (OASDI)

The United States does not have an equivalent of the first tier of the pension system in Canada—a universal demogrant like the OAS and income-tested supplement like the GIS. The U.S. Social Security through Old Age, Survivors and Disability Insurance (OASDI), covering over 90 percent of the U.S. workforce, is broadly comparable to the second tier of Canada's system, the CPP. OASDI, which dates back to 1935, consists of three components: Old Age or retirement (OA), Survivor (S), and Disability (DI) benefits. OASDI is financed by a payroll tax with equal contributions by the employer and employee. In 1994, the total contribution rate was set at 12.4 percent of earnings up to a ceiling of $60,600 .[10]

The full Old Age Security retirement benefit is available to employees who are *fully insured* by the year of their retirement.[11]   For individuals born in 1937 or earlier, the normal retirement age (that is, the age at which unreduced social security benefits are payable) is 65. For those born after 1937, the normal retirement age is gradually being increased. For those born in 1960 or later, the normal retirement age will be age 67. Retirement benefits are available to individuals as early as age 62 on an actuarially reduced basis. Benefits are increased for those working beyond the normal retirement age, up to age 70.

The pension benefit is based on the worker's Averaged Indexed Monthly Earnings (AIME) to which a formula is applied to determine the Primary Insurance Amount (PIA). The PIA is subject to an annual cost-of-living adjustment. Up to 85 percent of Social Security benefits are subject to income taxes for persons whose income exceeds a certain threshold amount. The exact proportion subject to taxes depends upon such factors as marital/tax filing status, and combined income from earnings, tax-exempt interest, and social security.

Those who continue employment after commencing receipt of benefits will have their benefit subject to a clawback. For those between the ages of 65 and 69, the benefit is reduced by one-third of earnings above $11,160 (in 1994). Those under age 65 experience a reduction in social security benefits of 50 cents for every dollar of earnings above $8,040.

Fully insured individuals and their spouses qualify for health benefits under Medicare, which covers in-patient hospital care, home nursing and health care services, and some types of hospice care. Deductibles and coinsurance payments apply for certain services. Those qualifying for Medicare may also opt (at a fee of $41.10 per month in 1994) for supplementary health benefits which cover a number of services not covered by the basic Medicare plan. There is an annual deductible and coinsurance for most charges.

Family members of persons receiving Social Security are also eligible for partial payments. Eligible family members include: spouses (including divorced spouses) who are at least 62 years old; spouses of any age who are caring for a child under the age of 16 or caring for a child who became disabled before the age of 22; unmarried dependent children (and sometimes grandchildren) under the age of 18 (under age 19 if the child is still in high school); and children of any age if they became disabled before age 22. The sum of these benefits are subject to a Family Maximum Benefit level. If the Social Security recipient is deceased, more generous survivor benefits are available to a slightly broader group of family members.

Pension Income as Component of Retirement Income: United States

Table 7 shows the relative contribution of OASDI benefits to the incomes of older Americans in 1979, 1989, and 1992. The median income level of those 65 years of age and older was $8,795 in 1979, $10,765 in 1989, and $10,200 in 1992. OASDI benefits accounted for about 42 percent of retirement income in both 1979 and 1992. The rel-

Table 7 Contribution of Public Pension Benefits to Incomes of Americans Aged 65 and Over, 1979, 1989, and 1992

% Income derived from	1979	1989	1992
Public OASDI	42.7	38.6	41.7
Private pension income	14.8	17.5	20.1
Investment income	21.5	25.2	20.5
Employment income	17.3	15.8	14.8
Other income	3.6	2.9	3.0

SOURCE: Yablonski and Silverman (1994, p. 29).

ative share of income from investment was about four percentage points higher in 1989 than in the other two years, presumably reflecting the relatively high returns on investment vehicles experienced at the time.

While definitional differences preclude strict comparisons with the Canadian figures given in Tables 4 and 5, some comparisons can be suggested. The share of retirement income derived from sources other than public pensions are remarkably similar in the two countries. This is best seen by comparing Table 5 for Canada with the latest year figures in Table 7 for the United States. The components are usually within 1–3 percentage points of each other. The overall public pension components, at about 41 percent of retirement income, are almost identical between OASDI in the United States and the combined OAS/GIS and CPP in Canada. Because the OAS/GIS in Canada is almost twice as large as the CPP component, this means that Canada delivers its public pensions in a more "progressive" fashion—that is, universal (OAS) and income-tested (GIS). As highlighted previously, the earnings-based CPP component in Canada is extremely modest.

The Income Replacement of Public Pension Programs in the United States

The effect of this greater progressivity in Canada as compared with the United States is highlighted when comparisons are made of the extent to which public pensions replace preretirement earnings for those who retire and have no further earnings. Like the Canadian sys-

Table 8 Income Replaced by Public Pension Programs in the United States

Individual's earnings, preretirement	OA benefit ($)[a]	Replacement rate (%)
Nil		
$6,450 (25%)	5,087	78.9
$12,900 (50%)	7,346	56.9
$19,350 (75%)	9,606	49.6
$25,800 (100%)	11,868	46.0
$51,600 (200%)	13,764	26.7
$129,000 (500%)	13,764	10.7

[a] The OA benefit calculation assumes that the worker retired at age 65 in 1994 with average indexed annual earnings shown in the first column.

tem, the U.S. Old Age benefit program is designed to replace a greater proportion of preretirement earnings for lower income workers. The effect of this policy is demonstrated in Table 8, which shows the income replacement rates for individuals with preretirement earnings levels corresponding to the Canadian levels given earlier in Table 6. Individuals earning the average Canadian industrial wage of $25,800 would have almost 50 percent of their preretirement earnings replaced by the OAS benefit. The replacement rate is higher at 79 percent for those earning one-quarter of the average industrial wage, and is lower at 27 percent for those who earn twice the industrial wage.

While the U.S. public pension system has elements of progressivity, it is much less so than the Canadian system. For persons at one-quarter of the industrial wage, the Canadian system replaces 130 percent of preretirement income, as compared with 79 percent in the United States. For persons at twice the industrial wage, the Canadian system replaces only 21 percent of preretirement income, as compared with 27 percent in the United States.

Intergenerational Transfers: United States

As of 1994, it has been estimated that the OASDI will require funding from other government revenues by the year 2013 and will become insolvent by 2029 (U.S. Department of Health and Human Services 1994). An increase in the contribution rate from the present 12.4 percent to 19.0 percent of earnings by 2070 would be required to fund the benefits at current levels. No contribution rate increases have been scheduled.

As a result of the 1983 reforms to the Social Security Act, the normal retirement age of individuals born after 1937 has been gradually increased. For those born in 1938, the normal age of retirement is 65 years and 2 months. For those born in 1960 and after, the normal retirement age is 67. Assuming that the normal retirement benefit remains at its January 1, 1995 level of $884, the impact of increasing the normal retirement age from 65 to 67 has been estimated to result in a reduction in the monthly benefit for an individual who chooses to retire at age 65, with average indexed monthly earnings of $2,000, from $884 to $766. This 13.3 percent reduction is due to the fact that those retiring at age 65 will be doing so early, given the increase in the normal retirement age to 67, and thus their benefit will be subject to the reduction formula applied to the benefits of those who retire prior to the normal retirement age. Similarly, those retiring at age 67 will receive a 6 percent smaller monthly payment in comparison to the pre-reform benefit because the increase in benefits due to late retirement would not be applied given the older normal retirement age (Salisbury and Silverman 1994).

POTENTIAL INCENTIVE EFFECTS

While a full mapping of the incentive effects of the public pension schemes in Canada and the United States is beyond the scope of this analysis, some broad characterizations can be suggested. More complete discussions of theory and empirical research into the work incentive effects of social security benefits can be found in popular labor economics texts such as Ehrenberg and Smith (1994) and Gunderson and Riddell (1993), and they are also contained in broader reviews of the pension literature including Mitchell and Fields (1982) and Lazear (1986).

Work Incentives

An analysis of the financial incentives contained in public (and private) pension benefits on the decision to retire from the labor market typically begins by calculating the discounted present value of the future stream of such benefits, commonly termed "pension wealth," at different points in the lifetime of the worker. In essence, pension wealth at time t is a measure of the future stream of pension payments due to the worker if the worker were to retire or otherwise terminate participation in the pension plan at time t. Other factors constant, it is assumed that workers seek to maximize their pension wealth.

The period-by-period changes in pension wealth, termed "pension accruals," embody the magnitudes of the financial incentives for the worker to remain in the labor force earlier in the life-cycle and then retire later in the life-cycle. For pension plans based on, for example, average earnings over some number of years of pensionable employment, an additional year of service generally brings about an increase in the monthly benefit payable to the worker. This increases pension wealth. Working against this, however, is the inevitable fact that every year the pension plan member gets a year older and the remaining years over which benefits can be received falls. In other words, over any period of time, while the monthly benefit payable to the worker may increase, the amount of time the worker has left to collect the benefit falls. As workers age, depending on the specific benefit formula of the pension plan, the positive impact on pension wealth of labor-market work becomes increasingly offset by the reduced amount of time remaining to receive the benefit. At some point, which again is influenced by the specific benefit formulae contained in the pension plan, pension payments foregone by not retiring are not offset by increased monthly benefits, and pension wealth accruals become negative—that is, pension wealth falls with increased work. At some point in time, the two effects are completely offsetting, at which point pension wealth is maximized. Delaying receipt of benefits beyond this point is associated with negative pension wealth accruals and, clearly, reductions in pension wealth (see Kotlikoff and Wise 1987; Lazear and Moore 1988; Pesando and Gunderson 1988; and Pesando, Hyatt and Gunderson 1992). Thus, as long as pension wealth accruals are positive, there is an incentive to continue work, or stated differently, there is no pension penalty to continued labor market employment. Holding pension wealth accruals constant, increases in pension wealth are expected to be associated with younger retirement ages.

If Social Security benefits are unexpectedly increased, but the post-retirement income clawback, the preretirement labor -market wage and other factors are all held constant, economic theory predicts that the retirement age will fall—that is, the increase in Social Security benefits will have a pure wealth effect, encouraging workers to consume leisure. Anderson, Burkhauser, and Quinn (1986) estimated that unanticipated increase in Social Security wealth significantly increases the probability of retiring earlier and significantly decreases the probability of retiring later, for a sample of men aged 58 to 63 in 1969.[12]

Some public pension plans, like U.S. Social Security, have postretirement earnings tests such that pension payments are clawed-back by some proportion for each dollar of labor-market income (usually over some threshold amount). These earnings tests effectively reduce the wage net of pension benefit reductions, thereby reducing the opportunity cost of retirement. Policies that reduce the clawback would increase time in labor-market work, thereby increasing the expected retirement age, but they would also result in greater wealth, thereby reducing the expected retirement age. Which of the two effects dominates is an empirical question that Gustman and Steinmeier (1991) addressed through a simulation analysis. Their results suggest that eliminating the Social Security clawback would have a small positive effect on the labor supply of those in the 65–69 age group.

In summary, Social Security can be expected to discourage continued labor-market work (i.e., encourage retirement) both because the income transfer enables the individual to afford to retire and because the clawback reduces the net returns to continued work. The income or wealth effect may be small because it is largely anticipated and hence can affect labor-supply decisions throughout the life-cycle, not just when the income is received after the normal retirement age. Nevertheless, income that is guaranteed in the later part of the life-cycle can be particularly important in facilitating retirement since it does not require the uncertainty of liquidating assets to pay for retirement—assets that can be bequeathed if not used and can be used up too quickly if one lives longer than expected.

While Social Security can discourage labor-force participation after the age of normal retirement, it can encourage labor-force participation in earlier stages of the life-cycle to build eligibility for the benefits. Furthermore, the wealth effects emanating from the intergenerational transfers can affect retirement decisions. Specifically, the older generations who are recipients of the transfers can more easily afford to retire. Future generations who are net payers may be less likely to afford to retire.

As indicated previously, the Canadian public pension system has a different set of incentives. The intergenerational wealth redistribution effects are likely to be similar because both involve transfers from younger generations to older generations. However, the more progressive nature of the Canadian system implies that lower income people in Canada may more easily be able to afford to retire.

More importantly, the absence of direct clawbacks on CPP in Canada means that there are less disincentives to keep working past the normal retirement age.[13] For lower income people who would otherwise receive the GIS supplement, however, the 50 percent clawback for that component could discourage continued work. In essence, there may be some tendency for the Canadian system to encourage retirement amongst lower income persons, both because the progressive nature of the system means that they can afford to retire and because the 50 percent clawback of the GIS supplement is likely to discourage work most amongst low-income persons. Overall, however, the absence of a direct clawback on CPP in Canada should mean that there is more incentive to continue working and not to retire.

Interestingly, the United States appears to facilitate continued working past the normal retirement age because of the legislated ban on mandatory retirement. However, it discourages continued working through the clawback of Social Security. In contrast, mandatory retirement in Canada is generally not banned[14]; however, continued labor-force participation is not discouraged through tax-back features of the public pension system (except possibly for low-income persons as indicated).

Payroll Taxes and the Demand for Labor

While most attention on incentive effects focuses on the labor-supply side, the payroll taxes used to finance the CPP in Canada and Social Security in the United States can also have important incentive effects reducing the demand for labor. The issue is complicated, however, by the fact that payroll taxes may be shifted back to labor in the form of lower wages in return for the pension benefits that are financed by the payroll tax.

Dahlby (1992), based on previous econometric studies, concluded that in the short-run, workers bear less than 50 percent of the payroll tax burden, increasing to at least two-thirds in the longer term.

Payroll taxes can affect the demand not only for the overall labor input but also for the different components of the labor input. Specifically, the ceilings on the payroll tax mean that the tax does not apply to earnings beyond the ceiling. This can create an incentive for firms who have employees at the ceiling to work them long hours (since no further payroll taxes are incurred) rather than to hire new recruits and to incur the payroll taxes. In essence, the ceilings create an element of quasi-fixed costs of employment that can discourage new employment and encourage firms to demand longer hours from existing employees. This can be a contributing factor, for example, to the tendency to work incumbent workers overtime hours on a regular basis rather than hiring new employees. Since the ceiling on CPP contributions in Canada is reached sooner (i.e., at $25,800) than the ceiling on Social Security contributions in the United States (i.e., $60,000), this constraint should be more binding in Canada than in the United States.

CONCLUDING OBSERVATIONS

There is a clear trend to early retirement that exists in both Canada and the United States. In both countries, in the immediate post-war period, the labor-force participation rates of males aged 65 and over were in the neighborhood of 47 percent. By the early 1990s, these had fallen to well under 20 percent and closer to 10 percent in Canada. Participation rates of older workers have consistently been higher in the United States than in Canada. Of note, however, is the fact that after 1985, U.S. participation rates began moving upwards, while Canadian rates continued their downward trend. Whether this reflects the impact of the legislated ban on mandatory retirement in the United States (a ban that did not occur in Canada) is an interesting and important question.

Overall, the following general conclusions emerge from this analysis.

- In addition to the earnings-based CPP (broadly comparable to OASDI in the United States), the Canadian public pension system also has a universal demogrant, the OAS, payable to all Canadians 65 and over, and an income-tested supplement, the GIS.

- As a source of retirement income, the OAS demogrant and the GIS supplement are more important than is the labor-market-based, earnings-related CPP. In fact, the target income replacement rate of the CPP is designed to be modest, at 25 percent of the average industrial wage. As a result, an individual who qualifies for the maximum CPP benefit, but who has no additional income other than the OAS pension, would qualify for some income-tested GIS benefits.

- The U.S. public pension system of OASDI, which is broadly comparable to the Canadian CPP, does not have a universal demogrant like the OAS, nor an income-tested supplement like the GIS. In spite of these differences, the public pension systems in both countries are remarkably similar as a source of retirement income, accounting for slightly over 40 percent of retirement income in both countries. Canada simply delivers more of its public pension under universal and income-tested components, while the United States delivers its public pension largely through the labor-market-related, earnings-based component.

- In both countries, the public pension systems are progressive or redistributive in that they involve higher income replacement rates for low-income persons and lower income replacement rates for higher income persons. In Canada, however, this is much more prominent. This reflects the fact that total public pension benefits are almost constant with respect to income: the OAS demogrant is completely flat and the CPP component, which is earnings-related, is modest, capped, and effectively subject to the 50 percent GIS clawback because CPP benefits are included in total income for purposes of that clawback.

- In the United States, the continuation of working past a normal retirement age is facilitated by the legislated ban on mandatory retirement, but it is discouraged by the clawbacks on Social Security that range from 0.33 to 0.50, depending upon age and income. In Canada, in contrast, mandatory retirement is not generally banned, but continued work is also not discouraged in the sense that there is no direct clawback from the CPP. There is only an indirect clawback for low-income people in the sense that any additional income (including CPP income) is subject to the 50 percent clawback of the GIS supplement.

- Payroll taxes that are used to finance public pensions can reduce the overall demand for labor. The ceilings on such payroll taxes can also create a quasi-fixed hiring cost that discourages new hiring (that would be subject to the payroll tax) and that encourages working the existing workforce long hours (since no further payroll taxes are incurred once the ceiling is reached). The impact of such taxes on the demand for labor, and on the demand for hours versus new hires, is complicated by the fact that the cost of a large portion of the payroll tax is ultimately shifted back to labor.

- In both Canada and the United States, public pension programs contain significant intergenerational transfers, to current from future generations, creating some uncertainty as to the willingness and ability of future generations to sustain future pension "obligations."

These conclusions highlight the substantial degree of variation in the key parameters of the public pension systems in the United States and Canada. This variation can potentially be exploited to understand examine the behavioral effects of public pensions in a way which is seldom possible in a single jurisdiction, unless that jurisdiction experienced a major change in policy regimes. This echoes the sentiment expressed by Card and Freeman (1993, p. 2) that, "(i)f one wants to study the impact of differing unemployment insurance, income maintenance, or labor laws on economic behavior and outcomes, comparisons of Canadian and U.S. experiences hold out the promise of relatively straightforward inferences."

There are at least two areas of research on public pensions that have the potential to realize some of the promise suggested by Card and Freeman. The first is an examination of the comparative labor demand effects induced by financing public pensions exclusively through a payroll tax, as is the case in the United States, or a combination of a payroll tax and general revenues, as is the case in Canada. It would also be possible to examine the extent of disemployment in Canada that results from the quasi-fixed cost of hiring created by the relatively low payroll tax ceiling in Canada. These features have competing implications for employment and hours. This first suggests that Canadian firms will hire more workers than U.S. firms, while the second suggests that rather than hire new workers, firms will try to amortize the quasi-fixed cost of the payroll tax by working its existing workforce longer hours. However, as we cautioned earlier, the impact on labor demand of a payroll tax depends on the ultimate incidence of the tax, which some evidence suggests may fall largely on workers in the form of lower wages.

Second, on the supply side, useful research would consider the impact of pension generosity on labor-force participation. It would be expected that labor-force withdrawal rates would be higher for low lifetime income earners in Canada than for their counterparts in the United States. Confounding considerations, such as the fact that mandatory retirement is still permitted in some provinces, would have to be addressed in the research design.

Both Canada and the United States have exhibited a dramatic trend towards retirement as exhibited by the falling labor-force participation rates of males age 65 and older. The role of public pensions (as well as private pensions and mandatory retirement policies) in stimulating, or facilitating, this trend remains an important topic of future research.

Notes

1. The Government of Canada also provides an additional tax credit (equal in 1993 to 54 percent of the basic personal tax credit) for those age 65 or over and additional tax credit for the first $750 of private pension income. In Quebec, the Canada Pension Plan is replaced by its equivalent, the Quebec Pension Plan.
2. There is also a Spouse's Allowance, which is income-tested and payable from age 60 to 65 to eligible widows, widowers, and spouses of OAS pensioners. In 1993, the maximum annual allowance was $6,160 to spouses and $6,801 to widows and widowers.
3. Additional income-tested benefits for those aged 65 and over provided by several provinces are also exempt from the GIS tax-back provisions. Indeed, receipt of GIS benefits is generally used as the eligibility criterion for these provincial supplements. As an example of a provincial supplement, Ontario paid a maximum supplement of $83.00 per month in 1994 to single retirees through its Guaranteed Annual Income System (GAINS) program. The supplement is scaled down based on a formula which takes into account other sources of income, such as interest and dividend payments, foreign pensions, CPP benefits, employment income, unemployment benefits, workers' compensation payments, and net rents from property.
4. The self-employed pay both employer and employee contributions. The CPP also contains death (including surviving spouse's) and disability benefits.
5. For those between the ages 60 and 65 who opt for early retirement, the normal retirement benefit is reduced by 0.5 percent for each month that early retirement precedes normal retirement to a maximum reduction of 30 percent. The worker must have substantially ceased working, meaning that the worker's employment earnings must be less than the maximum CPP benefit payable at age 65.
6. Of course, these costs can be shifted back to employees in the form of lower compensating cash wages in return for more generous pension benefits. Evidence on such cost shifting in union-based flat benefit plans in Canada is given in Gunderson, Hyatt, and Pesando (1992).
7. The contribution growth rate is expressed in nominal terms. This facilitates comparison with the CPP growth rate, which reflects both increases in the earnings base and increases in the contribution rate.
8. The retirement benefit payable under the CPP is linked to the worker's average lifetime earnings, updated to the three years prior to the worker's retirement. The mechanics are as follows: The ratio of the worker's earnings to the YMPE (set equal to one if earnings exceed the YMPE) is averaged for each year after the worker turned age 18 (or 1996). The resulting fraction (or the value one) is multiplied by the YMPE average for the year of retirement and the two previous years. This is called the worker's Average Pensionable Earnings (AYMPE). The procedure, in effect, updates the worker's lifetime earnings to their current equivalent. The worker's CPP benefit is equal to 25 percent of the worker's AYMPE. (If a worker earned more than the YMPE in every year, for, example, the worker's pen-

sion would equal 25 percent of the YMPE in the years in which the worker was 63, 64, and 65. If the worker has contributed for more than 10 years, 15 percent of the months in the contribution period can be dropped before the worker's AYMPE is calculated. In effect, this allows the worker to eliminate the periods of lowest earnings.

9. The contribution rates through the year 2016 were set in the 1990–1991 review of contribution rates, per agreement among the federal and provincial ministers of finance.

10. The self-employed pay both employer and employee contributions.

11. A fully insured individual is one who has (or whose spouse has) earned 40 credits in the year in which they reach age 62. In 1994, a credit is earned for every $620 of employment earnings, up to a maximum of four credits per year. The amount of employment earnings required to earn a credit increases annually, to reflect changes in the average industrial wage.

12. For an excellent discussion of these issues, see Ippolito (1990). Krueger and Pischke (1992) find only small effects of increases in Social Security wealth on labor-force participation of older workers.

13. As described earlier, to draw CPP benefits before age 65 an individual in Canada must have substantially stop working.

14. Except in the federal jurisdiction, which covers about 10 percent of workers, and in the provinces of Manitoba and Quebec.

References

Anderson, K., R. Burkhauser, and J. Quinn. 1986. "Do Retirement Dreams Come True? The Effect of Unanticipated Events on Retirement Plans." *Industrial and Labor Relations Review* 39 (July): 518–526.

Card, D., and R. Freeman, eds. 1993. *Small Differences that Matter: Labor Markets and Income Maintenance in Canada and the United States.* Chicago: University of Chicago Press.

Chiswick, B., ed. 1992. *Immigration, Language and Ethnicity: Canada and the United States.* Washington, D.C.: AEI Press.

Dahlby, B. 1992. "Taxation and Social Insurance." In *Taxation to 2000 and Beyond*, R. Bird and J. Mintz, eds. Toronto: Canadian Tax Foundation, pp. 110–156.

Ehrenberg, R., and R. Smith. 1994. *Modern Labor Economics: Theory and Public Policy*, 5th edition. New York: Harper Collins.

Galarneau, D. 1991. "Women Approaching Retirement." *Perspectives on Labour and Income* 3 (Autumn): 28–39.

Gunderson, M., D. Hyatt, and J. Pesando. 1992. "Wage-Pension Trade-Offs in Collective Agreements." *Industrial and Labor Relations Review* 46 (October): 146–160.

Gunderson, M., and W.C. Riddell. 1993. *Labour Market Economics*, third ed. Toronto: McGraw-Hill Ryerson.

Gustman, A., and T. Steinmeier. 1991. "Changing the Social Security Rules for Work After 65." *Industrial and Labor Relations Review* 44 (July): 733–745.

Health and Welfare Canada. 1992. *Income Security Programs, Monthly Statistics*, January 1992. Ottawa: Health and Welfare Canada.

Ippolito, R. 1990. "Toward Explaining Earlier Retirement After 1970." *Industrial and Labor Relations Review* 43 (July): 556–569.

Kotlikoff, Laurence, and David Wise. 1987. "The Incentive Effects of Private Pension Plans." In *Issues in Pension Economics*, Zvi Bodie et al., ed. Chicago: University of Chicago Press, pp. 283–336.

Krueger, A., and J.-S. Pischke. 1992. "The Effect of Social Security on Labor Supply: A Cohort Analysis of the Notch Generation." *Journal of Labor Economics* 10 (October): 412–437.

Lazear, E. 1986. "Retirement from the Labor Force." In *Handbook of Labor Economics*, Volume 1, O. Ashenfelter and R. Layard, eds. Amsterdam: North Holland, pp. 305–355.

Lazear, E., and R. Moore. 1988. "Pensions and Turnover." In *Financial Aspects of the United States Pension System*, Z. Bodie and J. Shoven, eds. Chicago: University of Chicago Press, pp. 163–188.

Mitchell, O., and G. Fields. 1982. "The Effects of Pensions and Earnings on Retirement: A Review Essay." *Research in Labor Economics* 5: 115–155.

Organization for Economic Cooperation and Development. 1992. *Private Pensions and Public Policy*. Paris: Organization for Economic Cooperation and Development.

Pesando, J., and M. Gunderson. 1988. "Retirement Incentives Contained in Occupational Pension Plans and Their Implications for the Mandatory Retirement Debate." *Canadian Journal of Economics* 21(2) 244–264.

Pesando, J., D. Hyatt, and M. Gunderson. 1992. "Early Retirement Pensions and Employee Turnover: An Application of the Option Value Approach." *Research in Labor Economics* 13: 321–337.

Salisbury, Dallas, and Celia Silverman. 1994. "Social Security and Medicare Programs Face Reform." *Employee Benefit Research Institute Notes* 15(June): 1–6.

Statistics Canada. 1994. *Pension Plans in Canada*, 1992. Ottawa: Supply and Services.

U.S. Department of Health and Human Services. 1994. *1994 Report of the Board of Trustees of the Federal Old-Age and Survivors Insurance and Disability Trust Funds*. Washington, D.C.: U.S. Government Printing Office.

Yablonski, Paul, and Celia Silverman. 1994. "Baby Boomers in Retirement: What Are Their Prospects?" Employee Benefit Research Institute Special Report SR-23, July.

11 Current Policy Issues towards Private Pensions in Canada and the United States

Stuart Dorsey
Baker University

Public policies toward private pensions in Canada and the United States share a common history and many current issues. Policymakers and analysts in both countries view the retirement income program as a "three-legged stool," with base incomes established by public pensions, supplemented by private pension benefits and individual retirement saving. Canada and the United States provide similar tax incentives for private pension saving, and both countries have regulations for vesting, funding, and fiduciary behavior designed to enforce and preserve private sector pension promises.

Although basic private pension policies are similar, there are important differences. Both countries limit tax-deductible contributions and benefits, but the ceilings established by Revenue Canada are considerably lower than those in the United States (although the difference has shrunk over the past decade). Another significant difference is the greater role for personal retirement accounts. Canadian Registered Retirement Savings Plans (RRSPs) have a longer history and enjoy more favorable tax treatment than do Individual Retirement Accounts (IRAs) in the United States. An important tax distinction is the greater responsibility placed upon actuaries by Revenue Canada to determine minimum and tax-deductible contributions to defined-benefit funds in Canada. Internal Revenue Service rules, in contrast, disallow contributions sufficient to fully fund future benefit obligations in many plans.

The uniformity of pension regulations is another difference. Non-tax pension rules are primarily enforced at the federal level in the United States, whereas pension regulation is a provincial responsibility in Canada. The result is that it is difficult to compare pension regulations in the United States with rules that differ between provinces in Canada. Vesting rules, for example, vary between British Columbia and Ontario. Also, only Ontario has mandatory pension insurance, whereas all defined-benefit pension sponsors in the United States are covered by the Pension Benefit Guaranty Corporation.

Canada and the United States share several current public policy issues. One of the most important is the increasing tension between policy goals of encouraging expansion of pension coverage and funding, and of minimizing revenue loss of preferential treatment of pension compensation. Both federal governments in recent years have established minimum funding requirements, but they also have developed regulations to discourage "overfunding" as a pure tax shelter. There also is concern in both countries that increasing regulation will continue to lead to the decline of defined-benefit pension coverage and its attendant advantages over the defined-contribution approach. One of the biggest public policy differences appeared in response to the inflation of the 1970s and early 1980s. The protection of pension benefits during an inflationary environment was the most keenly debated public policy issue in Canada. In the United States, in contrast, inflation protection drew very little attention. Public policy in the United States has been focused primarily on declining coverage, portability, and the effect of the pension tax preferences on the distribution of the tax burden.

This chapter compares public policies towards private pensions in Canada and the United States and examines relevant policy research from both countries. First, I review the evolution of private pensions and policies in each country. Although pension policies are similar, Canada (especially the province of Ontario) has tended to involve government in the private pension system earlier than the United States. Next, I describe and compare the most important pension tax and regulatory rules. In the remainder of the paper, I examine four common current public policy issues: coverage, portability, tax policy, and inflation indexing. The emphasis of this discussion is a review of relevant research on Canadian and U.S. outcomes. The volume of pension research has increased dramatically over the past two decades and, although most studies have focused on the United States, pension research in Canada has made important contributions, especially on the issue of mandatory inflation indexing.

The motivation for a joint discussion of private pension issues is that a comparison of research may shed light on pension outcomes and policy impacts in both countries. The similarities in pension systems suggest that outcomes of research in one country will be applicable to the other. Further, when possible, I try to identify differences in policies and institutions that provide an opportunity for comparative analysis. For example, a major issue in the United States is the decline in coverage rates. A review of Canadian coverage experience may inform the extent to which this decline reflects policy changes or changes in employment composition. Similarly, the continued popularity of defined-benefit pensions in Canada may suggest reasons why defined-benefit coverage has declined in the United States. This issue also is relevant in Canada, where many pension analysts are concerned that regulations will result in similar trends there.

EVOLUTION OF PENSION POLICY IN CANADA AND THE UNITED STATES

Retirement programs and tax and regulatory policies towards private pensions have a similar history in the United States and Canada. Both countries adopted universal public pension plans, extended favorable tax treatment to encourage expansion of private pensions, and later enacted broad regulations on pension outcomes. There have been important differences, however, in the evolution of private pension policies.

The first employer-sponsored pension in Canada was introduced by the Grand Trunk Railway in 1874, followed a year later by the first formal pension plan in the United States, sponsored by the American Express Company. Although employment shifts from agriculture into manufacturing created new pressures for explicit retirement saving vehicles, pension coverage grew slowly in both countries before 1910.[1] The first legislation in either country to encourage retirement savings was the Government Annuities Act of 1908, which authorized the

Canadian federal government to sell annuities to the public at favorable rates.

The period between 1910 and 1930 saw the widespread adoption of pension plans by the largest employers in the United States and Canada. Graebner (1980) attributed much of the early growth to management's view that pensions could reduce labor costs by lowering turnover and encouraging early retirement. The introduction of income tax systems during this period also provided a stimulus to coverage in both countries. The favorable tax treatment of pension contributions and earnings that continues to this day was put in place quickly in the United States. Payments to fund current retirement benefits were recognized as legitimate business deductions at the outset of the corporate income tax. The Revenue Acts of 1921 and 1926 explicitly exempted the earnings of assets in retirement funds from taxation, and the Revenue Act of 1928 allowed pension sponsors to deduct contributions to advance fund benefit accruals.

Employer contributions also were immediately exempted from the Canadian corporate income tax. In addition, the 1919 Income Tax War Act extended the exemption to employee contributions to pension funds.

Rapid growth in pension plans and compensation during World War II created fears that pensions were increasingly being adopted for the purpose of avoiding income taxation. In the United States, the result was the enactment of the first contribution limits in the Revenue Act of 1942. This legislation also established the first nondiscrimination rules to prevent the adoption of pensions for the primary benefit of high-wage employees. Employer contribution limits were first imposed in Canada in 1947. Because tax-qualified plan limits on contributions and benefits in Canada have been strict, Canada has not felt it necessary to adopt nondiscrimination rules.

A significant difference between tax policies is the more favorable treatment of individual contributions to retirement funds in Canada than in the United States. In addition to exempting employee contributions from taxation, Canada established personal retirement accounts in 1957. Canadian workers were allowed to make tax deductible contributions to RRSPs even if they were covered by a private pension plan. In the United States, IRAs were not generally available until 1981 and were strictly limited after 1986.

The existence and generosity of public pension benefits is an important factor in private pension coverage. Canada first enacted public pensions legislation in 1927. The Old Age Pension Act provided federal assistance to provinces that delivered means-tested pensions to the elderly. By 1951, the view that means-tested pensions were inadequate was widespread, and the Old Age Security Acts authorized a flat, universal retirement benefit. Canada did not adopt a universal, earnings-related public pension until the Canada/Quebec Pensions Plans in 1965. The Canadian incremental approach is in contrast to the United States Social Security program, which has been earnings-based since 1938.

Prior to the 1960s, private pension regulation was vested in each country's federal income tax codes, which established conditions for tax-qualified pension plans. The first important private pension regulations were approved in Ontario in 1963, establishing minimum vesting rules, funding requirements and, most notably, requiring all employers of more than 15 workers to provide pension coverage. Mandatory coverage was dropped with the revised Ontario Pension Benefits Act in 1965. However, the vesting standard of 45 years of age and 10 years of service was preserved. Most of the provinces subsequently adopted the major provisions of the Pension Benefits Act.

Significant pension regulation was not enacted in the United States for another decade. The Employees' Retirement Income Security Act of 1974 (ERISA) was more ambitious than the Pension Benefits Act. ERISA established standards for vesting, funding, and fiduciary behavior, as well as establishing a system of mandatory insurance for private sector, defined-benefit plans. Ontario is the only province in Canada that has mandatory pension insurance.

Several important changes in pension law were implemented in Canada during the 1980s. In the late 1970s, interest in private pension policy grew, as the ability of the public pension system to provide adequate income support for the elderly came into question. A number of government and private sector commissions issued reports containing various proposals for comprehensive pension policy reforms related to issues of coverage, vesting, tax treatment, and inflation indexing. This discussion has been referred to as the "Great Pension Debate," and it contributed to the passage of the Ontario Pension Benefits Act of 1987. This act reduced the minimum vesting period, required that vested benefits be locked in, and created options for transferability of benefits under defined-benefit plans. All other provinces have adopted similar regulatory legislation. A major change in the taxation of pension contributions was enacted in 1990, when the concept of integrated overall limits for contributions to defined-benefit plans, money purchase plans, and RRSPs was introduced.

Changes in pension policy were less extensive in the United States. The President's Commission on Pension Policy (1981) called for mandatory pensions and improvements in portability. This report was largely ignored, however, and there was no explicit national debate, as compared with Canada, on the adequacy of retirement income. Pension tax preferences, instead, were reduced in a piecemeal fashion. Contribution limits were lowered several times, most recently in 1993, and a controversial funding limit was adopted in 1987. In addition to lowering benefit limits, nondiscrimination rules also were tightened. The primary motivation for increased taxation of pensions was enhancing federal tax revenue, and the preference of Congress for broadening the tax base over raising marginal income tax rates. Critics of these changes warned, however, that their cumulative effect would be greater complexity and reduced attractiveness of pensions, especially defined-benefit plans.

PUBLIC POLICIES TOWARDS PENSIONS IN CANADA AND THE UNITED STATES

Among industrialized nations, Canadian and U.S. pension policies are perhaps the most uniform. Tax rules and vesting and funding regulations are broadly similar. There are important distinctions, however. Most notable are the integrated contribution limits that allow for greater individual retirement savings in Canada than in the United States and the provincial system of pension regulation, which allows for differences in nontax pension rules within Canada.

Taxes and Coverage

Tax codes in Canada and the United States both permit deductions of employer contributions to pension funds from current income and do not tax pension fund earnings until benefits are distributed. Favorable tax rules clearly have been a stimulus to the growth of pension coverage and assets. There is a tension in both countries, however, between the policy goals of encouraging retirement saving and limiting revenue losses. Therefore, both countries have ceilings on benefits that can be provided under preferential tax status.

In the United States, defined-benefit plans cannot provide participants with more than the lesser of 100 percent of the highest three-year average earnings or $115,641 (in 1993). In addition, there is an overall limit on annual compensation that can be used for benefit determinations. The compensation limit was lowered from $235,840 to $150,000 in the 1993 Omnibus Budget Reconciliation Act. Contributions to pension funds in excess of these limits are not deductible. Allowable contributions to defined-contribution plans may not exceed 25 percent of an employee's compensation or $30,000.

The contributions and benefit ceilings are lower in Canada. Under rules adopted in 1990, the old system of separate limits for defined-benefit plans, defined-contribution plans, and RRSPs was replaced by an overall contribution limit of 18 percent of earnings up to Can$15,500. This figure was designed to correspond to a maximum annual benefit of just over Can$60,000 per year and allowable compensation of Can$86,000 (Horner and Poddar 1992). An implied contribution amount is determined for workers who participate in a defined-benefit plan. The total of this amount plus contributions to the defined-contribution pension could not exceed the 18 percent/Can$15,500 ceiling. (In 1995, the budget plan announced reductions in maximum contributions.) The idea is to apply uniform ceilings to workers, regardless of the type of plan provided by their employer.

Both countries also limit employer contributions to fund benefits. The Internal Revenue Code allows a deduction for the "normal cost" plus amortization of any prior unfunded liabilities. However, contributions to plans having assets equal to or above 150 percent of current liabilities are not deductible.[2] Further, the tax code limits the range of actuarial assumptions that may be used to calculate pension liabilities.

Thus, sponsors cannot avoid the 150 percent funding limit by adopting a low discount rate.

Revenue Canada, in contrast, relies more heavily on the judgment of professional actuaries in determining deductible pension contributions. In Ontario, the Pension Commission of Ontario requires defined-benefit plans to be evaluated by a pension actuary every three years. The actuary's determination of the required contribution for full funding is used by Revenue Canada to determine allowable deductions. Contributions to pension funds determined to be overfunded are disallowed in Canada, as they are in the United States. It appears, however, that the two countries apply different definitions of "fully funded." Canadian actuaries are permitted to take into account future salary increases as well as possible postretirement benefit increases; that is, contributions are allowed to fully fund currently accrued benefits. The full-funding limit in the United States, in contrast, applies to current or termination liabilities, which can be substantially less than ongoing obligations in periods of significant inflation.

Employee contributions in Canada are also generally exempt from taxation as current income. In the United States, employee contributions are deductible only in special 401(k) plans.[3] A more important difference is the greater ability of Canadians to contribute to personal retirement accounts. The overall contribution limit of 18 percent or $15,500 also applies to RRSPs. Workers not covered by an occupational pension plans may contribute up to this limit to their RRSP; allowable contributions, however, are reduced dollar-for-dollar by implied contributions to defined-benefit or money-purchase plans on the employee's behalf. Contributions to RRSPs have grown rapidly over the past decade. The proportion of tax filers who made RRSP contributions rose from 13.8 percent in 1982 to 24.2 percent in 1991 (Statistics Canada 1992).

Individual Retirement Accounts were established by ERISA in 1974 for workers not covered by an employer-sponsored pension, but American workers who were pension participants could not contribute to a personal retirement account until 1981. Like Canadian RRSPs, IRAs are nonforfeitable, fully portable retirement funds. The Economic Recovery Tax Act allowed all workers to make tax-deductible contribution to IRAs. However, the Tax Reform Act of 1986 put limits on contributions of workers who were otherwise covered by a pension.

A married couple with adjusted gross income above $50,000 cannot make tax-deductible contributions to an IRA.[4]

The most rapidly growing pension vehicle in the United States is the 401(k) plan. Authorized by Congress in 1978, 401(k) plans allow employees the option of making tax-deductible contributions to a qualified profit-sharing or stock bonus plan. Typically, the employer matches voluntary employee contributions up to a percentage limit. The maximum employee 401(k) contribution is $8,994 in 1993; otherwise, 401(k) plans are subject to the same rules as other defined-contribution plans.

In summary, contribution limits to tax-qualified pension funds are stricter in Canada. Canadian workers, whether or not covered by an occupational pension plan, however, have a greater ability to make tax-favored contributions to personal retirement accounts.

Vesting and Portability

Although personal retirement accounts are more important in Canada than in the United States, pension wealth overall may be less portable in Canada due to the dominance of defined-benefit plans. About one-third of all private pension assets in Canada reside in RRSPs or money-purchase plans (Statistics Canada 1992). In the United States, however, defined-contribution plans have grown rapidly and now hold nearly 40 percent of pension assets (Turner and Beller 1992).

Portability of benefits has emerged as a major pension issue in both countries, with much of the focus on early vesting. In 1987, the Ontario Pension Benefits Act and the federal Pension Benefits Standards Act established vesting after two years of service, and five other provinces have since adopted this standard. Three provinces have a five-year requirement, and Newfoundland applies the "10 and 45" rule. In the United States, all defined-benefit sponsors are subject to the same vesting rules, which generally require vesting after five years.

The Ontario Pension Benefits Act also enhanced portability of vested defined benefits. Upon termination, the vested worker may have the present value of his pension benefit transferred into another plan or into a Registered Retirement Savings Plan. Generally, workers do not have similar access to lump-sum benefits in the United States. As I discuss in the next section, however, preserving the value of defined benefits depends less upon the portability of assets than upon the interest rate used to calculate the termination value, and neither country requires that distributions index for preretirement wage growth.

Portability outcomes also are a function of policies that encourage personal retirement accounts or defined-contribution plans. Tax policy in Canada is more favorable to RRSPs, but many analysts have argued that tax and regulatory changes over the past decade are responsible for the shift towards defined-contribution pensions (Clark and McDermed 1990). An indirect, and perhaps intended, effect of these policies has been to make pension benefits more portable.

PUBLIC POLICY ISSUES IN CANADA AND THE UNITED STATES

In this review I examine four public policy issues towards private pensions that have been prominent in the United States and Canada. The two countries share concerns about coverage, portability and preservation of benefits, the role of tax policy in promoting pensions, and inflation protection. My primary objective is to identify and briefly review relevant pension research from both countries. Most of the empirical research on private pensions has focused on outcomes in the United States. A number of studies, however, on the Canadian system have relevance for policy debates in the United States. In addition, there may be opportunities for comparative analysis, which exploits the different experiences of Canada and the United States, to improve our understanding of the private pension system and the effects of tax and regulatory policies in both countries. For example, research on trends in pension coverage in the United States generally uses time series methodology to evaluate the impacts of institutional, demographic, and public policy changes. Since Canadian policies and coverage outcomes have been different, however, a comparative analysis should be useful.

The discussion is organized around four policy issues: private sector coverage, portability and preservation of benefits, pension tax policy, and inflation indexing. I present an overview of the issue first, describing recent or proposed policy changes in each country. A brief review of relevant policy research is presented next. Finally, I discuss some implications of cross-national comparisons and make some suggestions for further comparative policy research.

Pension Coverage

The most fundamental policy debates in both countries center on the level of coverage. Governments in both countries historically have promoted private sector pensions with favorable tax policy. Despite these incentives, the expansion of coverage begun after World War II has stalled, with cross-section coverage rates less than 50 percent in both workforces.[5] The percentage of employed, private sector workers covered under an employer-sponsored pension plan is estimated to be 39 percent in Canada (Frenken and Maser 1992) and 42 percent in the United States (Beller and Lawrence 1992).[6] Incomplete coverage was cited as the primary weakness of private pensions during the Canadian Great Pension Debate. According to Sayeed (1984, p. 59), "The most important issue in the debate on pension reform [in Canada] is whether coverage should be improved by an expansion of the public system or . . . of the private system." Most of the commission reports recommended expansion of private sector pension coverage, and one called for mandatory pensions.[7]

Private pensions in the United States also have been criticized for incomplete coverage. The President's Commission on Pension Policy (1981) recommended mandatory pension coverage, and a 1988 report of a Department of Labor advisory group also recommended consideration of, among other options, mandatory coverage. More recent critics of incomplete pension coverage have made different recommendations, arguing for repeal of pension tax preferences on the grounds that the beneficiaries of pensions and tax preferences are disproportionately high-income individuals (Munnell 1991, 1992; Gravelle 1993).

A particular concern in the United States has been the apparent decline in private pension coverage since the late 1970s. Table 1 shows coverage rates declining slightly between 1979 and 1988.[8]   However, these averages mask two significant trends: an increase in pension coverage for women and a decline for younger males. Even and Macpherson (1994) calculated that coverage rates for females rose by more than 6 percentage points between 1979 and 1988; whereas, over the same

Table 1 Pension Coverage Rates, Canada and the United States (%)

| Year | United States | | Canada |
	Private sector	Civilian, public and private sector	Civilian, public and private sector
1979	43	46	
1982			46.5
1983	41	43	
1984			47.3
1986			46.0
1988	42	42	44.9
1990			44.8
1992			47.5

SOURCE: United States: estimates based on tabulations from May supplements to Current Populations Surveys by Beller and Lawrence (1992) for private sector and Piacentini (1989) for all civilian workers. Canada: *Statistics Canada* (1992).

period, the coverage rate fell 1.6 points for males between the ages of 35 and 55 and 6.6 points for males aged 21–35. Bloom and Freeman (1992) reported similar results.

Coverage rates in Canada appear to have been stable in comparison. Such a conclusion may be misleading, however. First, the source of time-series data on coverage rates in Canada is administrative data provided by plan sponsors, and coverage rate estimates from similar data in the United States also show stable private-sector coverage rates over the past decade, at about 46 percent (Beller and Lawrence 1992). Evidence for declining coverage rates in the United States has come from household surveys. A comparable trend might be found in Canada if household surveys were regularly repeated. Second, the stable coverage rates reported for Canada in Table 1 combine private and public sector employees. Unfortunately, an analysis of private sector coverage trends is not possible with Canadian data.[9]

More directly comparable are coverage rates for all civilians. Table 1 shows falling civilian coverage rates in the United States (see also Andrews 1985; Parsons 1991) relative to Canada. However, a given downward trend in private sector coverage would show less of an impact on civilian coverage rates in Canada because the proportion of covered public sector workers is greater in Canada than it is in the United States.

Why Has Coverage Declined? Several studies have examined the decline in male coverage rates in the United States. The two most widely cited explanations are structural changes in the labor market, and changes in tax and pension policy. The first explanation argues that coverage declined because employment shifted to labor markets with traditionally low coverage rates: small, nonunion firms in service industries. Another possibility, however, is that coverage declined due to increased regulatory costs, reductions in marginal tax rates, and the introduction of pension plans in which employee participation is voluntary. The results of these studies are relevant to Canada. Although overall civilian coverage rates have not declined, common trends are at work. Coverage rates for Canadian men declined slightly, from 53.7 percent to 51.8 percent between 1982 and 1992, while the coverage rate for females was up about 6 percentage points. There also is concern that new Canadian pension regulations may reduce coverage (see discussion in Frenken and Maser 1992).

Investigations of declining coverage in the United States build upon cross-section studies of the determinants of pension coverage. These studies have consistently shown that the probability of having a pension is higher for individuals who are union members and are employed by large, manufacturing-based firms (Mitchell and Andrews 1981; Dorsey 1982; Even and Macpherson 1994; Parsons 1994). Although the determinants of pension coverage in Canada have received less attention, the cross-section pattern is similar to that of the United States (Frenken and Maser 1992; Smith and Meng 1991; Currie and Chaykowski 1993).

On the basis of these patterns, Bloom and Freeman (1992) and Even and Macpherson (1994) attributed most of the decline in pension coverage to shrinking union membership, manufacturing employment, and increases in the relative importance of small firms.

Cross-section estimates also suggest that earnings and marginal tax rates are important determinants of pension coverage in the United States (Alpert 1983; Long and Scott 1982; Woodbury and Bettinger 1991). Currie and Chaykowski (1993) and Smith and Meng (1991) found coverage to be strongly related to earnings for Canadian workers as well. These results suggest that reduction in marginal tax rates during the 1980s may have lowered coverage rates in the United States. Bloom and Freeman argued that tax cuts could not explain the drop in coverage for younger, lower income workers because their tax rates declined the least. When the pension coverage decision is viewed in a lifetime context, however, tax cuts should have the greatest effect on younger workers. Older covered workers would have little incentive to drop pension coverage, but forward-looking younger workers would anticipate lower lifetime tax savings if the tax cuts were viewed as permanent.

Woodbury and Bettinger (1991) estimated that the decline in the tax price of pensions, due to reductions in marginal tax rates, explained about one-third of the drop in coverage between 1979 and 1988 and was nearly as important as declining union membership. Reagan and Turner (2000) attributed about one-fourth of the decline in coverage for young males to tax effects.

Even and Macpherson also argued that much of the fall in coverage for young males was due to the introduction of 401(k) plans, which allow workers to voluntarily participate. Their estimates indicated that the pension offer rate did not decline, but that the acceptance rate, given that a pension was in place, fell. Note that this theory also is consistent with the view that coverage fell due to an increased regulatory burden. Under this view, higher regulatory costs for defined-benefit plans induced employers to adopt 401(k) plans, indirectly leading to lower coverage rates.

This result is relevant for Canada, given the generous contribution limits for voluntary RRSPs. There is a corresponding concern that higher regulatory costs of defined-benefits will lead to substitution of voluntary pension coverage for defined-benefit plans (Hirst 1992), which could lead to similar reductions in coverage for young males in Canada.

A test of the 401(k) explanation for declining coverage would be a comparison of trends in coverage for young males in Canada and the United States. This theory predicts that coverage rates for young males should have declined less in Canada because RRSP limits were raised well after 401(k) plans were introduced. Unfortunately, there are no repeated household surveys that allow comparisons of coverage rates by age over time in Canada.

Another factor consistent with greater declines in coverage in the United States for all workers is the greater decline in unionization than in Canada.

Changes in Coverage Type. The structure of pension coverage also has changed dramatically in the United States. The percentage of covered workers who had a primary defined-benefit plan fell from 87 percent in 1975 to 68 percent in 1987. A similar decline has not been found in Canada: 94 percent of covered workers had a defined-benefit plan in 1982, as compared with 90 percent in 1992. Again, a time series on only private sector, defined-benefit coverage rates is not possible in Canada. But, given that about half of all covered workers are private sector employees, a decline in private sector, defined-benefit coverage similar to the United States would have lowered the overall defined benefit rate by more than 4 percentage points.

The shift in coverage type has become an important policy issue in the United States. Some analysts are concerned that the growth of defined-contribution plans will yield lower retirement incomes than defined-benefit plans, because savings rates are lower for defined-contribution plans and because of the likelihood that lump-sum distributions will be consumed before retirement (Paine 1993). Although defined-benefit coverage has not shrunk in Canada, some are concerned that pension and tax reforms, and especially the issue of the surplus in overfunded plans, may precipitate a similar movement toward defined-contribution plans.

The two main explanations for shifts in coverage are changes in the structure of employment and changes in sponsor preferences for defined-benefit plans. Studies of pension plan type in the United States have shown that defined-benefit plans are more common among large firms and in unionized, goods-producing industries (Dorsey 1987). Consistent with this, Gustman and Steinmeier (1992) estimated that over half of drop in defined-benefit coverage between 1977 and 1985 was due to shifts in the distribution of workers away from sectors that traditionally provide defined-benefit plans. Clark and McDermed (1990) found, in contrast, that only 21 percent of the decline in firms who offer defined-benefit plans is due to employment shifts. They attributed the remainder to changes in sponsor preferences and argued that changes in the tax and regulatory climate have been the primary reason for these shifts. A study by Hay/Huggins (1990) estimated that administrative costs per worker increased 181 percent between 1981 and 1991, but only 99 percent for defined-contribution plans.

An analysis of plan choice in Canada could be instructive in evaluating the relative effects of public policy versus employment shifts. Two significant differences in Canadian trends are a smaller decline in unionization and, at least during the decade beginning in the late 1970s, a less dramatic increase in regulatory costs of defined-benefit plans.

Portability and Benefit Preservation

The primary reason for encouraging private pensions is to raise retirement income, but critics of private pensions point out that even workers who are covered frequently receive low benefits due to imperfect portability and consumption of pension assets before retirement. Canada and the United States both have recently adopted policies to enhance portability of benefits and to "lock in" pension assets. Standards for vesting have been raised to five years in the United States, and two years for most Canadian provinces. New legislation provides Canadian workers with greater portability of defined-benefit assets upon a job change, and vested benefits in Canada also are locked-in. Although lump-sum distributions are increasingly common in the United States, there is a 10 percent excise tax on assets not rolled over into an IRA.

Policy towards portability and benefit preservation raises several issues besides the ability of pensions to support retirement consumption. Equity concerns arise because workers who change jobs frequently reach retirement with smaller benefits than those who spend their entire career with a single employer. Thus, imperfect portability may lower retirement income of females and low-income workers relative to high-wage males. The effect of pensions on economic efficiency also is relevant. Pensions are sometimes criticized for tying workers to jobs, thereby restricting job changes when technology or product demands change.

Despite shorter vesting periods, benefit losses when changing jobs can still be significant. A Hay/Huggins study (1988) projected that 59 percent of covered workers would lose pension wealth in a job change and that the average loss would be 23 percent of the benefits that would have been received if all years of service were credited to their final pension plan. The study estimated that immediate vesting would lower average portability losses by less than 1 percent. Most portability losses arise because very few plans in either country index the earnings of workers who separate from the firm before retirement. Thus, a worker who is continuously covered by a pension, but changes jobs frequently, receives a smaller benefit than a worker with the same years of service credited to one plan.

Several proposals have been made to further reduce portability losses (Turner 1993). Mandatory indexing of the earnings base, similar to public pensions, has been suggested in both countries. Such a policy would eliminate most portability losses but, of course, would raise the cost of funding benefits. Ozanne and Lindeman (1987) estimated that such a policy would increase annual defined-benefit costs between 6 and 28 percent. Alternatively, portability losses could be reduced by requiring employers to accept service credit earned on a previous pension. Clearly, this policy could substantially raise the cost of hiring workers who were covered by a pension on a previous job.

Munnell (1991) pointed out that enhanced portability of assets will not necessarily lower losses for workers who separate. If the present value of benefits is calculated with a nominal interest rate, the assets to be transferred do not reflect wage indexing, and the worker is no better off than if the credits were left with the original plan. In theory, pension losses from job change could be eliminated by requiring a preretirement distribution valued at a discount rate that assumes wage indexing. The Ontario Pension Benefits Act provides that the present value of the deferred pension may be transferred for an employee who has terminated, either to another plan or an RRSP. However, it is my understanding that the present value is calculated using a nominal interest rate. If so, this option would have little effect on benefit losses.

In contrast to recent changes in Canadian regulations, defined-benefit assets generally cannot be distributed prior to the retirement age in the United States. Sponsors may cash out job leavers with accrued benefits of less than $3,500, however. The Tax Reform Act of 1986 required such lump sums to be calculated with the interest rate used by the Pension Benefit Guaranty Corporation. The PBGC rate is less than the market rate generally used to determine current pension liabilities, and thus portability losses are lower. However, when larger distributions are permitted, sponsors may use a nominal interest rate.

Requiring sponsors to transfer pension assets of separated workers valued with a real interest rate in effect transforms the defined-benefit pension into a defined-contribution plan. A more direct policy to enhance portability is to encourage defined-contribution plans. Some analysts have argued that the increasing regulation of defined-benefit plans has been purposeful to encourage defined-contribution plans. Unfortunately, one consequence of the growth of defined-contribution plans in the United States has been increased consumption of pension assets before retirement.

Economic Effect of Enhanced Portability. The impact of policies to enhance benefit portability centers on two questions. Would greater portability increase retirement income? Second, would these policies have adverse effects on employee productivity?

Pesando's (1984a) discussion of pension reform proposals in Canada pointed out that economists and employee-benefit experts widely accept the view that higher pension costs must ultimately be borne by workers, either in the form of lower wages or less generous pensions. Whether retirement income rises on average depends upon whether workers understand that benefits are imperfectly portable. If workers are fully informed and the expected retirement benefit is consistent with their preferences, enhanced portability would lead to lower benefit generosity, and retirement income would not rise. But, if workers do not understand that job change lowers real benefits, the policy would lead to an increase in pension benefits but lower wages or other compensation.

Some have suggested that enhanced pension portability would create gains for workers who make frequent job changes at the expense of long-tenured employees, but Pesando pointed out that this would occur only if employers do not adjust the wage structure. If the reward for long tenure is intentional, perhaps to provide incentives for longevity, employers will respond by steepening the career wage profile.[10] If so, the distributional effects will be minimized. No studies, however, have attempted to estimate employer and employee responses to policies to reduce pension benefit losses.

The second question is based upon the premise that potential portability losses reduce employee turnover. Several studies in the United States have shown that pension coverage is associated with lower quit and layoff rates (Mitchell 1982; Ippolito 1986; Even and Macpherson 1991; Gustman and Steinmeier 1993; Allen, Clark, and McDermed 1993). Fewer studies have focused on the determinants of job change in Canada, but a study by Osberg, Apostle, and Clairmont (1986) found that Canadian workers were less likely to change employers when initially covered under a pension plan.

The pension-quit relationship has different interpretations, however. Even and Macpherson (1991) found that workers with defined-contribution pension coverage, whose benefits generally are fully portable, also were less likely to change jobs. Gustman and Steinmeier attributed most of the lower job change associated with pensions to wage premiums, rather than the potential portability losses. Their results suggest that pensions are associated with an efficiency wage and that enhanced portability would not increase quit rates. In contrast, Allen, Clark, and McDermed (1993) ascribed the significant decline in quits and layoffs to backloaded pension benefits, independent of wages.

The question of how policies to enhance pension portability would affect labor-market efficiency has received much less attention. For some time, analysts have been concerned that nonportable pensions would make workers less mobile in the face of demand and technological shocks. From this perspective, policies to make pension benefits more portable would improve allocative efficiency in the labor market. In contrast, most recent labor-market analysis is based upon gains from durable employment relationships or implicit contracts. Under this perspective deferred compensation plays an important incentive role in encouraging firm-specific investments in workers or reducing job shirking, and enhanced portability could reduce labor-market efficiency by encouraging worker quits and the loss of firm-specific job rents.

I found very little direct evidence on the productivity effects of nonportable pensions (Dorsey 1995). However, there is substantial indirect evidence that pensions may raise worker productivity. Two recent studies have shown that pension coverage is strongly related to worker training (Dorsey and Macpherson 1997; Johnson 1996). In addition, a number of empirical studies based upon a wide variety of data sets have established that pension coverage is associated with large wage premiums. To my knowledge, there also have been no studies of the effect of pensions on productivity in the Canadian workforce.

"Locking In." Proposals to "lock in" pension assets have received closer attention in the United States with the growth of defined-contribution plans. A major difference between defined-contribution and defined-benefit plans is that the former typically make lump-sum distributions to workers who separate prior to retirement. According to Turner (1993), consumption of these preretirement distributions results in a greater loss in retirement income than do losses due to imperfect portability.[11]

Estimates based on the 1988 May Current Population Survey showed that 8.5 million American workers reported a lump-sum distribution from a previous pension plan, averaging $8,300 in 1988 dollars (Piacentini 1990). Piacentini reported that only 11 percent rolled the entire sum over into a tax-qualified retirement plan, while 40 percent reported consuming at least a part of the distribution.

In Canada, defined-contribution plans have been less important, so presumably preretirement distributions have been quantitatively less significant. However, the 1987 Ontario Pension Benefits Act allowed separated workers to receive distributions from defined benefit plans. To make sure that these assets were used for income support in retirement, the law generally requires that vested benefits be locked in (Conklin 1990). There is no corresponding requirement that distributions in the United States be placed in another pension savings vehicle. However, since 1987, assets not rolled over into another tax-qualified retirement plan are subject to a 10 percent excise tax.

Many pension analysts are concerned that the growth in defined-contribution plans combined with the greater likelihood of spending lump-sum distributions will lower retirement income. Samwick and Skinner (1994), however, estimated that reductions in benefits due to consumption of defined-contribution distributions approximately matches portability losses from defined benefit plans. Overall, their results suggest that, under current policy, the substitution of defined-contribution plans will have little effect on retirement income.

Taxation of Pension Benefits

There is general agreement that the long-standing policy of preferential tax treatment has been an important factor in the development of private pensions in Canada and the United States. However, this basic policy has been quietly diluted in the United States since 1982 as the federal government looked for ways to raise revenue without raising tax rates. A more explicit debate over the advisability of pension tax preferences appears to be looming in both countries, reflecting a fundamental tension between the goals of encouraging retirement savings, horizontal tax equity, and limiting revenue loss.

Benefit and contribution ceilings in the United States have been lowered on several occasions since 1982. The Tax Equity and Fiscal Responsibility Act (TEFRA) of 1982 lowered limits on the annual benefit a defined-benefit participant could receive, from $136,425 to $90,000. The act also reduced the maximum contribution to defined-contribution plans. These limits again were lowered by the Deficit Reduction Act of 1984 and the Tax Reform Act of 1986. A limit on compensation that could be used for benefit calculation became effective in 1989 and was reduced from $235,000 to $150,000 by the Omnibus Budget Reconciliation Act (OBRA) of 1993. Perhaps the most controversial policy shift occurred with OBRA 1987, which limited pension funding to 150 percent of current pension liabilities, independent of contributions needed to fund future benefit promises. This change prevented many plan sponsors from making contributions and, in effect, required that future benefits be funded with after-tax dollars (Ippolito 1991b).

Reduced pension preferences have not been driven by an explicit reappraisal of federal retirement income policy, but instead by a continuous search for additional revenue combined with the perception that pension tax policy disproportionately benefits higher income workers. According to estimates produced by the Joint Committee on Taxation, the annual loss in revenue due to the exclusion of pension contributions and earnings was $56.5 billion in FY 1993, the largest of the so-called "tax expenditures." This figure has made pensions an enticing target for revenue enhancement, especially when a claim can be made that taxing pensions both raises revenue and improves horizontal equity.[12]

Many analysts have become concerned that retirement income policy has become too focused on short-run budgetary concerns, and that an explicit comparison of the costs and benefits of pension tax policy is overdue (Paine 1993). Two fundamental questions would be addressed by such a debate: Do the gains in private pension coverage and benefits justify the revenue loss? Are the benefits of current policy distributed too unfairly?

This explicit debate over pension tax policy is now being joined. Munnell (1991, 1992) argued that private pension coverage is too limited to justify favorable tax treatment, and she recommended taxing pension earnings or assets. Gravelle (1993) also criticized pension tax expenditures for disproportionately benefiting high-income individuals.

These criticisms have been challenged, however. For example, Goodfellow and Schieber (1993) and Salisbury (1993) argued that private pension coverage was never intended to be universal but must be evaluating according to its contribution to "three-legged" stool. Schieber and Goodfellow also argued that the bulk of pension tax expenditures accrue to middle-income households and that the progressivity of the entire retirement income system, including the Social Security system, should be considered.

A similar debate proceeded in Canada. During the "Great Pension Debate," some labor groups took the position that private pensions were fundamentally flawed due to incomplete coverage, nonportability, and the lack of indexed benefits. They argued that augmenting public pensions is more effective strategy for delivering retirement income. The federal and provincial governments elected, instead, to strengthen private pensions and individual retirement saving.

Recent changes in tax policy towards pensions in Canada have taken a much different direction than in the United States. The 1990 tax reforms were the result of an explicit debate over the adequacy of retirement income and the role of tax policy in encouraging private pensions (Horner and Poddar 1992). In other words, changes in tax policy have been less piecemeal and ad hoc than they have been in the United States. The basic approach was to set a consistent overall limit on contributions and benefits for each individual, regardless of whether they were covered by a defined-benefit, money-purchase, or individual savings plan. This integrated limit establishes a target benefit eligible for tax assistance, equal to an annual benefit limit of 18 percent of earnings up to a maximum of Can$15,500. Workers who accrue benefits below this limit in a defined-benefit plan or money-purchase plan may contribute the difference to a RRSP. Thus, workers who do not participate in an occupational pension plan may contribute Can$15,500 to a RRSP.

Some Canadian pension specialists are concerned that the new tax rules, designed to put money-purchase and RRSP plans on an equal footing with defined-benefit plans have, in conjunction with the cost of new regulations, created a disadvantage for defined-benefit plans (Hirst 1992). It must be kept in mind, however, that benefit limits still are much lower in Canada than in the United States. As a result, horizontal equity arguments for taxing pensions have less force in Canada.

Another important difference is that Canada has not adopted ad hoc limits on funding, comparable to the 150 percent rule of OBRA 1987. This represented a fundamental change in policy, for the sole purpose of raising revenue. The full-funding limit is difficult to justify on equity or efficiency grounds.

The debate over taxation of pensions apparently has begun in Canada. The 1995 budget lowered contribution limits to reduce revenue loss. The government has established the principle of limiting tax assistance to earnings up to 2.5 times the average wage. A proposal to tax investment earnings of pension funds was considered but rejected.

The Effect of Reducing Pension Tax Preferences.

The question of whether or not the benefits of expanded pension coverage justify the revenue loss from pension tax preferences is very complex. What is the effect of favorable tax treatment on pension coverage and benefits? If tax preferences were eliminated and pension covered declined, would individual retirement savings make up the difference? How elastic is retirement saving to the after-tax rate of return? Would revenue gained by taxing pensions be used to lower marginal tax rates or expand public pensions? Would taxing pensions make the income tax code and retirement income programs more progressive?

A number of studies cited previously suggest that pension coverage is quite sensitive to its tax price, implying that proposals to tax pension contributions and earnings would reduce coverage. A more direct prediction is made by Woodbury and Huang (1991). They estimated a simultaneous model of wages, health insurance, and pension benefits, and the results allowed them to simulate policy effects of several proposals to tax fringe benefits. Woodbury and Huang estimated that treating pension contributions and health insurance benefits as fully taxable income would have reduced pension coverage by over 60 percent in the simulation period. This simulation suggests that a policy of taxing *only* pensions, not other fringes, would have even greater effects on pension coverage, as workers would substitute health insurance for pension coverage.

The case that tax incentives matter for the private pension system is strong, but whether a decline in private pension coverage would lower retirement saving is theoretically ambiguous. Empirical estimates, however, suggest that the trade-off between pension and nonpension saving is less than dollar-for-dollar (Munnell and Yohn 1990). Ippolito (1986) estimated that at least one-quarter of pension contributions represents new saving (see also VanderHei 1992). The result hinges, in part, on whether savings has a positive interest elasticity. Several studies have examined the effect of changes in IRA limits in the United States on aggregate saving. Some found that a substantial amount of contributions were simply substitutions of other forms of savings (Gravelle 1991). However, studies by Venti and Wise (1990) and Carroll and Summers (1987) suggested that IRAs did increase net savings. Carroll and Summers estimated savings equations for the United States and Canada in an attempt to explain why Canadian personal savings rates increased relative to the United States beginning in the mid 1970s. The availability of RRSPs in Canada was found to be a statistically significant factor in the divergence of savings rates.

The impact of changes in tax policy on retirement saving depends crucially upon how the public pension system responds. It is always possible, as some have recommended, to expand the public retirement system to counter any loss in private retirement savings. Private pension advocates argue, in contrast, that one of its principle merits is to reduce pressure on public pensions (Paine 1993). The OASI trust fund in the United States is projected to face significant shortfalls as the baby boom generation begins drawing benefits, and increasing public pension generosity seems unlikely.

The equity effect of taxing pensions is also complicated. Given the patterns of coverage and progressive income tax rates in both countries, a disproportionate share of the pension tax expenditure accrues to high-income families,[13] but the treatment of pensions is only one factor in the progressivity of the tax code and retirement policies. Elimination of pension tax preferences may lead to pressure to reduce the progressivity of the tax code in other areas. Further, public pensions in both countries increase the progressivity of the total retirement income system. Estimates by Goodfellow and Schieber (1993) suggest that the higher share of pension tax expenditures is more than offset by a less than fair return on Social Security payroll taxes for high-wage workers. The redistributive nature of public pensions may reflect the disproportionate private pension benefits of high-income workers.

Evidence on Effects of the 1980s Changes. The reduction in benefit and contribution limits in the United States could be described as "nibbling at the edges" of the pension tax preference. The basic policy remains intact, so it is unlikely that tax policy changes directly reduced coverage during the 1980s.[14] Many have argued, however, that frequent changes in tax rules added to the complexity of administering defined-benefit plans and contributed to a shift towards defined-contribution and 401(k) plans.[15] As stated by Utgoff (1991), "It is often difficult for nonspecialists to comprehend just how complex our pension laws have become . . . nondiscrimination laws in particular." Frequent changes in nondiscrimination rules appear to have been especially burdensome for small employers, among whom the shift away from defined-benefit pensions has been the greatest.

The full-funding limit established by OBRA 1987 also has created concern. Ippolito (1991b) estimated that the 150 percent funding limit establishes, in effect, an excise tax on defined-benefit assets of 3 to 10 percent per year, with a nominal interest rate of 10 percent. The constraint is greatest for companies with a younger workforce and when nominal interest rates are higher. Ippolito estimated that, had this limit been applied since 1974, funding ratios, especially for growing firms, would have been dramatically reduced. It seems clear that this provision has significantly reduced pension funding. A study by the U.S Department of the Treasury found that half of all defined-benefit plan assets were affected by the limit.

Mandatory Inflation Protection

The issues discussed so far have been prominent in both countries. The debate over indexing private pension benefits, however, has occurred almost exclusively in Canada. The erosion of benefits by inflation was seen the principal weakness of private pensions by many participants in the Canadian pension debate. Before inflation subsided, there was widespread concern that, if private pensions were unable to guarantee some form of indexation, the public pension system would expand and eclipse private pensions. In response to this challenge, a series of studies were undertaken and proposals issued.[16] Public debate on indexing private pension benefits in the United States was minimal, in contrast, even before inflation declined.

Canadian Proposals and Background Analysis. A 1978 pension reform study for the Quebec government first proposed that "surplus" investment earnings be used to fund increases in benefits. This "excess earnings" approach was adopted by several other studies. The following year the Economic Council of Canada recommended that the federal government assume the risk of variations in inflation by offering price-indexed annuities to pension funds. The 1980 Report of the Royal Commission on the Status of Pensions in Ontario, however, rejected various proposals to mandate inflation protection, arguing that indexing would interfere with the more important goal of expanding pension coverage. A short time later, four commissions proposed that indexing be mandatory and favorably evaluated the excess earnings proposal.

Not all reports supported mandatory indexing. Business groups were critical of what they saw as an open-ended obligation. A report by the Ontario Economic Council (1984) criticized the excess earnings approach. Growing doubts about the excess earnings approach caused subsequent study groups to favor a partial or capped CPI adjustment. For example, an Ontario White Paper proposed a formula of 60 percent of CPI.

This flurry of activity had little ultimate effect on policy. Although the Ontario government is committed, in principle, to inflation protection for private pensions, inflation adjustments are not mandatory in any province.

Much of the economic analysis of mandatory indexing proposals in Canada was done by James Pesando (1984a). A series of papers focused on the conditions under which pension funds could provide inflation protection and remain viable. In his evaluation of the federal government's proposals, he noted that a portfolio composed entirely of Treasury bills could approximate a portfolio of index bonds, allowing sponsors to promise index benefits without assuming inflation risk. Pesando suggested that the general absence of such lower return portfolios, however, suggests that employees may be unwilling to pay the market price for avoiding inflation risk.

In this and a later study (Pesando 1988), he was especially critical of the excess earnings approach, which pegs inflation adjustments to current bond interest rates, not yields. Under this approach, when inflation and nominal interest rates rise, pension funds are required to increase benefits, even though their value has declined. Although pension funds could avoid inflation risk by holding only Treasury bills, the real interest rate required by the excess earnings proposal was well above the equilibrium rate for such a riskless portfolio.

What is the Nature of the Pension Contract? The debate over mandatory indexing goes to the heart of a question that is fundamental for pension policy. What are the implicit promises of defined-benefit sponsors to employees? Is there an implicit promise of a real retirement benefit? While fewer than 5 percent of plan sponsors promise automatic indexation, evidence suggests that ad hoc post-retirement benefit increases, which sponsors are under no legal obligation to provide, are widespread but incomplete. Allen, Clark, and Sumner (1986) found that 75 percent of retirees in the United States received such an adjustment during the 1970s; however, the average increase was only about 40 percent of price increases over the period. A later study by Allen, Clark, and McDermed (1992) found that fewer plans raised benefits during the 1980s, but inflation adjustment was more complete. Conklin (1990) reported that ad hoc adjustments also were common in Canada and cited a study suggesting that the average increase offset about one-fourth of price increases between 1977 and 1986.

Thus, the evidence is not consistent with a contract that guarantees real pension benefits. Periodic adjustments are sufficiently common, however, to suggest some kind of implicit agreement. Pesando

(1984b) and Pesando and Hyatt (1992) have argued against the traditional notion that the risk of pension fund performance is borne entirely by shareholders. They suggest an implicit contract model in which workers and, presumably, retirees share in favorable and unfavorable investment performance. The finding that benefits are not fully indexed reflects the sharing by workers in a decline in the performance of the pension fund.

Evidence for this type of contract is mixed, however. The studies by Allen, Clark, and McDermed (1992, 1993) both find that larger firms are more likely to provide ad hoc adjustments, consistent with the contract model. However, they found no evidence that financial performance altered the likelihood that plans would provide benefit increases during the 1980s. In addition, strong pension fund performance during the 1980s should have made adjustments more, rather than less, likely. Pesando and Hyatt (1992), on the other hand, presented informal evidence and case studies to suggest that employees are negatively affected by adverse plan performance in Canada, where sponsors are required to quickly amortize experience deficiencies through increased contributions.

A closely related issue is the appropriate discount rate for valuing pension liabilities. If the beneficiaries bear no investment risk, the risk-free rate is appropriate, regardless of the assets held by the fund. If the implicit contract calls for workers to share in investment risk, the appropriate rate is instead related to the risk characteristics of the fund. Petersen (1994) attempted to infer from the discount rate chosen by plan sponsors the extent to which risk is born by workers. Given legal limitations on the choice of discount rates in the United States, an analysis of rates used by Canadian actuaries may be more instructive, however.

Allen, Clark, and McDermed (1992) raised the possibility that slowing benefit increases during the 1980s may reflect increased propensity to renege on the implicit contract, by terminating pension plans and acquiring surplus assets. Ownership of surplus assets is another aspect of the implicit pension contract, which is a matter of legal and public policy interest in both countries. Recent legislation in the United States has taken the view that pension surpluses belong to workers and has imposed large penalties on sponsors who terminated plans with surplus assets. The view that surplus assets are owned by plan participants is consistent with the view that workers share in the investment risk of pension funds. Until recently, plan sponsors in Canada could more easily acquire surplus funds. However, the Pension Commission of Ontario has enforced a freeze on surplus assets.

Why is There Less Concern about Indexing in the United States?

A striking difference between the pension policy debate in Canada and the United States is has been the attention paid to mandatory indexing. Inflation protection was perhaps the central private pension policy issue in Canada through the mid 1990s. Indexing of private pensions has drawn far less interest in the United States. Given the similarities of systems and other policy concerns, what explains the difference in emphasis on indexing?

A likely candidate is the conflict between encouraging retirement income and minimizing federal revenue losses. This policy trade-off exists in both countries and helps explain why indexing proposals have not been implemented in Canada. Short-run revenue concerns appear to have been more powerful in the United States, however. Utgoff (1991) described how *any* policy to expand private pension benefits increases the reported pension tax expenditures and, under current budget rules, requires a spending offset or revenue increase. During the 1980s, the budget rules were informal but no less binding. In short, the U.S. federal budget deficit dominated any pension-related debates.

Second, the "Great Pension Debate" in Canada was largely over the adequacy of retirement income, and benefit erosion is clearly a key factor. The United States has experienced no similar fundamental debate over retirement income policy probably, again, due to the immediacy of the revenue concerns.

A reason cited by the Canadian Task Force on Inflation Protection is that most of the attention in the United States on retiree benefits was focused on health care insurance. More recently, of course, the health insurance debate has dominated any policy analysis of employee benefit issues.

Consider also that, at the time that mandatory indexing was being debated in Canada, cost-of-living increases for federal workers in the United States were being reduced in order to minimize the budget deficit, and various proposals were circulating which would limit indexing of social security benefits. Automatic indexing—of retirement benefits or the tax code—was viewed quite negatively by much of Congress, as part of the entitlement "problem." No doubt contributing to this perception was the "double-indexing" of Social Security benefits during the 1970s, which contributed to the solvency problems of the OASI trust fund and created very unpleasant transitional problems.

Finally, comparison of the policy debate in both countries gives the impression that there is greater consensus in Canada for an active government role in guaranteeing retirement income. A frequently voiced concern in Canada was that, unless private pensions could do a better job of providing inflation protection, indexed government pensions would be likely to expand. In the United States, expansion of the Social Security to overcome perceived deficiencies in private pensions seems quite unlikely. If anything, private pensions are seen as reducing the pressure to increase Social Security benefits.

CONCLUSIONS

The policy stance of the governments of Canada and the United States towards private pensions is similar. Both view private pensions as a primary source of retirement income, along with public pensions and individual saving. Tax and regulatory policies are fundamentally the same in each country. There are small, but important, differences however. One of the most important is that contribution limits are integrated and lower in Canada than they are in the United States. The integrated limits establish a greater ability to save for retirement outside of an employer-sponsored plan in Canada. The lower overall limits in Canada also have resulted in an absence of nondiscrimination rules; the complexity of these rules is cited as an important factor in declining defined-benefit coverage in the United States, especially among small employers.

The most significant portability policy difference is that preretirement distributions are locked-in in Canada, whereas they only are subject to a penalty tax in the United States. This is important because the consumption of lump-sum distributions has created fears that the shift towards defined-contribution plans threatens basic retirement income.

Canada and the United States share most current pension policy issues. The most basic policy issue facing both countries over the next decade is pension coverage and, in particular, the appropriate role of tax and regulatory policy. There is a fundamental tension in both countries between the goals of encouraging private pension coverage and benefits and minimizing revenue losses. This conflict already has produced significant effects on pension outcomes in the United States. A more explicit debate on fundamental pension tax policy appears to be developing in Canada and the United States. In both countries, the sides will be drawn between those who believe private pensions are fundamentally flawed and favor the expansion of public pensions, and advocates who view private pensions as an essential leg of the retirement "stool." Such an explicit debate would be welcome, especially in the United States, where recent tax policy has been driven by short-run revenue concerns with little regard to impacts on the retirement income system.

The two most important trends in coverage in the United States are a decline in overall private sector coverage, especially for young males, and the dramatic fall in the relative share of coverage provided by defined-benefit plans. An unresolved question is whether or not Canada is experiencing similar trends. There has not been an overall decline in coverage rates in Canada; however, current data cannot address whether there has been a similar large drop in private sector coverage for young males, a drop that has been driving the falling coverage in the United States. A comparison of coverage trends for young males would be helpful in evaluating the importance of policy changes versus employment shifts since there have been differences in the latter between the two countries.

A time-series for private sector, defined-benefit coverage is not available in Canada; however, it is clear that coverage shifts have been much greater in the United States. Again, a comparative analysis may shed light on the causes of this trend. A theory of the decline in defined-benefit coverage is that it reflects shifts in employment away from large, unionized, manufacturing firms. However, Canada has had similar shifts, with the exception that unionization rates have fallen less. If the shift to defined-contribution plans has been primarily a result of changes in tax and regulatory policies, the United States experience may be relevant in Canada. There is concern that recent regulatory changes in conjunction with expanded contribution limits for RRSPs may cause a similar drop in defined-benefit coverage there.

Finally, my overall impression is that there is a greater consensus for regulation of pension outcomes in Canada. Canada had earlier and stricter vesting standards than the United States and does not allow workers to consume vested benefits. Most recently, the seriousness of the debate over mandatory indexing stands in contrast to the lack of interest in regulating inflation protection in the United States.

Notes

The author wishes to thank Keith Horner for many helpful comments on an earlier draft of this paper.

1. The most extensive survey of early pension coverage combined data from the United States and Canada (Latimer 1932). It is likely that early trends were similar in both countries, however. According to Ezra (1983), the introduction of pensions in Canada resulted primarily from decisions of firms headquartered in the United States.
2. Contributions to these "overfunded" plans are subject to a 10 percent excise tax.
3. While most mandatory contributions are not deductible, interest earnings do accumulate tax-free.
4. However, each working spouse may make up to a $2,000 nondeductible contribution, and the investment earnings are not subject to taxation.
5. Cross-section coverage rates understate the percentage of workers who earn credit for pension benefits at some point in their career, due to the typical life cycle pattern of coverage. Tabulations reported by Goodfellow and Schieber (1993) tabulations from the March 1991 Current Population Survey showed that 61 percent of all persons aged 45 to 59, whether working or not, were either participating or receiving benefits from a private pension plan in the United States.
6. Estimates of private sector coverage rates can vary significantly in each country. One reason is different databases. The Frenken and Maser estimate is based upon the 1989 Labour Market Activity Survey. Other coverage rates estimates for Canada are derived from a biennial plan sponsor survey. The latter, however, do not allow an estimate of private sector coverage. In the United States, several surveys and methodologies are used to calculate coverage rates, and the estimates differ by definition of coverage, public versus private sector, and other factors. See Doescher (1994) for a comprehensive discussion and comparison of differences in pension coverage statistics in the United States.
7. See Sayeed (1984) for a review of pension commission recommendations. Only the Canadian Labour Congress opposed expanded private coverage, favoring expansion of public pensions instead.

8. The extent to which coverage has declined in the United States is a matter of some debate. Other surveys have shown a larger drop in coverage; for example, see Parsons (1994). In contrast, establishment surveys have indicated constant coverage rates (Beller and Lawrence 1992). In general, comparisons of coverage and trends are quite sensitive to the form of the survey question and population definition. See Doescher (1994) for a review of pension coverage surveys in the United States. Since different surveys yield different results, even with the United States, international comparisons of coverage rates should be undertaken with great care.

9. Turner and Dailey (1990) estimate that Canadian private sector coverage rates were unchanged between 1970 and 1988. Their figure of 28 percent coverage, however, is well below the estimate of 39 percent reported by Frenken and Maser (1992).

10. However, as noted by Ippolito (1991a), a steepened career wage is a less efficient vehicle for delivering deferred compensation incentives than is a pension.

11. Samwick and Skinner (1994) pointed out, however, that workers may use these distributions to purchase consumer durables or to pay down debt, which will increase retirement resources. Workers obtain no benefit from portability losses.

12. For example, during the debate on TEFRA, Congressional staff generally referred to the reduction in compensation limits as "loophole closers."

13. However, as pointed out by Schieber (1990), the share of tax expenditures always is more skewed than the share of pension benefits, given that higher income families face greater marginal tax rates. A dollar of benefits provides a larger tax benefit to families with greater tax liability. He also estimated that more than half of the benefits accrue to families with incomes less than $50,000 per year.

14. However, as noted above, the decline in marginal income tax rates may have had an important effect.

15. As discussed above, the growing popularity of 401(k) plans may have been an important factor in declining coverage. To the extent that tax and regulatory changes encouraged the adoption of these plans, these policies have indirectly reduced pension coverage.

16. A chronology of recommendations from no fewer than 12 study groups is provided by the Ontario Economic Council (1988).

References

Allen, Steven G., Robert L. Clark, and Ann A. McDermed. 1992. "Post Retirement Benefit Increases in the 1980s." In *Trends in Pensions,* John Turner and Daniel Beller, eds. Washington, D.C.: U.S. Government Printing Office.

_____. 1993. "Pensions, Bonding, and Lifetime Jobs." *Journal of Human Resources* 28(3): 463–481.

Allen, Steven G., Robert L. Clark, and Daniel A. Sumner. 1986. "Post Retirement Adjustment of Pension Benefits." *Journal of Human Resources* 21 (Winter): 118–137.

Alpert, William T. 1983. "Manufacturing Workers' Private Wage Supplements: A Simultaneous Equations Approach." *Applied Economics* 15 (June): 363–378.

Andrews, Emily S. 1985. *The Changing Profile of Pensions in America.* Washington, D.C.: Employee Benefits Research Institute.

Beller, Daniel J., and Helen Lawrence. 1992. "Trends in Private Pension Plan Coverage." In *Trends in Pensions,* John Turner and Daniel Beller, eds. Washington, D.C.: U.S. Government Printing Office.

Bloom, David, and Richard Freeman. 1992. "The Fall in Private Pension Coverage in the United States." *American Economic Review* 80(May): 539–545.

Carroll, Chris, and Lawrence Summers. 1987. "Why Have Private Savings Rates in the U.S. and Canada Diverged?" *Journal of Monetary Economics* 20(September): 249-280.

Clark, Robert L., and Ann A. McDermed. 1990. *The Choice of Pension Plans in a Changing Regulatory Environment.* Washington, D.C.: American Enterprise Institute.

Conklin, David W. 1990. "Pension Policy Reforms in Canada." In *Pension Policy: An International Perspective*, John A. Turner and Lorna Dailey, eds. Washington, D.C.: U.S. Government Printing Office.

Currie, Janet, and Richard Chaykowski. 1993. "Male Jobs, Female Jobs, and Gender Gaps in Benefits Coverage in Canada." Unpublished paper, Queen's University.

Doescher, Tabitha. 1994. "Are Pension Coverage Rates Declining?" In *Pension Coverage Issues for the '90s*, John Hinz, ed. Washington, D.C.: U.S. Government Printing Office.

Dorsey, Stuart. 1982. "A Model and Empirical Estimates of Worker Pension Coverage in the U.S." *Southern Economic Journal* 49(October): 506–520.

_____. 1987. "The Economic Function of Private Pensions: An Empirical Analysis." *Journal of Labor Economics* 5(4): S171–S89.

_____. 1995. "Pension Portability and Labor Market Efficiency: A Review of the Literature." *Industrial and Labor Relations Review* 48(2): 276–292.

Dorsey, Stuart, and David Macpherson. 1997. "Pensions and Training." *Industrial Relations* 36(1):81–96.

Even, William, and David Macpherson. 1990. "The Gender Gap in Pensions and Wages." *Review of Economics and Statistics* 72(2): 259–65.

_____. 1991. "Pensions, Labor Turnover, and Employer Size." Unpublished paper, Miami University.

_____. 1994. "The Pension Coverage of Young and Mature Workers." In *Pension Coverage Issues for the '90s*, John Hinz, ed. Washington, D.C.: U.S. Government Printing Office.

Ezra, D.D. 1983. *The Struggle for Pension Wealth.* Toronto: Pagurian Press.

Frenken, Hubert, and Karen Maser. 1992. "Employer-Sponsored Pension Plans—Who Is Covered?" *Perspectives on Labour and Income* (Winter): 27–34.

Goodfellow, Gordon P., and Sylvester Schieber. 1993. "Death and Taxes: Can We Fund for Retirement between Them?" In *The Future of Pensions in the United States,* Ray Schmidt, ed. Philadelphia: The Pension Research Council.

Graebner, William. 1980. *A History of Retirement.* New Haven: Yale University Press.

Gravelle, Jane. 1991. "Do Individual Retirement Accounts Increase Savings?" *Journal of Economic Perspectives* 5: 133–148.

_____. 1993. Statement Before the Committee on the Budget, U.S. Senate.

Gustman, Alan L., and Thomas L. Steinmeier. 1992. "The Stampede Towards Defined Contribution Pension Plans: Fact or Fiction?" *Industrial Relations* 31(Spring): 361–369.

Gustman, Alan L. and Thomas L. Steinmeier. 1993. "Pension Portability and Labor Mobility: Evidence from the SIPP." *Journal of Public Economics* 50(3): 299–323.

Hay/Huggins Company, Inc. 1988. *The Effect of Job Mobility on Pension Benefits.* Report to the U.S. Department of Labor.

_____. 1990. *Pension Plan Expense Study for the Pension Benefit Guarantee Corporation.* Washington, D.C: Pension Benefit Guarantee Corporation.

Hirst, Peter C. 1992. "Pension Coverage in Canada: A Looming Crisis." *Employee Benefits Digest* 29(February): 3–8.

Horner, Keith, and Satya Poddar. 1992. *Pension Reform in Canada.* Photocopy. Ottawa, Canada: Department of Finance.

Ippolito, Richard. 1986. *Pensions, Economics and Public Policy.* Homewood, IL: Dow Jones-Irwin.

_____. 1991a. "Encouraging Long-Term Tenure: Wage Tilt or Pensions?" *Industrial and Labor Relations Review* 44(3): 520–35.

_____. 1991b. "The Productive Inefficiency of New Pension Tax Policy." *National Tax Journal* 64(September): 405–417.

Johnson, Richard. 1996. "The Impact of Human Capital Investments on Pension Benefits." *Journal of Labor Economics* 14(3): 520–554.

Latimer, Murray W. 1932. *Industrial Pension Systems in the United States and Canada.* New York: Industrial Relations Counselors, Inc.

Long, James E., and Frank Scott. 1982. "The Income Tax and Nonwage Compensation." *Review of Economics and Statistics* 64(May): 211–219.

Mitchell, Olivia, and Emily S. Andrews. 1981. "Scale Economies in Private Multi-Employer Pension Systems." *Industrial and Labor Relations Review* 34(4): 522–30.

Mitchell, Olivia. 1982. "Fringe Benefits and the Cost of Changing Jobs." *Journal of Human Resources* 17(Spring): 286–298.

Munnell, Alicia. 1991. "Are Pensions Worth the Cost?" *National Tax Journal* 44(September): 393–403.

_____. 1992. "Current Taxation of Qualified Pension Plans: Has the Time Come?" *New England Economic Review* (March/April):12–25.

Munnell, Alicia, and Frederick Yohn. 1992. "What is the Impact of Pensions on Savings?" In *Pensions and the Economy*, Zvi Bodie and Alicia Munnell, eds. Philadelphia: University of Pennsylvania.

Ontario Economic Council. 1984. *Pensions Today and Tomorrow: Background Studies*. Toronto: Ontario Economic Council.

_____. 1988. *Report of the Task Force on Inflation Protection for Employment Pension Plans*. Toronto: Ontario Economic Council.

Osberg, L., R. Apostle, and D. Clairmont. 1986. "Job Mobility, Wage Determination, and Market Segmentation in the Presence of Sample Selection Bias." *Canadian Journal of Economics* 19(May): 319–346.

Ozanne, Larry, and David Lindeman. 1987. *Tax Policy for Pensions and Other Retirement Savings*. Washington, D.C.: Congressional Budget Office.

Paine, Thomas. 1993. "Appraising Public Policy for Private Retirement Plans." In *Pension Funding and Taxation*, Dallas Salisbury and Nora Super Jones, eds. Washington, D.C: Employee Benefit Research Institute.

Parsons, Donald O. 1991. "The Decline in Private Pension Coverage in the United States." *Economic Letters* 36(September): 419–423.

_____. 1994. "Recent Trends in Pension Coverage Rates." in *Pension Coverage Issues for the '90s*, John Hinz, ed. Washington, D.C.: U.S. Government Printing Office.

Pesando, James E. 1984a. "An Economic Analysis of the Green Paper Proposals for the Reform of Employer-Sponsored Plans." In *Pensions Today and Tomorrow*, David Conklin, Jalynn Bennett, and Thomas Courchene, eds. Toronto: Ontario Economic Council.

_____. 1984b. "Employee Valuation of Pension Claims and the Impact of Indexing Alternative." *Economic Inquiry* 22(January): 1–17.

_____. 1988. "Assessment of Alternative Formulas for Delivering Inflation Protection." *Report of the Task Force on Inflation Protection for Employment Pension Plans, Research Studies, Vol. 1*. Ontario Economic Council.

Pesando, James, and Douglas Hyatt. 1992. "The Distribution of Investment Risk in Defined Benefit Pension Plans: A Re-Examination of the Evidence." Unpublished paper, University of Toronto.

Petersen, Mitchell. 1994. "Allocating Assets and Discounting Cashflows: Pension Plan Finance." Unpublished paper, Northwestern University.

Piacentini, Joseph S. 1989. "Pension Coverage and Benefit Entitlement: New Findings from 1988." Employee Benefit Research Institute Issue Brief No. 94, September.

————. 1990. "An Analysis of Pension Participation at Current and Prior Jobs, Receipt and Use of Lump-Sum Distributions, and Tenure at Current Job." Report to U.S. Department of Labor.

President's Commission on Pension Policy. 1981. *Coming of Age: Toward a National Retirement Income Policy.* Washington, D.C.: U.S. Government Printing Office.

Reagan, Patricia, and John A. Turner. 2000. "Did the Decline in Marginal Tax Rates during the 1980s Reduce Pension Coverage?" Chapter 13 in this volume.

Salisbury, Dallas. 1993. "The Costs and Benefits of Pension Tax Expenditures." In *Pension Funding and Taxation,* Dallas Salisbury and Nora Super Jones, eds. Washington, D.C: Employee Benefit Research Institute.

Samwick, Andrew, and Jonathan Skinner. 1994. "How Will Defined Contribution Plans Affect Retirement Income?" Working paper, National Bureau of Economic Research.

Sayeed, Adil. 1984. "A Survey of Pension Reform Recommendations." In *Pensions Today and Tomorrow,* David Conklin, Jalynn Bennett, and Thomas Courchene, eds. Toronto: Ontario Economic Council.

Schieber, Sylvester J. 1990. *Benefits Bargain: Why We Should Not Tax Employee Benefits.* Washington, D.C.: Employee Benefit Research Institute.

Smith, Douglas A., and Ronald A. Meng. 1991. "Pension Coverage in Ontario: The Roles of Collective Bargaining and Firm Size." *Proceedings of the 27th Conference of the Canadian Industrial Relations Association.*

Statistics Canada. 1992. *Pension Plans in Canada.* Ottawa: Statistics Canada.

Turner, John A. 1993. *Pension Policy for a Mobile Labor Force.* Kalamazoo, Michigan: W.E. Upjohn Institute for Employment Research.

Turner, John A., and Daniel Beller. 1992. *Trends in Pensions.* Washington, D.C: U.S. Government Printing Office.

Turner, John A., and Lorna Dailey. 1990. *Pension Policy: An International Perspective.* Washington, D.C.: U.S. Government Printing Office.

Utgoff, Kathleen. 1991. "Toward a More Rational Pension Tax Policy: Equal Treatment for Small Business." *National Tax Journal* 64(September): 383–391.

VanDerhei, Jack. 1992. "Pensions, Social Security, and Savings." Employee Benefit Research Institute Issue Brief No. 129, September.

Venti, Steven, and David Wise. 1990. "Have IRAs Increased U.S. Savings? Evidence from Consumer Expenditure Surveys." *Quarterly Journal of Economics* 105: 661–698.

Woodbury, Stephen A., and Douglas R. Bettinger. 1991. "The Decline of Fringe Benefit Coverage in the 1980s." In *Structural Changes in U.S. Labor Markets in the 1980s: Causes and Consequences*, Randall W. Eberts and Erica Groshen, eds. Armonk, N.Y.: M.E. Sharpe.

Woodbury, Stephen A., and Wei-Jang Huang. 1991. *The Tax Treatment of Fringe Benefits*. Kalamazoo, MI: W.E. Upjohn Institute.

12 Labor-Market Effects of Canadian and U.S. Pension Tax Policy

James E. Pesando
University of Toronto

John A. Turner
U.S. Department of Labor

By providing favorable tax treatment to pensions, as compared with other assets, Canadian and U.S. tax policies encourage firms to offer pension plans. Such tax policy is common among countries in the Organization for Economic Cooperation and Development. All countries with well-developed pension systems grant tax preferences to saving through pensions (Turner and Watanabe 1995).

The tax treatment of pensions results from compromises legislators make between competing political goals. Those goals include interpersonal equity in tax deductions and deferrals, as well as minimization of revenue loss from foregone taxes. While the broad goals of governments concerning pension tax policy are similar across developed countries, major differences occur within this framework.

In this regard, Canada and the United States are particularly interesting to compare. The two countries are similar enough to make comparisons of differences useful: both have social security systems with moderate benefit levels that leave room for a private pension system to develop and both have voluntary private pension systems.

The level of family income in Canada and the United States is roughly equivalent. While average family income is slightly higher (by 2.2 percent) in the United States, median family income is slightly lower (by 4.4 percent), reflecting the greater income inequality in the United States (Wolfson and Murphy 1994).[1]

The elderly in the United States, however, have considerably higher income than their counterparts in Canada—19 percent higher for couples aged 65 to 74. The mix of income among the elderly also differs. Social security benefits are higher in Canada—6 percent higher for couples aged 65 to 74, accounting for 40 percent of the income of that group—in comparison with 31 percent for U.S. couples of that age. Income from private sources (earnings from working, pensions, and savings) is higher in the United States (Wolfson and Murphy 1994).[2]

In both countries, workers in unions, manufacturing, large firms, and the public sector are more likely to be covered by a pension plan than are other workers. In the United States, the percentage of the private sector workforce that is unionized has declined considerably, to about 11 percent in the late 1990s. In Canada, the percentage is roughly the same or perhaps slightly higher.[3] Public sector employment is more important in Canada than in the United States.

Because of their proximity and similar income and culture, one might think that the two neighbors would have similar tax policy toward pensions. In fact, important differences exist that may have caused differences in their private pension systems. Insights can be gained into the tax treatment of pensions in both countries by examining the differences.

The tax codes in both Canada and the United States place requirements on pension plans to qualify for favorable tax treatment. These include the requirement that the pension benefits of plan members must vest within a minimum number of years. These requirements have a strictly regulatory function, rather than being a revenue-raising aspect of tax policy. While regulations influence or determine some features of pension plans, we choose to ignore regulatory aspects of the tax code. We analyze instead how marginal tax rates affect pensions as a form of employee compensation.

OVERVIEW

Employer contributions to pension plans in Canada and the United States are treated similarly to wages—both are tax deductible under the corporate income tax. Book reserve financing, where an employer could receive a tax deduction without having made a contribution, is not allowed.[4] Investment earnings in pension funds accumulate tax free, and pension assets and liabilities are not taxed.[5]

Workers are not taxed at the time their employer contributes to a pension fund; however, all distributions from pension funds to workers are taxable under the personal income tax. In Canada, retirees receive a tax credit for the first Can$1,000 of pension income. Pension distributions in both countries are not subject to the social security payroll tax. Worker contributions are treated differently in the two countries and are discussed later. Both countries also offer workers individual plans not tied to a particular employer: Registered Retirement Savings Plans (RRSPs) in Canada and Individual Retirement Accounts (IRAs) in the United States.[6]

The tax system affects the role of pensions in the compensation of workers.[8] We examine how the tax treatment of pensions affects four pension policy issues: 1) pension coverage rates, 2) the generosity of pension benefits, 3) employer versus employee contributions, and 4) defined-benefit versus defined-contribution plans.[9]

PENSION COVERAGE

The pension coverage rate is the percentage of the workforce covered by a pension. Although the concept is simple, the coverage rate is measured in considerably different ways, producing a range of statistics.

Empirical comparisons of private sector workers in Canada and the United States, such as the earlier comparison of the percentage of unionized workers, are difficult because the distinction between the private and public sector is less clear in Canada than it is in the United States. It appears that some public sector Canadian workers who work for institutions such as universities, hospitals, and public corporations (such as Air Canada), rather than traditional government bureaucracies, respond in household surveys that they are private sector workers. Because of this, Canadian data for the entire workforce are much more reliable than are data that attempt to distinguish between the public and private sectors. Because the public sector is relatively larger in Canada, however, and because pension coverage rates are considerably higher in the public than the private sector, empirical comparisons across the two countries are difficult. The coverage rate for the entire workforce has the advantage that it indicates the percentage of the workforce in the two countries that has an employer-provided pension that supplements social security. It has the disadvantage that the rate is influenced by government policy concerning the relative size of the public sector.

Dailey and Turner (1992) attempted to comparably measure private pension coverage for Canada and the United States. They found that, for many years, the private pension coverage rate was about 50 percent higher in the United States than in Canada. Since 1975, the pension coverage rate for full-time private sector workers has varied between 28 and 30 percent in Canada and between 44 and 46 percent in the United States.

Several problems caused those figures to overstate the difference in private sector coverage rates between Canada and the United States. In 1990, Statistics Canada determined it was impossible to accurately determine private sector pension coverage rates because of difficulties in determining who was in the private sector, and that previous figures underestimated pension coverage. The U.S. figures are overstated relative to those of Canada because the Canadian figures include the unemployed as part of the labor force, while the U.S. figures include only wage and salary workers, not the unemployed. After adjusting for these factors based on a somewhat subjective assessment of the magnitude of their effects, it still appears that the private sector pension coverage rate was at least 5 percentage points higher in the United States than it was in Canada.

By contrast, when examining pension coverage provided by both private and public sector employers, the coverage rates by income for all workers are higher in Canada for all income levels except the lowest, where the rate is slightly lower (Table 1). The coverage rates are 10 to 20 percentage points higher in the middle income categories; in the highest income category, the difference is only 4 percentage points.

Because one goal of pension tax policy is to encourage pension coverage, an important pension policy issue is the extent to which differences in pension coverage in Canada and the United States arise

Table 1 Pension Coverage Rates by Income, All Workers

Earnings (U.S.$)	Canada (%) 1989	United States (%) 1993
1 – 14,999	27	28
15,000 – 22,499	59	48
22,500 – 29,999	72	52
30,000 – 44,999	82	62
45,000 or more	73	69

SOURCE: Canada—Franken and Maser (1992, p. 29); United States—unpublished tabulations from the 1993 Current Population Survey Special Pension Supplement.

because of differences in the tax treatment of pensions. In both Canada and the United States, the tax system encourages employers to offer pensions. Workers reduce their total lifetime taxes when they receive some compensation as a pension rather than taking all compensation as wages. In both countries, pension coverage rates increase with income, presumably at least partially because tax rates increase with income.

Marginal Income Tax Rates

If an individual's marginal income tax rate is the same in the preretirement and postretirement periods, the individual earns the pretax rate of return on pension saving in both Canada and the United States. This occurs because the investment earnings on pension funds are untaxed. The incentive that the tax system provides for participating in a pension is thus higher with higher marginal income tax rates. The "wedge" between the pretax and the after-tax rate of return is higher in Canada for most workers because income tax rates are higher in Canada and the top rates are reached at much lower levels of income.

Provincial tax rates differ in Canada but to a lesser extent than do state income tax rates (Alpert, Shoven, and Whalley 1992). About 40 percent of Canadian employees work in the province of Ontario, and thus Ontario is a major component of the Canadian experience. In 1996, the maximum tax rate—federal plus provincial—was 53 percent in Ontario (Table 2). This maximum rate was reached at a taxable

Table 2 Marginal Federal Plus Provincial or State Income Tax Rates in Canada and the United States

Family taxable income (U.S.$)	Canada (%)		United States (%)
0 – 22,749	(up to)	27	19
22,750 – 55,099	(up to)	53	33
55,100 –114,999		53	36
115,000 – 249,999		53	42
250,000 and up		53	46

NOTE: Data for Canada are from the Province of Ontario; data for the United States represents a national average. Provincial income tax rates are much higher in Canada than are state income tax rates in the United States. The average state income tax rates are calculated from the Current Population Survey Special Pension Supplement, April 1993 for the tax year 1992. For the income brackets in the table, they are, respectively, 3.8%, 4.6%, 5.1%, 5.9% and 5.9%. Because of top coding of income in the data, there is no income reported greater than $250,000. The average state income tax rate for the preceding category is used for the top income category in this table.

income of $49,990. (Unless indicated otherwise, all amounts are expressed in U.S. dollars, at the exchange rate of U.S.$0.75 for each Canadian dollar.)

In both Canada and the United States, marginal federal income tax rates were reduced during the 1980s. In Canada, they were reduced from 65 percent in 1980 to 29 percent in 1987. It should be noted, however, that provincial income tax rates are much higher than state income tax rates. For this reason, comparing only marginal federal tax rates is misleading because the federal/provincial split of income tax is far different than the federal/state split in the United States.

In the United States, the Tax Reform Act of 1986 reduced the top federal rate on the highest-income households to 28 percent. The highest rate was 33 percent, which applied for some middle income taxpayers. The top rate in 1980 had been 70 percent. Marginal tax rates have since risen. The highest marginal federal income tax rate in 1994, applied to families with income above $250,000, was 39.6 percent (Table 2). In addition, taxpayers are liable for state income tax, which in some states reaches as high as 11 percent. Thus, the highest marginal income tax rate in the United States (state plus federal rates) is currently 51 percent, but only the top few percent of families pay that rate. Workers with family income of $50,000 would pay, on average, a marginal tax rate (federal plus state) of about 33 percent and thus have marginal tax rates about 20 percentage points lower than in Canada.[9]

These comparisons do not include social security taxes. Social security is largely funded through general revenues in Canada, while it is funded by a payroll tax in the United States. When social security taxes are included, the share of social security and personal income taxes in GNP in 1987 was 18.0 percent in Canada and 19.5 percent in the United States (Wilson 1992). The social security payroll tax rate in Canada in 1993 was 5 percent, shared equally by employers and employees. This compares to 12.4 percent shared equally by employers and employees in the United States (U.S. Department of Health and Human Services, Social Security Administration 1994). In both cases, it is presumed that employees bear the incidence of the payroll tax. However, to the extent social security benefits are related to earnings, some workers may view the true social security tax rate as being lower than the statutory rate (Burkhauser and Turner 1985).

Empirical studies in the United States have shown that higher marginal income tax rates encourage the provision of pensions. In their study of pension coverage in 1979, 1988, and 1993, Reagan and Turner (2000) found that, on average, a 1 percentage point increase in marginal income tax rates increases pension coverage rates by 0.4 percentage points.[10] This finding suggests that, based solely on marginal income tax rates, pension coverage would be roughly 5 to 7 percentage points higher in Canada than in the United States.

Income Tax Progressivity

As well as being affected by the level of marginal income tax rates, the tax incentive for pensions is greater with a greater progressivity of the tax system. Workers generally have lower income in retirement than while working. The more progressive the tax system, the more their reduced income during retirement will lower the marginal tax rate they pay on their pension benefits.

Because the highest marginal rate starts at a much lower income in Canada, marginal rates are more "compressed," so that it might appear that higher income Canadians are less likely than Americans to face *lower* marginal rates in their retirement years than while working.

In the United States, however, the tax system is also not very progressive but for a different reason. The top marginal bracket begins at a high income level, and a single marginal rate covers a wide range of the distribution of income. Reagan and Turner (2000) found that, in their regression sample of males aged 21 to 55, the marginal tax rate (federal plus state) in 1979 was 32 percent, with a standard deviation of 13 percentage points. These figures had declined in 1993 to a marginal rate of 25 percent with a standard deviation of 9 percentage points. Thus, it appears that neither the Canadian nor the U.S. tax system is very progressive, and differences in the progressivity of the income tax systems cannot explain the lower pension coverage rates for private sector workers in Canada.

Tax Subsidies for High-Income Workers

To further examine coverage rate differences between the two countries, we focus separately on the tax treatment of high- and low-income workers. The centerpiece of tax reform in Canada in the early 1990s was the establishment of a comprehensive limit to tax-assisted pension saving. All workers are permitted to contribute the *lesser* of 18 percent of their earned income (in the previous calendar year) or a maximum dollar amount (if lower) to an RRSP. In 1995, this dollar amount equalled $11,625, or 18 percent of $64,550. The latter is the level of earned income above which there is no tax-assisted pension saving for members of defined-benefit pension plans.

For individuals with relatively high incomes, the tax assistance provided to pension savings is considerably higher in the United States. In the United States, from 1993 to 1996, the maximum compensation that could be used for calculating pension benefits that receive preferential tax treatment was $150,000, with this figure being raised to $160,000 in 1997.[11]

Some benefits consultants have argued that a low ceiling on compensation used for calculating pension benefits reduces the incentive for employers to provide pensions because the personal benefit to high-income employers is reduced. This argument is most likely to be valid for the owners of successful small firms, where the owner may weigh the amount that he or she can accumulate in a pension versus the cost of providing pensions to his or her employees. If this argument is valid, it may partly explain why pension coverage appears to be lower in the private sector in Canada.

In the United States since 1984, some higher income taxpayers have faced an implicit tax on their pension benefits in addition to the personal income tax. Up to 50 percent of social security benefits could be included in taxable income for persons with adjusted gross income plus certain nontaxable income above $25,000 for individuals and $32,000 for married couples. Under the 1993 Omnibus Budget Reconciliation Act, a two-tier tax liability was established, so that the taxable proportion of social security benefits for retirees with income in the second-tier range was increased to 85 percent. Thus, for some workers at the margin, increases in pension benefits are taxed at the worker's marginal tax rate and cause the worker's social security benefits to become taxable. Eighteen percent of families with social security benefits pay taxes on those benefits, but more than half of families in the eighth, ninth, and tenth deciles are taxed (Pattison 1994). The net result is that many higher income workers pay an implicit tax on pension benefits of 20 to 40 percent due to the taxation of their social security benefits.

Housing as an Alternative Investment for High-Income Workers

Housing ownership is taxed differently in the two countries (Poterba 1992). In Canada, mortgage interest is not tax deductible, but capital gains are not taxed. In the United States, mortgage interest is tax deductible, but capital gains are taxed when a person sells their residence and does not purchase a residence of equal or greater value. The tax liability is subject to a lifetime exclusion of $150,000. Since Canadians must pay the before-tax rate of interest on their mortgages, they can in effect receive the before-tax rate of return by paying down their mortgage. Thus, housing provides an alternative vehicle for investing at the before-tax rate of return. In the United States, homeowners in effect pay the after-tax rate of return on their mortgages because they can deduct their mortgage interest payments. Thus, it is relatively more favorable to finance housing with debt than equity in the United States, making pension investments relatively more favorable in the United States. This is especially true for high-income workers with high tax rates.

Two-thirds of Canadian elderly own their own homes and 86 percent of those have homes that are mortgage free (Chappell 1990). The comparable figure for the United States is 70 percent home ownership, 57 percent of which are mortgage free (Struyk, Turner, and Ueno 1988). Thus, it appears that the different tax treatment of mortgages causes elderly Americans to be much more likely to have one.

In sum, high-income workers in Canada face a greater tax incentive to invest in tax-sheltered assets than they do in the United States. However, the amount they can shelter through pensions is lower, and housing is relatively more favorable an equity investment in Canada.

Implicit Taxes on Low-Income Workers

In addition to explicit taxes, implicit taxes may also reduce the net receipt of pension benefits. For Canadians with low lifetime earnings, the income-tested component of the social security system *discourages* participation in an employer-sponsored pension plan. All Canadians aged 65 and over, independent of their work history, receive a flat-rate Old Age Security (OAS) benefit. As of January 1, 1994, these benefits were worth $3,472 per year. Canadians with no other source of income also receive income-tested benefits from the Guaranteed Income Supplement (GIS), worth a maximum of $4,127 per year. For each dollar of retirement income in excess of the flat rate OAS benefits, GIS benefits are reduced by 50 cents.

The *maximum* pension payable from the earnings-related component of Canada's public retirement system, the Canada Pension Plan (CPP) was $6,250 as of January 1, 1994. The maximum Canada Pension Plan benefit would be received by individuals whose lifetime earnings (in 1994 dollars) average $25,800 per year. Thus, an individual who receives the *maximum* CPP benefit would still qualify for partial GIS benefits if the individual had no other retirement income than the flat-rate OAS benefits. So, too, would individuals not entitled to the maximum CPP benefit.

The net result is that Canadians with low lifetime earnings face a 50 percent tax rate on private pension income during retirement, this rate being in addition to federal and provincial income taxes. These public pension provisions, in effect since 1966, thus discourage low-income workers from participating in an employer-sponsored pension plan.[12] A similar disincentive exists in the United States because of the income testing for eligibility for Supplemental Security Income, but that program only affects very low income workers.

Individual Pension Plans

The Canadian government has set contribution limits for defined-contribution plans—money-purchase plans and RRSPs—equivalent to the limits for defined-benefit plans. Also, the federal tax rules treat employer and employee contributions the same, regardless of the type of pension plan.

A primary objective of the Canadian tax treatment of pensions is to provide equitable tax assistance for retirement, regardless of whether a worker participates in a company-sponsored pension plan or in an individual account pension plan. In Canada, workers who set up a RRSP can access the same amount of tax assistance as do workers who participate in an employer-provided plan.

Registered Retirement Savings Plans also enjoy other advantages over IRAs. Since Canadian tax reform in 1990, failure to contribute to a RRSP by the deadline does not cause the deduction to be lost. Unused contribution amounts, subject to a seven-year limit, may be carried forward and deducted later when made. No such carry-forward provision exists for IRAs in the United States.

Participation in RRSPs has increased greatly in Canada. In 1970, 2 percent of the total population aged 18 to 70 contributed to a RRSP. By 1988, 25 percent of all tax filers contributed to a RRSP, with an average contribution of Can$3,545 (Venti and Wise 1995).

Since 1990, the tax treatment of RRSPs has meant there is no tax advantage to participating in an employer-provided plan since an equal amount could be contributed to either type of plan. This change should cause a reduction in pension coverage rates in Canada. However, a study of data prior to the change found no negative relationship between the amount of employer-provided pension assets held by an individual and their RRSP assets (Venti and Wise 1994). In 1987, for example, 37 percent of tax filers who contributed to a pension plan also contributed to a RRSP, versus only 16 percent of tax filers who did not contribute to a pension plan (Franken 1990).

In the United States, no attempt has been made to equalize the treatment between employer-sponsored plans and individual plans. Employers in the United States have a near monopoly in the provision of tax-favored pension benefits. Since 1981, the maximum an individual can deduct for contributions to an IRA has been frozen at $2,000.[13] Inflation has reduced the real value of the tax deduction for IRAs by more than half since 1981.

Summary and Other Explanations

The higher marginal income tax rates in Canada would—other things equal—cause pension coverage rates to be roughly 5 to 7 percentage points higher in Canada than in the United States. This effect may be offset somewhat by higher social security tax rates in the United States. An explanation for relatively lower pension coverage rates at lower income levels in Canada is that the income-tested provisions of the Canadian social security system place an implicit tax of 50 percent on the pension benefits of workers with low lifetime earnings.

Other factors besides taxes affect pension coverage. While it is beyond the scope of this chapter to fully investigate other possible factors, several are mentioned that would cause pension coverage rates to be lower in Canada than in the United States. Social security is moderately more generous in Canada than it is in the United States, which would lower pension benefit levels and probably also pension coverage rates in Canada. The United States, through nondiscrimination rules, requires employers that offer pensions to offer them to most of their employees. This regulation is one way that public policy attempts to expand coverage. Canada has no such regulation.

In Canada, pension benefits are locked in after vesting, and workers cannot access them until retirement. In the United States, workers can often take a lump-sum distribution from their pension plan when they change jobs. Some U.S. policy analysts have argued that prohibiting preretirement lump-sum distributions would reduce pension coverage because it would reduce the flexibility that workers have to use those funds for various purposes. These locking-in provisions, which are contained in provincial legislation, have been in effect in most provinces since only 1987.

THE GENEROSITY OF PENSION PLANS

While pension coverage measures one dimension of the extent to which pension plans are provided, the generosity of pension plans measures another. One measure of pension plan generosity is the level of pension benefits being paid to current retirees. The level of pension benefits, however, does not directly measure the generosity of pension benefit formulas because other factors also affect benefit levels. For example, if a pension system is immature, workers having participated in it for less than their full career, it will pay lower retirement benefits than an equally generous system that is fully mature. While it is not evident that the Canadian and U.S. pension systems differ in their maturity, such a difference could cause average benefits to differ.

Canadian private pension plans are slightly less generous than U.S private plans in the level of benefits they provide. Canadian pensions in the late 1980s provided slightly less and U.S. pensions provided slightly more than $6,000 in annual benefits (Dailey and Turner 1992).

Canada and the United States differ considerably in the maximum amount that a worker can save through the pension system. In Canada, the maximum percentage of earnings that a worker can save is lower and, as indicated earlier, the maximum earnings that can be used in determining pension benefits is much lower.

The maximum limit in Canada for contributions to a defined contribution plan is 18 percent of worker earnings, based on the previous year's earnings. In Canada, the maximum benefit for a defined-benefit plan is the lesser of $45,185 per year or 70 percent of the participant's earnings in the three highest years.

Both the defined-contribution and defined-benefit limits are higher in the United States. The maximum contributions to a defined-contribution plan in 1997 are the lesser of 25 percent of earnings or $30,000 a year. For a defined-benefit plan, the maximum benefit is the lesser of $125,000 a year or 100 percent of the participant's average compensation for his or her three highest earnings years. For high-income workers, the maximum pension benefit in Canada is about half of that in the United States.

The lower maximum contributions and benefits, however, may be of little economic significance if few workers are constrained by the limits. The difference is most likely to be constraining for older workers and higher income workers who, because of the ceiling on social security benefits, are more likely to wish to save a relatively large fraction of their income for retirement.

If the 18 percent maximum is not a binding constraint, the higher marginal income tax rates in Canada would encourage middle income workers to save more in pensions than they do in the United States.

EMPLOYER VERSUS EMPLOYEE CONTRIBUTIONS

In Canada, a major tenet of pension policy is equal treatment of different options. This consideration has been considerably less important in the United States. One aspect of the policy of equal treatment is that employees in Canada can make tax-deductible contributions to both defined-benefit and defined-contribution plans. In the United States, employee contributions to defined-benefit plans and to most types of defined-contribution plans are not tax deductible.

In the United States, employee contributions are only tax deductible if made to a type of defined-contribution plan called a salary reduction plan. The most common type of salary reduction plan is the 401(k) plan.[14] As a result of the tax rules, few employees contribute to pension plans other than 401(k) plans.

Even for 401(k) plans, however, employee contributions are taxed more heavily than employer contributions. Employee contributions are subject to the social security payroll tax, while employer contributions are not.[15] Employee contributions are subject to the payroll tax on the grounds that to do otherwise would erode the payroll tax base, causing an increasingly small percentage of compensation to be subject to the payroll tax.

The feature permitting deductible employee contributions to 401(k) plans favors those plans relative to other types of plans, and they have grown considerably. Between 1984 and 1993, 401(k) plans gained 15.6 million participants, while defined-benefit plans and all other types of defined-contribution plans lost participants (U.S. Department of Labor 1997).

Economic theory suggests that, due to compensating differentials, workers pay for employer contributions through reductions in wages and other compensation. While this theory has proven difficult to test empirically, some studies have found evidence supporting it (Montgomery, Shaw, and Bennedict 1992). If workers do pay for employer pension contributions through reduced wages, the distinction between employer and employee contributions is unimportant. Assuming labor markets adjust imperfectly, however, or workers have imperfect knowledge, there may be some effects. Benefits consultants frequently argue that workers undervalue employer pension contributions relative to their own contributions because they are less aware of, and thus tend to understate, the amount of employer contributions necessary to provide the benefits they will receive.

In spite of the argument that the distinction between employer and employee contributions is economically unimportant, provincial pension legislation throughout Canada, as well as pension legislation in the United States, treats employee contributions differently from employer contributions. In Canada, a universal provision in provincial pension regulation is that employer contributions must pay for at least 50 percent of the accrued value of defined-benefit pensions at the date of the employee's termination, retirement, or death. Employee "excess" contributions may (depending upon the jurisdiction) be reimbursed, transferred, or used to increase benefits. To implement this provision, a minimum rate of interest is imputed to employee contributions, through regulation or statute.

Except for the flat benefit plans that predominate among unionized workers in the private sector, employees as well as employers contribute to most pension plans in Canada. Virtually all public sector plans are contributory, while about one-half of plan members in the private sector are in contributory plans.

DEFINED-BENEFIT VERSUS
DEFINED-CONTRIBUTION PLANS

In the United States, there has been a major shift from defined-benefit plans towards defined-contribution plans. While the number of participants in defined-benefit plans was slightly lower in 1993 than in 1984, the number of participants in defined-contribution plans grew by 11 million over that period due to the growth of 401(k) plans (U.S. Department of Labor 1997). In Canada, there has also been a trend towards defined-contribution plans, but that trend has been much weaker. Between 1982 and 1995, for example, the percentage of pension participants who belonged to money-purchase plans rose from 5.3 percent to 10.0 percent, while the percentage who belonged to defined-benefit plans declined from 93.7 to 88.6 percent.[16] This section examines the extent to which differences in tax policy can account for the much more pronounced trend towards defined-contribution plans in the United States.

Tax reform in Canada, implemented in 1990, seeks to "level the playing field" with regard to the tax assistance provided to pension saving in different types of plans. The maximum amount of tax assistance provided to members of employer-sponsored defined-benefit and defined-contribution plans, as well as to individual RRSPs, is intended to be equal. Further, through the introduction of new carry-forward provisions, individuals are provided with greater flexibility in the timing of RRSP contributions. These provisions were enacted because firms who sponsor defined-benefit plans can make retroactive enrichments in their plans.

In Canada, the 18 percent maximum allowable contribution to a defined-contribution plan was chosen because it is roughly equivalent to the defined-benefit limit. The defined-benefit limit is 2 percent of final earnings per year of service, with a maximum of 70 percent of highest earnings (Wyatt Company 1990).

In the United States, the defined-benefit limit does not vary with years of service, as it does in Canada. The maximum benefit that can be received from a defined-contribution plan, in both Canada and the United States, necessarily increases with service because the maximum benefit is based on the accumulation of contributions and investment earnings over time. Because the U.S. limit does not vary with service, short-service workers in the United States can receive higher benefits through a defined-benefit plan than through a defined-contribution plan. For long-service workers, the situation is the reverse.

Within its lower contribution limits, Canada allows individuals greater flexibility in the timing of their contributions. In Canada, an individual's unused contribution allowance in each year is carried forward indefinitely for use in subsequent years, subject to certain dollar limits. Similarly, contributions not deductible in the year in which they are paid may be deducted in subsequent years.

This flexibility for defined-contribution plans was introduced to bring them on equal footing with the flexibility that is available to employers for contributions to defined-benefit plans. This flexibility occurs, however, at the cost of increased complexity of administration of pension plans.

In the United States, contributions not deductible in the year paid are subject to a 10 percent excise tax. Before 1987, a credit carry-forward was available when an employer's contributions to a profit-sharing plan were less than the maximum allowed (McGill and Grubbs 1989, p. 652). That carryforward is no longer available. Flexibility is provided, however, by the higher limit on contributions, so it is not clear which system effectively provides the greater flexibility.

As indicated earlier, in the United States, employee contributions are only tax deductible for defined-contribution plans and then only for contributions to 401(k) plans. This feature of the tax code may favor defined-contribution plans. In Canada, employee contributions are tax deductible to defined-benefit plans.

The Tax Benefit of Overfunding Defined Benefit-Plans

In assessing the reasons why employers might prefer to sponsor defined-benefit plans rather than defined-contribution plans, financial economists (Tepper 1981) have drawn attention to the tax advantages to shareholders of overfunding such plans. In the United States, the Omnibus Reconciliation Act of 1987 (OBRA) reduced the desirability of defined-benefit plans relative to defined-contribution plans by reducing the amount that could be contributed to overfunded defined-benefit plans (Ippolito 1990).

Under the OBRA rules, employer contributions are not tax deductible if the plan is overfunded by 50 percent *on a termination basis*. This reduces the flexibility firms have in managing defined-benefit plans, and it reduces the amount that can be sheltered from tax. Termination liabilities are calculated as if the plan were to terminate immediately. For plans with a typical age structure of workers, these liabilities are considerably less than the liabilities calculated assuming that the plan will continue in existence. Those liabilities for ongoing plans recognize that currently accruing benefits are based on future wages, in final average pay plans. Under the OBRA rules, many defined-benefit plans cannot contribute sufficient amounts to a pension plan to cover the current accrual of liabilities. This creates a tax disadvantage for defined benefit plans because, by comparison, in defined contribution plans firms can contribute an amount equal to the full current accrual of liabilities.

In Canada, too, the tax authorities seek to limit the amount of overfunding in defined-benefit plans. However, the restrictions are less onerous than those now in effect in the United States. In Canada, employer contributions are tax deductible so long as the surplus in the plan is no more than 10 percent of actual plan liabilities or twice the annual value of current service contributions. However, the plan's liabilities are *not* valued on a termination basis for the purpose of this calculation. Indeed, if the plan has a history of cost-of-living or similar adjustments, these may be taken into account in determining the plan's liability if it is reasonable to assume that such adjustments will continue. These adjustments would include *ad hoc* increases for pensioners and increases in accrued benefits under career average earnings plans and flat benefit plans. In Canada, a potentially more important constraint on the extent of overfunding is the uncertainty that may exist as to the ownership of surplus assets.

Summary

In Canada, an effort has been made to equalize the treatment of defined-benefit and defined-contribution plans. As a result, employee contributions are tax deductible for both defined-benefit and defined-contribution plans, while they are only tax deductible to (one type of) defined-contribution plans in the United States. Defined-benefit plans also receive more favorable tax treatment in Canada than in the United States in terms of allowable maximum funding. Greater flexibility is allowed for contributions to defined-contribution plans in Canada than in the United States, in order to try to equalize the degree of flexibility that employers and employees have to contribute to both types of plans. On balance, tax policy in Canada is relatively more favorable to defined-benefit plans than it is in the United States.

CONCLUSIONS

Major differences in the tax treatment of pensions in the United States and Canada may help explain differences in the pension systems in the two countries. They may account for differences in pension coverage and the prevalence of defined-benefit plans relative to defined-contribution plans.

In Canada, high marginal tax rates on income at upper income levels suggest that pension coverage should be higher among upper income workers in Canada than it is in the United States. However, the maximum benefit that an upper income worker can receive in Canada is much less than in the United States.

The high effective tax rates on private pension incomes of low-income retirees due to the earnings-testing of retirement benefits in Canada suggest that coverage rates should be lower in Canada than they are in the United States for low-income individuals.

Tax reform in Canada in 1990 sought to "level the playing field" with regard to the tax assistance provided pension savings. In particular, and unlike the United States, the self-employed and those *not* covered by an employer-provided pension plan are—through the vehicle of the Registered Retirement Savings Plan—provided with more equal access to tax assistance.

Employee contributions to occupational pension plans in Canada are tax deductible, unlike the case for employee contributions to defined-benefit plans in the United States. In both countries, employee contributions are treated differently by pension law than are employer contributions. This fact, in turn, focuses attention on the issue of the ultimate incidence of *employer* contributions. Implicit in pension law in Canada appears to be the assumption that the ultimate incidence of employer contributions does *not* fall upon employees.

Defined-benefit plans receive more favorable tax treatment in Canada than they do in the United States. In Canada, the tax treatment of defined-benefit plans is also more favorable relative to the tax treatment of defined-contribution plans. The move towards defined-benefit plans has been much weaker in Canada.

While assessment of the magnitude of the effects of these differences in tax policy is difficult, in part because the tax treatment of pensions differs in a number of ways, we believe that important insights concerning the possible range of the parameters of pension tax policy can be gained by comparing Canada and the United States.

Notes

The material in this chapter is the responsibility of the authors and does not represent the position of the institutions with which they are associated. Patricia Reagan has made valuable comments.

1. This study used the 1988 purchasing power parity of Can$1 equals U.S.$0.80. We use the slightly lower value of U.S.$0.72 for making comparisons.
2. The lower average Social Security benefits in the United States may arise in part because more older Americans are working and not receiving Social Security benefits.
3. It is difficult to determine a precise estimate of the private sector unionization rate in Canada because of difficulties in measuring the private sector workforce, a topic that is discussed later.
4. Such financing is allowed in Germany and Japan by simply recording the liability for the pension plan on the company's financial books.
5. In the United States, premium payments to the Pension Benefit Guaranty Corporation are based on the unfunded liabilities of pension plans. This is also true for the Guarantee Fund in Ontario. We are not considering these levies as taxes.
6. For a more complete discussion of taxation of pensions in Canada, see Jobin et al. (1991).
7. Generally, a tax policy affecting a workers' decisions distorts economic activity from what it would have been without taxes. However, in a system with multiple taxes, one aspect of taxation may correct distortions introduced by another aspect. The optimality of pension tax policy in terms of creating or correcting distortions is not discussed here (Ippolito 1990).
8. We thus do not discuss, for example, the effects of taxation of pensions on income distribution, government revenues, or the capital market.

9. The higher marginal personal income taxes in Canada are reflected in personal income taxes being about 25 percent larger as a percentage of GNP in Canada than they are in the United States (Wilson 1992).

10. The marginal effect is probably lower at higher tax rates. See also Woodbury (1983), Woodbury and Bettinger (1991), and Woodbury and Huang (1991).

11. An explanation for the more favorable tax treatment for pensions of high-income workers in the United States may be that with its higher income inequality, there are relatively more high-income workers in the United States, and they therefore presumably have more political power.

12. This issue has important implications, as well, for public policy. In Canada, the fact that pension coverage is far from universal is often cited by critics as proof of the inadequacy of the private pensions system and the need, therefore, to expand the public pension system or to mandate private pension coverage. (In 1990, 49.6 percent of males and 33.1 percent of females who participated in the labor force belonged to an occupational pension plan. [Statistics Canada 1990, Text Table D, page 8].) However, the absence of universal coverage is perhaps best seen as a statement about workers' revealed preferences rather than as a "failure" of the private pension system.

    The introduction of a mandatory private pension plan, inclusive of part-time as well as full-time workers, is likely to reduce the lifetime resources available to those with low lifetime earnings. The incidence of employer contributions to a mandatory private pension plan (if it is not retroactive) is likely to fall ultimately on the employee. Workers, including those with low lifetime earnings, will be required to allocate a larger fraction of their lifetime earnings to provide for their retirement years. On one hand, this will gradually reduce the likelihood of future claims on income-tested programs such as GIS. On the other hand, by forcing persons with low lifetime earnings to provide a larger share of their own retirement incomes, this proposal may redistribute income away from those with low lifetime earnings.

    In this context, two facts merit note. First, persons whose current earnings are low are less likely to be members of occupational pension plans. To the extent that current earnings are positively correlated with lifetime earnings, this fact suggests that those with low lifetime earnings are less likely to be covered by an occupational pension plan. Second, Canadians with low current incomes generally choose not to contribute to RRSPs. Given the low value to them of the tax subsidy associated with RRSP contributions together with the likelihood that they would be substituting their own savings for retirement for benefits available from income-tested public programs, this decision is probably rational.

13. The amount is $2,500 for a worker whose spouse does not also contribute to an IRA.

14. These plans are named after the enabling section of the Internal Revenue Code.

15. Because both tax payments and future benefits are increased by increases in earnings, for some workers the payroll tax may not be a tax when viewed in a life-cycle setting (Burkhauser and Turner 1985).

16. These figures do not add to 100 percent due to the presence of "composite and other plans."

References

Alpert, William T., John B. Shoven, and John Whalley. 1992. "Introduction." In *Canada–U.S. Tax Comparisons*, John B. Shoven and John Whalley, eds. Chicago: University of Chicago Press.

Burkhauser, Richard V., and John A. Turner. 1985. "Is the Social Security Payroll Tax a Tax?" *Public Finance Quarterly* 13(July): 253–267.

Chappell, Neena L. 1990. "Housing for Canadian Elders: Current Directions and Future Innovations." Paper presented at the conference Choices Today, Options Tomorrow, Senior Housing for the '90s. Canadian Mortgage and Housing Corporation, Vancouver, British Columbia, June.

Dailey, Lorna M., and John A. Turner. 1992. "U.S. Pensions in World Perspective, 1970–1989." In *Trends in Pensions 1992*, John A. Turner and Daniel J. Beller. eds. Washington, D.C.: U.S. Government Printing Office.

Frenken, Hubert. 1990. "RRSPs: Tax-Assisted Retirement Savings." In *Perspectives on Labour and Incomes*. Ottawa: Statistics Canada, pp. 9–20.

Frenken, Hubert, and Karen Maser. 1992. "Employer-Sponsored Pension Plans—Who is Covered?" In *Perspectives on Labour and Income*. Ottawa: Statistics Canada.

Ippolito, Richard A. 1990. *An Economic Appraisal of Pension Tax Policy in the United States*. Homewood, IL.: Irwin.

Jobin, Guy A., Raymond Koskie, Patrick Longhurst, and Mark Zigler. 1991. *Employee Benefits in Canada*. Brookfield, Wisconsin: International Foundation of Employee Benefit Plans.

McGill, Dan M., and Donald S. Grubbs, Jr. 1989. *Fundamentals of Private Pensions*, sixth ed. Philadelphia: University of Pennsylvania Press.

Montgomery, Edward, Kathryn Shaw, and Mary Ellen Benedict. 1992. "Pensions and Wages: An Hedonic Price Theory Approach." *International Economic Review* 33(February): 111–128.

Pattison, David. 1994. "Taxation of Social Security Benefits Under the New Income Tax Provisions: Distributional Estimates for 1994." *Social Security Bulletin* 57(Summer): 44–50.

Poterba, James M. 1992. "Taxation and Housing Markets." In *Canada–U.S. Tax Comparisons*, John B. Shoven and John Whalley, eds. Chicago: University of Chicago Press.

Reagan, Patricia B., and John A. Turner. 2000. "Did the Decline in Marginal Tax Rates during the 1980s Reduce Pension Coverage?" Chapter 13 in this volume.

Statistics Canada. 1990. *Pension Plans in Canada 1988*. Ottawa: Statistics Canada.

Struyk, Raymond J., Margery A. Turner, and Makiko Ueno. 1988. *Future U.S. Housing Policy.* Washington, D.C.: The Urban Institute Press.

Tepper, Irwin. 1981. "Taxation and Corporate Pension Policy." *Journal of Finance* 36: 1–13.

Turner, John A., and Noriyasu Watanabe. 1995. *Private Pensions: Systems and Policies.* Kalamazoo, Michigan: The Upjohn Institute for Employment Research.

U.S. Department of Health and Human Services, Social Security Administration. 1994. *Social Security Programs Throughout the World—1993.* Washington, D.C.: U.S. Government Printing Office, May.

U.S. Department of Labor. 1997. *Abstract of the Form 5500.* Washington, D.C.

Venti, Steven F., and David A. Wise. 1995. "RRSPs and Saving in Canada." Unpublished paper, Dartmouth College.

Wilson, Thomas A. 1992. "Reflections on Canada-U.S. Tax Differences." In *Canada–U.S. Tax Comparisons*, John B. Shoven and John Whalley, eds. Chicago: University of Chicago Press.

Wolfson, Michael C., and Brian B. Murphy. 1994. "Kinder and Gentler: A Comparative Analysis of Incomes of the Elderly in Canada and the United States." In *Economic Security and Intergenerational Justice: A Look At North America*, Theodore R. Marmor, Timothy M. Smeeding, and Vernon L. Greene, eds. Washington, D.C.: The Urban Institute Press.

Woodbury, Stephen A. 1983. "Substitution Between Wage and Nonwage Benefits." *American Economic Review* 73(March): 166–182.

Woodbury, Stephen A., and Douglas R. Bettinger. 1991. "The Decline of Fringe-Benefit Coverage in the 1980s." In *Structural Changes in U.S. Labor Markets: Causes and Consequences*, Randall W. Eberts and Erica L. Groshen, eds. Armonk, New York: M.E. Sharpe, pp. 105–138.

Woodbury, Stephen A., and Wei-Jang Huang. 1991. *The Tax Treatment of Fringe Benefits.* Kalamazoo, Michigan: W.E. Upjohn Institute for Employment Research.

Wyatt Company. 1990. *Special Memorandum.* Toronto, Ontario: The Wyatt Company.

13 Did the Decline in Marginal Tax Rates during the 1980s Reduce Pension Coverage?

Patricia B. Reagan
Ohio State University

John A. Turner
U.S. Department of Labor

After years of constancy or increase, private pension coverage rates declined during the 1980s. Because private pensions are an important source of retirement income, the decline in their coverage raises concern over the adequacy of future retirement income.[1] Between 1979 and 1988, the percentage of full-time male private sector employees participating in a pension plan fell from 55 to 51 percent, where it remained in 1993 (Beller and Lawrence 1992; U.S. Department of Labor 1994).

The coverage decline was particularly large for young males. Coverage for full-time male private sector employees aged 25 to 29 declined by nearly a quarter, from 53 percent in 1979 to 41 percent by 1993 (U.S. Department of Labor 1994).

Because the decline in pension coverage rates has been particularly great for young males, researchers have looked for determinants of coverage that changed more for that group than for older males. Bloom and Freeman (1992) and Even and Macpherson (1994) used this approach to argue that the decline in coverage for young males is explained primarily by disproportionately large declines in their unionization and contemporaneous real income.[2] The fact that marginal tax rates declined most for high-income workers while coverage declined most for younger low-income workers led these researchers to ignore the potentially important effect of contemporaneous declines in marginal tax rates.[3]

The tax code encourages both pension coverage and generosity by exempting pension savings from the double taxation associated with other savings vehicles (Turner 1981; Woodbury and Bettinger 1991; Woodbury and Hamermesh 1992; Gentry and Peress 1995).[4] Workers' earnings are taxed, for example, before they contribute to savings accounts. The returns on savings are again taxed when they are realized (Munnel 1982). In contrast, pension contributions made by firms on behalf of workers are not taxed. Pension benefits are only taxed when they are disbursed, thereby avoiding double taxation.

Preferential tax treatment causes the tax advantage of pensions to increase with marginal income tax rates. Workers with high marginal tax rates tend to seek jobs with pensions, suggesting that pension coverage was reduced by declines in marginal tax rates during the 1980s and early 1990s. Woodbury and Bettinger (1991) found that decreases in marginal tax rates did reduce pension coverage for a sample pooled by gender and age. Woodbury and Huang (1991) and Feldstein (1997) found that the large cuts in marginal income tax rates encouraged high-income workers to take less compensation as fringe benefits and more as income.[5]

Because the tax expenditure for pensions is the largest tax expenditure for individuals in the federal budget, it is important to understand the effects of that expenditure on pension coverage.[6] The tax expenditure for pensions could lead to increased national savings through increased pension coverage, but of itself reduces government revenue, reducing savings.

We examine whether the decline in marginal tax rates during the 1980s caused a decline in pension coverage rates. We empirically test the assertion that tax changes cannot explain the disproportionate decline in coverage for young males because "the 1980s fall in coverage was smallest among high-income (older) workers, for whom marginal tax rates declined the most" (Bloom and Freeman 1992, p. 543). We explore causal links between declines in tax rates and observed declines in pension coverage using cross-sectional data over a 15-year period, from the 1979, 1988, and 1993 Current Population Surveys.[7]

Our estimates suggest that, on average, a 1 percentage point increase in the marginal tax rate leads to a 0.4 percentage point increase in private pension coverage. Declining tax rates explain almost 20 percent of the total decline in coverage for young males between 1979 and 1988. Our model predicts that changes in exogenous variables lowered coverage rates 7.3 percentage points for young males between 1979 and 1988. Declining tax rates account for 1.4 percentage points of the total predicted decline in coverage. Declining unionization accounts for only 0.9 percentage points of the predicted decline, whereas declining earnings account for 5.7 percentage points of the predicted decline.

We test the robustness of our results by reestimating the coverage equation for a sample of female private sector workers. In contrast to the males, who experienced declining coverage rates in the 1980s and early 1990s, females experienced slightly rising coverage rates during this period. Our results from the female sample corroborate our earlier conclusions that on average a 1 percentage point increase in the marginal tax rate leads roughly to a 0.4 percentage point increase in pension coverage.

In the next section, we discuss the empirical specification. We then discuss the data and variables, with special attention to the problem of endogeneity of tax rates, and we estimate our model for males and then for females. In the final section, we offer concluding comments.

EMPIRICAL SPECIFICATION

Observed compensation packages consisting of wages and fringe benefits result from decisions made by firms and workers, subject to market and regulatory constraints. Woodbury (1983) and Woodbury and Huang (1991) estimated a demand equation for pensions as a share of total compensation. They modeled the determinants of pension provision and other nonwage compensation by assuming that employers offer a menu of compensation packages, given their costs. Utility-maximizing workers then choose their preferred compensation packages from the menu of available alternatives. As suggested by Deaton and Muellbauer (1980), the authors cited above specified a flexible form expenditure function, from which they derive a system of demand equations for wages and pension benefits as a share of total compensation. Since share data are more readily available at the firm level, they variously used the establishment and the two-digit industry as the unit of observation. Explanatory variables are firm or industry average characteristics.

Other studies, such as Woodbury and Bettinger (1991), Bloom and Freeman (1992), and Even and Macpherson (1994), focused on accounting for changes over time in observed coverage rates. These studies used household data and the individual as the unit of observation. Household data sets, however, do not contain information about the amount that the firm contributes to an individual's retirement pension. The data available are discrete and measure whether an employer offers a pension and, if so, whether the employee participates in the plan. These authors estimated a discrete model of the probability that a worker with given economic and demographic characteristics, employed at a firm with given attributes, is covered by a pension. The coverage equation is interpreted as the probability of a pension coverage outcome and is not interpreted as a behavioral equation. The estimated coefficients in the coverage equation, appropriately transformed, measure the effect of a change in an exogenous variable on the probability that a worker/firm match leads to coverage for the worker.

Like Woodbury and Bettinger, Bloom and Freeman, and Even and Macpherson, we use household data to estimate a pension coverage equation. However, Bloom and Freeman and Even and Macpherson do not include a tax variable and maintain the hypothesis that changing tax rates have no effect on coverage. Woodbury and Bettinger, on the other hand, include a tax variable, but pool by age and gender. None of these authors have tested whether declines in tax rates contributed to the decline in coverage for young males. They also have not tested the hypothesis that declining tax rates put downward pressure on coverage rates for women, during a time period where observed coverage rates for women were rising.

To formalize the model, let Z represent a vector of worker and firm characteristics that affect the probability of coverage.[9] The equilibrium outcome is represented by an indicator variable, P, which takes a value of 1 if the worker is covered by a pension plan offered by the worker's firm. Let e represent a random variable interpreted as unobserved heterogeneity in the rates at which firms and workers are willing to substitute pension benefits for wages. We can write the probability that worker i employed at firm j has pension coverage as:

$$\text{Prob}(P=1) = F(Zg + e > 0) = F(-Zg) \tag{1}$$

where F is a cumulative distribution function and g is the vector of parameters to be estimated. We assume that e has a normal distribution and estimate a probit model.

Rather than report the estimated probit coefficients, $\hat{g}$, we report the marginal effects of the continuous variables and the delta effects of the dichotomous variables.[9] The delta effect is the discrete analog of the marginal effect. We report t-statistics for the marginal and delta effects themselves.[10]

DATA, VARIABLES, AND ENDOGENEITY

We use data from the 1979 and 1988 May Current Population Surveys (CPS) and the 1993 April CPS, which include a special survey of workers concerning pension plan coverage and other employer attributes. These data have been matched to the March CPS of the same year, which provides income and other economic and demographic data. The sample is limited to full-time employed, private, wage and salary workers aged 21 to 55 who did not work in agriculture or the railroad industry and had valid responses to questions relevant for this study.

The dependent variable is worker self-reported pension plan participation, which includes participation in both defined-benefit and defined-contribution plans. This is the best definition of pension coverage for our purposes because it represents the worker's intention to use a plan for retirement. Some workers who are in defined-contribution plans, which are like savings accounts, may intend to use those plans for preretirement consumption rather than for retirement and respond that they are not covered by a pension plan.

Most of our explanatory variables are standard in equations estimating pension coverage. They include age, race, firm size, education, marital status, years with employer, and union status (Table 1). We also use nine industry and four occupation dichotomous variables.

In addition, we use two variables not universally included in pension coverage equations—the predicted combined state and federal marginal income tax rate and predicted yearly earnings at age 55. To avoid bias due to the endogeneity of earnings and thus marginal income tax rates, we use the predicted value of both variables.[11]

We calculate the predicted marginal income tax rate, reflecting both state and federal income taxes, using current predicted family income (rather than actual family income), marital status, and number of children. These predicted tax rates are not subject to endogeneity bias arising from idiosyncratic variations in labor supply and earnings. To calculate marginal tax rates, we use the income tax codes for each of the 50 states for each of the three years of analysis. Marginal tax rate variability across states provides exogenous variation in tax rates.

Table 1 Variable Definitions

Variable	Definition
Covered	Equals 1 if covered by a pension on the current job
Tax	State plus federal marginal income tax rate based on current predicted family earnings
Age	Age in years
Pearn55	Predicted yearly earnings at age 55 in 1993 dollars, assuming real earnings from the cross-sectional age/earnings profile grow 1 percent annually
African American	Equals 1 if African American
Married	Equals 1 if married with spouse present
Newhire	Equals 1 if worked for current employer for no more than one year
Union	Equals 1 if covered by a collective bargaining agreement
Mult1000	Equals 1 if employer operates at more than one location and employs 1,000 or more workers

Since the family income question in the CPS is retrospective, we use tax rates for the year prior to each CPSs.[12]

The average predicted marginal income tax rate, state plus federal, for male workers aged 21–35 in our regression sample fell from 30.8 percent in 1979 to 26.0 percent in 1988 and rose slightly to 26.1 percent in 1993. The average for workers aged 36–55 fell from 35.3 percent in 1979 to 30.4 percent in 1988 and to 29.8 percent in 1993 (Table 2).

In addition to controlling for marginal tax rates, it is important to control for wealth or lifetime income. The argument for including such a measure is based on the normality of consumption during retirement. Individuals who have greater earnings or wealth over their lifetime wish to consume more during retirement and thus have a higher demand for pension coverage. Because income and marginal income tax rates are positively correlated, if income is not adequately controlled for, a finding of a significantly positive effect of marginal income tax rates on coverage could merely indicate that higher income workers have a higher demand for coverage.

Some authors, particularly Bloom and Freeman (1992) and Even and Macpherson (1994), include current earnings as a variable explaining pension coverage. However, current earnings are endogenous and so the coefficient estimate on this variable is biased. The direction of the bias cannot be determined *a priori*. The estimated coefficient is likely to be upward biased if unobserved heterogeneity in ability is positively correlated with both earnings and pension coverage. However, compensating differentials for pension coverage would cause the coefficient on earnings to be downward biased since unobservables that are positively correlated with pension coverage may be negatively correlated with earnings.

Instead of using current earnings, we use the instrumental variables approach suggested by Dorsey (1982) and Woodbury and Bettinger (1991). First, for each data set we estimate an earnings equation, with a standard human capital formulation. Included in the explanatory variables is potential experience, measured as age minus years of education minus 6. Using current job characteristics, we predict earnings for each individual at age 55. To do so, we assume that, in addition to age/earnings growth due to greater work experience as indicated by cross-sectional age earnings profiles, there is a 1 percent growth rate in real earnings over the life cycle.[13]

Table 2 Variable Means for Male Workers
        (standard deviations of continuous variables in parentheses)

Variable	Ages 21–35			Ages 36–55		
	1979	1988	1993	1979	1988	1993
Covered	0.569	0.481	0.453	0.694	0.674	0.657
Tax	30.8	26.0	26.1	35.3	30.4	29.8
	(8.0)	(9.3)	(8.7)	(7.9)	(9.0)	(7.5)
Pearn55[a]	31.52	29.08	26.80	36.73	36.85	33.90
	(9.75)	(10.85)	(10.86)	(11.08)	(13.46)	(13.48)
Union	0.285	0.169	0.128	0.343	0.250	0.196
Mult1000	0.423	0.403	0.397	0.469	0.485	0.469
African American	0.055	0.058	0.056	0.054	0.050	0.057
Married	0.705	0.611	0.584	0.880	0.831	0.785
Newhire	0.206	0.188	0.193	0.074	0.094	0.095

SOURCE: 1979 and 1998 March and May Current Population Surveys and 1993 March and April Current Population Surveys. 1978 tax rates are from Commerce Clearinghouse (1979). 1987 and 1992 rates are from Advisory Commission (1988 and 1993).

NOTE: The sample includes all full-time, male, private, wage and salary workers aged 21 to 55. The sample is further restricted to those who have valid responses to questions relevant to this study. The sample size is 5,496 in 1979, 6,241 in 1988, and 6,157 in 1993.

[a] Predicted earnings at age 55, in units of 10,000 1993 dollars. The variable used in the regressions was transformed by taking logarithms.

The predicted earnings measure is affected not only by changes in the worker's current earnings but also by changes in the entire age/earnings profile for workers of that gender for the given year. It is also affected by changes in the rate of return to experience, unionization, industry of employment, and firm size.

This measure of predicted earnings is then included as an explanatory variable in the coverage equation. In addition to circumventing the endogeneity problem associated with current earnings, the instrumental variable approach measures (although imperfectly) the earnings power of all individuals at the same age. The imprecision is greater for young workers, for whom we project for more years.

Predicted earnings at age 55 for young male workers fell by $2,400 (1993 dollars) between 1979 and 1988 and fell another $2,300 between 1988 and 1993. The fall during the 1980s occurred because young males were moving to lower paid occupations and industries in greater numbers than older males. In addition, young males experienced relatively large declines in unionization and in employment in large firms.[14]

COVERAGE ESTIMATES FOR MALE WORKERS

In this section, we present evidence from our data on the effect of the decline in income tax rates on the pension coverage of males. We examine effects separately for young and older workers for each of the three years of data.

We tested whether we could pool our data by age group, gender, or year, and the equality of coefficients across groups was always rejected. This result is in itself interesting because pension antidiscrimination rules limit firms' ability to target specific groups of workers. Whether a firm provides a pension to a worker should depend on the collective characteristics of the workers in the firm rather than the individual characteristics of the worker. Sorting in the labor market may account for the differing coefficients across age and gender groups.

Table 2 contains variable means for the three sample years while Tables 3 (young males) and 4 (older males) contain the estimates of the marginal effects for the continuous variables and the delta effects for the discrete variables.

A decline in marginal tax rates can result in reduced pension coverage rates through several paths. Some firms may decide to terminate plans that have diminished value to their workers. New firms that otherwise would have offered a pension plan may decide not to do so. Workers may change jobs, leaving firms offering a pension plan and moving to firms without one. Workers in firms where pension participation is optional may choose not to participate. Finally, workers entering the job market who would have otherwise sought firms offering a pension plan may instead seek employment with nonpension firms.

The extent to which workers change their pension coverage status in reaction to a change in marginal tax rates depends on the extent of job change within the economy, which depends on the phase of the business cycle. It also depends on the length of time workers have had to adjust to tax rate changes and the length of time workers expect those new tax rates to be in effect. Workers in firms offering only a 401(k) plan can adjust their pension status more quickly than other workers because they can simply decide not to participate in the plan. We do not attempt to distinguish by which path a change in marginal income tax rates influences pension coverage. Because of dynamic aspect of these factors, however, we expect the estimated tax coefficients to vary over time.

The estimated coefficient on marginal tax rates is positive and significant in all six of the male samples (Tables 3 and 4).[15] Thus, these results suggest that the decline in marginal tax rates during the 1980s reduced pension coverage for both young and older males.

The coefficient on predicted earnings at age 55 is positive and significant for all samples.[16] Given the positive correlation between marginal income tax rates and employee income, the finding of significant positive effects for predicted earnings as well as taxes is important because it suggests that we have isolated separate income and tax effects.[17]

One way to quantify the predicted effect of changes in tax rates on pension coverage is to multiply the estimated marginal effect of taxes by the observed change in taxes. This approach is equivalent to taking the difference in the predicted probabilities of coverage with mean tax in the base year and mean tax in the comparison year, evaluated at the means of the other variables in the base year. The difference in the predicted probabilities gives the change in the estimated probability attributable to the tax change for an "average" individual.

This approach has the weakness that the sum over changes in all variables does not equal the change in coverage predicted by the model. Even and Macpherson (1990) developed a technique without this defect for calculating the predicted effect of changes in one variable. With their technique, the sum over changes in all variables is constrained to equal the total predicted change.

Table 3 Marginal And Delta Effects for Young (age 21–35) Male Pension Coverage Probit, 1979, 1988, and 1993 (*t*-statistics in parentheses)

Variable	1979	1988	1993
Tax	0 .0040 (2.34)	0.0036 (2.03)	0.0043 (2.32)
Pearn55	0.467 (3.97)	1.071 (371.99)	1.064 (222.71)
Union	0.303 (17.29)	0.156 (15.54)	0.166 (25.81)
Mult100	0.278 (24.48)	0.180 (35.82)	0.123 (25.83)
African American	0 .055 (3.19)	–0.180 (0.64)	–0.013 (1.35)
Married	0.147 (33.48)	0.010 (31.60)	0.129 (21.26)
Newhire	–0.192 (36.10)	–0.205 (18.11)	0.029 (3.16)
Intercept	–0.863	–1.744	–1.877
Log likelihood	–1492.9	–1534.3	–1524.1
N	3008	2931	2949

SOURCE: 1979 and 1988 March and May Current Population Surveys and 1993 March and April Current Population Surveys. The 1978 tax rates are from Commerce Clearinghouse (1979), 1987 and 1992 rates are from Advisory Commission (1988 and 1993).

NOTE: The sample includes all full-time, male, private, wage and salary workers aged 21 to 55. The sample is further restricted to those who have valid responses to questions relevant to this study. The probit equation also contains four controls for education, four controls for occupation, and nine industry controls. All controls were coded as dichotomous variables.

**Table 4 Marginal and Delta Effects for Older (age 36–55) Male
Pension Coverage Profit, 1979, 1988, and 1993
(*t*-statistics in parentheses)**

Variable	1979	1988	1993
Tax	0.0033	0.0066	0.0048
	(1.97)	(4.18)	(2.86)
Pearn55	0.370	0.627	0.662
	(5.28)	(18.76)	(24.01)
Union	0.224	0.195	0.154
	(11.74)	(9.64)	(7.81)
Mult100	0.237	0.190	0.224
	(14.67)	(13.95)	(17.14)
African American	−0.023	−0.033	0.148
	(0.78)	(1.26)	(5.02)
Married	−0.021	0.077	0.035
	(0.85)	(5.01)	(2.90)
Newhire	−0.150	−0.126	−0.012
	(10.74)	(8.80)	(0.44)
Intercept	−0.628	−1.137	−1.312
Log likelihood	−1102.9	−1248.4	−1452.9
N	2516	2886	3213

SOURCE: 1979 and 1988 March and May Current Population Surveys and 1993
March and April Current Population Surveys. The 1978 tax rates are from Commerce
Clearinghouse (1979), 1987 and 1992 rates are from Advisory Commission (1988
and 1993).

NOTE: The sample includes all full-time, male, private, wage and salary workers aged
21 to 55. The sample is further restricted to those who have valid responses to questions relevant to this study. The probit equation also contains four controls for education, four controls for occupation, and nine industry controls. All controls were coded
as dichotomous variables.

The predicted change in coverage between 1979 and 1988 is calculated:

$$EXP = \sum_{i=1}^{N88}\Phi(Z_{i88}\hat{g}_{88}) - \sum_{i=1}^{N79}\Phi(Z_{i79}\hat{g}_{79}), \tag{2}$$

where $N88$ is the number of observations in 1988, $N79$ is the number of observations in 1979, and Φ is the standard normal cumulative distribution function. EXP is the average predicted coverage rate in 1988 minus the average predicted coverage rate in 1979. Using 1988 as the base year, the portion of the predicted change attributable to changes in variable Z_k is

$$EXP_k = EXP * (\bar{Z}_{k88} - \bar{Z}_{k79})\hat{g}_{k88} / \left[(\bar{Z}_{88} - \bar{Z}_{79})\hat{g}_{88}\right] \tag{3}$$

where $\bar{Z}_{79}$ and $\bar{Z}_{88}$ are the vectors of variable means in 1979 and 1988; and $\bar{Z}_{k79}$ and $\bar{Z}_{k88}$ are the means of variable k in 1979 and 1988. A similar formula applies for base year 1988 in comparison to 1993.

Calculations of the effects of the changes in selected variables are presented in Table 5. These calculations indicate that the changes in marginal income tax rates, in the earnings measure, and in the percentage of the workforce covered by a union help explain the decline in pension coverage.[18] Our results regarding the effects of declining unionization and earnings are comparable to those found by Bloom and Freeman (1992) and by Even and Macpherson (1994). However, we find that between 1979 and 1988, the effect of declining taxes was twice as large for young workers as for older workers. Between 1988 and 1993, for both young and older workers, the estimated effect is so small as to be economically insignificant.

A calculation indicates that pension coverage rate for males aged 21 to 36 was 1 percentage point lower in 1993 than it would have been had the marginal tax rates in 1979 been in effect.[19] Dividing the estimated effect due to the change in tax rates by the change in tax rates, we find that a 1 percentage point increase in marginal tax rates on average leads to a 0.4 percentage point increase in pension coverage rates for this group.

As a test of robustness, we reestimate the model for males making three changes in the regression (Table 6). First, we pool the data. Sec-

Table 5 Predicted Changes in Male Pension Coverage Attributed to Changes in Observed Characteristics

Variable	Age 21–35		Age 36–55	
	1979–1988	1988–1993	1979–1988	1988–1993
Total predicted change	−0.073	−0.041	−0.011	−0.026
Change explained by				
Tax	−0.014	−0.3–e5	−0.007	−0.6–e3
Union	−0.009	−0.002	−0.004	−0.002
Pearn55	−0.057	−0.038	−0.004	−0.019

NOTE: These predicted changes are calculated using the 1988 estimates of the probability of coverage. Qualitatively similar predicted changes are found using the 1979 estimates of the probability of coverage. The percentage change attributable to changes in representation in manufacturing predicted a decline of 0.002 for young male workers and a rise of 0.002 for old male workers. Since the predicted change in coverage is sufficiently close to zero, we do not report the percentage of total predicted change attributable to underlying variables.

ond, we test for the effect of lagged taxes. Third, we use the log of current salary rather than our permanent earnings variable. Our measure of lagged taxes is the tax rate that would have applied in the second and third years of our data had the tax laws applying to the first or second years of the data prevailed. The interpretation of the lagged variable is complicated. It can indicate the effect of a lag in adjustment to taxes. It can also indicate for a particular time period that workers view lagged taxes to be more representative of the long run tax regime than they view current taxes.

COVERAGE ESTIMATES FOR FEMALE WORKERS

We test the robustness of our estimated tax effects for males by reestimating the model using data on females from the 1979, 1988, and 1993 CPS. The additional estimates of the marginal effect of taxes on pension coverage are an independent measure to assess the plausibility of our estimated tax effects for males. These comparisons across gender are particularly useful because changes in average tax rates were

Table 6 Estimated Marginal Tax Effects from Probit Regressions for Females, 1979, 1988, and 1993 (*t*-statistics in parentheses)

Sample	1979	1988	1993
Young females	0.0046	0.0048	0.004
	(2.28)	(2.63)	(2.09)
Older females	0.0073	0.0046	0.0040
	(2.30)	(2.11)	(1.90)

SOURCE: 1979 and 1988 March and May Current Population Surveys and 1993 March and April Current Population Surveys. The 1978 tax rates are from Commerce Clearinghouse (1979), 1987 and 1992 rates are from Advisory Commission (1988 and 1993).

NOTE: The sample includes all full-time, female, private, wage and salary workers aged 21 to 55. The sample is further restricted to those who have valid responses to questions relevant to this study. The probit equation also contains four controls for education, four controls for occupation, and nine industry controls. All controls were coded as dichotomous variables.

similar for both men and women, while changes in coverage rates were not. While coverage for men declined, women generally experienced rising coverage rates during the 1980s.[20]

We estimate female pension coverage equations using the same specification used for males. To economize on space, we summarize results concerning tax effects (Table 6). Coverage rates for females in our sample rose by 0.5 percentage points between 1979 and 1988 and by 2 percentage points between 1988 and 1993.[21] The mean tax rates in each year are virtually identical to those of men and display a similar trend.[22]

Predicted earnings at age 55 for females rose over the period. The increase in predicted earnings reflects the rising wages and narrowing of the gender gap in wages that women have experienced from the late 1970s. In addition, the percentage of the workforce that is unionized fell by 50 percent between 1979 and 1993. The overall percentage decline in unionization is comparable to the percentage decline for men, although in absolute levels men are twice as likely to be unionized.

The percentage of women who were new hires, defined to have less than one year of tenure with the employer, fell from 19 to 18 percent between 1979 and 1988 and then fell to 14 percent in 1993. Since eligibility for coverage usually requires some minimum level of tenure, the 4 percent decline in new hires is potentially important in explaining women's rising coverage rates between 1988 and 1993.

The estimated coefficient on marginal tax rates is positive and significant in five of the six female samples.[23] It is similar in magnitude to the estimated coefficients in the male regressions.

Table 7 presents the total predicted change in coverage and the predicted change in coverage attributable to changes over time in marginal tax rates. As we did for men, we use the 1988 coefficients as the base from which to extrapolate. The change in coverage for women predicted by our model is much smaller than it is for men, consistent with their smaller change in coverage.

Table 7 Predicted Changes in Female Pension Coverage Attributed to Changes in Observed Characteristics

	Age 21–35		Age 36–55	
	1979–1988	1988–1993	1979–1988	1988–1993
Total predicted change	0.024	–0.035	0.013	0.030
Change explained by				
Tax	–	–0.002	–0.001	–0.0–e3
Union	–	0.005	–0.004	–0.001
Pearn55	–	–0.045	0.018	0.026

NOTE: These predicted changes are calculated using the 1988 estimates of the probability of coverage. Qualitatively similar predicted changes are found using the 1979 estimates of the probability of coverage. Although the model predicts a 2.4 percentage point decline in coverage for young women between 1979 and 1988, almost all the change came about by changes in the estimated coefficients in the two years and not from changes in variable means. The decomposition described by Eq. 5 is meaningful only if the denominator is not close to zero. When this occurs, the predicted change attributed to any one variable becomes implausibly large because of division by a number close to zero. Therefore, we do not report predicted changes attributable to individual variables for young women between 1979 and 1988.

CONCLUSIONS

Private pension coverage rates for males declined during the 1980s, especially for young males. Previous studies of pension coverage for young males have ignored the decline in marginal income tax rates. Using data from the 1979, 1988, and 1993 CPS Pension Supplements, we find that the probability of coverage for an individual, in both our young and older samples, increases with increases in the marginal income tax rate. Declining marginal income tax rates are found to be nearly as important as the decline in unionism in explaining trends in coverage for young males. While our estimates vary, a rough summary indicates that a one percentage point increase in marginal tax rates causes a 0.4 percentage point increase in pension coverage rates. We find comparable tax effects for women.

Our results indicate that workers and firms react to changes in marginal income tax rates when making decisions concerning pension plans. Higher pension tax expenditures associated with higher marginal income tax rates "pay for" increased pension coverage.

Our results have implications for a number of issues not directly addressed in the paper. The decline in generosity of pension plans that many analysts believed occurred during the 1980s may have been due in part to the fall in marginal income tax rates. To the extent that pension saving is new saving, rather than replacing saving that would have occurred in another form, the decrease in marginal tax rates may have caused a decrease in savings. Finally, our results suggest that the reduction in tax rates partially paid for itself because the lower tax rates were associated with reduced tax expenditures on pensions.

Notes

We have received helpful comments from Daniel Beller, Tasneem Chipty, Stephen Cosslett, William Even, William Gale, Richard Hinz, David McCarthy, Donald Parsons, Alan Viard, participants at the Center for Pension and Retirement Research conference at Miami University of Ohio, and participants at seminars at the University of Vienna, the University of Southern California, the American Economic Association meetings, the Tax Economists Forum, and the Congressional Budget Office. Tzu-Kuang Hsu and Zooyob Anne provided excellent research assistance. Patricia Reagan thanks the Center for Labor Research at the Ohio State University for financial support.

The opinions expressed in this paper are the responsibility of the authors and do not represent the position of the U.S. Department of Labor.

1. See Doescher (1994) for an extensive survey of studies on pension coverage.
2. We follow traditional usage and define coverage to indicate that a worker is a participant in an employer-provided pension plan. When discussing 401(k) plans, we draw the distinction between being offered a plan and choosing to participate in it.
3. The primary legislative change in tax rates during the 1980s occurred with the passage of the Economic Recovery Tax Act of 1981, which cut the top federal marginal income tax rate from 70 percent to 50 percent and reduced marginal income tax rates in all other brackets by 23 percentage points over three years. The Tax Reform Act of 1986 reduced the top rate on wealthiest households to 38 percent, effective 1988. It provided for a transitional top rate of 38.5 percent, effective 1987. The highest rate in 1988 was 33 percent, which applied that year for single (unmarried head of household) [married couple] households with taxable income between $44,315 and $100,480 ($61,650 and $156,550) [$71,900 and $192,930]. The brackets increased in subsequent years.
4. The basic tax rules concerning pensions were established in the Internal Revenue Acts of 1922, 1926, and 1928. Employer contributions to private pension plans are not treated as income to workers. The investment earnings on those contributions accrue tax free. Benefits are taxed under the federal and state personal income taxes when received.
5. If managers of firms decide on whether to offer pension plans based, in part, on the desirability of pension benefits to themselves, the decline in tax rates at upper income levels will also affect the probability that lower income workers have pension coverage.
6. In 1979, 26 percent of all male workers with tax rates below 10 percent were covered. Coverage rates rose to 75 percent for the 40–49 percent tax bracket. A similar profile emerges from the 1988 and 1993 data.
7. We follow the convention of referring to the data by the year of the survey that it is from. The income data, and the income tax rate data derived from it, are for the year preceding the survey.
8. Since the unit of observation is a match between worker i and firm j, we should subscript the vector and subsequent stochastic terms by ij. However, for ease of notation we suppress these subscripts.
9. The probit estimates are available from the authors on request.
10. The practice of reporting marginal effects of continuous regressors is standard to the literature (see Even and Macpherson 1994). The authors, however, use the same formula to calculate the marginal effects of discrete regressors. We instead report delta effects for discrete variables. We also report t-statistics based on standard errors of the marginal and delta effects. These differ from the t-statistics on the coefficient estimates of the probit equation. We believe that our approach represents a technical improvement over previous work. The variance-covariance matrix for the marginal and delta effects is calculated by pre- and post-multiply-

ing the variance-covariance matrix of the probit estimates by the matrix of the derivatives of the vector of marginal and delta effects with respect to the elements in the vector g. The code is available on request.

11. Gustman, Mitchell, and Steinmeier (1994) criticized previous studies for not addressing the issue of the endogeneity of marginal tax rates. In principle, the worker's expected marginal income tax rates for all future years affect the demand for pensions. We do not pursue that approach empirically because of colinearity.

12. State tax data for 1987 and 1992 are contained in reports of the Advisory Commission on Intergovernmental Relations (1988, 1993). Data for 1978 were supplied by Commerce Clearing House (1979). The marginal income tax rate is calculated as follows. First, we take the family income data from the CPS, which is categorical, and replace it with the mean family income in each category. Since the data on family income is top coded, we use IRS Statistics of Income tables to obtain average family income conditional on income exceeding the maximum reported by the CPS. We then use information on marital status and number of children in the family from the CPS, coupled with information about allowed exemptions and deductions from the federal and state income tax codes to obtain a measure of taxable income. Taxable income was calculated separately for state and federal tax purposes. The combined federal and state tax rates take into account the deductibility of state income taxes in computing federal income tax rates.

13. We experimented with a 2 percent growth rate and found our results to be robust to the assumption of 1 percent growth.

14. Unionism is another variable that previous studies have found to have an important effect on pension coverage. Between 1979 and 1988, the percentage of workers covered by a union contract dropped 11.7 and 9.3 percentage points for young and old workers, respectively. Between 1988 and 1993, these rates dropped an additional 4.1 and 5.4 percentage points. Although older workers are more likely to be covered by union contracts in all years, the magnitude of the decline in unionization was large for both groups.

15. We found statistically significant positive effects for all samples when we entered marginal tax rates calculated from actual family earnings rather than predicted family earnings.

16. The reported t-statistics are for the marginal and delta effects. The marginal and delta effects and their t-statistics are calculated by a nonlinear transformation of the probit estimates. Because of the nonlinearity of the transformation, it does not preserve the t-values in the probit estimates. The transformation increases the t-value for variables with already large t-values, explaining the very large reported t-values for some of the earnings coefficients.

17. In addition, we find the standard results that pension coverage increases with earnings, education, firm size, union status, and a marital status dichotomous variable (1=married). When we entered age in regressions not shown, it is insignificant, age having been controlled for already in the choice of samples.

18. For the calculations for both 1979 to 1988 and 1988 to 1993, we use 1988 as the base year. These calculations are entirely based on statistically significant estimated coefficients.
19. We calculate this by multiplying the predicted tax effect on coverage rates by the number of male full-time private sector wage and salary workers not covered by a pension plan (U.S. Department of Labor 1994).
20. Between 1988 and 1993, young women experienced a slight decline.
21. As with males, the coverage rates within the sample exceed the population coverage rates due to restrictions on valid responses to questions used in the regression analysis.
22. This is not surprising since marginal tax rates are based on family income.
23. The predicted earnings at age 55 is positive and significant, which suggests that the tax effect has been isolated.

References

Advisory Commission On Intergovernmental Relations. 1988. *Significant Features of Fiscal Federalism*, 1988 Ed. Vol. I. Washington, D.C.

Beller, Daniel J., and Helen H. Lawrence. 1992. "Trends in Private Pension Plan Coverage." In *Trends in Pensions 1992*, John A. Turner and Daniel J. Beller, eds. Washington, D.C.: U.S. Government Printing Office, pp. 59–96.

Bloom, David E., and Richard B. Freeman. 1992. "The Fall in Private Pension Coverage in the U.S." *American Economic Review* 82(May): 539–545.

Commerce Clearing House. 1979. *1979 U.S. Master Tax Guide*, Chicago, Illinois: Commerce Clearing House.

Deaton, Angus, and John Muellbauer. 1980. *Economics and Consumer Behavior*. Cambridge, England: Cambridge University Press.

Doescher, Tabitha. 1994. "Are Pension Coverage Rates Declining?" In *Pension Coverage Issues for the '90s*, Richard P. Hinz, John A. Turner, and Phyllis Fernandez, eds. Washington, D.C.: U.S. Government Printing Office.

Dorsey, Stuart. 1982. "A Model and Empirical Estimates of Worker Pension Coverage." *Southern Economic Journal* 49(October): 506–520.

Even, William E., and David A. Macpherson. 1990. "Plant Size and the Decline of Unionism." *Economics Letters* 32(April): 393–398.

_____. 1994. "The Pension Coverage of Young and Mature Workers." In *Pension Coverage Issues for the '90s*, Richard P. Hinz, John A. Turner, and

Phyllis Fernandez, eds. Washington, D.C.: U.S. Government Printing Office.

Feldstein, Martin. 1997. "The Effect of Marginal Tax Rates on Taxable Income: A Panel Study of the 1986 Tax Reform Act." National Bureau of Economic Research Working Paper No. 4496.

Gentry, William M., and Eric Peress. 1995. "Taxes and Fringe Benefits Offered by Employers." Presented at the American Economic Association meetings, Washington, D.C., January 7, 1995.

Gustman, Alan L., Olivia S. Mitchell, and Thomas L. Steinmeier. 1994. "The Role of Pensions in the Labor Market: A Survey of the Literature." *Industrial and Labor Relations Review* 47(April): 417–438.

Munnell, Alicia H. 1982. *The Economics of Private Pensions*. Washington, D.C.: The Brookings Institution.

Turner, John A. 1981. "Inflation and the Accumulation of Assets in Private Pension Funds." *Economic Inquiry* 19(July): 10–425.

U.S. Department of Labor. 1994. *Pension and Health Benefits of American Workers: New Findings from the April 1993 Current Population Survey.* Washington, D.C.: U.S. Department of Labor, Pension and Welfare Benefits Administration.

Woodbury, Stephen A. 1983. "Substitution Between Wage and Nonwage Benefits." *American Economic Review* 73(March): 166–182.

Woodbury, Stephen A., and Douglas R. Bettinger. 1991. "The Decline of Fringe-Benefit Coverage in the 1980s." In *Structural Changes in U.S. Labor Markets: Causes and Consequences*, Randall W. Eberts and Erica L. Groshen, eds. Armonk, New York: M.E. Sharpe, pp. 105–138.

Woodbury, Stephen A. and Daniel S. Hamermesh. 1992. "Taxes, Fringe Benefits and Faculty." *Review of Economics and Statistics* 74(May): 287–296.

Woodbury, Stephen A. and Wei-Jang Huang. 1991. *The Tax Treatment of Fringe Benefits*. Kalamazoo, MI: W.E. Upjohn Institute for Employment Research.

Author Index

497

Subject Index

518

About the Institute

The W.E. Upjohn Institute for Employment Research is a nonprofit research organization devoted to finding and promoting solutions to employment-related problems at the national, state, and local levels. It is an activity of the W.E. Upjohn Unemployment Trustee Corporation, which was established in 1932 to administer a fund set aside by the late Dr. W.E. Upjohn, founder of The Upjohn Company, to seek ways to counteract the loss of employment income during economic downturns.

The Institute is funded largely by income from the W.E. Upjohn Unemployment Trust, supplemented by outside grants, contracts, and sales of publications. Activities of the Institute comprise the following elements: 1) a research program conducted by a resident staff of professional social scientists; 2) a competitive grant program, which expands and complements the internal research program by providing financial support to researchers outside the Institute; 3) a publications program, which provides the major vehicle for disseminating the research of staff and grantees, as well as other selected works in the field; and 4) an Employment Management Services division, which manages most of the publicly funded employment and training programs in the local area.

The broad objectives of the Institute's research, grant, and publication programs are to 1) promote scholarship and experimentation on issues of public and private employment and unemployment policy, and 2) make knowledge and scholarship relevant and useful to policymakers in their pursuit of solutions to employment and unemployment problems.

Current areas of concentration for these programs include causes, consequences, and measures to alleviate unemployment; social insurance and income maintenance programs; compensation; workforce quality; work arrangements; family labor issues; labor-management relations; and regional economic development and local labor markets.